The EU under strain?

Europe under Strain

Series Editors
Mechthild Roos and Daniel Schade

Volume 1

The EU under strain?

—

Current crises shaping European Union politics

Edited by
Mechthild Roos and Daniel Schade

DE GRUYTER

ISBN 978-3-11-162719-9
e-ISBN (PDF) 978-3-11-079033-7
e-ISBN (EPUB) 978-3-11-079047-4
ISSN 2750-8366
e-ISSN 2750-8374

Library of Congress Control Number: 2023932374

Bibliographic information published by the Deutsche Nationalbibliothek
The Deutsche Nationalbibliothek lists this publication in the Deutsche Nationalbibliografie; detailed bibliographic data are available on the Internet at http://dnb.dnb.de.

www.degruyter.com

Table of Contents

Part III: **The EU in a changing world**

Part IV: **European policy fields shaped by crisis**

List of authors

Piotr Bodganowicz, Professor in European Law, University of Warsaw.

Alexandra Bousiou, Senior Researcher at the Center for Global Migration, University of Gothenburg.

Desmond Dinan, Professor of Public Policy and Ad personam Jean Monnet Professor, George Mason University.

Andreas Eisl, Research Fellow on European Economic Policy, Jacques Delors Institute.

Sören Keil, Academic Head at the International Research and Consulting Centre IRCC, Institute of Federalism, University of Fribourg.

Lucy Kinski, Postdoctoral Researcher in Political Science, Salzburg Centre of European Union Studies, University of Salzburg.

Paulette Kurzer, Professor of Political Science, University of Arizona.

Benjamin Leruth, Assistant Professor in European Politics and Society, University of Groningen.

Martijn Mos, Assistant Professor of International Relations, Leiden University.

Mechthild Roos, Lecturer in Comparative Politics, University of Augsburg.

Jeffrey Rosamond, PhD student and Researcher at the Department of Public Governance and Management, Ghent University.

Daniel Schade, Assistant Professor of Europe in Global Affairs, Leiden University.

Frank Schimmelfennig, Professor of European Politics, ETH Zurich.

Linnea Schleyer, MA student, Institut Barcelona d'Estudis Internacionals & University of Gothenburg.

Michael H. Smith, Honorary Professor in European Politics, University of Warwick.

Bernhard Stahl, Professor of International Politics, University of Passau.

Mattia Tomay, Legal and Policy Officer, European Commission.

Simon Usherwood, Professor of Politics and International Studies, The Open University.

https://doi.org/10.1515/9783110790337-001

Part I: **Contextualising the EU and crises**

Mechthild Roos & Daniel Schade

1 Introduction: The EU under strain

Abstract: Policy-making in the European Union has been shaped – if not dominated – by a wide variety of different types of crises in recent years. Accordingly, much political activity by the EU and related actors has had a certain urgency, occurred under intense economic and societal strain, and required responses in policy areas where the EU traditionally only holds fragmented competencies. Shifting priorities, short-term policy responses, and adapted implementation schedules showcase that EU governance now most often occurs in reaction to unforeseen events, rather than following mid- to long-term planning as originally foreseen by its foundational actors and the underlying institutional set-up in calmer times. Building on a concise overview of some of the most impactful recent crises from an EU perspective, this introductory chapter provides a conceptual framework for the analysis of European crisis governance. While the chapter catalogues and categorizes a variety of different crises, it conceptualises crisis governance not as an exception to the regular functioning of the EU's political system, but instead as a regular feature of how the EU works nowadays. In so doing, it offers a conceptual basis for the following chapters of this volume, as well as for further empirical studies on the impact of crises on EU policies and politics more generally. Following these considerations, the chapter outlines and explains the volume's structure which considers (1) crises related to the legal and democratic foundations of the EU; (2) the EU's role and behaviour as an international actor in a changing world; and (3) the origins and impacts of crises in various EU policy areas.

Setting the scene: Crisis as the new normal in the EU?

When EU member states signed the Treaty of Lisbon in 2007, they did not anticipate the manifold crises that would ensue over the course of the following years. Instead of the intended consolidation of a Union which had just gone through its biggest round of enlargements, the EU faced the financial and economic crises of 2007–2008, the European debt crisis of the early 2010s, the Arab Spring and ensuing

Acknowledgments: The authors would like to express their profound gratitude to Julia Simon for her most constructive and helpful feedback on this chapter, and to Jamie L. Kaup for her excellent work in proofreading all chapters of this volume.

https://doi.org/10.1515/9783110790337-002

instability in the EU's wider neighbourhood, Russia's annexation of Crimea and subsequently rising tensions in the EU's Eastern neighbourhood, the Brexit referendum of 2016 and its aftermath, the so-called 'migration crisis' of 2015–17, strained transatlantic relations under US President Donald Trump, the global repercussions of the Covid-19 pandemic, the Taliban's takeover in Afghanistan, as well as internal threats to the EU's fundamental principles, values and legal order, and most recently Russia's re-invasion of and war in Ukraine, to name only some of the most impactful events. Beyond these, a number of more long-term and slowly evolving developments, such as the ever-increasing impact of the climate emergency, as well as the intensification of the EU's so-called rule of law crisis have further put the EU's system and its internal cohesion under strain.

These events and developments have pushed EU policy-making in many areas into a permanent mode of crisis management. In this context, political and institutional actors often had to prioritise one crisis over another and weigh the urgencies of (re)action against each other. They felt pressured to acknowledge rising tensions and increasing levels of politicization in more and more emotionally charged public, economic, and political debates when making decisions on short- as well as long-term policies. These tensions and the ensuing politicization often developed alongside, or were shaped by, the rise of 'Eurosceptic' political positions at the national level, which have increased sharply since the 1990s (Down & Wilson 2008).

Accordingly, policy-making in the EU has been shaped – if not dominated – by the above-mentioned wide variety of endogenous and exogenous crises in recent years, both in areas with well-established EU competences and in areas for which the treaties provide only fragmentary, if any, EU involvement, yet in which calls for a unified European response arose under the impression of events unforeseen by any treaty or piece of legislation. As a consequence, European integration has evolved in different ways and speeds within different policy areas, as a growing corpus of literature on EU crisis response and on differentiated integration in the EU shows (see also Chapter 4 by Leruth). In a similar vein, different actors' involvement in European policy-making and resulting power balances have changed frequently, but not necessarily in a lasting manner, or in a way that is synchronized across policy areas over the course of the last years.

It is precisely these various dynamics that this volume seeks to examine, contextualise, and conceptualise. In so doing, it aims to provide a research guide that will help develop a deeper understanding of EU policy-making under the impression of (poly)crisis both in the past and future, as current and ongoing global developments and scientific predictions give little reason to expect smoother, less crisis-informed sailing in European politics for years to come. To this end, this introductory chapter offers a conceptual toolkit for further research on EU policy-making under strain.

Most of the strain arising out of the various crises identified above not only affects the EU system in and of itself but also has repercussions at the national level below and for the international community above the EU's political system. Nonetheless, to provide a clearer focus, this chapter and ultimately this edited volume place the EU level at the core of analysis. While there are important interactions between EU-level politics and policy and those at other levels, and such interactions are indeed considered throughout the volume, the actual relevance of EU politics and the interconnectedness of its crisis governance across different types of strain can arguably be best explored when focusing on the EU system as its own level of analysis.

The remainder of this introductory chapter is structured as follows: Building on a discussion of key terms and concepts, the central section of the chapter develops a conceptual framework for the analysis of European crisis governance, both for the following chapters of this volume and for empirical studies on the impact of crises on EU policies and politics more generally. Following these considerations, a section elaborates on how the contributions to the volume are embedded in and add to this framework, and explains their grouping in three topical parts – on the legal and democratic fundaments of the EU (1), the EU's role and behaviour as an international actor in a changing world (2), and the impact of select crises on specific European policy areas (3) – and provides an overview of the themes and developments covered by the individual contributions.

Conceptualising crisis and European-level responses

Crises have often been framed as fundamental challenges to European integration, questioning not merely the EU's ability to thrive but to survive in the face of unexpected events and developments with far-reaching political, economic and social repercussions (for a state-of-the art discussion of the literature on EU crises see Riddervold et al. 2021b; also Davis Cross 2017). Yet, this black-and-white framing of crisis as a fundamental challenge to European integration has arguably prevented scholars from developing a more fine-grained conceptualisation of crisis phenomena and their impact on EU politics and policies.

Davis Cross (2017, 24; emphasis in the original) undertakes a fundamental step in this direction by distinguishing "crisis and *existential crisis*", with the former being a state of affairs "constructed through negative and heightened characterizations of events involving conflict", and the latter being understood (in the context of EU crises) as "marked by widespread belief that the EU's very existence and/or core characteristics are seriously under threat". Yet, even this dichotomous distinction does not go far enough, as it does not allow us to capture other relevant properties of crises, such as their origin or how the EU's political system has reacted to them. The EU has – by now – demonstrated a convincing level of stamina in overcoming, or at least muddling through, the multitude of crises it has faced since its creation. Resulting European crisis responses have often been identified in the recent literature as a 'failing forward' of European integration (see e.g. Jones et al. 2021), where a lacklustre initial crisis response leads to further crises evoking a similar response, thus moving European integration forward if on an imperfect basis.

In light of the ever-changing, but arguably never entirely abating crisis context within which EU politics take place, we argue that it is time to consider crises as a feature rather than a bug of European integration. After all, "the EU has reached a stage in its development where it has sufficiently consolidated to adapt to and cope with multiple and simultaneous crisis situations" (Riddervold et al. 2021b, 6). The 'new normal' that the latter has come to signify comes not least with the EU's widening and deepening: the larger its competences and the wider its geographical extent, the more possibilities are there for crises to directly affect European politics. With this in mind, it is particularly important, from a European studies perspective, to move beyond a perspective that sees the presence or absence of crises as binary variables, and to develop conceptual approaches allowing one to systematically grasp different kinds of crises, their life cycle and impact on European policies and politics. It is based on this that we develop a conceptual framework that allows for a more systematic understanding of triggers, processes, sequences, and consequences of crises at the EU level.

To this end, what is first required is a definition of the term 'crisis' itself. In very general terms, crisis can be understood as "a (radical) rupture in the status quo" (Barthoma & Çetrez 2021, 6), including even the mere intensification of likeliness, i.e., the palpable threat of such a rupture. Namely, as its most crucial characteristic, crisis constitutes a juncture calling into question an established order, be it institutional, political, economic, societal, normative, or other; in a manner that is unexpected by its contemporaries. Even if actors expect similar kinds of crises to happen at some point in the future (if, for instance, economists predict a stock market crash to take place again at some point, or if political pundits express worries about the likelihood of major societal unrest), an inherent element of crisis is the unpredictability of its occurrence, of its precise extent, as well as of its repercussions. Moreover, a crisis is defined as requiring a response to the uncertainties it has raised. While this typically raises the need for concerned actors to alter course under time pressure (Davis Cross 2017, 23; Riddervold et al. 2021a, 7), both the immediate urgency of a crisis and the extent of a required response may vary as the following sections outline.

Beyond its inherent characteristics, a crisis is also ultimately defined by it being *framed and understood* as such by involved actors, the media, and not least the public, for it to qualify as a genuine crisis rather than a mere additional challenge on regular political agendas. It is this dimension related to a crisis needing to be understood as such, which can explain "why various events on the road to EU integration have built up into crises while others have not" (Davis Cross 2017, 30). Indeed, the construction, framing and reading of certain developments as a crisis is something that merits much more enquiry in its own right. A number of chapters in this volume discuss examples where actors' perception of certain instances of strain influenced their respective crisis responses – among them Mos (Chapter 13) on EU member states' differing responses to violations of minority rights, Bousiou & Schleyer (Chapter 11; see also Simon 2022) on the effects of the securitization of forced migration and of different understandings of/references to solidarity during the 'migration crisis', and Schimmelfennig (Chapter 2) on the relevance of actors' varying crisis management preferences. It should be noted, however, that the selection of crises addressed in the chapters of this volume is largely limited to developments affecting the EU which have generally been accepted and described as crisis by policy-makers and researchers alike.

Going beyond the identification of such basic crisis characteristics as addressed above, politicians and researchers have in recent years taken the concept of crisis to a somewhat more complex level when trying to assess the multi-layered and multi-issue nature of crises facing the EU. Here, the total of challenges that the EU has been confronted with since the sovereign debt crisis of the late 2000s has frequently been referred to as polycrisis. This term was prominently introduced by then-European Commission President Jean-Claude Juncker in a public speech (2016) and then found its way into academic discourse. While the term originally referred "to the confluence of multiple, mutually reinforcing challenges facing the EU" (Zeitlin et al. 2019, 973, footnote 1), today it seeks to capture and conceptualise the fact that "several simultaneous crises are now affecting multiple policy domains and fracturing the cohesion of the Union's member states across new and changing cleavages" (Zeitlin et al. 2019, 963).

These cleavages emerge and deepen not least as an inherent characteristic of the EU's confederal nature: the different crises which together form the larger picture of polycrisis tend to affect different member states in distinct ways and to different degrees. Examples for such janus-faced crises abound, with the sovereign debt crisis, the so-called migration crisis and the EU's rule of law crisis affecting all EU members in some manner, yet leaving a mark on individual EU member states, institutions, and policy areas, and thus public perception across the union, in different ways.[1] Throughout the many crises Europe has faced, however, it soon became evident that there are some patterns in how individual crises affect different member states and various parts of the EU's political system. Depending on the crisis at hand, divisions could be seen unfolding for instance on a roughly North-South dimension in the EU regarding fiscal policy, or a cleavage between Western European and Central European member states over the issue of migration (Zeitlin et al. 2019, 963–64). These divisions, particularly in the context of the Eurozone crisis, have also been somewhat problematically labelled as a core-periphery divide in academic analysis (Magone et al. 2016) and political discourse alike (Ervedosa 2017), thus speaking to the EU fragmentation potential inherent to these crises.

Such varying degrees of affectedness, in turn, impact coalition-building, relations between individual member states and EU institutions, and dynamics of differentiated integration (the varying participation in EU policies of different groups of member states) which evolve ever further among member states (see the Chapter 4 by Leruth). To understand such dynamics and evolving patterns of relations, the different sub-strands of the EU's polycrisis ultimately need to be disentangled and understood, both in their individual roots, scopes, and consequences as well as their interconnectedness. Through the crisis typology developed in the following, as well as in its individual contributions, this volume seeks to contribute to this process of disentanglement and understanding.

A typology of crises

While we consider crises as a regular feature of today's EU governance, lumping different *kinds* of crises together to be able to invoke their collective relevance for today's EU would be analytically harmful. Thus, it is necessary to categorize crises to better comprehend how they affect the EU and its underlying political system, or how they may even be caused by it. So as to trace similarities and differences in their roots, sequence, and consequences, our typology considers different crisis parameters, with notable attributes being crisis origin, temporality, perception, delineation, as well as impact. Each of these different foci allows us to indi-

---

1 See e.g. the contributions to the special issue 'The Effects of the Eurozone Sovereign Debt Crisis' (discussed in the special issue editorial by Schweiger & Magone 2014), and also several chapters in this volume, e.g. Bousiou & Schleyer on different countries' affectedness in the context of the 'migration crisis', and Mos on the varying effects of strain in the areas of diversity and minority rights and the rule of law as part of the EU's larger 'values crisis'.

vidually specify different crisis types, as is necessary for a more complex exploration of their relevance in and beyond the EU's political system.

Crisis origin

The first distinction to be made relates to whether a crisis is constituted through an *exogenous* development that then affects the EU indirectly or directly, or is *endogenous* to the EU and its political system. In adopting this distinction, we argue that crises do not always have to be some exogenous "property" or "chain of events" that "hit [the EU's] institutions, politics, and policies" (Riddervold et al. 2021a, 8), but can equally be produced within the institutional, economic and societal system(s) of the Union and its member states. Among the clearest examples of such endogenous crises are Brexit, and the EU's internal rule-of-law crisis (see Chapter 9 by Usherwood and Chapter 5 by Bogdanowicz). Endogenous crises are not an exclusively recent phenomenon but can be found throughout the history of the EU and its predecessors. Indeed, it could be argued that in the history of the EU endogenous states of "[c]risis arose whenever the Member States resisted (further) transfer of political authority to the EU level or opposed EU interference into their domestic affairs even though joint action at the EU level appeared to be clearly needed" (Börzel 2016: 10). Schimmelfennig (Chapter 2) specifies the delimitation of exogenous vs. endogenous crisis origins even further by distinguishing *policy failures* – as result of exogenous shocks, the impact of which exposes deficiencies of existing EU policies – from *polity attacks* as endogenous events which originate from Eurosceptic actors within the EU political system, who seek to undermine EU core institutions and constitutional principles.

Overall, however, it is not always possible to clearly distinguish exogenous from endogenous crises. Some crises may originate outside of the EU's political system and their effects may then trigger an internal crisis for the EU. In the recent past, this was notably the case for the Great Recession which began in the United States towards the end of 2007 and ended on a global scale by the end of the decade. This originally exogenous crisis – albeit facilitated by structural characteristics of the Eurozone – then caused the interlinked yet separate (endogenous) Eurozone crisis which began in 2009 and from which the EU still has not fully recovered.

Additionally, some EU crises may have their roots in exogenous phenomena which may not have qualified as a crisis originally in and of themselves. While independently these phenomena may only cause some political strain, or indeed contain merely the potential for bringing a system under strain, they may transform into an endogenous crisis within the EU's political system based on the latter's structure and functioning, or because of a specific context in which they coincide with other, strain-reinforcing events and developments. For instance, European actors may come to perceive events or developments outside the EU as questioning its fundamental values, thus risking contagion in intra-EU processes, even though these same events and developments may not trigger or constitute a crisis in and of themselves in their place of origin. In turn, endogenously created crises – such as Brexit – may not remain purely endogenous phenomena, but can have impacts beyond EU politics and policies, such as for the EU's relations with third countries, or indeed larger shifts of power on the global political stage and in international markets, such as engendered by the EU's loss of influence as a result of Brexit, e.g. manifested in its loss of a permanent seat at the table of the UN Security Council.

Similarly, certain aspects of EU political strain, which may not amount to an endogenous EU crisis in and of itself, may cause crises outside of the EU's own political system. For instance, while the question of rapid EU enlargement to the Western Balkans has caused some political strain amongst EU member states, the delay to further EU enlargement caused by this has led to various government crises in countries such as North Macedonia which hope to join the EU (see Chapter 8 by Keil & Stahl).

In short, examining and disentangling the origins of crises can help in understanding – and possibly even anticipating, as regards ongoing developments – their scope, evolution, and multidimensional impact. At the same time, any scholar conducting research in this wider area always needs to be aware that even careful analysis cannot always neatly disentangle crises as endogenous or exogenous in origin. Beyond the above-mentioned dynamics of – often enough unpredictable – interconnections, actors within the EU political system may seek to alleviate the effects, or even the mere visibility, of one crisis by (over)emphasising the need of reacting to another. In such instances, actors may, for instance, purposefully single out an exogenous crisis in their pursuit of overcoming an endogenous one. An example for such behaviour is discussed in Michael H. Smith's contribution to this volume (Chapter 7), namely the strengthening of the EU's powers in the area of external action and diplomacy as 'antidote' to internal tension regarding the possible redesign of the EU's and its actors' shifting balance of competences.

Temporality and prominence of crisis

When it comes to the temporality of crises, several distinct categorizations related to the factor of time can be made. Firstly, some crises are *long-lasting*, whereas others can be very *short* in nature, either due to a solution being found or their origin disappearing at one point in time. An exemplary area for long-lasting crises are the ever-ongoing power struggles between supranational and (inter)governmental actors at the EU level, with the former typically seeking to extend the respective institutions' remit of competence, and the latter pursuing the preservation of their decision-making power. This question of the division of competencies within the EU has never been fully resolved given different readings of the EU's treaties and altered demands by various actors across time. This is despite various attempts by both sides to address these issues, such as through the 1966 Luxembourg compromise which enshrined national veto rights to Community decision-making, or later on phase-in periods to enable further majority voting. The type of short-lived crisis is exemplified by the Presidency of Donald Trump in the United States, which led to a significant rift in transatlantic relations, but which mostly disappeared – at least temporarily – with the election of Joe Biden in 2020 (see Chapter 10 by Schade).

A related yet not entirely similar categorisation of crises can also be found in the literature on EU crisis governance. Schmidt (Schmidt 2020, 1177; emphasis added), for instance, makes a distinction between "Europe's *fast-burning crises*" starting "with the sovereign debt crisis in 2010, continued with the migration crisis that exploded in 2015, and followed with the British vote to exit the EU in 2016", and its "*slow-burning crises*" such as "the on-going security crisis, the simmering climate crisis, and the steady rise of populist anti-system parties which challenged the existence of the euro, the EU, and the tenets of liberal democracy and the rule of law in the EU and its member-states".

The distinction between these two types of crises lies not only in the pace at which a response is required, with crisis developments unfolding rapidly for fast-burning crises and requiring immediate attention, whereas reacting to slow-burning crises has the potential to be more gradual and thought-out, but also whether these are – portrayed and perceived as – *dominant* or *latent* in the EU's political system. For instance, while issues such as the Covid-19 pandemic or Russia's re-invasion of Ukraine have dominated the EU's political system, the climate crisis has until recently rarely been the focal point of the EU's entire political activity (see chapter 14 by Rosamond). Dominant crises tend to be of a fast-burning nature (e.g. Brexit, especially in its initial phase; the sovereign debt crisis; and Russia's re-invasion of Ukraine), and latent crises of a slow-burning nature (e.g. the EU's diversity and minority rights crisis, see chapter 13 by Mos). However, the chapters in this volume also shed light on cases of dominant yet mostly slow-burning crises (e.g. the rule of law crisis) and latent yet – at times, at least – fast-burning crises (e.g. the EU's political representation crisis, especially around European elections; see Chapter 6 by Kinski).

Importantly, most EU crises do not constantly unfold as fast- or slow-burning crises, or indeed dominant or latent crises. Carstensen & Schmidt (2018, 611; emphasis added) "differentiate between fast- and slow-burning *phases*" of crises, with the former "requir[ing] quick responses from actors in a position to decide", and the latter "allowing more time for reflection on optimal solutions". Similarly, while a particular crisis can dominate the EU's political system, it can transform into a latent one when a temporary workaround is found, or when another crisis begins to dominate the EU's political system, as happened in February of 2022 when Russia's re-invasion of Ukraine made the EU's Covid-19 recovery discussions take a back seat, despite the pandemic's ongoing impact on member states' economies and healthcare systems.

Similarly, some slow-burning latent crises in the EU, such as constant tensions over institutional competencies and inter-institutional relations which can be traced back to the 1950s, occasionally see fast-burning phases in which they dominate the EU's political activity. In the case of conflictual institutional relations, occasions such as the 2014 and 2019 European Parliament elections have temporarily brought these to the fore given the European Parliament's insistence on establishing the so-called *Spitzenkandidaten* procedure for the election of the European Commission President, with the European Council attempting to circumvent such efforts (Heidbreder & Schade 2020). Overall, crises can thus combine various of these temporal aspects, and even move between types over time.

Scope and nature of crisis effects

As already demonstrated through the distinction of dominant vs. latent crises, it is helpful analytically to examine not only the origins and duration but also the situatedness and effects of different types of crises within a political system. This helps in better grasping their (potential) impact on the system, understanding their inherent characteristics as compared to other crises, and thus contextualising their appearance, evolution, and possible disappearance. In this vein, it is conducive also to delineate what is affected by individual crises. Here, one can distinguish between crises that are *isolated* in nature, being of relevance only for individual EU policy areas or institutions, and *all-encompassing* crises that affect a whole host of areas of EU activity, or indeed the EU's entire political system.

While examples for the latter kind abound, such as how Brexit affected not only almost every single EU policy but also led to concerns about the EU's future composition (see Chapter 9 by Usherwood), those for the former are increasingly hard to find as the contributions to this volume show. One historical example of an isolated crisis would be the corruption scandal in the Santer Commission in the late 1990s, which led to the collective resignation of the College of Commissioners, and thereby threatened the credibility of this particular institution, yet which did not have a long-lasting effect on EU policy-making or the EU's political system in a broader sense. Instead, this crisis merely acted as a temporary highlight in the still ongoing contestation and underlying strain related to inter-institutional relations (Ringe 2005; Spence 2000).

At the same time, many crises may neither fully qualify as isolated nor all-encompassing. This is not only a characteristic of factors such as crisis origin and temporality explored above but also ultimately mitigated by the internal structure of the EU. Given the EU's current differentiated set-up (as discussed in Chapter 4 by Leruth), with not all EU member states participating in all EU policies and some non-EU countries partaking in individual EU policy areas, it may thus be important to consider whether a crisis is *differentiated* in nature or not. Here, the sovereign debt crisis can serve as an example in which only those EU members which had adopted the Euro as their currency and those EU institutions and bodies linked to Eurozone governance were directly affected.

Moreover, much like crises can move from being dominant to being latent in nature, their delineation can also change. For instance, while the so-called migration crisis of 2015 initially unfolded within the scope of the EU's asylum policy, it would soon affect related policy areas, such as the governance of the Schengen area, relations to key third countries such as Turkey, and the EU's development policy. Furthermore, the impact of the crisis on Schengen can be considered a prime example of the potential *spillover effect* of crises: a crisis that originally affected only one part of EU activity or of the EU's political system may subsequently begin to have effects on others (Niemann & Speyer 2018). Given the set-up of the Schengen area, in the case of the so-called migration crisis this also turned the crisis from one affecting the EU collectively to one that was differentiated in nature, and where a crisis related to a largely intergovernmental area of EU activity, namely migration policy, then hindered the effective governance of a more supranationally integrated area of EU activity, namely Schengen.

Beyond the *extents* of crises' impact, we can also consider *how* distinct crises have affected the EU's political system. Specifically, crises may show distinct characteristics as regards the broad type of impact and effect that they have on the EU, in that they *disrupt* existing EU activity in a particular area, and thus add strain to or intensify existing tensions in the EU's political system. Alternatively, crises may ultimately have a *shaping* effect on policies and/or politics, thus opening up new avenues for European-level cooperation, whether organized or more ad-hoc in nature. Much like how crises can move from slow-burning to fast-burning phases, so can a crisis originally have a principally disrupting effect, before later on setting the foundations for shaping EU policies or the EU's political system further. This links closely to different types of crisis responses which are discussed and distinguished in the following subsection.

To illustrate the distinction between a disrupting and a shaping crisis with an example, one can use the phase of European integration of the 1970s which was determined by multiple economic and financial shocks, and has been characterised as a period of 'Eurosclerosis'. At the time, this phase of interlinked crises was principally disrupting in nature, as many attempts to progress on European integration were stalled, such as in the realm of social and employment policy (Varsori & Mechi 2007). Later on, the larger and longer-term background effects then transformed this crisis into a shaping one, allowing not least to set the foundation for the establishment of the European Council, and producing momentum for the creation of the Economic and Monetary Union and European Political Cooperation, culminating thus in the later dynamisation of the European integration process from the early 1980s (Mourlon-Druol 2012). The Covid-19 pandemic constitutes a more recent example, initially causing a surge in intra-EU tensions as member states first chose swift national over common European action, leading not least to border closures and competition in the area of medicine, equipment, and vaccine procurement. Over the course of the pandemic, however, the impression of economic and social strain shared across the EU led to the evolution of previously unreached levels of integration, not least in the areas of health and debt policy (see Chapter 12 by Kurzer, and Chapter 15 by Eisl & Tomay).

Distinguishing between types of crisis response

Beyond characteristics in their origin, temporality, and effect on the EU's political system, crises can also be distinguished by the type of crisis *response* that they elicit by political actors involved in the EU's political system. Here, crises are typically expected by those studying them in the EU context to have an impact on the EU's governance system either by furthering European integration (if constituting a shaping crisis) or weakening it (if being principally disrupting in nature), or indeed to introduce further differentiation into the EU system (Riddervold et al. 2021a, 5). In light of this apparent connection between the occurrence of crises and the character of the respective crisis responses, scholars have tried to grasp causal pathways between different types of crises, the response that they engender, and the effect that this has on European integration as a whole.

Existing research has already developed a tripartite conceptualisation of distinct kinds of EU crisis response, with crisis possibly contributing to the (at least) partial breakdown of the EU as a response (1); providing incremental progress by "muddling through" (2); or indeed by catalysing radically new solutions (3)

(Riddervold et al. 2021a, 8). While this conceptualisation of crisis response helps to provide answers as to crises' wider impact on overall European integration, akin to how grand theories of European integration try to explain the overall evolution of the EU (see Chapter 2 by Schimmelfennig), it is less helpful in trying to understand how far crisis-driven activity has become a regular feature of day-to-day activity of the EU system akin to the explorations of middle-range theories of European integration.

To better understand crises as a now regularized feature of the EU's political system, we consider two distinct modes of crisis response by the EU, namely *crisis management* and *crisis governance*. The first of these two concepts, crisis management, describes a type of crisis response that sees EU actors react to an ongoing crisis on a largely confined and ad-hoc basis which arises out of the immediate need to urgently answer developments caused by the crisis. However, this type of response does not see the EU deliberately develop or adapt its toolkit to be able to respond more systematically to the next potential phase of said crises, or to similar crises moving forward.

In contrast to this, crisis governance sees the EU act in a more structured manner, with equal consideration being given to resolve the crisis at hand, all while equipping the EU with the necessary tools to also act in a more structured manner going forward. While crisis governance can occur immediately after the onset of a crisis, it may also happen later on, after initially attempting to contain a crisis through crisis management. For instance, while the EU's reaction to the sovereign debt crisis was initially shaped by crisis management, thus trying to deal with the immediate fallout of the crisis, later reforms to areas such as EU economic and fiscal policy and banking supervision have equipped EU actors with a new governance toolkit allowing a (theoretically) more systematic response to the issues which were at the core of the initial crisis (Haas et al. 2020; Howarth & Quaglia 2020).

Rather than adopting a course of either crisis management or governance, individual EU actors may of course also choose not to act at all upon a crisis at hand – that is, to adopt a course of *crisis ignorance*. This may happen in particular when every possible response to the crisis at hand would be more uncomfortable to the respective actor, would come with higher costs, and be (perceived as) going more against their interests, than not acting at all. Whilst this form of crisis (non-)response can hardly be found across the board of all European actors (at least some – even if powerless – agencies or individual members of EU institutions typically speak up and call for a more proactive response), the contributions to this volume trace a number of examples, for instance in the cases of the EU's political representation crisis (Kinski in Chapter 6), rule of law crisis (Bogdanowicz in Chapter 5), or migration (administration) crisis (Bousiou & Schleyer in Chapter 11). Just like crisis management and governance, ignorance may be only one stage of EU actors' overall crisis response, potentially being replaced at a later stage by either crisis management or governance measures.

In addition to these crisis response options, it would also be possible to consider a further category in which the EU would not react to or *act upon* a crisis, but instead, take action through *crisis prevention*. Such preventive action might take shape through anticipation of a possible crisis based on previous experience in another policy field, which has been affected by crisis or elevated strain in the past, causing a response at the EU level either in the form of crisis management or crisis governance. Considering the potential for a similar/comparable crisis in another policy field, EU actors may then adopt preventative action even though the respective area has not yet experienced a phase of crisis, e.g. by providing for accelerated decision-making procedures, or by outlining a detailed plan of action for the case that a swift response to the anticipated crisis is required. Such preventative action might even take the shape of treaty reform, allowing for instance for faster, more efficient, or also (more) differentiated policy-making wherever needed.

While individual institutions have attempted to enable crisis prevention in individual areas, such as the European Commission in the field of migration (Simon 2022: 6–9), we have been unable to find examples of the EU collectively having decided to provide itself with a toolkit to prevent a potential future crisis from unfolding. Instead, all crisis-related governance changes have ultimately been introduced as a prevention mechanism to avoid similar crises from happening again in the future. This can be exemplified in the now established frameworks allowing the EU to negotiate the withdrawal of a member state from the union, as triggered by Brexit (see Usherwood in Chapter 9), or the set-up of the so-called Temporary Protection Directive which was not established to pre-empt the kind of migration crisis caused by Russia's reinvasion of Ukraine, but instead as a reaction to the migration crisis triggered by the dissolution of Yugoslavia and the associated conflicts (see Bousiou & Schleyer in Chapter 11).

Whether the EU reacts or acts in response to a crisis through crisis management or crisis governance depends mainly on how affected actors perceive the crisis and the existing EU tools, where they see the need for action, as well as what public, economic and political repercussions they expect (see Hadj Abdou & Pettrachin 2022; Pettrachin 2021 for examples related to the EU's so-called migration crisis). Crucially, even where parts of a majority of the EU's political system may see the need for the introduction of tools allowing for crisis governance, instead of crisis management, this may ultimately be prevented by the lack of support on the matter from member states or institutions with the power to stall or even block related processes.

For the most part, crisis governance should be easiest for a crisis affecting the EU in areas where a strong degree of supranational integration has occurred, reducing the effect that (limited) diverging views and perceptions by individual actors on a crisis can have on the strength of the EU's crisis response. Conversely, crisis management is likely bound to occur most for those crises which unfold in policy areas principally outside of the core competencies of the EU, where the EU's continued intergovernmental nature requires a unanimous position to establish the necessary toolkits. If such a united position cannot be achieved, then the EU's response to a crisis will – at least initially – resemble a muddling-through reaction, with only those steps taken that everyone deems necessary, leading the EU's crisis response to reflect the position of the actor least keen for the EU to (re)act on the crisis collectively. It is also this underlying tension that can see crisis governance move to the realm of differentiated integration, or indeed partly or entirely outside of the scope of the EU's institutions, as is the case to some extent for the EU's sovereign debt crisis, in the European-level reaction to which the International Monetary Fund, alongside some national governments, the Commission and the European Central Bank, took centre stage in the pursuit of leading the EU and its member states out of the crisis (Véron 2016).

Both crisis management and governance have in recent years been shaped by a certain degree of *learning*. As the number and variety of crises grow which the EU and its member states have faced, so does intra- and interinstitutional, political as well as procedural experience in dealing with situations of elevated strain and urgent need for (re)action. Such experience may then be – and has over the past repeatedly shown to be – transformed into crisis responses resembling reactions to previous crises. Indeed, such learning processes and resulting similarities in crisis response strategies have proven to take shape not just between crises of similar origins, or affecting the same areas of EU policy-making, but also between very different types of crises and affected areas. A range of examples is addressed in the contributions to this volume, such as common debt schemes developed as an answer to the Eurozone crisis and then once again in the context of the Covid-19 pandemic (Eisl & Tomay in Chapter 15); the incorporation of climate objectives in economic recovery schemes within the crisis contexts of the Covid-19 pandemic and thereafter also of Russia's invasion of Ukraine (Rosamond in Chapter 14); and the idea first of a European Confederation (in the wake of the fall of the Iron Curtain) and then, more recently, of a European Political Community (under the impression of Russia's invasion of Ukraine) as institutionalised fora of cooperation between EU/European Community member states on the one hand and (mostly) Central and Eastern European countries (largely) with the ultimate aim to join the Union/Community on the other (Chapter 4 by Leruth, and Chapter 8 by Keil & Stahl).

Not least via such learning processes, which through repetition, adaptation and refinement may result in the institutionalisation of crisis response measures, crisis governance can contribute to the *formal* and permanent evolution of the EU's institutional superstructure where existing mechanisms and formats have proven unable to guide a sufficient EU crisis response. Yet, important hurdles to altering the EU's institutional superstructure through treaty reform exist. Here, only some smaller integration steps can be made by groups of willing member states as so-called enhanced cooperation, thus furthering the differentiated nature of European integration. Given the difficulty of such formal changes, crisis response thus typically occurs as more *informal* steps where this is deemed necessary or inducive. The type of crisis response is then also determined by whether it leads to further *intergovernmental* cooperation amongst the EU's member states, or whether this provides the opportunity for further *supranational* integration steps.

Typically, one would expect formal supranational integration steps to be a rather long-term effect of EU crises, following the pace of EU treaty reform. Informal steps can, however, also occur on a much more rapid basis. For instance, while health policy is an area of activity framed by very limited EU competencies, the Covid-19 pandemic has nonetheless contributed to the EU becoming a much more active player in this regard (see Chapter 12 by Kurzer). It also constitutes an example of a crisis where some further informal supranational cooperation has occurred amidst difficulties to formalise EU powers in the primarily concerned area.

Even where supranationalisation is not the aim, and where the crisis response has technically remained intergovernmental in nature, can a crisis set a precedent contributing to the shape of the EU's overall development going forward. For instance, the EU's Next Generation EU instrument as part of its Covid-19 response under which collective debt has been issued, was notionally described as a one-off process – not least to get sceptical governments to support it, against previously held opposition to common debt issuance. At the same time, this development has already served as a precedent in discussions surrounding the EU's energy crisis following Russia's reinvasion of Ukraine (see prominently Breton & Gentiloni 2022).

Lastly, it is important to point out that a crisis *response* need not necessarily be limited or genuinely linked to the respective crisis at hand. Instead, the prevalence of various crises can also serve for so-called *crisis-washing* in which a particular crisis is used to justify and legitimize EU activity in areas that have no genuine linkage to the crisis at hand. This may then allow political actors to take political decisions which would have been deemed inconceivable otherwise. One example is how the onset of the Covid-19 pandemic has led to an instance of 'Covid-washing' thus aggravating the EU's rule of law crisis. Here, the governments of both Poland

and Hungary instrumentalised the state of crisis caused by the pandemic to adopt an emergency governance modus and vastly rule by decree and with significantly limited parliamentary oversight, thus justifying a significant reduction of civil liberties as means to combat the pandemic (Drinóczi & Bień-Kacała 2020). When considering the closely connected concept of securitization, that is, the justification of policy action by actual or constructed security threats, similar developments could also be observed for the EU's migration policy (see Chapter 11 by Bousiou & Schleyer).

EU crises across this volume

The individual chapters in this edited volume help explore the type, prevalence, and impact of different types of crises across various aspects of EU activity. Whilst the introductory part seeks to provide a conceptual and theoretical framework for the study of the interconnections of EU governance and crisis, the following three thematic parts of this volume contain a wide range of case studies of specific crises which currently shape EU policies and politics, and often enough also have the potential to impact the EU polity as a whole. In the chapter following this introduction, Schimmelfennig develops a novel conceptualisation approach offering a key to distinguish the ways in which different types of crises may predominantly affect either EU policies, or the union's core institutions and principles. Based also on a critical discussion of the grand theories of European integration's explanatory power when it comes to the study of crises in a European context, Schimmelfennig thus provides a valuable theoretical toolkit for further research in the larger thematic area of this volume.

Part II, which opens the triad of thematically structured case studies on European crisis responses, is principally concerned with crises affecting the foundations of EU integration. Here, Desmond Dinan outlines the difficulties underlying EU treaty change, thus affecting the EU governance system at large. Benjamin Leruth considers in his chapter how another core feature of EU integration, namely differentiation, has been the product of EU crises and can potentially contribute to their resolution going forward. The remaining two chapters of this section are then concerned with the EU's core values and its democratic foundation. Piotr Bogdanowicz elaborates on the EU's increasing difficulties to uphold the rule of law across the union. Lucy Kinski takes a different perspective and focuses on the EU's continuing difficulty to ensure citizen representation.

Part III of the volume then explores the EU's perspective on and role in strain and crises with a global dimension. The chapter by Michael H. Smith provides a broad overview of the evolution of the EU's standing in the wider world, including how this is determined by developments affecting the EU internally. Two chapters then focus on the EU's neighbourhood, with Simon Usherwood considering processes of disintegration and the shrinking of the EU through Brexit, while Sören Keil and Bernhard Stahl discuss the roots and effects of the EU's stalled enlargement policy. The remaining chapter of this part considers strain in the EU's international affairs beyond the immediate neighbourhood, as Daniel Schade outlines the parallel presence of different kinds of strain in the transatlantic relationship between the United States and the EU, which is shaped by international issues within and beyond the transatlantic sphere, and also by the relations of both with select third countries, such as – recently and increasingly – China.

The last part of the volume sheds light on key areas of EU activity that have been affected by crises over the course of the last decade. Here, Alexandra Bousiou and Linnea Schleyer consider the wider effects of the so-called migration crisis of 2015 within the fields of asylum policy, border control management, and beyond. Paulette Kurzer then discusses EU health policy amidst the Covid-19 pandemic, and thus another area of EU activity shaped and affected by a major crisis in recent years. As a contrasting case study to such fast-burning and dominant crises, Martijn Mos' analysis of minority rights across the union provides an example of a latent crisis for the EU, yet one which affects the very foundations of its societies and fundamental value system. Thereafter, Jeffrey Rosamond sheds light on the EU's response to the climate emergency, and how this slow-burning crisis links up with other recent EU crises. Focusing on EU finance and debt policy, Andreas Eisl and Mattia Tomay lastly consider an area of EU activity that gained particular relevance in the aftermath of the Eurozone crisis, and which has again been shaped in important ways by a crisis in recent years, namely by the Covid-19 pandemic.

In their variety of crisis roots and origins, affected policy areas and institutions, consequences and responses, the different examples of strain studied in the contributions to this volume provide examples for almost all of the types of crisis characteristics conceptualised in this introductory chapter. Table 1.1 provides an overview of the types of crises' origins, temporality, prominence, effects, and response mechanisms covered in the following chapters.

Many of the crises mentioned in Table 1.1 are addressed in several chapters (see the volume's index for a comprehensive list of respective mentions). However, to keep the table as clear and concise as possible, it lists only those contributions which put a primary focus on the respective crises. In the same vein, the table does not contain the categories crisis learning, formal & informal responses, and supranational & intergovernmental responses: considering that such crisis response processes appear(ed) in all crises covered, virtually all chapters would need to be listed under each of the categories, which would be detrimental to the table's clarity and comprehensibility. The table also leaves out the categories crisis prevention, given that no occurrence could be identified, as discussed above, and crisis-washing, since no case thereof is addressed in any of the contributions to this volume.

While all of these chapters vary in the crises that they consider, as well as the overall focus that these bring to the discussion, they nonetheless contribute to a broader discussion on the interrelations of crises and the EU present throughout this volume, and speak to one another in important ways. Overall, the volume thus serves as a map of the broad landscape of strain and crises affecting the EU. When utilizing the typology developed here it can also serve as a guide to link similar types of crises and their effects more clearly, as well as to distinguish those whose defining underlying characteristics differ substantially. Lastly, the volume illustrates that crises are (now) part and parcel of the development of the EU and cannot be considered an exception to an otherwise harmonious process of European integration.

Table 1.1: Crisis characteristics from the conceptual framework developed in this chapter, with examples covered in the contributions to this volume

Crisis characteristics	Examples (chapter in this volume)
Origins	
Exogenous	Climate crisis (Rosamond)
	Covid-19 pandemic (Kurzer)
	Global political turmoil (Smith)
	Transatlantic relations crisis (Schade)
Endogenous	Brexit (Usherwood)
	Rule of law crisis (Bogdanowicz)
	Crisis of political representation in the EU (Kinski)
Mix of (relatively balanced) exogenous and endogenous causes	Sovereign debt crisis (Eisl & Tomay)
	Migration crisis (Bousiou & Schleyer)
	Enlargement (Keil & Stahl)
Temporality and prominence	
Long-lasting	Climate crisis (Rosamond)
	Crisis of political representation in the EU (Kinski)
	Crisis to uphold diversity and minority rights in the EU (Mos)
Short	Covid-19 pandemic (Kurzer)
	Migration crisis & refugee emergency following Russia's re-invasion of Ukraine (Bousiou & Schleyer)
	Transatlantic relations crisis under the Trump presidency (Schade)

Table 1.1: Crisis characteristics from the conceptual framework developed in this chapter, with examples covered in the contributions to this volume *(Continued)*

Crisis characteristics	Examples (chapter in this volume)
Fast-burning (dominantly)	Brexit (Usherwood; at least in its initial phase) Covid-19 pandemic (Kurzer) European sovereign debt crisis (Eisl & Tomay) Migration crisis & refugee emergency following Russia's re-invasion of Ukraine (Bousiou & Schleyer) Transatlantic relations crisis (Schade)
Slow-burning (dominantly)	Climate crisis Rule of law crisis (Bogdanowicz; with occasional fast-burning phases – notably when colliding with other crises such as Covid-19 and Russia's re-invasion of Ukraine) Crisis to uphold diversity and minority rights in the EU (Mos)
Dominant	Brexit (Usherwood; at least in its initial phase) Covid-19 pandemic (Kurzer) Migration crisis (Bousiou & Schleyer) Russia's re-invasion of Ukraine (Smith)
Latent	Climate crisis (Rosamond) Crisis to uphold diversity and minority rights in the EU (Mos) Crisis of political representation in the EU (Kinski)
Effects	
Isolated	Brexit (Usherwood) Migration crisis (Bousiou & Schleyer)
All-encompassing	Russia's war on Ukraine (Bousiou & Schleyer; Leruth; Smith) Treaty articles and Treaty changes both as possible effect and root of/fuel for crisis (Dinan) Rule of law crisis (Bogdanowicz) Crisis of political representation in the EU (Kinski) Climate crisis (Rosamond; although long treated by EU actors as isolated crisis)
Differentiation	Brexit & Russia's war on Ukraine (Leruth)
Spillover	Covid-19 pandemic (Kurzer) Climate crisis: EU crisis governance to some extent hampered, but also facilitated by coinciding crises such as Covid-19 and Russia's re-invasion of Ukraine (Rosamond) Global turmoil and its effects first on the EU's external action, but gradually its entire political system and internal functioning (Smith) Effects of EU enlargement policy in third countries (Keil & Stahl)

Table 1.1: Crisis characteristics from the conceptual framework developed in this chapter, with examples covered in the contributions to this volume *(Continued)*

Crisis characteristics	Examples (chapter in this volume)
Disrupting	Brexit (Usherwood)
	Covid-19 pandemic (Kurzer; especially in its initial phase)
	Global political turmoil (Smith; Schade)
	Migration crisis (Bousiou & Schleyer)
	Rule of law crisis (Bogdanowicz)
Shaping	Climate crisis (Rosamond)
	Covid-19 pandemic (Kurzer, see also Eisl & Tomay; in its later phase)
	Crisis of political representation in the EU (Kinski)
	Differentiation as a shaping effect of crises (Leruth)
Responses	
Crisis management	Brexit (Usherwood; especially in its early phase)
	Global turmoil and shifting world order in immediate consequence of ruptures such as Brexit, US Presidency of Donald Trump, Russia's re-invasion of Ukraine (Schade; Smith)
	Migration crisis (Bousiou & Schleyer)
	Rule of law crisis (Bogdanowicz)
	Sovereign debt crisis & Covid-19 pandemic (Eisl & Tomay; Kurzer)
Crisis governance	Brexit (Usherwood; especially in its later phase)
	Shifting world order and global power balance in the aftermath of global turmoil and ruptures (Smith)
	Treaty change and reinterpretation/novel usage of Treaty provisions (Dinan)
Crisis ignorance	Climate crisis (Rosamond)
	Crisis to uphold diversity and minority rights in the EU (Mos)
	Crisis of political representation in the EU (Kinski)

References

Barthoma, Soner & Çetrez, Önver A. (2021): 'Introduction', in Soner Barthoma & Önver A. Çetrez (eds.): *RESPONDing to Migration: A Holistic Perspective on Migration Governance*, Uppsala University Library, 1–12.

Börzel, Tanja A. (2016): 'From EU Governance of Crisis to Crisis of EU Governance: Regulatory Failure, Redistributive Conflict and Eurosceptic Publics', *Journal of Common Market Studies*, 54:S1, 8–31.

Breton, Thierry & Gentiloni, Paolo (2022): 'Germany's latest response to energy crisis raises questions', The Irish Times, 3 October 2022. https://www.irishtimes.com/opinion/2022/10/03/germanys-latest-response-to-energy-crisis-raises-questions/ (Last access: 6 December 2022).

Carstensen, Martin B. & Schmidt, Vivien A. (2018): 'Power and Changing Modes of Governance in the Euro Crisis', *Governance*, 31:4, 609–24.

Davis Cross, Mai'a (2017): *The Politics of Crisis in Europe*, Cambridge University Press.

Down, Ian & Wilson Carole J. (2008): 'From 'Permissive Consensus' to 'Constraining Dissensus': A Polarizing Union?', *Acta Politica*, 43:1, 26–49.

Drinóczi, Tímea & Bień-Kacała, Agnieszka (2020): 'COVID-19 in Hungary and Poland: extraordinary situation and illiberal constitutionalism', *The Theory and Practice of Legislation*, 8:1–2, 171–1.

Ervedosa, Clara (2017): 'The Calibanisation of the South in the German public 'Euro crisis' discourse', *Postcolonial Studies*, 20:2, 137–162.

Haas, Jörg S., D'Erman, Valerie J., Schulz, Daniel F. & Verdun, Amy (2020): 'Economic and fiscal policy coordination after the crisis: is the European Semester promoting more or less state intervention?', *Journal of European Integration*, 42:3, 327–344.

Hadj Abdou, Leila & Pettrachin, Andrea (2022): 'Exploring the EU's Status Quo Tendency in the Migration Policy Field: A Network-Centred Perspective', *Journal of European Public Policy*, Online first.

Heidbreder, Eva G. & Schade, Daniel (2020): '(Un)Settling the Precedent: Contrasting Institutionalisation Dynamics in the Spitzenkandidaten Procedure of 2014 and 2019', *Research & Politics*, 7:2.

Howarth, David & Quaglia, Lucia (2020): 'One money, two markets? EMU at twenty and European financial market integration', *Journal of European Integration*, 42:3, 433–48.

Jones, Erik, Kelemen, Daniel R. & Meunier, Sophie (2021): 'Failing forward? Crises and patterns of European integration', *Journal of European Public Policy*, 28:10, 1519–36.

Juncker, Jean-Claude (2016): 'Speech by President Jean-Claude Juncker at the Annual General Meeting of the Hellenic Federation of Enterprises (SEV)', European Commission. https://ec.europa.eu/commission/presscorner/detail/en/SPEECH_16_2293 (Last access: 10 December 2022).

Magone, José, Laffan, Brigid & Schweiger, Christian (eds.) (2016): *Core-Periphery Relations in the European Union: Power and Conflict in a Dualist Political Economy*, Routledge.

Mourlon-Druol, Emmanuel (2012): 'Regional Integration and Global Governance: the Example of the European Council (1974–1986)', *Les cahiers Irice*, 9:1, 91–104.

Niemann, Arne & Speyer, Johanna (2018): 'A Neofunctionalist Perspective on the "European Refugee Crisis": The Case of the European Border and Coast Guard', *Journal of Common Market Studies*, 56(1), 23–43.

Pettrachin, Andrea (2021): 'Responding to the "Refugee Crisis" or Shaping the "Refugee Crisis"? Subnational Migration Policymaking as a Cause and Effect of Turbulence', *Journal of Immigrant & Refugee Studies*, Online first.

Riddervold, Marianne, Trondal, Jarle & Newsome, Akasemi (2021a): 'European Union Crisis: An Introduction', in Marianne Riddervold, Jarle Trondal & Akasemi Newsome (eds.): *The Palgrave Handbook of EU Crises*, Palgrave Macmillan, 3–47.

Riddervold, Marianne, Trondal, Jarle & Newsome, Akasemi (eds.) (2021b): *The Palgrave Handbook of EU Crises*, Palgrave Macmillan.

Ringe, Nils (2005): 'Government-Opposition Dynamics in the European Union: The Santer Commission Resignation Crisis', *European Journal of Political Research*, 44:5, 671–96.

Schmidt, Vivien A. (2020): 'Theorizing Institutional Change and Governance in European Responses to the Covid-19 Pandemic', *Journal of European Integration*, 42:8, 1177–93.

Simon, Julia (2022): 'The crisis discourse's blind spot: EU-level politicization and the endogenization of the migration crisis', *Journal of European Integration*, Online first.

Schweiger, Christian & Magone, José M. (2014): 'Differentiated Integration and Cleavage in the EU under Crisis Conditions', *Perspectives on European Politics and Society*, 15:3, 259–265.

Spence, David (2000): 'Plus ca Change, plus c'est La Meme Chose? Attempting to Reform the European Commission', *Journal of European Public Policy* 7(1), 1–25.

Varsori, Antonio & Mechi, Lorenzo (2007): 'At the origins of the European structural policy: the Community's social and regional policies from the late 1960s to the mid-1970s', in Jan van der Harst (ed.): *Beyond the Customs Union: The European Community's Quest for Deepening, Widening and Completion, 1969–1975*, Bruylant, 223–50.

Véron, Nicolas (2016): *The International Monetary Fund's role in the euro-area crisis: financial sector aspects*, Bruegel, Policy Contribution no. 13. https://www.bruegel.org/sites/default/files/wp_at tachments/PC-13-2016.pdf (Last access: 10 December 2022).

Zeitlin, Jonathan, Nicoli, Francesco & Laffan, Brigid (2019): 'Introduction: The European Union beyond the Polycrisis? Integration and Politicization in an Age of Shifting Cleavages', *Journal of European Public Policy*, 26(7): 963–76.

Frank Schimmelfennig

2 Polity attacks and policy failures: The EU polycrisis and integration theory

Abstract: For more than a decade, the European Union has been in perpetual crisis. The 'polycrisis' has amounted to a fundamental threat to the EU's core domains of post-Cold War integration. It has also turned attention to integration theories and their strengths and weaknesses in explaining integration crises. In the first section, the chapter suggests that the major integration theories make important contributions to the study of integration crises but also suffer from systematic gaps. As a remedy, I propose a functionalist synthesis of liberal intergovernmentalism and neofunctionalism and an elaboration of postfunctionalism. In the second section, the chapter distinguishes two types of integration crises – policy failures and polity attacks – which differ in their origins and produce diverse crisis dynamics and outcomes. I further suggest a theoretical division of labour: policy failures are best explained by the synthetic functionalist theory, whereas polity attacks are best accounted for by the expanded postfunctionalist theory. The chapter concludes with brief and illustrative case studies of the euro, migration, and corona crises (policy failures) and the Russia, Brexit, and rule of law crises (polity attacks) in order to demonstrate the empirical plausibility of the proposed typology and theoretical synthesis.

Keywords: Crisis, European integration, European Union, integration theory

Introduction

The immediate post-Cold War period was a period of massive growth in European integration. The European Union (EU) established its internal market and the common currency, aiming to crown economic integration and make it irreversible. Beyond economic integration, it built an 'Area of Freedom, Security and Justice', combining the free movement of persons across internal borders with common migration and justice policies. In addition, it pursued the grand project of reunify-

Acknowledgments: The author gratefully acknowledges financial support from the Jacques Delors Centre, Hertie School of Governance, Berlin (Michael Endres Visiting Professorship 2020/2021). I thank Christian Freudlsperger, Hanspeter Kriesi, and Berthold Rittberger as well as the audience at the ECPR SGEU conference in Rome in 2022 for comments on earlier versions.

https://doi.org/10.1515/9783110790337-003

ing Europe after decades of geopolitical and ideological division, more than doubling its membership and associating further countries in its neighbourhood.

All these flagship projects of post-Cold War European integration have experienced severe crises. The Brexit crisis challenged the integrity of the internal market, and the euro crisis put the monetary union at risk. The migration crisis threatened the 'Schengen' area of free travel and the common asylum policy. The Covid-19 pandemic combined challenges to the free movement of goods and persons with an economic and fiscal threat to the member states. Internally, the record of enlargement was tainted by the erosion of the rule of law in some new member states. Externally, it clashed with Russian revisionism in Eastern Europe. In 2016, when its full scale could not yet be known, Commission President Jean-Claude Juncker termed the dire state of the union a 'polycrisis'.[1] While earlier integration crises had mainly stopped or delayed plans for deeper integration from the European Defence Community to the Constitutional Treaty. The polycrisis, however, has threatened already deeply integrated policies with disintegration. In the EU context, threats of disintegration correspond to the definition of Boin et al. (2016: 5): a social system in crisis 'experiences an urgent threat to its basic structures or fundamental values'.

The polycrisis has also presented a formidable challenge to the theory of European integration. For one, the debate between the grand theories of European integration, which had been vibrant throughout the 1990s and early 2000s, had largely subsided ahead of the polycrisis. Under the assumption that the EU had reached a stable institutional setting and that major new integration projects were not on the horizon, integration theories focusing on polity change appeared to lose relevance, and the attention shifted to steady-state EU politics and policymaking.

Moreover, integration crises have not been the focus of the main contemporary integration theories. Liberal intergovernmentalism concentrated on explaining the 'major steps toward European integration' from Messina to Maastricht (Moravcsik 1998: 4). Supranational institutionalism emphasized gradual institutionalization dynamics driving integration forward (Stone Sweet & Sandholtz 1997). Whereas postfunctionalism (Hooghe and Marks 2009) is closer to a crisis perspective on integration, it analyses the domestic politicization and scepticism of European integration rather than EU-level crisis management and outcomes.

The polycrisis has refuelled interest in and controversy among theories of European integration (see, e.g., Hooghe & Marks 2019; Ioannou et al. 2015; Niemann &

---

1 'Speech by President Jean-Claude Juncker at the Annual General Meeting of the Hellenic Federation of Enterprises (SEV)', 21 June 2016, available at https://ec.europa.eu/commission/presscorner/detail/en/SPEECH_16_2293 (last access 16 December 2022).

Zaun 2018). While most contributions have analysed individual crises, a few studies have shifted towards comparing several crises from the vantage point of a single integration theory or in the framework of theory competition (see, e.g., Börzel & Risse 2018; Jones et al. 2016; Schimmelfennig 2014, 2018a, 2018b; Webber 2018). These studies do not establish overwhelming evidence in favour of a single theory. In a survey article, Hooghe and Marks portray integration theories as 'partial attempts to shed light on a multi-faceted phenomenon' (2019: 1113) but also call for mining integration theories 'for conflicting hypotheses that can be systematically tested against each other' (2019: 1128). In response to the apparent heterogeneity of integration crises, Ferrara and Kriesi (2022) have engaged in theoretical synthesis rather than competition, spelling out scope conditions under which different theories hold. This chapter follows the same strategy.

First, it argues that each grand theory makes an important contribution to the study of integration crises but also suffers from systematic explanatory gaps. Whereas liberal intergovernmentalism has the tools to examine and explain the intergovernmental preference formation, negotiation, and institutional design processes at the heart of crisis decision-making, its confidence in the efficiency and stability of integration and its neglect of feedback processes make it a weak candidate for the analysis of crisis origins and endogenous crisis management conditions. By contrast, neofunctionalism focuses on the feedback processes of integration. Its conceptualization of 'spillovers' can serve as a starting point for theorizing the origins of integration crises and its analysis of the institutionalization processes triggered by integration provides potential explanations for the crisis response and resilience of integrated policies. In turn, however, neofunctionalism has little to say about crisis decision-making. Postfunctionalism offers a rival account of endogenous crisis origins. In contrast to the neofunctionalist focus on functional deficits, it emphasizes the domestic politicization of integration. Furthermore, whereas neofunctionalism theorizes transnational and supranational stabilizers of integration, postfunctionalism highlights domestic destabilizers. However, postfunctionalism does not theorize EU-level negotiations and responses to crisis beyond emphasizing domestic constraints. In conclusion, I suggest a functionalist synthesis of liberal intergovernmentalism and neofunctionalism that combines the strengths of both theories and an elaboration of postfunctionalism that extends the assumptions and propositions of this theory to the EU responses to politicization.

Second, I propose a typology of integration crises – distinguishing policy failures and polity attacks – and a concomitant theoretical division of labour. Whereas policy failures result from exogenous shocks that expose deficiencies of EU policies, polity attacks originate with Eurosceptic actors taking determined action against core institutions and constitutional principles of the EU. Polity attacks correspond closely with postfunctionalist theorizing, whereas functionalist theories are better at explaining the management of policy failures. The chapter further suggests that polity attacks and policy failures produce different crisis processes that correspond to postfunctionalist and functionalist assumptions and hypotheses.

I conclude the paper with an illustrative classification and brief description of the individual crises of the EU's polycrisis. I categorize the euro, migration, and corona crises as policy failures and the Brexit, rule of law, and Russia crises as polity attacks – and I argue that the main process features exhibited by these crises fit with functionalist and postfunctionalist expectations, respectively.

Integration theories and the crisis challenge: functionalist synthesis and postfunctionalist elaboration

This section[2] focuses on the three major contemporary theories of European integration: (liberal) intergovernmentalism, neofunctionalism, and postfunctionalism. Neofunctionalism and intergovernmentalism are the canonical theories going back to the early period of European integration. Postfunctionalism has established itself as the major alternative to the older theories, emphasizing the democratic mass politics that they neglect.

Liberal intergovernmentalism proposes a three-stage explanation for European integration (Moravcsik 1998): national integration preferences form in a context of international interdependence and domestic interest group conflict; substantive policy agreements result from intergovernmental negotiations shaped by the constellation of issue-specific preferences and bargaining power and governments establish supranational institutions to secure the integrated policy. This three-stage explanation of integration is easily transferable to crisis decision-making. Integration crises are situations of intergovernmental negotiations and decision-making under conditions of particularly intense and acute interdependence. Governments form preferences on how the EU should deal with the threat of disintegration; they negotiate the collective response to the crisis, and introduce institutional reforms to overcome the threat and stabilize integration. States calculate their individual disintegration risk and form their crisis management preferences based on the balance of disintegration costs and benefits. The states that are hardest hit by

---

2 The section builds on Schimmelfennig (2022a).

the crisis find themselves in a weak bargaining position and are most willing to compromise (Moravcsik 1998: 3). If the crisis demonstrates that existing institutions are incomplete or insufficient to preserve the integrated policy, states will be open to reforming them.

Yet, for two main reasons, liberal intergovernmentalism has little to say about the origins of integration crises and the endogenous conditions of crisis management. For one, liberal intergovernmentalism does not theorize the feedback processes and effects of integration. It analyses European integration as a sequence of independent intergovernmental negotiation episodes, each of which ends with a distributional and institutional integration outcome. Liberal intergovernmentalism, therefore, lacks the theoretical tools to examine and explain integration crises as endogenous effects of, and crisis negotiations as informed and constrained by, earlier integration decisions and practices.

Moreover, liberal intergovernmentalism regards integration crises as rare and random events. It assumes that integration outcomes are efficient and mutually beneficial (Moravcsik 1998: 51; Moravcsik 2018: 1653). Rational actors calculate the longer-term consequences of integration with considerable certainty (Moravcsik 1998: 491). National preferences are stable (Moravcsik 1998: 493), and societal losers of integration are weakened in the process of European economic integration because of competitive elimination or structural adjustment (Moravcsik 1998: 490). Supranational institutions not only stabilize governments' commitments to the agreed policies but also deal with 'incomplete contracting', i.e., with particular or unanticipated situations, for which the treaties and legislation do not specify detailed rules (Moravcsik 1998: 73). Correspondingly, EU institutions can detect risks of failure and react to them before they develop into full-blown integration crises. To conclude, liberal intergovernmentalism has the tools to examine and explain the intergovernmental preference formation, negotiation, and institutional design processes at the heart of crisis decision-making; yet its confidence in the efficiency and stability of integration and its neglect of feedback processes make it a weak candidate for the analysis of crisis origins and endogenous conditions of crisis management.

Neofunctionalism focuses on the feedback ('spillover') processes of integration that liberal intergovernmentalism neglects. In Haas' early theorizing, spillover resulted from unanticipated and unintended consequences of integration but was thought to produce gradual, incremental, and positive change rather than crises (Haas 1958: 283–317). By contrast, Schmitter's revised neofunctionalism (1969; 1970) included 'crisis-induced decisional cycles' as a regular, endogenous feature of the integration process and regarded the outcome of integration crises as open (including disintegration or 'spillback'). Schmitter identified three main mechanisms of endogenous crisis. First, according to the 'spillover hypothesis', crisis may result from 'frustration and/or dissatisfaction generated by unexpected performance ... in a sector' (Schmitter 1969: 162). Second, integrated policies may 'elicit a reaction from adversely affected outsiders' who 'may threaten reprisals against the regional unit'. This is the 'externalization hypothesis' (Schmitter 1969: 165). Finally, according to the 'politicization hypothesis', the 'controversiality of joint decision-making goes up', which 'in turn is likely to lead to a widening of the audience or clientele interested and active in integration' (Schmitter, 1969: 166). Each integration crisis triggers a new 'decisional cycle' in the process of integration. Crises 'compel national or regional authorities to revise their respective strategies and, collectively, to determine whether the now joint institution(s) will expand or contract' (Schmitter 1970: 842).

However, in theorizing crisis decision-making, Schmitter (1970: 851–7) focuses predominantly on structural factors affecting national strategies (such as the size and domestic structures of states, the strength of transnational groups, and supranational bureaucracies or the structure of transactions within and beyond the region). Conversely, the theory has little to say on the issue-specific preferences and power of the actors, on the one hand, and on processes of negotiation and decision-making, on the other.

The 'supranational governance' approach (Sandholtz & Stone Sweet 1998; Stone Sweet & Sandholtz 1997) further elaborated neofunctionalism – not least by incorporating historical-institutionalist theorizing (Pierson 1996) – but again focused on incremental progress in integration rather than integration crises. However, the processes of transnational group formation and supranational institutionalization they highlight are in line with Schmitter's factors of crisis-induced integration, and the historical-institutionalist mechanism of path-dependence substantiates Schmitter's (1969: 163; 1970: 861) expectation that integration crises are less likely to result in disintegration as integration progresses. Neofunctionalism thus not only regards recurrent crises as an endogenous feature of European integration but also points to endogenous remedies: the increasing relevance of a transnational and supranational pro-integration constituency, the 'lock-in' of integration processes, and the stickiness of EU institutions. Yet, the neofunctionalist focus on the transnational and supranational politics of integration goes together with neglect of domestic politics, government preferences, and intergovernmental conflict and negotiations – all of which take centre stage in the EU's crisis response. Showing that transnational and supranational processes effectively constrain and influence intergovernmental agreements is not sufficient for dispensing with the analysis of national preferences and intergovernmental negotiations altogether.

The foci and gaps in intergovernmentalist and neofunctionalist theorizing on integration crises thus complement each other. Whereas intergovernmentalism has the tools to analyse preference formation, bargaining, and institution-building in the crisis management process, neofunctionalism addresses the feedback processes of integration that generate integration crises but also constrain the crisis response and outcomes transnationally and supranationally. It thus makes sense to synthesize both theories into a *functionalist theory of integration crisis*. Such a synthetic account has been suggested in recent contributions to the theoretical analysis of EU crises and integration (Freudlsperger & Jachtenfuchs 2021; Jones et al. 2016; Moravcsik 2018; 1665–6; Schimmelfennig 2018b); and it has received a further impetus by the advent of postfunctionalism, which treats both liberal intergovernmentalism and neofunctionalism as variants of 'functionalism'.

By contrast, *postfunctionalism* assumes that 'governance is [...] an expression of community. [...] Communities demand self-rule, and the preference for self-rule is almost always inconsistent with the functional demand for regional authority' (Hooghe & Marks 2009: 2). As economic integration has deepened and expanded to the domain of core state powers, it has turned into a challenge for the self-determination of national communities and into a positional issue in the 'transnational' divide that has come to increasingly structure political conflict in European societies (Hooghe & Marks 2018; Marks et al. 2021). The politics of integration has shifted from the elite arena of issue-specific negotiations – involving interest groups, executives, and supranational bodies in the distribution of the policy gains of integration – to the mass arena of identity politics. In this arena, social movements, parties, and mass media become relevant actors of European integration, and identities and values rather than policy-specific interests and cost-benefit calculations shape integration preferences (Hooghe & Marks 2019: 1116). Eurosceptic parties have been able to exploit the new cleavage and the shift to the mass arena. As a result, postfunctionalism expects 'to see downward pressure on the level and scope of integration', a 'constraining dissensus' limiting governments' room to manoeuvre, and a mismatch of functionally efficient and politically feasible European policies (Hooghe & Marks 2009: 21–23).

Even though Hooghe and Marks published their postfunctionalist theory of integration before the polycrisis began and did not explicitly frame it as a crisis theory, postfunctionalism is closer to a theory of integration crises than either intergovernmentalism or neofunctionalism. In contrast to the other two theories, postfunctionalism discusses disintegration ('downward pressure') as an expected outcome of integration – not as an unlikely accident. It also theorizes the rise of anti-integrationist domestic politicization, for which the contemporary versions of intergovernmentalism and neofunctionalism do not have a systematic place.

Yet, postfunctionalism is predominantly a theory of domestic constraints on European integration. It has much less to say about intergovernmental and supranational decision-making as such – the substantive and institutional choices that governments and other negotiators prefer and make in EU policymaking (Moravcsik 2018: 1660–1661). This general theoretical limitation also affects the use of postfunctionalism as a theory of integration crisis. Whereas postfunctionalism expects that domestic politicization delays crisis decisions and 'narrow[s] the options for responses to Europe's crises' (Marks et al. 2021: 190), it does not explain which responses European crisis actors actually take and under which conditions crises produce integrative or disintegrative outcomes.

This systematic gap in postfunctionalist theorizing calls for the further elaboration of postfunctionalist integration theory. For one, an *extended postfunctionalist integration theory* could draw, for instance, on accounts of two-level negotiations that provide the analytical link between domestic politicization and intergovernmental negotiations (see Biermann & Jagdhuber 2022; König 2018). The study of EU-level bodies reacting strategically to bottom-up politicization pressures (Bressanelli et al. 2020) is another fruitful venue. In addition, however, a complete postfunctionalist crisis theory needs to apply the same assumptions about community-oriented preferences and behaviour, which it uses for domestic politics, to the transnational and supranational level.

In principle, the ideological and identity conflict about European integration is an open contest between nationalists and transnationalists (Hooghe et al. 2019: 19). It pits the defenders of national communities against the defenders of supranational community. In line with postfunctionalist assumptions, in crises of integration, transnationalists are similarly driven by their supranational identities, their concerns about the survival, integrity, and self-determination of the supranational community as nationalists are driven by national identities and committed to the autonomy and sovereignty of the national community. In response to integration crises threatening the supranational community with disintegration, transnationalists rally around the (European) flag, ostracize nationalists, and ideologize and institutionalize contested supranational values and norms. In the process, they may strengthen the competence and capacity of supranational actors for the defence of the supranational community. In contrast to the mainstream postfunctionalist expectations of stagnation and disintegration, the elaborated postfunctionalist theory thus suggests that the mobilization of transnationalists and the defence of supranationalist community can actually strengthen European integration (Schimmelfennig 2022b).

The synthetic functionalist theory and the elaborated postfunctionalist theory can then be tested against each other in the explanation of integration crises. But rather than claiming that a single integration theory is superior to the other, I suggest a division of labour: the explanatory power of the theories depends on the type of integration crisis.

Integration theories and types of crises: policy failures and political attacks

I distinguish two types of integration crises: *policy failures* and *political attacks*.[3] Policy failures are crises of efficiency. Exogenous shocks expose flaws in the design, instruments, and capacity of the EU's integrated policies. Even though the shock itself is not an effect of European integration, the fact that it triggers a crisis indicates a failure of anticipation and preparation. Such unanticipated shocks can push EU policies to the verge of breakdown, without any EU actor having provoked the crisis or called for disintegration. By contrast, polity attacks are crises of legitimacy. Political actors opposed to supranational integration take determined action aimed at disintegration. Polity attacks are typically endogenous, i.e., caused by the integration process itself: they respond to policies of the EU that (supposedly) reduce the autonomy and go against the political preferences of the attackers. Moreover, they address core values and institutions of the EU rather than, or in addition to, specific policy regimes. Put differently, the polycrisis hit some EU flagship projects because their integration had not gone far enough to effectively weather exogenous shocks (policy failures), and others because their integration had gone too far for the taste of nationalist opponents to supranational integration (polity attacks).

The dichotomy of polity attacks and policy failures has important theoretical implications. For one, polity attacks and policy failures not only have different origins but are also likely to produce different preference constellations, conflicts, negotiation dynamics, and crisis outcomes. In other words, if we know the origins of the crisis and are thus able to classify it as a policy failure or a polity attack, we are also able to explain important features of the crisis management process. Moreover, polity attacks correspond with postfunctionalist theorizing about European integration, whereas functionalist theories are more suitable for explaining the emergence and management of policy failures. Table 2.1 contrasts the main postfunctionalist propositions on polity attacks with the functionalist propositions on policy failures.

Crisis origins. In line with postfunctionalist assumptions, polity attacks originate in threats to national self-determination. Such threats are most likely to emerge in societies with pronounced exclusive national identities and with nationalist governments that are sceptical toward supranational integration on principle. Attacks also generally have their origin in community-relevant policies. Such pol-

---

3 This section builds on Schimmelfennig (2022b).

Table 2.1: Functionalist and postfunctionalist crisis expectations compared

	Postfunctionalism	Functionalism
Crisis type	Polity attack	Policy failure
Crisis origins		
- trigger	Endogenous principled rejection of supranational integration	Exogenous shocks exposing deficits of supranational policies
- countries	Nationalist governments and societies	Vulnerable states and societies
- policies	Community-relevant policies	Low-capacity policies
Crisis management preferences		
- interests	Ideological polity interests	Material policy interests
- constellations	Disagreement on polity preservation	Agreement on policy preservation
Crisis negotiations		
- type	Ideological and disintegrative	Distributive and integrative
- objective	Defence of the integrity and autonomy of communities	Minimization and redistribution of preservation costs
- bargaining power	Depends on ideological determination	Depends on affectedness, indispensability, and alternative options
Crisis outcomes	Defence of polity; integration of defenders and disintegration of attackers	Preservation of policy; integration (if functionally needed)

icies concern internal and external security, immigration, social sharing as well as cultural and morality issues. By contrast, policy failures result from exogenous shocks that expose or exacerbate flaws in the design and instruments of an integrated policy. They typically originate in policies characterized by weak supranational financial, administrative, and coercive shock-absorbing capacity, and in those member states that are most vulnerable to shocks and lack national capacity.

Crisis management preferences. According to functionalism, actors form their crisis management preferences based on their issue-specific risk from disintegration. They prioritize tangible, predominantly material, policy interests and weigh the costs of policy preservation against the costs of policy reversal (disintegration). Faced with policy failure, member states are likely to agree on the desirability of policy preservation. For one, failures are unintended and affect policies that member states had supported before the shock. Moreover, functionalism assumes that path dependence and loss aversion bias actors in favour of policy preservation (Pierson 1996). Member states are likely to have made major investments in policy integration, adjusted national institutions and policies, and deepened their transnational interdependence. In this situation, they are typically willing to invest further in the consolidation of the policy rather than facing the uncertainties of dis-integration.

By contrast, postfunctionalism assumes ideological polity interests that derive from identity-based general attitudes towards European integration rather than issue-specific risk calculations. Actors who prioritize ideological polity interests ex-hibit reduced sensitivity to policy costs and material losses. Whereas policy failures hit states that are predisposed towards policy preservation, polity attacks produce disagreement on policy preservation from the start. Disintegration is the explicit objective of the attacking governments, whereas the defenders seek to protect the polity.

Crisis negotiations. Correspondingly, crisis negotiations responding to polity at-tacks tend to be ideology-laden and driven by the determination of both sides to defend the integrity and autonomy of their political communities. Actors regularly forgo policy benefits of cooperation for the sake of self-determination gains. Bar-gaining power is shaped by the relative ideological determination of both sides. A 'constraining dissensus' (Hooghe & Marks 2009) obtains if the intergovernmental search for compromise is undermined by the domestic dominance of ideological Eurosceptics. Crisis negotiations tend to exhibit a polarizing and disintegrative dy-namic driving attackers and defenders further apart.

In the case of policy failure, in which governments typically agree on policy preservation, negotiations focus on the distribution of preservation costs. In dis-tributive bargaining, power reflects asymmetrical interdependence. The less states are negatively affected by the policy failure and the more that their consent and capabilities are needed for preserving the policy, the better they can shape the dis-tributive outcome in their favour. In addition, states that have viable unilateral and international alternatives to policy integration within the EU enjoy higher bargain-ing power (Moravcsik 1998). Obviously, distributional conflict can exhibit polariz-ing dynamics, too. In contrast to polity attacks, they are constrained, however, by the overriding common interest in avoiding disintegration.

Crisis outcomes. From the functionalist perspective, governments that are faced with unintended policy failure and have policy interests biased by path de-pendence and loss aversion typically agree on and stand a good chance of achiev-ing policy preservation. The common goal of avoiding disintegration constrains hard distributive bargaining and generates a willingness to strengthen suprana-tional institutions to the extent necessary to end the policy failure and consolidate the integrated policy. The likelihood of policy preservation and further integration increases with the extent of international interdependence, the risks of disintegra-tion, and the capacity of supranational organizations to intervene in favour of pol-icy preservation (Schimmelfennig 2018a).

By contrast, political attacks typically have a dual outcome. On one hand, they run a high risk of escalating to the actual disintegration of the attacker – typically producing a form of exit or exclusion that is highly inefficient from a functional, policy-oriented perspective. On the other hand, attacks promote further integration. They induce unity and cohesion among the defenders, buttress the supranational capacity to respond to attacks, and reassert the values and norms of integration and membership.

Crises in comparison: polity attacks and policy failures in the EU polycrisis

This section provides a brief illustration and initial empirical plausibility test of the typology. Starting from the distinction of polity attacks and policy failures in Table 2.1, I classify the integration crises of the EU's polycrisis and describe their main features in Table 2.2. Accordingly, the EU has experienced three policy failures (the euro, migration, and corona crises) and three political attacks (the Russia, Brexit, and rule of law crises) during its polycrisis.

Crisis origins

In all three cases of policy failure, the crisis was triggered by exogenous shocks hitting the most vulnerable integrated countries. The euro crisis broke out at the end of a chain reaction starting with the US subprime mortgage crisis in 2007, which triggered a global financial crisis and a European banking crisis followed by a sovereign debt crisis in the mostly southern countries of the Eurozone. In the migration crisis, armed conflict and political repression in the Middle East significantly increased migration numbers and overwhelmed the Mediterranean countries of first entry. Finally, the Covid-19 pandemic spread from China to Europe in early 2020. In response, EU member states introduced lockdown measures at a time when they had not yet fully recovered from the euro crisis, causing an economic slump and debt levels that exceeded those of the euro crisis. The southern European countries were again hit particularly early and hard.

None of these crises resulted from a targeted attack against the EU's supranational policies, but each crisis exposed the lack of EU crisis management capacities. The EU had liberalized capital markets and delegated monetary policy to an independent central bank with a primary mandate to ensure price stability. By contrast, fiscal resources, and policy as well as the oversight of banks remained under national control. The Eurozone thus lacked effective European rules and mechanisms for the rescue or resolution of systemically relevant banks and the rescue of member states in severe balance-of-payment crises (Copelovitch et al. 2016). The EU asylum regime was not prepared to deal with a massive influx of refugees. The Schengen agreements abolished internal border controls and established a common external border. Yet, the policing of the external borders and the handling of asylum requests remained under the authority of individual member states. The 'Dublin rules' further allocate responsibility to the country of first arrival in the Schengen area. De facto, these rules put the burden of implementing the EU's asylum regime seekers on the EU's border states, many of which suffered from inadequate border protection and asylum-processing capacities. Moreover, they could not count on adequate EU financial or operational support (Bousiou & Schleyer in Chapter 11; Kriesi et al. 2021: 334–335). The corona crisis was both a health and an economic crisis. Yet, health policy had remained a predominant competence of the member states (Kurzer in Chapter 12). As for the economic crisis, member states could benefit from the instruments that had been created during the euro crisis: the credit-based European Stability Mechanism (ESM) and the bond-purchasing programs of the ECB. It soon became clear, however, that these instruments were insufficient in the face of an even deeper economic crisis and the already high levels of debt in the southern member states.

By contrast, the three cases of polity attack originated in the resistance of nationalist and Eurosceptic actors against core principles of European integration and the loss of national control resulting from supranational integration in community-relevant domains. Russia attacked Ukraine in 2014 after the Euromaidan protests had ousted a Russia-friendly government, the new Ukrainian government had signed an association agreement with the EU, and Ukraine appeared to escape the Russian sphere of influence for good. With the all-out war against Ukraine in 2022, Russia sought to regain full control over Ukrainian territory. Russian imperial ambitions clashed with the expansion of the EU's regulatory space and liberal international order.

The Brexit crisis started in a member state with a particularly strong exclusive national identity that had consistently obtained opt-outs from the supranational integration of community-relevant policies. Apart from principled concerns about national sovereignty, the attack focused on the one community-relevant EU policy, from which the UK had not opted out: internal migration. High numbers of EU migrants not only gained high public salience but also benefited the United Kingdom Independence Party (UKIP) electorally, which linked the immigration issue to its traditional anti-EU stance. To deflect the UKIP challenge and appease Eurosceptics within his Conservative party, Prime Minister Cameron promised to renegotiate the terms of UK membership and to hold an exit referendum.

Table 2.2: Functionalist and postfunctionalist crisis expectations compared

	Euro crisis	Migration crisis	Corona crisis	Russia crisis	Brexit crisis	Rule of law crisis
Crisis type	Policy failure			Polity attack		
Crisis origins						
- trigger	Exogenous shock of global financial crisis	Exogenous shock of Mediterranean migration	Exogenous shock of Covid-19 pandemic	Endogenous rejection of EU expansion	Endogenous rejection of supranational integration	Endogenous rejection of liberal democracy norms
- countries	Deficit countries	Frontline countries	Fiscally weak countries	Imperialist power	Nationalist country	Nationalist governments
- policies	Monetary union: lack of fiscal capacity	Asylum policy: lack of joint border control and asylum processing capacity	Lack of common health policy and fiscal support capacity	Association and membership	Internal migration	Rule of law
Crisis preferences						
- interests	Financial interests based on fiscal position	Restriction of migration based on geography	Financial interests based on fiscal position	Autonomy and democracy	Autonomy and integrity	Liberal values
- constellations	Agreement on preservation of Eurozone; disagreement on financial burden-sharing	Agreement on preservation of Schengen; disagreement on refugee burden-sharing	Agreement on preservation of Eurozone; disagreement on financial burden-sharing	Disagreement about European order	Disagreement about market integrity	Disagreement about independence of the judiciary
Crisis negotiations						
- type	Distributive (rescue and adjustment costs)	Distributive (allocation of asylum-seekers)	Distributive (recovery costs)	Disintegrative (sanctions)	Disintegrative (exit)	Disintegrative (sanctions)

Table 2.2: Functionalist and postfunctionalist crisis expectations compared *(Continued)*

	Euro crisis	Migration crisis	Corona crisis	Russia crisis	Brexit crisis	Rule of law crisis
- objective	Minimization of fiscal burden and adjustment	Minimization of asylum burden	Minimization of fiscal burden	Revision/defence of liberal order	Defence of sovereignty vs. market integrity	Defence of sovereignty vs. community values
- bargaining power/escalation dominance	Fiscally strong countries	Transit and by-stander countries	Fiscally strong countries	Russian revisionists	Hard Brexiteers	Backslider governments
Crisis outcomes	Preservation of Eurozone; capacity-building	Preservation of Schengen/Dublin; externalization	Preservation of Eurozone; capacity-building	Russia-EU disintegration; EU unity and Ukraine integration	UK-EU disintegration; EU-27 unity	Gradual internal ostracism

Finally, the rule of law crisis resulted from an attack of nationalist backsliding governments in Hungary and Poland on internal checks of their rule, in particular the independence of the judiciary (Bogdanowicz in Chapter 5). Because the rule of law is a fundamental value of the EU, and a prerequisite of its integration through law, governments that systematically weaken the rule of law at home not only undermine national democracy but also pose a disintegration threat to the EU. Clearly, none of these crises resulted from a failure of integrated policies, but from the perception of the attackers that supranational integration had been too effective for their taste.

Crisis management preferences

In the management of the policy failures, member states predominantly pursued self-centred and policy-specific material interests. Whereas they aimed at policy preservation, they also sought to minimize their contribution and shift the burden to other member states. In the euro crisis, high interdependence of the financial sector, significant risks of contagion, and the massive economic costs of a breakdown of the monetary union generated a common interest in preserving the Eurozone. At the same time, governments held conflicting views on the best means of rescue, which reflected divergent financial market and fiscal positions and vulnerabilities (Schimmelfennig 2015). A northern coalition of fiscally healthy surplus countries led by Germany propagated domestic austerity, fiscal discipline, stricter budget surveillance, and credit- as well as conditionality-based financial support. These measures put the bulk of the adjustment burdens on the deficit countries. By contrast, the southern coalition led by France sought to shift the rescue costs to the surplus countries. They favoured European risk sharing, budget expansion, and transfers as the way out of the crisis, e. g., in the form of Eurobonds or unlimited purchases of debt by the ECB. The start of the corona crisis saw a return of the north-south divide of the euro crisis on the issues of joint bonds (now termed 'corona bonds'), conditional vs. unconditional, and loan- vs. grant-based support (Eisl & Tomay in Chapter 15).

In the migration crisis, the member states generally sought to minimize their own burdens of processing asylum requests and hosting refugees. State interests resulted mainly from affectedness, which in turn mirrored geography and national asylum conditions. Because of their geography, frontline states like Greece and Italy were most immediately affected by the migrant flows. Destination states like Germany and Sweden, prosperous countries with a comparatively liberal asylum regime, were strongly affected by secondary migrant movement owing to attractive asylum conditions. Transit countries such as Hungary and Slovenia lay on

the migration routes from the frontline to the destination states. By-stander countries in the east and west were located off-route and therefore not directly affected.
Correspondingly, the heavily affected frontline and destination states pushed for
the redistribution of refugees across the EU, whereas transit and by-stander countries opposed relocation (Biermann et al. 2019).

By contrast, in the polity attacks, both the attackers and the defenders pursued
principled polity interests – and generally did so at the expense of issue-specific
material benefits. In the Russia crisis, the Russian government has prioritized its
polity interests of restoring imperial control and curbing democratic rule in its
neighbourhood. In response, the EU has imposed sanctions including travel
bans, asset freezes, import restrictions, and embargoes. Whereas the sanctions
after the 2014 intervention remained limited, those after the 2022 attack on Ukraine were unprecedented in scope. Even though Russia did not attack the EU directly and was unlikely to attack EU member states in NATO, the EU was prepared
to incur significant economic costs in defence of its international order.

In the Brexit crisis, from a functionalist perspective, the UK and the EU would
have been expected to make the best of the referendum (threat) and strive for a
compromise solution that would minimize policy costs. Instead, the British side insisted on an economically detrimental hard Brexit after the referendum to 'restore
[…] our national self-determination'.[4] In turn, the EU insisted on the integrity of the
internal market and ruled out a sector-by-sector approach. A formal UK opt-out
from the freedom of movement, or even the possibility to introduce an immigration quota under exceptional conditions, might well have changed the outcome of
the referendum given the centrality of the issue and the defection of leading Conservatives to the Leave camp after the New Settlement negotiations (Evans &
Menon 2017: 50). And whereas an integrated EU-UK market without the freedom
of movement for persons would have been both technically feasible and economically preferable to a mere free-trade agreement, the EU declared the four market
freedoms to be 'indivisible'.

In the rule-of-law crisis, the conflict has been slow to develop. While advocating 'illiberal democracy' and national sovereignty over the national constitutional
order, backsliding governments have not demanded their renegotiation. Moreover,
the domestic weakening of the rule of law has not had an immediate impact on EU
governance. For these reasons, the defenders of the supranational community
have initially been willing to go easy on the attackers. Over time, however,

---

4 Prime Minister's letter to Donald Tusk triggering Article 50, https://www.gov.uk/government/pub-
lications/prime-ministers-letter-to-donald-tusk-triggering-article-50 (last access 16 December 2022).

value-oriented actors in the EU's supranational institutions have gained ground on the EU side as well.

Crisis negotiations and outcomes

In all crises of the policy failure type, crisis management negotiations focused on the international distribution of the costs associated with preserving the integrated policy. In line with functionalist assumptions, superior bargaining power accrued to the states that were least affected by the crisis and whose cooperation was most needed to overcome the crisis. Because the preservation of the integrated policy was a shared goal, however, the distributional conflict was constrained. Moreover, integrative solutions were most likely where negotiations took place in a context of high international interdependence, and weak national and strong supranational capacity (Schimmelfennig 2018a).

In the euro crisis, negotiations focused on the distribution of rescue and adjustment costs between the surplus and deficit countries of the Eurozone. In these negotiations, the northern coalition, and Germany in particular, which was less affected by the crisis but whose cooperation was required to bail out the deficit countries, was able to largely shape the terms of policy preservation (Schimmelfennig 2015). Whereas the northern countries agreed to the necessary bailout measures whenever financial market pressure threatened to drive a Eurozone member state into insolvency, they refused the introduction of Eurobonds or any other formally mutualized sovereign debt and insisted on making the bailouts conditional on strict austerity. Moreover, the combination of massive disintegration costs, weak national capacity in the deficit countries, and a European Central Bank that could leverage high decision-making autonomy and monetary capacity, the crisis resulted in significant additional integration: the European Stability Mechanism, the European Banking Union, and stricter monitoring of national budgetary discipline.

In the corona crisis, negotiations shifted from bailouts, which were not necessary thanks to instruments created in the euro crisis, to recovery support, again pitting northern and southern countries against each other. However, in May 2020, the German government dropped its resistance against a recovery fund that would be borrowed by the Commission and distributed as grants through the EU budget for the benefit of the most affected sectors and regions, citing 'the extraordinary nature of the corona crisis being no one's fault, posing great dangers to the EU's cohesion and requiring a common European response (Krotz & Schramm 2022: 534). The German shift weakened the bargaining power of the remaining northern 'frugals'. The outcome not only preserved the Eurozone once again but also strengthened the fiscal capacity and solidarity of the EU (Eisl & Tomay, this volume).

In the migration crisis, distributive negotiations focused on the allocation of asylum-seekers across the EU. Here, the transit and by-stander countries wielded superior bargaining power: they were not or only transitorily affected by the migrant flows, but their willingness to accept refugees was necessary to alleviate the burden on the frontline and destination countries. Because several transit and by-stander countries have blocked Commission proposals for a burden-sharing reform of the EU asylum system since 2015, the crisis negotiations shifted towards externalization. The member states strengthened the EU's external border control capacities and outsourced responsibility for refugees to third countries such as Turkey (Kriesi et al. 2021: 343–345; Ripoll Servent & Zaun 2020; see also Bousiou & Schleyer, this volume). In contrast to the euro crisis, however, supranational integration among the member states was not functionally necessary. Rather, national measures and externalization were sufficiently effective (Genschel & Jachtenfuchs 2018). Even vulnerable member states could reduce their affectedness by national means: border controls, fences, and the 'waving through' of migrants. By contrast, states threatened by sovereign default in the euro crisis could not have coped without an international bailout. In addition, the costs of re-establishing internal Schengen borders were moderate by comparison. And the Schengen/ Dublin regime lacked powerful supranational organizations that could have pushed for more integrative solutions (Schimmelfennig 2018a).

By contrast, the crisis management of the polity attacks has been driven by ideological principles and commitments rather than distributional interests, and the insensitivity of ideologically motivated actors to material policy losses has accorded them escalation dominance. Polity attacks have consequently exhibited a disintegrative dynamic. In the Russia crisis, the revisionist zeal of the Putin regime has been initially met with attempts by major EU member states (above all, France and Germany) to ring-fence the intervention in Ukraine diplomatically, accompanied by mild sanctions and continued attempts to build mutually beneficial economic relations (as with the North Stream II pipeline). It was only after the February 2022 attack that the EU has taken an uncompromising stance. Subsequent waves of sanctions have cut most ties between the EU and Russia.

In the Brexit negotiations, polity interests trumped policy interests as well. Initially, and in line with functionalist expectations, the EU was able to use its superior material and institutional bargaining power in the intergovernmental withdrawal negotiations (Schimmelfennig 2018c). Accordingly, the government of Prime Minister Theresa May made a series of concessions to the EU, not only on process but also regarding internal market access (culminating in the Chequers Plan of July 2018) and the 'Irish backstop'. Yet, each concession of the UK government to the EU eroded its support among the defenders of national integrity and sovereignty at home: members of the government resigned, the withdrawal agreement failed in Parliament, and May had to step down. In line with postfunctionalist expectations, the constraining domestic dissensus about the autonomy price to pay for economic gain undermined efficient intergovernmental bargaining (Biermann & Jagdhuber 2021). In the negotiations on the future EU-UK relationship, the UK government sought again to maximize sovereignty, whereas the EU strove to protect the integrity of its internal market. In a few years, the UK went from full participation in the internal market to the Trade and Cooperation Agreement of December 2020, which represents the most minimal degree of economic integration with any West European non-member state.

In contrast to the UK, the attackers in the rule of law crisis do not wish to exit from the EU. Nevertheless, the crisis has set in motion a disintegrative dynamic as well. Despite the unlikely success, the Commission triggered Art. 7 against Poland in 2017; in 2018, the EP did the same against Hungary. In 2020, the EU passed a regulation establishing rule-of-law conditionality for the EU budget. Moreover, the Commission has withheld approval of Hungary's and Poland's plans for payments under the Covid-19 Recovery and Resilience Facility, totalling more than EUR 30 billion. Yet, the EU's increasing assertiveness has not induced the rule-of-law backsliders to comply – even though both countries reap large net benefits from the EU budget. Rather, the ideological defiance of the rule-of-law backsliders has hardened and the rift in the EU's membership has deepened (Bogdanowicz, this volume).

Conclusion

The brief empirical sketches of six EU integration crises have served as a plausibility probe for the main argument of this paper: that integration crises come in two major varieties and that functionalist and postfunctionalist integration theories are each suited to describe and explain one of these varieties. Overall, the dominant preference constellations, negotiation dynamics, and outcomes in policy failures and polity attacks have been in line with functionalist and postfunctionalist expectations, respectively.

But obviously, a proper empirical test would require a more detailed and nuanced engagement with the cases. Moreover, whereas policy failures generally led to policy preservation and polity attacks produced disintegrative dynamics between attackers and defenders, the degree of integration and disintegration varies within the classes of policy failures and polity attacks. This variation requires further explanation.

It is also worth noting that the crisis typology starts from a rather narrow definition of crisis as (manifest) threats of disintegration to integrated EU policies. Clearly, this definition does not cover all political challenges to the EU discussed as 'crises' in political discourse or academic analysis – including the 'strains' examined in this volume. For instance, the worsening of EU relations with the US during the Trump presidency (Schade, this volume) or with China under Xi Jinping did not immediately threaten the EU itself or any of its policies with disintegration. However, such external challenges to European integration by nationalist and illiberal great powers could develop into polity attacks – such as in the Russia crisis – and generate pressure on established policies such as enlargement policy (Keil & Stahl, this volume). Likewise, conflicts about diversity and minority rights (Mos, this volume) would qualify as a polity attack if they became manifest. By contrast, the climate crisis qualifies as a 'slow-burning' environmental crisis that could eventually generate a policy failure (Rosamond, this volume).

References

Biermann, Felix, Guérin, Nina, Jagdhuber, Stefan, Rittberger, Berthold & Weiss, Moritz (2019): 'Political (Non)reform in the Euro Crisis and the Refugee Crisis: a Liberal Intergovernmentalist Explanation', *Journal of European Public Policy*, 26:2, 246–266.

Biermann, Felix & Jagdhuber, Stefan (2022): 'Take it and Leave it! A Postfunctionalist Bargaining Approach to the Brexit Negotiations', *West European Politics*, 45:4, 793–815.

Börzel, Tanja A. & Risse, Thomas (2018): 'From the Euro to the Schengen crises: European integration theories, politicization, and identity politics', *Journal of European Public Policy*, 25:1, 83–108.

Boin, Arjen, t'Hart, Paul, Stern, Eric & Sundelius, Bengt (2016): *The Politics of Crisis Management. Public Leadership under Pressure*, Cambridge University Press.

Copelovitch, Mark, Frieden, Jeffrey & Walter, Stefanie (2016): 'The Political Economy of the Euro Crisis ', *Comparative Political Studies*, 49:7, 811–840.

Evans, Geoffrey & Menon, Anand (2017): *Brexit and British Politics*, Polity Press.

Ferrara, Federico Maria & Kriesi, Hanspeter (2021): 'Crisis Pressures and European Integration', *Journal of European Public Policy*, 29:9, 1351–1373.

Freudlsperger, Christian & Jachtenfuchs, Markus (2021): 'A member state like any other? Germany and the integration of core state powers', *Journal of European Integration*, 43:2, 117–135.

Genschel, Philipp & Jachtenfuchs, Markus (2018): 'From Market Integration to Core State Powers: The Eurozone Crisis, the Refugee Crisis and Integration Theory', *Journal of Common Market Studies*, 56:1, 178–196.

Haas, Ernst B. (1958): *The Uniting of Europe: Political, Social and Economic Forces, 1950–1957*, Stanford University Press.

Hooghe, Liesbet, Lenz, Tobias & Marks, Gary (2019): *A Theory of International Organization*, Oxford University Press.

Hooghe, Liesbet & Marks, Gary (2009): 'A Postfunctionalist Theory of European Integration: From Permissive Consensus to Constraining Dissensus', *British Journal of Political Science,* 39:1, 1–23.

Hooghe, Liesbet & Marks, Gary (2018): 'Cleavage Theory Meets Europe's Crises: Lipset, Rokkan, and the Transnational Cleavage', *Journal of European Public Policy,* 25:1, 109–135.

Hooghe, Liesbet & Marks, Gary (2019): 'Grand theories of European integration in the twenty-first century', *Journal of European Public Policy,* 26:8, 1113–1133.

Ioannou, Demosthenes, Leblond, Patrick & Niemann, Arne (2015): 'European integration and the crisis: practice and theory', *Journal of European Public Policy,* 22:2, 155–176.

Jones, Erik, Kelemen, R. Daniel & Meunier, Sophie (2016): 'Failing Forward? The Euro Crisis and the Incomplete Nature of Integration', *Comparative Political Studies,* 49:7, 1010–1034.

Kelemen, R. Daniel (2017): 'Europe's Other Democratic Deficit. National Authoritarianism in Europe's Democratic Union', *Government and Opposition,* 52:2, 211–238.

König, Thomas (2018): 'Still the Century of Intergovernmentalism? Partisan Ideology, Two-Level Bargains and Technocratic Governance in the post-Maastricht Era', *Journal of Common Market Studies,* 56:6, 1240–1262.

Kriesi, Hanspeter, Altiparmakis, Argyrios, Bojar, Abel & Oana, Ioana-Elena (2021): 'Debordering and re-bordering in the refugee crisis: a case of "defensive integration"', *Journal of European Public Policy,* 28:3, 331–349.

Krotz, Ulrich & Schramm, Lucas (2022): 'Embedded Bilateralism, Integration Theory, and European Crisis Politics: France, Germany, and the Birth of the EU Corona Recovery Fund', *Journal of Common Market Studies,* 60:3, 526–544.

Marks, Gary, Attewell, David, Rovny, Jan & Hooghe, Liesbet (2021): 'Cleavage Theory', in Marianne Riddervold, Jarle Trondal & Akasemi Newsome (eds.): *The Palgrave Handbook of EU Crises,* Palgrave Macmillan, 173–193.

Moravcsik, Andrew (1998): *The Choice for Europe: Social Purpose and State Power from Messina to Maastricht,* Cornell University Press.

Moravcsik, Andrew (2018): 'Preferences, Power and Institutions in the 21st Century', *Journal of Common Market Studies,* 56:7, 1648–1674.

Niemann, Arne & Zaun, Natascha (2018): 'EU Refugee Policies and Politics in Times of Crisis: Theoretical and Empirical Perspectives', *Journal of Common Market Studies,* 56:1, 3–22.

Pierson, Paul (1996): 'The Path to European Integration. A Historical Institutionalist Analysis?', *Comparative Political Studies,* 29:2, 123–163.

Ripoll Servent, Ariadna & Zaun, Natascha (2020): 'Asylum Policy and European Union Politics', *Oxford Research Encyclopedia of Politics,* https://oxfordre.com/politics/view/10.1093/acrefore/9780190228637.001.0001/acrefore-9780190228637-e-1057 (last accessed 16 December 2022).

Sandholtz, Wayne & Stone Sweet, Alec (eds.) (1998): *European Integration and Supranational Governance,* Oxford University Press.

Schimmelfennig, Frank (2014): 'European Integration in the Euro Crisis: the Limits of Postfunctionalism', *Journal of European Integration,* 36:3, 317–337.

Schimmelfennig, Frank (2015): 'Liberal Intergovernmentalism and the Euro Area Crisis', *Journal of European Public Policy,* 22:2, 177–195.

Schimmelfennig, Frank (2018a): 'European Integration (Theory) in Times of Crisis. A Comparison of the Euro and Schengen Crises', *Journal of European Public Policy,* 25:7, 969–989.

Schimmelfennig, Frank (2018b): 'Liberal Intergovernmentalism and the Crises of the European Union', *Journal of Common Market Studies,* 56:7, 1578–1594.

Schimmelfennig, Frank (2018c): 'Brexit: Negotiating Differentiated Disintegration in the EU', *Journal of European Public Policy*, 25:8, 1154–1173.

Schimmelfennig, Frank (2022a): 'European Integration Theories and Crises', in Neill Nugent, William E. Paterson, & Mark Rhinard (eds.): *The European Union: Crises and Challenges*, Bloomsbury, forthcoming.

Schimmelfennig, Frank (2022b): 'The Brexit Puzzle: Polity Attacks and External Rebordering', *West European Politics*, Online first.

Schmitter, Philippe C. (1969): 'Three Neo-Functional Hypotheses about International Integration', *International Organization*, 23:1, 161–166.

Schmitter, Philippe C. (1970): 'A Revised Theory of International Integration', *International Organization*, 24:4, 836–868.

Stone Sweet, Alec & Sandholtz, Wayne (1997): 'European integration and supranational governance', *Journal of European Public Policy*, 4:3, 297–317.

Webber, Douglas (2018): *European Disintegration? The Politics of Crisis in the European Union*. Palgrave Macmillan.

Part II: **The legal and democratic fundaments of the EU**

Desmond Dinan

3 Crisis-driven EU reforms in and beyond treaty limits: Is it time for a treaty change?

Abstract: The idea of crisis as opportunity is a recurring theme in the European Union. Although crises may sometimes have been beneficial for the EU, they have rarely impelled treaty change, one of the main vehicles for EU reform and renewal. None of the major treaty changes in the history of the European Community, and later the European Union, was due primarily or even largely to a prevailing crisis. Those major treaty changes, culminating in the Lisbon Treaty of 2007, proved politically costly, which greatly reduced the appetite among national governments for further treaty change. It is striking that the EU undertook only one treaty change – a relatively minor reform of Economic and Monetary Union – during the series of crises that has buffeted the EU since 2010 (the so-called poly-crisis). Recent developments, notably the conclusion of the Conference on the Future of Europe, Russia's invasion of Ukraine, and the revival of interest in EU enlargement, have prompted efforts to reopen the door to further treaty change. Given the legacy of the long and difficult road to the Lisbon Treaty, however, and the capacity of the Lisbon Treaty to meet new challenges, the possibility of further, far-reaching treaty change seems remote.

Keywords: Crisis/crises; Poly-crisis; Treaty/treaties; Reform

Introduction

Crises are endemic in the European Union (EU). Rather, events described as crises are endemic in the EU. Despite being inherently harmful, crises are generally seen as potentially beneficial; as providing an opportunity for EU reform and renewal, often by means of treaty change. This has been a constant supposition throughout EU history. Yet, the origins of treaty change are rarely rooted in crises. Even during the recent so-called poly-crisis – the series of crises that has buffeted the EU since 2010 – treaty change was almost non-existent. The exception that proves the rule is a minor revision of a treaty article in order to facilitate the establishment of the European Stability Mechanism during the euro crisis.

Change can come in many ways. Indeed, the EU is a dynamic polity; it is constantly in flux. For one thing, its membership has increased dramatically over

https://doi.org/10.1515/9783110790337-004

time. For another, its scope has broadened over the years, as more and more policy fields have come within the orbit of the EU. At the same time, the EU has adapted its institutional arrangements, not least because of the need to cope with the expansion of its membership and the extension of its policy scope. An additional and related development, which further propelled institutional adaptation, has been the acquisition by the EU of a constitutional character based on liberal democratic norms and values, and the need for the EU to strengthen its political legitimacy.

Those major maturations of the EU polity have come about largely, but by no means exclusively, through the negotiation, ratification, and implementation of new treaties or changes to existing treaties, notably the founding treaties of the European Communities and the EU. Since the Single European Act (SEA) of 1986, the trend in EU treaty change has been towards more ambitious and extensive reforms, notwithstanding the relatively narrow Amsterdam Treaty of 1997 and Nice Treaty of 2000, culminating in the Lisbon Treaty of 2007, an all-encompassing change that altered the EU's policy reach, institutional arrangements and effectiveness, and constitutional complexion.

Looking at the record of treaty change, a number of driving forces become apparent. One is the mobilization of political support for a big project requiring deeper European integration, such as completion of the single market (in the case of the Single European Act of 1986) or the launch of monetary union (in the case of the Treaty on European Union of 1992). Other, usually complementary, reasons include a desire to deepen European integration or strengthen cooperation among member states in other policy fields, such as the environment, science and technology, or foreign and security policy; to improve the efficiency of legislative decision-making, notably by the more widespread use of qualified majority voting; and to tackle the problem of weak democratic legitimacy, for instance by extending the power of the European Parliament.

In view of their multi-faceted origins, and in light of EU history, this chapter explores the extent to which treaty revisions have been linked to crises. Related to this is the extent to which the current crises besetting the EU may drive new treaty changes and whether, instead or as well, they may bring about reform through means other than treaty change. First, it briefly discusses the mantra of crisis as opportunity for the EU. It then notes the absence of major treaty change during the poly-crisis, with the exception of the euro crisis. The chapter next goes back in time, before the poly-crisis, to examine the relationship between crises, reform, and treaty change, notably with respect to the Empty Chair Crisis of 1965–1966 and the SEA. A subsequent section looks at the role of crises, if any, in post-SEA reform and treaty change, including the long road to the Lisbon Treaty. The final substantive section discusses current prospects for treaty change, not least because of the impact of Russia's invasion of Ukraine and the momentum generated by the Conference on the Future of Europe. The conclusion ties the preceding sections together.

Crisis as opportunity?

It is difficult to know what, exactly, constitutes a crisis for the EU (Dinan et al. 2018). The difficulty is compounded by a tendency to use the word "crisis" liberally to describe events and developments of varying seriousness or consequence affecting the EU. Whereas the same may be true of all political systems, perhaps because of journalistic embellishment or political opportunism, the liberal use of the label "crisis" with respect to the EU is deeply embedded in the history and political culture of European integration. One of Jean Monnet's most quoted aphorisms is: "Europe will be forged in crisis and will be the sum of the solutions adopted for those crises." It is ironic that the founding father of the European Community, an entity that sought to transcend national politics and develop a serene, technocratic, supranational demeanor, inculcated in the new, post-war project a veneration of crises as a driving force of deeper integration.

At face value, Monnet's aphorism has merit. Crises provide a jolt to the system. They threaten the status quo. They may require urgent action and innovative solutions. Moreover, Monnet was writing at a time when Europe was deeply unsettled by the experience of World War II and by the onset of the Cold War. Europe faced the challenges of reconstruction, of a shortage of dollars with which to buy capital and consumer goods, and of the "German Question" – how to incorporate what became the new, Federal Republic of Germany into a stable, prosperous, and secure (West) European state system.

The Marshall Plan and the North Atlantic Treaty were parts of the solution; so was the Schuman Plan. The Marshall Plan and the North Atlantic Treaty were unprecedented in scale and scope, but were otherwise traditional instruments of international relations. The Schuman Plan, by contrast, and the European Coal and Steel Community to which it gave rise, were novel initiatives involving supranational governance, that could only have come about in the peculiar post-World War II environment of acute challenges and perceived crises, and in the shadow of the disastrous failure of the post-World War I settlement.

Regardless of the impetus that post-World War II crises (real or perceived) may have provided to the launch of the European Community, the idea of "crisis as opportunity" became ingrained in the consciousness of advocates of deeper integration. If every crisis provides an opportunity, then a tendency to describe events as crises is understandable. This may help to explain the long list of supposed crises in the EC and EU, ranging from the crisis of the failure of the European Defence Community in 1954, to the crisis of the rejection of the Lisbon Treaty, following a referendum in Ireland in June 2007.

Clearly, some so-called crises were more serious than others. They constituted a crisis in the generally-accepted sense of providing a shock to the system, perhaps even threatening economic upheaval, political instability, or regime-change. The adjective "existential" is often used to convey the highest level of political risk associated with a crisis. By definition, an existential crisis has the potential to destroy a polity. History is replete with instances of crises bringing national regimes to an end. Recent European examples include the end of the German Third Reich, due to defeat and occupation in 1945; and the collapse of the French Fourth Republic, due to an attempted military coup in 1958.

Such extreme events seem unlikely to afflict the EU, but EU crises may nonetheless be existential. Certainly, the component parts of the poly-crisis that has beset the EU since 2010 – the euro crisis, Russia/Ukraine crisis, migration crisis, Brexit crisis, rule of law crisis, COVID-19 crisis, and the climate crisis – are serious and potentially destabilizing. Whether they are existential is debatable, although that label has generally been used to describe most of them. (On the use of existential" with respect to the euro crisis, see Menéndez 2013; the COVID-19 crisis, see Deen & Kruijver 2020; the migration crisis, see Balfour 2016; the external relations crises, see Duke 2014; and the rule of law crisis, see van Middelaar 2020). No less an authority than Commission President Jean-Claude Juncker declared, in his 2016 State of the Union speech, that: "Our European Union is ... in an existential crisis." Perhaps realizing how extreme such a statement may have sounded, however, Juncker included a qualification: his full statement was that: "Our European Union is, *at least in part*, in an existential crisis." (Juncker 2016: 6; emphasis added).

The absence of major treaty change during the poly-crisis

In order to cope with such serious challenges and crises, whether before or after 2010, whether existential or not, the EU has had to react. Its reaction has included far-reaching measures and reforms, but has rarely involved treaty change. The most clear-cut instance of treaty-change emanating directly from a crisis – perhaps the only such instance in EU history – happened during the poly-crisis, with respect to Economic and Monetary Union (EMU), in the context of facilitating the establishment of the European Stability Mechanism as the permanent Eurozone bailout fund. This was one of only two uses made so far of a 'simplified' treaty revision procedure included in the Lisbon Treaty, in Article 48 of the Treaty on European Union (TEU).

The procedure in question is applicable exclusively to Part Three of the Treaty on the Functioning of the European Union (TFEU), pertaining to the internal policies and action of the Union, and may be used only if the proposed amendment does not lead to an increase in the EU's competences. It allows the European Council to agree unanimously on a treaty amendment without having to convene a Convention and an intergovernmental conference (IGC), although the agreement must be ratified in all member states.

The other 'simplified' method of treaty reform, so far unused by the EU, is the so-called *passerelle* procedure, under which the European Council may agree, by unanimity, to allow a change from unanimity to qualified majority voting (except for decisions with military implications or those in the area of defence) or from a special legislative procedure to the ordinary legislative procedure. There are also specific *passerelle* clauses in the treaties relating to a number of policy fields. The *passerelle* procedure for treaty reform does not require national ratifications, but gives national parliaments the ability to delay or possibly prevent implementation of the proposed change.

The idea of amending Article 136 TFEU was not uncontroversial. Whereas national leaders generally agreed on the desirability of establishing a permanent bailout fund, most were skittish about embarking on treaty reform, however specific, so soon after a fraught period of wide-ranging treaty change spanning the years 2001 to 2009, from the Laeken Declaration to the eventual implementation of the Lisbon Treaty, a period that included the failure of the Constitutional Treaty. It took a concerted effort by German Chancellor Angela Merkel and French President Nicolas Sarkozy, including a Franco-German Declaration in October 2010, to provide the necessary political push for the treaty change to happen. Leaders agreed to the treaty change – a mere two sentences – at the European Council on 25 March 2011 (European Council 2011). Ratification went smoothly, not least because there were no referendums on the matter, and the treaty change came into effect on 1 May 2013. Fear of ratification, and of ratification referendums, proved an enduring legacy of the odyssey of treaty reform during the previous decade (Mendez et al. 2014). It is still prevalent today, notwithstanding the successful outcome of the Danish referendum of 1 June 2022 on opting fully into the EU's Common Security and Defence Policy.

The revision of Article 136 TFEU was not intended to be the only treaty change stemming from the euro crisis. Indeed, at the same time that leaders agreed to that reform, Chancellor Merkel was advocating a more ambitious change: the inclusion in the Lisbon Treaty of a so-called Fiscal Pact, a set of binding rules on national deficits and debts intended to bolster the foundations of monetary union by strengthening fiscal discipline. At the December 2011 meeting of the European Council, however, entrenched opposition from UK Prime Minister David Cameron thwarted agreement on revising the Lisbon Treaty in order to incorporate the Fiscal Pact. The other leaders decided instead to negotiate the pact as an intergovernmental arrangement, outside the formal EU framework, which, arguably, was tantamount to a minor treaty change. All of the then member states, except the Czech Republic and the UK, signed the Fiscal Pact, formally called the Treaty on Stability, Coordination and Governance in the Economic and Monetary Union on 2 March 2012.

Taking the Fiscal Pact outside the EU treaty framework facilitated the ratification process. Because it was not an EU treaty reform, the Fiscal Pact was not subject to the usual ratification procedure, and did not require ratification in all member states in order to come into effect. Accordingly, the new treaty entered into force on 1 January 2013 for the 16 states that had completed ratification by that time.

The establishment of the European Stability Mechanism and implementation of the Fiscal Pact were two of a number of significant steps taken by the EU and its member states in response to the euro crisis. Others include the Euro Plus Pact on stronger economic policy coordination, and legislative measures to strengthen the Stability and Growth Pact. Still, the EU did not go as far in reforming EMU as some national leaders, such as French President Emmanuel Macron, and the Presidents of the EU institutions called for. More far-reaching, fundamental reform would have required more far-reaching, fundamental treaty changes, which most national leader were unwilling to undertake.

Before the poly-crisis: from the Empty Chair crisisto the Single European Act

Looking before the era of the poly-crisis, it is clear that crises often triggered changes in the EU, but not necessarily the kind of change championed by advocates of "crisis as opportunity," and not necessarily treaty change. Indeed, instances of treaty change in the history of the EU seem unrelated to crises. Two cases are nonetheless worth discussing. One is the Empty Chair Crisis of 1965–1966, perhaps the most serious political and constitutional crisis in EU history. The other is the Single European Act, the first major treaty-change in EU history. What kind of change did the Empty Chair Crisis cause, and was it beneficial for the European Community? Did the crisis provide an opportunity to advance European integration? And was the SEA propelled, to some extent or other, by crisis? Was it a crisis-driven EU reform?

Empty Chair crisis

The empty chair crisis pitted France, under French President Charles de Gaulle, against the five other member states of the nascent European Community (EC), over the rules of decision-making in the Council of Ministers (Ludlow 2006: 71–93; Palayret et al. 2006). Though not the proximate cause of de Gaulle's boycott of the Council (hence the empty chair), which began in July 1965, the extension of majority voting to new policy areas, due to take place in January 1966 under the terms of the treaty establishing the EC (the Rome Treaty), became the make-or-break issue. For practical, policy-related reasons, as well as principled opposition to supranationalism, de Gaulle wanted to maintain the status quo, whereby decisions in the Council were taken largely on the basis of unanimity. By attempting to block the transition to majority voting, de Gaulle challenged both a core value and a legal obligation of EC membership. Accordingly, the political and constitutional stakes were high. Here was a crisis genuinely worthy of the name, as the outcome could have wrecked the EC, or at least fundamentally changed its character.

As it was, France needed the Community too much for de Gaulle to risk its destruction. In the face of domestic disquiet and a strong show of unity by the other member states, de Gaulle relented. Nevertheless, he wrung a significant concession from his EC partners. Under the terms of the Luxembourg Compromise – a political agreement among the member states – a government could delay or possibly prevent recourse to majority voting in the Council by claiming that "very important interests are at stake" (the text of the Luxembourg Compromise is reproduced in Palayret et al. 2006: 321–322). Though the treaty remained unchanged, the political effect was to give governments a veto in Council decision-making.

The empty chair crisis has been studied in great detail. There is general agreement that it was indeed grave, but there is less agreement on its long-term impact. Some say that the Council continued with business as usual; most argue that the threat or use of a national veto stymied decision-making for years to come. None claim that the outcome strengthened the Community by providing an opportunity for deeper integration. Moreover, none of the protagonists advocated treaty change. De Gaulle wanted only the suspension of an existing treaty provision.

For Luuk van Middelaar, a prominent Dutch public intellectual and former EU official, the significance of the Luxembourg Compromise is not only that it provided a clever way out of a political cul-de-sac, thereby allowing "the Community to continue to exist," but also that it fundamentally transformed the EC by "allowing it to operate in a brave new world between the strict interpretation of treaties and the geopolitical world of international relations – the intermediate sphere of the [member states]" (Van Middelaar 2013: 88–89). Thus, the Luxembourg Compromise, "a political accord of historical importance," marked "a decisive moment of passage for the European order as a whole" (Van Middelaar 2013: 92, 94).

While not endorsing the view of crisis as opportunity, this interpretation highlights a beneficial, though unintended, consequences of the dramatic events of 1965–66. The EC was indeed a new kind of polity with a new kind of politics, which were only beginning to take shape in the 1960s. Even before the crisis, the EC seemed to be moving in the direction that Van Middelaar described. The crisis may have hastened that move, without necessarily having caused it. Regardless, even Van Middelaar concedes that the impact of the crisis on day-to-day decision-making was far from benign. The shadow of the veto (the possibility that a government would invoke the Luxembourg Compromise) hung over the Council for the next two decades, until eventually displaced by the shadow of the vote (the possibility that the Council Presidency would call for a vote to be taken) in the aftermath of the SEA. Few proponents of crisis as opportunity in the history of European integration cite the events of 1965–66 to bolster their case.

Single European Act

The Single European Act was a major breakthrough in the history of European integration, one that was built on treaty change (Gillingham 2003: 228–58). Completion of the single market programme, a core objective of the European project, was the centerpiece of the SEA. Political pressure to complete the single market had been building since the early 1980s, fueled by an elite, transnational business lobby; shifting ideological winds; and a convergence of national interests.

The record of European integration had been mixed during the previous decade. Within the EC, as elsewhere, widely fluctuating exchange rates were a feature of the 1970s, as were sluggish growth, soaring inflation, and high unemployment, although national experiences varied considerably. Frequent financial and economic shocks generated an atmosphere of chronic crisis among European decision-makers. Protectionism was on the rise, and efforts to break down national barriers to cross-border economic activity through EC legislative measures were hobbled by frequent recourse to the Luxembourg Compromise. This was the era of "Eurosclerosis."

The most notable institutional initiative with response to these developments was the launch of the European Council in 1975 (Wessels 2015). The European Council, which would later become a powerful EU institution, began as an informal arrangement for national leaders to meet occasionally in order to direct Community affairs. Born at a time of economic instability, the European Council initially saw itself as a crisis management mechanism. Its original purpose was to hold the Community together, not to provide a means to drive European integration forward.

The most striking policy initiative of the late 1970s was in the monetary sphere. Then Commission President Roy Jenkins, who first proposed what became the European Monetary System (EMS), deliberately exploited what he saw as an opportunity to revive both European integration and the fortunes of the Commission. Having been taken over by French President Giscard d'Estaing and German Chancellor Helmut Schmidt, what eventually emerged as the EMS, in March 1979, was not as ambitious as what Jenkins had called for, and operated outside the EC treaty framework. The EMS nonetheless helped to rescue European integration and contributed to the eventual achievement of EMU (Mourlon-Droul 2012: 132–260).

By the early 1980s, buoyed by the apparent success of the EMS, weary of persistent economic underperformance, concerned about Western Europe's declining global competitiveness, and lobbied by a group of elite business leaders, national leaders began to coalesce around the idea of deeper market integration. Jacques Delors, who became Commission President in 1985, seized this opportunity and fashioned a legislative agenda – the famous White Paper – to fully liberalize the movement of goods, services, and capital within the Community (Cockfield 1994). For Delors, the single market programme was a means towards the greater end of EMU and, ideally, political union. Delors was ambitious and opportunistic, though the opportunity that he exploited in 1985 existed because of a decade-long series of economic and financial setbacks, not because of an immediate crisis.

It was one thing for the single market programme to enjoy broad political support; it was another for national governments to take the necessary steps to bring it about. The decision-making rule of unanimity, in some cases, and the ability to invoke the Luxembourg Compromise, in other cases, stood in the way. A possible solution was for governments to reach an informal agreement to enact the legislation specified in the White Paper, as well as other decisions on regulatory harmonisation, on the basis of qualified-majority voting in the Council, regardless of the formal rules and informal practices. This is what UK Prime Minister Margaret Thatcher, a leading proponent of the single market, proposed. In her view, the obstacle of the Luxembourg Compromise, which had bedeviled decision-making in the Council, could easily be removed by a political agreement among national leaders to do so. After all, the Luxembourg Compromise was itself a political agreement. Thatcher did not see any need for a treaty change, being fearful that negotiations among governments to revise decision-making rules in the treaty, in order to facilitate completion of the single market, would open a Pandora's Box of other treaty changes (Thatcher 1993: 551–554). She lost the argument, and the vote in the European Council in June 1985, on whether to hold an IGC to reform the Rome Treaty.

As Thatcher feared and as proponents of deeper integration, such as French President François Mitterrand, German Chancellor Helmut Kohl, and Commission President Delors, hoped, the ensuing IGC did, indeed, result in far-reaching treaty change, covering the EC's institutional arrangements and policy scope. The impact of the SEA, which emerged out of the IGC, and which finally came into effect in July 1987, was immediately apparent. The extension of majority voting to specific single market measures had a knock-on effect on decision-making in other policy areas. Clauses in the SEA covering environmental policy, social policy, and cohesion policy spurred unexpected advances in those fields. The SEA became synonymous with the acceleration of European integration and set the stage for another leap forward within a surprisingly short time (Dinan 2012). But the single market and the SEA represented an imaginative response to internal and external economic challenges confronting the Community, not to a particular crisis. Moreover, the single market programme, at the heart of the SEA, could well have been implemented without treaty change.

Post-SEA reform and treaty change

Implementation of the SEA and the success of the single market programme provided a major impetus for further European integration. The Commission promoted EMU as spillover from the single market and most national governments agreed on the desirability of having a single currency. The UK was again an outlier. Governments had already agreed to hold another IGC, this one on EMU, by the time that seismic geopolitical shocks reverberated through Central and Eastern Europe. The fall of the Berlin Wall on 9 November 1989, was a crisis for the German Democratic Republic (East Germany) and the Soviet Union, but was a gift to the Federal Republic of Germany and the EC, albeit one that required careful handling under extraordinary circumstances. The EC responded, in part, by deciding to hold a separate IGC to include additional policy fields and institutional arrangements, not least with a view to clarifying the putative EU's constitutional character and addressing concerns about its political legitimacy. The ensuing Maastricht Treaty transformed the EC into the EU and marked an ambitious new phase in the process of European integration. The road to Maastricht was full of challenges but free of crises.

Ironically, the road from Maastricht was almost blocked by a crisis: the crisis of treaty ratification caused by the negative outcome of the Danish referendum on 2 June 1992. Unless ratified by all member states, the treaty could not have come into effect. National governments overcame the crisis by giving Denmark opt-outs from provisions of the treaty that were controversial domestically (European Council 1992). This facilitated the success of the second Danish referendum on 18 May 1992. But the crisis portended deep public dissatisfaction with the European project throughout the embryonic EU. Although leaders had tried, in the Maastricht Treaty, to address concerns about the so-called democratic deficit, they would forever find themselves playing catch-up with respect to the alleged weakness of the EU's democratic legitimacy. The EU would introduce a host of measures based on subsequent treaty changes in an effort to bolster its democratic credentials. These ranged from reforming and extending the procedure for legislative co-decision, to establishing the office of European Ombudsman, to linking the outcome of European Parliament elections directly to the nomination of the next Commission President (the so-called *Spitzenkandidaten* process). If the democratic deficit constituted a crisis for the EU, then it triggered several treaty changes. Rather than constituting a crisis, however, weak democratic legitimacy has posed a chronic challenge for the EU that may be inherent in the novel nature of supranational governance.

Apart from the challenge of democratic legitimacy, the challenge of institutional efficiency, accentuated by the prospect of large-scale post-Cold War enlargement, drove subsequent EU reforms and treaty changes. A negative lesson of the Luxembourg Compromise and a positive lesson of the single market project was the utility of qualified majority voting for efficient Council decision-making and effective policy output. Having more member states would mean having more policy preferences and, without the widespread use of QMV, more veto players. The desire to improve the efficiency of Council decision making, which was not new in the EU, became pressing in view of imminent post-Cold War enlargement.

The two treaty reforms that followed in the decade after the Maastricht Treaty were nonetheless disappointing. The Amsterdam Treaty of 1997 was partly a tidying up exercise, notably with respect to the treaty's provisions for the Common Foreign and Security Policy and the incorporation into the treaty of the Schengen acquis (the rules and regulations governing the unrestricted movement of people among countries participation in the so-called Schengen free travel area), that nonetheless included important clarifications concerning the EU's constitutional and political nature (Laursen 2002). The Nice Treaty of 2000 attempted to manage institutional arrangements that were left over from the IGC that resulted in the Amsterdam Treaty, but was generally seen as being unsatisfactory (Laursen 2006).

The rocky road to Lisbon

Disappointment with the outcome of the 1996–1997 and 2000 IGCs contributed directly to the announcement by EU leaders, in the Laeken Declaration of 15 December 2001, that "In order to pave the way for the next Intergovernmental Conference as broadly and openly as possible, the European Council has decided to convene a Convention composed of the main parties involved in the debate on the future of the Union" (European Council 2001). The Convention would consist of representatives of national and EU institutions, from the existing and prospective member states, who would explore the possibility of wide-ranging treaty change. At no point did the Laeken Declaration refer to a crisis or to the EU being in crisis.

The Convention on the Future of Europe, also known as the Constitutional Convention, met in Brussels in 2002–2003, and produced a Draft Constitutional Treaty. This contained a host of amendments to the original treaties and merged them into a single text. In general, the Draft Constitutional Treaty's provisions were a significant improvement on the existing treaties, promising a more efficient, effective, and democratic EU (Magnette & Nicolaidis 2004).

Although the Convention carried out extensive preparatory work for further treaty reform, an IGC was nonetheless required to negotiate treaty change. National governments were not willing merely to rubber-stamp the Draft Treaty. In particular, they disagreed among themselves on some of the Draft Treaty's institutional provisions. By the time of the June 2004 meeting of the European Council, only a small number of issues remained unresolved. As in the closing stages of the Amsterdam and Nice negotiations, those included the proposed new system for qualified majority voting, and the size and composition of the Commission. The agreement eventually reached on qualified majority voting was for a double majority of 55 per cent of the Member States and 65 per cent of the population of the EU. The Commission would retain one Commissioner per member state until 2014, when it would be limited to a number of Commissioners corresponding to two-thirds of the number of EU countries. Altogether, the IGC approved 80 amendments to the Convention's Draft Treaty. Nevertheless, the successful conclusion of the negotiations and agreement on the Constitutional Treaty represented a major step forward politically and constitutionally for the EU.

What happened next is well known. Signed in Rome on 29 October 2004, the Constitutional Treaty foundered on the rock of ratification, notably after its rejection in referendums in France and The Netherlands, in mid-2005. Here was another treaty ratification crisis, this one more serious than the others because of the greater importance of the Constitutional Treaty and because Dutch and French opposition could not be overcome simply with opt-outs and the promise of a second referendum (Hobolt & Brouard 2011).

Notwithstanding the ratification setback, most EU leaders were loath to let the Constitutional Treaty go. They had invested too much time and political capital in the Convention and in the IGC. Their response was to put things on hold and launch a "period of reflection," before trying to rescue as much as possible of the Constitutional Treaty in a new "Reform Treaty." Another IGC would therefore be necessary. Leaders resolved, however, to keep it as short as possible and modify the Constitutional Treaty in ways that might make the text of an alternative treaty change more widely acceptable to EU citizens.

Many of the proposed changes were symbolic, such as dropping the adjective "constitutional" and deleting the mention of "European symbols" – the flag, anthem, and celebration of Schuman Day. Another suggestion was to incorporate as much as possible of the rejected treaty into the existing TEU and a Treaty on the Functioning of the European Union. This would help ratification prospects and go some way toward easing public concerns about the allegedly over-ambitious Constitutional Treaty.

Accordingly, the new IGC was not really a negotiation but an exercise in redrafting the Constitutional Treaty in a limited, technical way. Nevertheless, the concluding summit of the IGC, held in Lisbon in October 2007, was not without drama, as the Eurosceptic Czech and Polish governments, in particular, brought up some touchy, last-minute issues. The most serious of these was Poland's concern about the "double majority" formula for QMV. Poland preferred to retain the status quo – the arrangement included in the Nice Treaty whereby Poland's share of the total number of Council votes almost equaled Germany's. In the end, Poland was assuaged with a slight concession and the IGC ended with approval of what became the Lisbon Treaty (Phinnemore 2013).

Implementation of the Lisbon Treaty was delayed by yet another ratification crisis, this one caused by the negative result of the Irish referendum of 12 June 2008. EU leaders resorted to tried and trusted measures to overcome this setback: they offered concessions to Ireland, relating to the treaty, that would enable a second referendum and help to ensure a positive result. One of the concessions was to keep the Commission at one member per member state, something that many Irish citizens, and the citizens of other small member states, felt strongly about. On the basis of this and other reassurances, Ireland held a second referendum on 2 October 2009, this time with a different outcome (Curtin 2009).

The Lisbon Treaty included most of the institutional and other innovations originally contained in the Constitutional Treaty. Although the Lisbon Treaty is long, complicated, and difficult to read, the EU that it describes is, in many respects, more coherent and comprehensible than the EU that it reformed. The Lisbon Treaty struck a better balance between efficiency and democratic legitimacy. It also recast the balance between the main institutions, with the European Council in the ascendant. This would become apparent during the series of crises that would soon beset the EU. Like every preceding treaty change, the Lisbon Treaty was not optimal, but reflected the art of the possible at a particular moment in EU history.

Valuable though the Lisbon Treaty undoubtedly is, it came at the cost of further souring public sentiment on the EU. It is also debatable whether the Convention provided more legitimacy for the treaty reform process (Risse & Kleine 2007). Undoubtedly, it failed to arouse much public interest. The negative results in the French and Dutch referendums in 2005, though due in large part to domestic political considerations, exposed deep-seated public dissatisfaction with the EU's direction. Reaction to the Constitutional Treaty confirmed the impression that the permissive consensus in public attitudes toward the EU was long gone.

The protracted process of treaty revision, lasting almost a decade, robbed national governments of their appetites, and European publics of their patience, for further large-scale treaty reform. Apart from a reluctance to invest the time and effort required to negotiate more than minor treaty modifications, governments were now fully aware of the pitfalls of ratification, especially if it involved referendums. When given an opportunity to vote in a referendum on treaty change, opponents of deeper integration could easily exploit public unease about unrelated issues, thereby derailing the proposed amendments, as had occurred in France and the Netherlands in 2005, and in Ireland in 2008. The conduct and outcome of the Brexit referendum in June 2016, was another salutary lesson for the EU.

Fortunately, the Lisbon Treaty leaves plenty of scope for further EU adaptation, thereby obviating, in many cases, the need for more treaty change. The *passerelle* clauses, which have not yet been used, come immediately to mind. So does the *Spitzenkandidaten* process, which the EP introduced before the 2014 elections, based on its astute interpretation of Article 17 TEU and Declaration 11, on Article 17 TEU (Tilindyte 2019). Further treaty change may well have been desirable, but arguably was not essential in the aftermath of the lengthy process of treaty reform that came to an end in 2009, with implementation of the Lisbon treaty. The experience of the poly-crisis bears out that point.

Another treaty change? – The Conference on the Future of Europe

Nevertheless, the possibility of treaty change returned to the EU's agenda in 2022. The proximate cause was the report of the Conference on the Future of Europe (CFE), submitted in May. Other reasons were the growing frustration in certain member states with the debilitating impact of unanimity on decision making in the Council with respect to the Common Foreign and Security Policy, including the Common Security and Defence Policy, especially following Russia's invasion of Ukraine in February. Discussions about Ukraine's possible EU membership, in the broader context of another round of EU enlargement, notably in the Western Balkans, also contributed to the new debate on possible reform of Council decision-making by means of treaty change.

The Conference on the Future of Europe was an exercise in direct, deliberative democracy at the EU level. President Macron, in particular, was keen to engage citizens in discussions about EU reform. In an op-ed published in several media outlets in March 2019, Macron called, among other things, for the convening of "a Conference for Europe in order to propose all the changes our political project needs, with an open mind, even to amending the treaties." The conference "will need to engage with citizens' panels and hear academics, business and labour representatives, and religious and spiritual leaders. It will define a roadmap for the European Union that translates … key priorities into concrete actions" (Macron 2019).

The EP has long been a leading proponent of far-reaching EU reform and of greater citizen participation in EU governance. EP interest in both grew at the time of the 2019 elections. Ursula von der Leyen tapped into this sentiment in her speech to the EP on 16 July, when she asked MEPs to support her candidacy for President of the Commission. Von der Leyen assured MEPs, having "heard your concerns, your hopes and your expectations," that she wanted "European citizens to play a leading and active part in building the future of our Union. I want them to have their say at a Conference on the Future of Europe" (Von der Leyen 2019).

The possibility of such a Conference, involving extensive citizen participation, percolated throughout the EU in the following months (Kotanidis 2019; Ålander et al. 2021). In November 2019, the French and German governments released a "non-paper" expressing support for the idea and recommending that the conference focus on a wide range of policies as well as institutional issues. However, the Franco-German paper did not mention possible treaty change, suggesting only that "The final document with *recommendations* should be presented to the EUCO (European Council) for debate and implementation" (EUlawlive 2020; emphasis in original).

The Franco-German suggestion that the Conference be "chaired by a senior European personality" was potentially divisive. President Macron was known to favour Guy Verhofstadt, a close political ally, a leading Euro-federalist, and a prominent MEP. Leaders did not devote much time to the issue at their December 2019 summit. Keen to affirm its institutional prerogative, the European Council declared in the summit conclusions that "priority should be given to implementing the Strategic Agenda agreed in June, and to delivering concrete results for the benefit of our citizens." In other words, regardless of the desirability of holding a Conference, the European Council had a special responsibility for directing the EU, which it was determined to assert (European Council 2019).

Inevitably, the outbreak of the Covid-19 pandemic, in early 2020, hobbled inter-institutional planning for the Conference. Nonetheless, the Council managed to agree a position on the arrangements for the Conference in June 2020, paving the way for the opening of discussions with the Commission and the EP (Council of the EU 2020). It took another nine months before the three institutions issued a Joint Declaration on launching the Conference (Council of the EU, European Parliament, and European Commission 2021). The ongoing Covid-19 crisis contributed to the delay, but also masked a protracted inter-institutional squabble over the purpose, scope, and organization of the Conference. A key dispute concerned the Conference presidency. Most national leaders opposed Verhofstadt's candidacy, fearing that he would push a federalist agenda and privilege the interests of the EP, or at least those MEPs most in favour of deeper European integration. The compromise eventually reached was for a Joint Presidency made up of the Presidents of the Commission, the EP, and the Council, supported by an Executive Board co-chaired by representatives of the institutions (Conference on the Future of Europe 2021).

The Joint Declaration included a list of possible topics, such as health, climate change, social fairness, digital transformation, the EU's role in the world, and how to strengthen democracy and EU governance. It committed the three institutions "to examine swiftly how to follow up effectively to [the final] report, each within their own sphere of competences and in accordance with the Treaties" (Council of the EU, European Parliament, and European Commission 2021). In deference to most member states, the Joint Declaration did not mention possible treaty change.

The Conference finally began in April 2021, fully a year later than expected. It included a multilingual digital platform for citizens to share ideas and send online submissions. There were also decentralized events – online, in-person, and hybrid – held by non-governmental organisations as well as national, regional and local authorities across the EU. Eight hundred citizens, chosen randomly from the 27 member states, with due regard to location, gender, age, socioeconomic background, and level of education, participated in the Conference. They were organized into four Citizens' Panels organized on thematic lines, each with 200 people.

The Plenary included 20 representatives from each Citizens' Panel, as well as strong EU institutional representation. Based on input from the citizens' panels, the multilingual digital platform, and other sources, the Plenary drafted proposals for the Executive Board, which drew up the final report (Conference on the Future of Europe 2022a).

The Conference did not attract much attention during its deliberations. Media coverage tended to dismiss it as extravagant and inconsequential. Overshadowed initially by the COVID crisis, in its final months the Conference seemed eclipsed entirely by Russia's invasion of Ukraine. Nonetheless, the Conference made a surprising splash at its final plenary session, in Strasbourg, on 9 May 2022, when the Executive Board presented the Conference report to the President-in-office of the Council, who happened to be Emmanuel Macron, as well as to the Presidents of the Commission and the EP (French Presidency of the Council 2022). The report included over 200 recommendations for strengthening the EU and improving its effectiveness. These ranged from deeper integration in areas such as climate, social, and health policy, to extending the use of majority voting in the Council in all policy areas (Conference on the Future of Europe 2022b).

For Macron, the presentation of the final report was an emotional occasion. After all, the Conference had been his brainchild. Having just won the second round of the French presidential election, but not yet been battered in the parliamentary elections, Macron looked forward to a second five-year term in the Elysée pursuing an ambitious agenda on European integration. The Conference report could prove useful in that regard.

Most of the recommendations in the final report were neither innovative nor radical. Almost all could be implemented through existing procedures and unused (or under-used) provisions of the Lisbon Treaty. Only a few, such as giving the EP the right of legislative initiative, making health policy a shared competence, or extending the use of qualified majority voting to all policy fields, would require treaty change. A particular benefit of potential treaty change was nonetheless increasingly apparent. For some time, advocates of a more credible and effective EU foreign, security, and defence policy had been calling for the abolition of the national veto in decision-making in these areas. Such calls increased in frequency in early 2022, following Russia's invasion of Ukraine (Blockmans 2022; Russack 2022).

MEPs in favor of deeper integration quickly picked up on the possibility of treaty change. This culminated in a resolution by the EP on 9 June, endorsing the outcome of the Conference and calling for the convening of a Convention, under Article 48 TEU, for the revision of the treaties (European Parliament 2022). Broadly, the EP wanted to see reform of Council voting procedures; more competences transferred to the EU in policy fields such as health, energy, defence, and the economy; full co-decision for the EP on the EU budget; and stronger procedures to protect the values on which the EU is founded. Specifically, the EP called for two treaty changes extending the use of qualified majority voting in the Council in order to impose EU sanctions (Article 29 TEU); and the use of qualified majority voting in the European Council in order to allow decisions to be taken in the Council by a qualified majority in areas where the treaties provide for the Council to act only by unanimity (Article 48(7) TEU).

In a communication on 17 June, the Commission noted that treaty change "should not be an end in itself and for the vast majority of measures, there is much that can and will need to be done under the existing treaties. Just like constitutional texts of the Member States, the EU treaties are living instruments." At the same time, the Commission endorsed the EP's call for a Convention: "the Commission will always be on the side of those who want to reform the European Union to make it work better, including through Treaty change where that may be necessary … The Commission stands ready to fully play its institutional role in the procedure set out in Article 48 TEU, and in particular to give its opinion in response to a consultation by the European Council" (European Commission 2022).

Most national governments remained equivocal about treaty change, if not outright opposed to it. No sooner had the Conference concluded than 13 countries (Bulgaria, Croatia, the Czech Republic, Denmark, Estonia, Finland, Latvia, Lithuania, Malta, Poland, Romania, Slovenia, and Sweden) issued a non-paper on 9 May, lauding the Conference method and advocating EU reform, while noting firmly that "Treaty change has never been a purpose of the Conference." The non-paper warned that "unconsidered and premature attempts to launch a process towards Treaty change … would entail a serious risk of drawing political energy away from the important tasks of finding solutions to the questions to which our citizens expect answers and handling the urgent geopolitical challenges facing Europe … The EU's handling of the crises in recent years …have clearly shown how much the EU can deliver within the current Treaty framework" (Government of Sweden 2022).

In response, six member states (Germany, Belgium, Italy, Luxembourg, the Netherlands, and Spain) issued their own non-paper on 23 May. They also praised the work of the Conference, especially in light of developments in Ukraine, which reinforced "the goal of increasing Europe's ability to act, strengthening its shared foundation of values, as well as making it more democratic, social and citizen-oriented" (Tweede Kamer 2022). The authors of the non-paper argued that a distinction should be made between proposals that "are already being implemented, [that] can be implemented quickly within the framework of existing treaties and [that] would require treaty changes," and "remain in principle open to necessary treaty changes that are jointly defined" (Tweede Kamer 2022). This hardly amounted to a ringing endorsement of revising the Lisbon Treaty. Because it was in the Council Presidency, France did not join either of the non-papers, but was clearly aligned with the non-paper issued by the six member states.

Apart from an understandable reluctance to open a possible Pandora's Box of treaty reform, there were compelling reasons why governments were not too keen on changing the decision-making rules for foreign and security policy, regardless of the outcome of the Conference or the developing situation in Ukraine. As Jim Cloos, a former EU official who is a veteran of many meetings of the European Council, asked rhetorically: "Do we want a CFSP with an increasing number of areas where not all the twenty-seven are on board? Or is the idea to have QMV decisions binding for all?" His view was that "This is unrealistic … In the present situation, countries who want the strongest possible sanctions against Russia are frustrated by the need for unanimity. But there can be cases where they could be outvoted on what they consider vital interests in [their] relations with Russia. We have had situations in the past where Greece and Cyprus have blocked decisions on Turkey. Are we sure that we would solve the problem by simply outvoting them?" (Cloos 2022).

The June 2022 European Council provided the first opportunity for national leaders to discuss the outcome of the Conference, explore the possibility of treaty change, and respond to the EP's call for a Convention. They chose not to do so. Instead, the European Council merely praised the Conference as "a unique opportunity to engage with European citizens," and took note of the proposals in the Final Report (European Council 2022). Clearly, the possibility of initiating treaty change was not a priority for most national leaders. Without their agreement, launching the process of treaty change was simply not possible.

Conclusion

Like any polity, the EU has evolved over the years in response to everyday events, longer-term changes, challenges, and crises – however broadly defined. But the EU is unlike other polities because of several unique characteristics, including its supranational nature and its ever-increasing membership, despite the departure of the UK in 2020. Over the years, the EU has adapted to frequent rounds of enlargement and to other significant developments in formal and informal ways that have strengthened its institutional capacity and defined its political character.

Perhaps the most striking method of formal adaptation has been through treaty change, although this has almost never originated because of an immediate crisis. Having been brought into existence by far-reaching changes to the founding treaties of the European Communities, the EU has gone through a number of treaty changes in its relatively short life, culminating in the Lisbon Treaty of 2007. Getting to Lisbon, however, was extremely arduous for all concerned. The cost of treaty change has been high, not least because of ratification difficulties that have exposed deep-rooted public dissatisfaction with the EU.

As a result, national leaders have become extremely reluctant to engage in further treaty change. Nor have they had to, even during the poly-crisis. With the exception of a technical amendment to EMU, engineered through the use of a simplified procedure for treaty change, leaders have been unwilling – and have not found it necessary – to incur the high political cost of treaty reform by means of the ordinary revision procedure, which would necessitate convening a Convention, conducting an IGC, and undertaking national ratification proceedings. Even after the initial excitement generated by the conclusion of the Conference on the Future of Europe, including the EP's call for a Convention in order to initiate the process of treaty change, and after Russia's invasion of Ukraine, which highlighted procedural deficiencies in the formulation of the EU's response, the European Council has shown scant interest in pursuing further treaty change.

References

Ålander, Minna, von Ondarza, Nicolai, & Russack, Sophia (eds.) (2021): *Managed Expectations: EU Member States' Views on the Conference on the Future of Europe*, EPIN, June 2021: https://www.ceps.eu/wp-content/uploads/2021/06/EPIN-Report_EU-Member-States-Views-on-CoFoE.pdf (Accessed 23 November 2022).

Balfour, Rosa (2016): "Why are Europe's crises 'existential'?" German Marshall Fund https://www.gmfus.org/news/why-are-europes-crises-existential (Accessed 23 November 2022).

Blockmans, Steven (ed.) (2022): *A Transformational Moment: the EU's response to Russia's war in Ukraine*, CEPS, May 2022: https://www.ceps.eu/download/publication/?id=36541&pdf=A-transformational-moment_The-EUs-response-to-Russias-war-in-Ukraine.pdf) (Accessed 23 November 2022).

Cloos, Jim (2022): "Should the EU Embark on Treaty Change after the Conference on the Future of Europe?" TEPSA, 31 May 2022: https://www.tepsa.eu/should-the-eu-embark-on-treaty-change-after-the-conference-on-the-future-of-europe-cofoe/ (Accessed 23 November 2022).

Cockfield, Arthur (1994): *The European Union: Creating the Single Market*, Wiley.

Conference on the Future of Europe (2021): "Rules of Procedure of the Conference on the Future of Europe:" https://futureu.europa.eu/uploads/decidim/attachment/file/9340/sn02700.en21.pdf (Accessed 23 November 2022).

Conference on the Future of Europe (2022a): Website: https://futureu.europa.eu/?locale=en (Accessed 23 November 2022).

Conference on the Future of Europe (2022b): Report on the Final Outcome, May 2022: https://futureu.europa.eu/pages/reporting (Accessed 23 November 2022).

Council of the EU (2020): "Conference on the Future of Europe: Council agrees its position," 24 June 2020: https://www.consilium.europa.eu/en/press/press-releases/2020/06/24/conference-on-the-future-of-europe-council-agrees-its-position/ (Accessed 23 November 2022)

Council of the EU, European Parliament, and European Commission (2021): "Joint Declaration on the Conference on the Future of Europe: engaging with citizens for Democracy", 10 March 2021: https://ec.europa.eu/info/sites/default/files/en_-_joint_declaration_on_the_conference_on_the_future_of_europe.pdf (Accessed 23 November 2022).

Curtin, Deirdre (2009): 'The Irish 'No' to the Lisbon Treaty: Ireland's Voice and Europe's Exit?' *Zeitschrift für Staats- und Europawissenschaften*, 7:1, 31–50.

Deen, Bob & Kruijver, Kimberley (2020): 'Corona: EU's existential crisis. Why the lack of solidarity threatens not only the Union's health and economy, but also its security,' *Clingendael Alert*, April 2020.

Dinan, Desmond, Nugent, Neill, & Paterson, William (eds.) (2018): *The European Union in Crisis*, Palgrave.

Duke, Simon (2014): 'The EU's existential crisis: far from Academic,' *Eipascope*, 2014, 17–22.

EUlawlive (2019): "Conference on the Future of Europe: Franco-German non-paper on key questions and guidelines," 26 November 2019: https://eulawlive.com/special-reports/franco-german-non-paper-26-november-2019/ (Accessed 23 November 2022).

European Commission (2022): "Communication on the Conference on the Future of Europe: putting vision into concrete action," June 17: https://ec.europa.eu/info/files/communication-conference-future-europe_en (Accessed 23 November 2022).

European Council (1992): Conclusions of the Presidency, 11–12 December: https://www.consilium.europa.eu/media/20492/1992_december_-_edinburgh__eng_.pdf (Accessed 23 November 2022).

European Council (2001): Presidency Conclusions: European Council Meeting in Laeken, 14–15 December 2001: https://www.consilium.europa.eu/media/20950/68827.pdf (Accessed 23 November 2022).

European Council (2004): Presidency Conclusions, 17–18 December: https://www.europarl.europa.eu/summits/pdf/bru0404_en.pdf (Accessed 23 November 2022).

European Council (2011): Conclusions, 25 March 2011: https://data.consilium.europa.eu/doc/document/ST-10-2011-INIT/en/pdf (Accessed 23 November 2022).

European Council (2019): Conclusions, 12 December 2019: https://www.consilium.europa.eu/media/41768/12-euco-final-conclusions-en.pdf (Accessed 23 November 2022).

European Council (2022): Conclusions, 23–24 June 2022: https://www.consilium.europa.eu/media/57442/2022-06-2324-euco-conclusions-en.pdf (Accessed 23 November 2022).

European Parliament (2022); 'Call for a Convention for the revision of the Treaties,' Strasbourg, 9 June 2022: https://www.europarl.europa.eu/doceo/document/TA-9-2022-0244_EN.html (Accessed 23 November 2022) (Accessed 23 November 2022).

French Presidency of the Council (2022); "The Conference on the Future of Europe concludes its work," 9 May 2022: https://presidence-francaise.consilium.europa.eu/en/news/press-release-the-conference-on-the-future-of-europe-concludes-its-work/ (Accessed 23 November 2022).

Gillingham, John (2003): *European Integration, 1950–2003: Superstate or New Market Economy?* Cambridge University Press.

Government of Sweden (2022): "Non-paper by Bulgaria, Croatia, the Czech Republic, Denmark, Estonia, Finland, Latvia, Lithuania, Malta, Poland, Romania, Slovenia, and Sweden on the outcome of and follow-up to the Conference on the Future of Europe," 9 May 2022: https://www.government.se/information-material/2022/05/non-paper-by-bulgaria-croatia-the-czech-re public-denmark-estonia-finland-latvia-lithuania-malta-poland-romania-slovenia-and-sweden/ (Accessed 23 November 2022).

Hobolt, Sara & Sylvain Brouard, (2011): 'Contesting the European Union, Why the Dutch and the French Rejected the European Constitution,' *Political Research Quarterly*, 64:2, 309–322.

Juncker, Jean-Claude (2016), *State of the Union 2016*, European Commission, Directorate-General for Communication, Publications Office, 2016: https://data.europa.eu/doi/10.2775/968989 (Accessed 23 November 2022).

Kotanidis, Silvia (2019): "Preparing the Conference on the Future of Europe," EPRS, December 2019: https://www.europarl.europa.eu/RegData/etudes/BRIE/2019/644202/EPRS_BRI(2019)644202_EN. pdf (Accessed 23 November 2022).

Laursen, Finn (ed.) (2002): *The Amsterdam Treaty: National Preference Formation Interstate Bargaining and Outcome*, University Press of Southern Denmark.

Laursen, Finn (ed.) (2006): *The Treaty of Nice: Actor Preferences, Bargaining and Institutional Choice*, Brill.

Ludlow, Piers N. (2006): *The European Community and the Crises of the 1960s: Negotiating the Gaullist Challenge*, Routledge.

Macron, Emmanuel (2019): "For European Renewal," 4 March 2019: https://www.elysee.fr/en/emma nuel-macron/2019/03/04/for-european-renewal (Accessed 23 November 2022).

Magnette, Paul & Nicolaidis, Kalypso (2004): 'The European Convention: Bargaining in the Shadow of Rhetoric,' *West European Politics*, 27:3, 381–404.

Mendez, Fernando., Mario Mendez, & Vasiliki Triga (2014): *Referendums and the European Union: A Comparative Inquiry*, Cambridge University Press.

Menéndez, Agustín José (2013): 'The Existential Crisis of the European Union,' *German Law Journal*, 14:5, 453–526.

Mourlon-Droul, Emmanuel (2012): *A Europe Made of Money: The Emergence of the European Monetary System*, Cornell University Press.

Palayret, Jean-Marie, Helen Wallace & Pascaline Winand (eds.) (2006): *Visions, Votes and Vetoes: The Empty Chair Crisis and the Luxembourg Compromise Forty Years On*, Peter Lang.

Phinnemore, David (2013): *The Treaty of Lisbon: Origins and Negotiation*, Palgrave.

Risse, Thomas, & Kleine, Mareike (2007): 'Assessing the Legitimacy of the EU's Treaty Revision Methods,' *Journal of Common Market Studies*, 4:1, 69–80.

Russack, Sophia (2022): "The good, the bad and the ugly of the Conference on the Future of Europe," CEPS, 12 May 2022: https://www.ceps.eu/the-good-the-bad-and-the-ugly-of-the-confer ence-on-the-future-of-europe/ (Accessed 23 November 2022).

Thatcher, Margaret (1993): *The Downing Street Years*, HarperCollins.

Tilindyte, Laura (2019): *Electing the President of the European Commission: Understanding the Spitzenkandidaten Process*, EPRS Briefing, April 2019: https://www.europarl.europa.eu/RegData/ etudes/BRIE/2018/630264/EPRS_BRI(2018)630264_EN.pdf (Accessed 23 November 2022).

Twede Kamer (2022): 'Non-paper submitted by Germany, Belgium, Italy, Luxembourg, the Netherlands, and Spain on implementing the proposals of the Plenary on the 'Conference on the Future of Europe',' 23 May 2022: https://www.tweedekamer.nl/kamerstukken/detail?id= 2022D20911&did=2022D20911 (Accessed 23 November 2022).

Van Middelaar, Luuk (2013): *The Passage to Europe: How a Continent Became a Union*, Yale University Press.

Van Middelaar, Luuk, (2020): 'Europe's existential crisis,' *Politico*, 10 December: https://www.politico. eu/article/europe-existential-crisis-rule-of-law-hungary-poland/ (Accessed 23 November 2022).

Von der Leyen, Ursula (2019): 'Opening statement in the European Parliament plenary session by Ursula von der Leyen, candidate for President of the European Commission,' 16 July 2019: https://ec.europa.eu/commission/presscorner/detail/en/SPEECH_19_4230 (Accessed 23 November 2022).

Wessels, Wolfgang (2015): *The European Council*, Palgrave Macmillan.

Benjamin Leruth

4 What happened to the idea of 'Ever Closer Union'? Differentiation as a persistent feature of European integration

Abstract: The Brexit process effectively opened a new chapter in the history of European integration. Indeed, for the first time, a member state unilaterally triggered Article 50 of the Treaty on European Union to withdraw from the Union following the outcome of a heated (and controversial) referendum. Brexit is best understood as a process of differentiated disintegration, which combines two strains of European studies: differentiation, a phenomenon that gained traction following the ratification of the Maastricht Treaty; and European disintegration, a concept that scholars started focusing on following the 2007–08 Great Recession and subsequent waves of crises across the European Union.

The war in Ukraine also created significant challenges for the future of European integration. The EU swiftly approved Moldova's and Ukraine's requests to be considered as accession candidates; yet, there is no genuine 'fast track' option to join the Union. Differentiation may offer some temporary or permanent options to strengthen ties with neighbouring countries. The European Political Community proposed by Emmanuel Macron in May 2022 aims at filling an institutional void that would pave the way for more differentiation across Europe, with the risks and opportunities this would entail.

This chapter focuses on differentiation, understood as an umbrella term covering heterogeneous modes and strategies of integration and disintegration in the European Union, and its consequences for the future of European integration. It is argued that differentiation is now a persistent and mainstream feature in Europe and that it remains difficult to understand the full consequences it entails as these can be specific to the empirical context. As a result, differentiation should not be inherently considered as good or bad for the European Union. The chapter concludes by offering a theoretical reflection on where to draw the line between what is deemed acceptable for the European institutions and EU member states, and what can be harmful for the future of European integration, especially in line with the recent rule of law crises in Poland and Hungary.

Keywords: Differentiation; European Union; Disintegration; European Political Community; crisis.

https://doi.org/10.1515/9783110790337-005

Introduction

The idea of an 'Ever Closer Union' is deeply rooted in the history of European integration, and certainly drove the process for the past five decades. Yet, with the increasing politicization of Europe, the transformation of the Community into a full-fledged political Union and the end of the permissive consensus (under which citizens let political elites shape the process of European integration) gave way to constraining dissensus (in which citizens are warier of the processes of deepening and widening; Hooghe & Marks 2009; Moland 2022), the European Union became progressively more differentiated, with member states opting out of core policies and non-EU member states cooperating closely with Brussels, for instance through European Economic Area membership. In 2016, Brexit undoubtedly opened a new chapter in the history of European integration, as this was the first instance of a member state triggering a process of differentiated *disintegration.* The full consequences of the United Kingdom's withdrawal from the European Union are yet to be felt, as both parties still try to reconcile their views amidst successive periods of political turmoil.

Over the past three decades, successive crises have moulded the prospects for differentiation in the European Union. More recently, Russia's invasion of Ukraine reopened a long-standing debate over whether more flexibility should be granted to cooperate with non-EU member states, leading French President Emmanuel Macron to propose the creation of a so-called 'European Political Community' in May 2022. Following Ukraine's formal application to join the European Union under what Ukrainian authorities hoped would be an accelerated procedure, the idea was initially met with scepticism but also significant interest (e.g., Grant 2022; Mucznik 2022). Fundamentally, Brexit (as a form of differentiated disintegration) and the war in Ukraine (triggering prospects of accelerated cooperation or enlargement) reopened a long-standing debate within the European Union: how flexible should the European Union be to accommodate different interests and needs? And, more broadly, what are the risks and opportunities differentiation entails for the future of European integration?

This chapter focuses on differentiation as a mainstream and persistent feature of European integration. It first offers a broad definition and a brief history of the development of differentiation in the European Union, highlighting that although differentiation as an idea can find its roots back to the Treaty of Rome, it became a salient and prominent issue from the 1990s onwards. The chapter then explains the drivers of differentiation, drawing on a supply and demand model which encompasses different modes and strategies of differentiation to make sense of its dynamics, and explains that over the past thirty years, crises of different natures have been used to solve political conundrums. As differentiation (understood here as an umbrella term) entails different risks but also opportunities for different actors, the chapter then moves on to discuss how the academic literature assessed such flexibility mechanisms, to emphasise the lack of consensus on the matter which tends to be context-specific. Given the challenges posed by Brexit and Russia's invasion of Ukraine for the future of European integration, the chapter subsequently focuses on what the creation of the European Political Community means for Europe, before concluding that differentiation is a persistent feature of the European Union that should be considered the norm, as long as it does not impact the Union's core values, especially the rule of law.

What is differentiation in the European Union?

Differentiation is a broad phenomenon that covers multiple types of arrangements and concepts, ranging from EU member states' opt-outs of specific EU policies to non-member states' opt-ins, and including temporary de facto or de jure exemptions in primary or secondary law. For this reason, differentiation is best understood as an umbrella term referring to heterogeneous modes and strategies of integration and disintegration in the European Union (Leruth et al. 2022). In other words, differentiation encompasses a wide range of centrifugal and centripetal 'movements' towards and away from the so-called 'core' of the European Union.

Differentiation is far from being a new phenomenon in the European Union. In fact, one can trace its roots back to the Treaty of Rome, although back then, differentiation was strongly limited in scope and time. In the 1970s, in the midst of a series of economic, social, and political crises commonly referred to as the 'Eurosclerosis' period, differentiation was tabled by Belgian Prime Minister Léo Tindemans (1975) in the form of a multi-speed Europe. But it is only in the early 1990s that proper attention started being paid to differentiation as a mechanism to deepen and widen European integration prospects. On the one hand, with the creation of the European Economic Area, countries that did not seek to join the Union (such as Iceland and Liechtenstein) could enjoy the benefits of joining the Single Market as outsiders. On the other hand, reluctant member states could mark their opposition to participating in new policies without triggering a new era of integrational stagnation by negotiating opt-outs, as the United Kingdom and Denmark did in the context of the ratification of the Maastricht Treaty. As such, the early 1990s marked the beginning of the 'differentiation studies' era, in which scholars and policy-makers attempted to make sense of such flexibility mechanisms.

One of the pioneering studies of differentiation is Stubb's (1996) categorisation of differentiated integration. By analysing discussions and negotiations taking place at the European level, Stubb managed to make sense of what he referred to as the 'semantic indigestion' surrounding some differentiation-related concepts by proposing three categories of differentiated integration, all relating to one dimension of European integration. The first one is the so-called 'multi-speed' Europe model, according to which differentiation is temporary. The second one is the 'concentric circles' model, according to which avant-garde member states form a pioneering group within the EU's 'inner core' and other reluctant member states form the 'outer core' of the Union by negotiating opt-outs. The third model has a functional dimension, as participation in European integration varies depending on the policy area, with 'à la carte Europe' (also understood as 'cherry-picking') being the main model of differentiation.

Since then, new models of differentiation have emerged. In the late 1990s, the mechanism of enhanced cooperation, which allows a minimum of nine member states to cooperate within the EU framework without forcing the hand of reluctant ones, became constitutionalised (Kroll & Leuffen 2015). This mechanism inspired subsequent policy developments, such as the creation of the Permanent Structured Cooperation (also known as PESCO) in 2018. Additional concepts capture diverse processes of differentiation that are context-specific, such as instrumental or capacity differentiation (i.e., imposing differentiation to new member states for a specific period; Schneider 2007; Schimmelfennig 2014), constitutional or sovereignty differentiation (i.e., processes of differentiation that follow treaty revisions and lead to opt-outs from reluctant member states; Schimmelfennig & Winzen 2014; Bellamy & Kröger 2021) or experimental differentiation (i.e. small-scale, short-term policies or programmes that fall under the scope of EU institutions to test whether cooperation can be deepened or widened in specific policy areas; Leruth 2023). These reflect the wide range of differentiated mechanisms of integration, which all entail different consequences. It would therefore be wrong to assess differentiation as good or bad, as such assessment should be concept- and context-specific (see Leruth et al. 2019a).

In the early 2010s, in the midst of the EU's so-called polycrisis (Zeitlin et al. 2019), academic discussions started focusing on conceptualising and theorising European disintegration (Fossum 2015; Leruth et al. 2019b; Webber 2014; Zielonka 2014). Vollaard (2014: 1143) for instance highlighted the lack of studies on disintegration processes in the European Union, stating that differentiated integration studies 'only explain why some member states do not join all integrative steps, and not whether the EU could become less integrated'. The absence of such debates in the

academic literature also contributed to some scholarly confusion over the consequences of the United Kingdom's surprise vote to leave the European Union.[1]

Brexit effectively created an unprecedented challenge for Europe. Effectively,
the Brexit vote triggered a long process of differentiated disintegration, which is
best understood as "the selective reduction of a state's level and scope of integration" (Schimmelfennig 2018: 1154). Chopin and Lequesne (2016), Jones (2016), and
Rosamond (2016) were among the first scholars to reflect on the Brexit vote, arguing that ideas of European disintegration and differentiation ought to be analysed
to understand the consequences Brexit will have on the future of European integration. Initial discussions focused on a potential 'domino effect', with pundits
wondering which EU member state will leave the Union next given the increasing
prominence of Eurosceptic leaders across Europe. In sum, Brexit acted as a 'wake-
up call' for academics to study European disintegration.

As a response to these different challenges, the European Commission (2017)
released a much-discussed White Paper on the Future of Europe, which aimed
at reflecting on the way forward for the European Union ahead of the 2019 European Parliament elections. Rather than offering a long-term vision for Europe, this
White Paper laid out five broad scenarios for the short-term future of European
integration, i.e., reflecting on what the European Union would look like in 2025.
The first scenario is 'carrying on': in line with the EU's successful experiences in
muddling through crises, the EU's current course of action should proceed as plan-
ned and the polycrisis should not alter the current pace and depth of European
integration. The second scenario is 'Nothing but the Single Market': in this scenario, the EU's competences would be drastically reduced to revert these back to
pre-Maastricht levels, thereby excluding areas such as migration, security, and defence (i.e., a form of homogeneous disintegration). The third one is entitled 'Those
who want more do more': in this scenario, the principles underlying the mechanism of enhanced cooperation would be expanded to become more prominent,
thereby creating a constellation of concentric circles within the EU. The fourth option is 'Doing less more efficiently': in contrast to the second scenario, this would
imply both integration and disintegration at the same time, by increasing cooperation in areas that are deemed beneficial (such as expanding the scope of the Single Market). Finally, the fifth idea is 'Doing much more together', with the aim of
significantly deepening the process of European integration across policy areas. To
these five scenarios, then European Commission President Jean-Claude Juncker

---

1 It is worth noting that the Brexit vote is not the first instance of a surprising outcome in EU-related referendums, as illustrated by the Danish initial rejection of the Maastricht Treaty, as explained below. One may therefore find the lack of theoretical debates over the prospects of European disintegration quite surprising.

(2017) will add a sixth idea in his 2017 State of the Union address, namely 'a Union of Values' in which three principles would be 'unshakeable': freedom, equality, and the rule of law. This scenario, however, does not elaborate on its possible institutional or integrationist consequences. Although none of the above-mentioned scenarios explicitly mention the idea of differentiation, the third scenario does cover core principles underlying differentiated integration (rather than disintegration) and is reflected in the institutional design of PESCO. While no clear-cut conclusions or follow-up discussions were made by the Juncker Commission regarding this White Paper (see Gänzle et al. 2020), it did bring debates over the future of European integration back to the table ahead of the 2021–22 Conference on the Future of Europe. The European Commission funded three Horizon 2020 projects focusing on differentiated integration that deepened our understanding and knowledge of the causes and consequences it entails (EU IDEA, EU3D, and InDivEU).

What are the dynamics behind differentiation? While scholars have been struggling to find a consensus on the consequences it broadly entails for the future of European integration given its diverse forms, the existing literature extensively covered its roots and causes (see e. g. Leuffen et al. 2012; Holzinger & Schimmelfennig 2012; Piris 2012; Leruth & Lord 2015). Schimmelfennig and Winzen (2020) proposed a model that broadly summarises the dynamics behind differentiation: put simply, for differentiation to occur, one needs *suppliers* and *demanders*. The suppliers consist of governments from the above-mentioned 'inner core' of the European Union who are willing to accept moves away from homogeneous integration. Supply, the authors argue, varies depending on the size of this inner group (which needs to be large enough to create patterns of integration), the perceived consequences of differentiation by this group (i. e., whether it may create positive or negative externalities), and decision-making rules in place, with precedents leading to a path-dependent process of differentiation that may vary per policy area. The demanders of differentiation are governments (sometimes pressed by other actors, such as political parties, interest groups, or the public by means of a referendum) that seek to move away from uniformity due to one or several forms of heterogeneities: these can be heterogeneities of preference, for instance, if governments believe participation in a specific policy would harm their national sovereignty; heterogeneities of dependence, if governments believe that participation in a specific EU policy would not benefit them because the country's needs are different; and heterogeneities of capacity, if governments believe their countries do not have the financial or technological tools to implement a specific policy. In the latter case, demands tend to have a temporal dimension, triggering demands for a multi-speed form of integration.

Differentiation as a response to crises

This supply and demand model for differentiation is particularly useful to understand the dynamics behind differentiation, especially in times of crisis. Leruth (2021) applied this model to four instances of political crises since the early 1990s: Denmark's initial rejection of the Maastricht Treaty via referendum in 1992; Sweden's rejection of Eurozone membership via referendum in 2003; and Iceland and Greece's experiences of the Great Recession, which respectively triggered integrationist and disintegrationist movements (see also Taylor-Gooby et al. 2017). In the Danish case, the surprising outcome of the referendum created a political crisis that caught both Danish and European elites off guard and led the European Council (as suppliers of differentiation) to consider a series of scenarios including a withdrawal of Denmark from the European Community. European institutions were particularly concerned about the lack of progress to deepen the process of European integration after almost two decades of political stagnation. Scrapping the proposed Maastricht Treaty would have meant entering yet another period of political uncertainty for the European Community, which Brussels wanted to avoid at all costs. This crisis, however, was swiftly managed by Danish political parties who drafted demands for opt-outs in four fields: Economic and Monetary Union (effectively allowing Denmark to stay out of the Eurozone), Justice and Home Affairs, Security and Defence, and the more symbolic EU citizenship, to provide reassurance that it would not replace national citizenship. These were ultimately accepted by the European Council in the so-called 1992 Edinburgh Agreement, which paved the way for a second referendum to be held in Denmark. Ultimately, 56.7 percent of the Danish voters approved the ratification of the Maastricht Treaty, thereby suggesting that differentiation was an effective strategy to get out of a political crisis that would have affected both Denmark and the European Union.

In Sweden, demands for differentiation were driven by two sets of public actors. Firstly, the Sweden government, which initially decided to *postpone* participation in the Eurozone based on the advice of the Calmfors commission in 1997, thereby triggering demands for multi-speed differentiation. Such demands were also driven by internal divisions within the ruling Social Democratic Party. Secondly, public opinion was reluctant to the idea of abandoning the Swedish Króna. This was confirmed in 2003, as 55.9 percent of Swedish voters opposed Economic and Monetary Union membership. European institutions opted to tolerate the outcome of this referendum, by granting a form of informal (or de facto) differentiation; still, Sweden is legally bound to join the Eurozone sooner or later, making this form of differentiation therefore unstable and based on the goodwill of the suppliers' group. As such, the strategy used by European institutions was more passive than in the Danish context, with the European Commission (2003) 'taking note' of the outcome and being 'confident that the Swedish Government will choose the way forward to keep the euro project alive in Sweden'.

In Iceland, a long-standing member of the European Economic Area, the government demanded a form of 'de-differentiation' by seeking full EU membership as a response to the global financial crisis (also called the Great Recession). Such demands followed an early election that saw the first left-wing, pro-European government in Iceland's history enter office. Although accession talks started swiftly and seemed promising, they could not make progress with regard to fisheries policy, with Iceland's negotiating team seeking an opt-out from the Common Fisheries Policy to maintain Iceland's exclusive economic fishing zones. This demand was not accepted by the European Union, and subsequent negotiations were significantly slower in making progress. Eventually, as the national economy progressively recovered from the financial crisis, the country withdrew its application six years later following an ideological change in the composition of the government. In Greece, although there were no formal demands in this respect, temporary differentiation in the form of a much-debated Grexit (understood as a temporary withdrawal from the Eurozone) was advocated by then German finance minister Wolfgang Schäuble, but the insider group was strongly divided on the matter and a form of accidental or forced differentiated disintegration was avoided following a compromise between the Greek government and the European institutions, during the Eurozone crisis that followed the Great Recession.

These four examples illustrate that differentiation has been advocated and used as one of the strategies to respond to political or economic crises, even if this does not become a reality as illustrated in the case of Greece. Yet, where it is being implemented, differentiation can act as a double-edged sword. History has proven that differentiation has been difficult to rollback, as illustrated by successive Danish governments' unsuccessful attempts to transform opt-outs into opt-ins. It was only in the context of the war in Ukraine that Denmark opted into the Common Security and Defence Policy following a referendum held on 1 June 2022.

Brexit is a particularly complex case. As mentioned above, the vote to leave the European Union held on 23 June 2016 triggered a long and unprecedented process of differentiated disintegration, effectively opening a new chapter in the history of European integration. Initially, however, demands from the British government targeted more differentiation for the United Kingdom while staying inside the EU. These demands mostly focused on symbolic issues, such as an opt-out from the notion of an 'Ever Closer Union', or domestically salient policy issues, such as the introduction of a so-called emergency brake to restrict access to in-work benefits for EU citizens for a period of 4 years and halting the payment of childcare benefits overseas. Overall, these demands did not cross any of the suppliers' 'red lines' (despite some reluctance regarding the 'Ever Closer Union' opt-out which, in some governments' views, could set up a dangerous precedent), and an agreement was found between then British Prime Minister David Cameron and President of the European Council Donald Tusk, which laid grounds for the Brexit referendum campaign. These demands were accepted, yet did not prove to be sufficient in containing a well-organised 'Vote Leave' campaign (despite the absence of debate on the type of differentiated disintegration that would be sought by its proponents), while the pro-remain 'Stronger In' campaign suffered from internal divisions (Oliver 2018). Ultimately, differentiated disintegration was triggered by different actors who constituted the 'demand side': Eurosceptic Conservative front- and backbenchers most notable from the European Research Group, who put significant pressure on David Cameron (and Theresa May during post-referendum negotiations with the European Union); the UK Independence Party, a single issue party that managed to politicise the issue to the point of putting pressure on the UK government despite its an almost invisible presence in Westminster (with only two Members of Parliament, both Conservative defectors, at its peak); and ultimately the public who decided on the outcome of the referendum.

Differentiation, therefore, takes a wide range of forms. From initial discussions on temporal flexibility that can be found in the roots of the European integration project, differentiation has progressively become a constellation of strategies that serve different purposes, ranging from deepening integration without 'forcing' reluctant member states to join policies (e.g., through enhanced cooperation) to disintegration as illustrated in the case of Brexit.

The risks and opportunities differentiation entails

Although differentiation still remains the exception to the rule, it has become a permanent and mainstream feature within the European Union. As mentioned above, it would be wrong to argue that differentiation as a whole is 'right' or 'wrong' for the European Union, as it encompasses a wide range of strategies and modes of (dis)integration that are very context-specific. For instance, one cannot compare instrumental differentiation (i.e., temporary forms of differentiation for new member states to adapt and accommodate) with enhanced cooperation, as these modes of differentiation have different roots and objectives. When assessing the risks and opportunities differentiation entails, it is therefore worth specifying which mode or strategy one focuses on. Yet, one specific form of differentiation has been the focus of much scholarly and political debate, namely the opt-outs that have been granted (either *de facto* or *de jure*) to some member states. This is arguably the most visible type of differentiation, and also the one that constituted the core of differentiation studies from the early 1990s onwards. Furthermore, in the context of the Eurozone crisis and the potential existence of two membership 'classes' based on participation in the third stage of the Economic and Monetary Union (see e.g. Piris 2012), assessing the risks and opportunities such opt-out entails are significant to understanding the impact differentiation may have on the future of European integration.

Several studies have attempted to assess and map out the pros and cons of differentiation, although its long-term consequences remain difficult to grasp. Kölliker (2001) posited that differentiation is likely to create centripetal effects in the long run, especially in the case of excludable networks and club goods.[2] Piris (2012) also argued in favour of institutionalised differentiation through the creation of two formal 'clubs' of member states: an avant-garde group of Eurozone members, and another group that would *temporarily* play a less active role in shaping the European Union (given that Piris argues in favour of a *two-speed* Europe rather than for a permanent form of differentiation, with opt-outs being constrained in time under a multi-speed model). Bellamy and Kröger (2021) argued that different modes of differentiated integration (instrumental and constitutional) can be considered 'fair' from a demoicratic perspective[3] when it fosters a European Union in which member states "can simultaneously meet their obligations to their own people as well as to EU citizens and the peoples of other member states by not integrating when the latter might conflict with the former". Reflecting on Brexit and the experience of the Covid-19 pandemic, Trondal et al. (2022) argued that differentiation can contribute to the long-term sustainability and institutional robustness of the Union. In contrast, Walker (1998: 387) was among the first academics to call differentiated integration a 'non-project' which could lead to "increased fragmentation, legal indeterminacy, declining democracy and political failure". Another well-known risk of differentiation is dominance. Eriksen (2018) among others posited that differentiation undermines the conditions for democratic self-rule through non-participation or (self-)exclusion from decision-making bodies. This is best exemplified by non-EU member states' participation in the European Economic Area, as these countries (Iceland, Norway, and Liechtenstein) are

---

2 Subsequent empirical developments would however nuance this theory, as illustrated by the Brexit vote.
3 In European Studies, demoicracy refers to a European Union of peoples, understood both as states and as citizens, who govern together but not as one (hence the plural form of demos; see Nicolaïdis 2013).

not represented in the European institutions. As a result, Norway's relationship with the European Union has sometimes been referred to as a 'fax democracy', mirroring the fact that Oslo receives directives and regulations from Brussels and Norway ought to implement without having participated in the decision-making process (Leruth et al. 2019a).

In an attempt to make sense of diverging academic views towards differentiation, Kröger and Loughran (2021) ran an expert survey that yielded 95 responses. Their findings indicated ambivalent views: while most experts agree that differentiation is useful to ensure the long-term future of European integration, Eastern Europe-based scholars tend to be more critical of differentiation, being of the view that opt-outs from the Economic and Monetary Union for instance lead to the domination of Western European member states by creating or reinforcing existing power asymmetries between member states.

These divergences of opinion on the risks and opportunities differentiation entails are expected, as they may be connected to one's vision of the future of European integration as a whole. There is therefore a strong normative component to attitudes towards differentiation. As such, the more 'Euro-federalist' the subjects, the less likely they will support differentiation. Yet, there is a wide-ranging agreement between scholars regarding where to draw the line, as core EU values such as the rule of law should not be compromised. In sum, while there is no clear consensus over whether differentiation has been and continues to be a useful tool to foster European integration, perhaps Kelemen (2021: 680) makes the most sense of these lasting and yet ongoing debates over the effects of flexibility mechanisms in the European Union: "[l]ike most habits and even vices, [differentiation] is not threatening if engaged in with moderation".

Recent developments: The war in Ukraine and the European political community

In the first years of the presidency of Commission President Ursula von der Leyen, the European Union has had to face a new wave of crises. The first one is what is best conceived as a 'creeping crisis', or a challenge that has been ongoing for decades and progressively becomes more urgent to address: climate change. Following a series of deadly floodings across France, Germany, Belgium, and the Netherlands in 2021, the summer of 2022 was marked by a heatwave that resulted in Europe's largest drought in five centuries, water shortages across several European countries, and uncontrolled wildfires. The second challenge is the Covid-19 pandemic, which caught most EU member states off guard: while it originally resulted in unilateral actions when it comes to closing borders (what one could conceive as a form of 'disorganised differentiation'), European institutions managed to muddle through difficult months to organise the purchase of vaccines[4] and implement an EU-wide Digital Covid Certificate, resulting in mostly homogenous action to tackle the crisis. The third, and even more complex challenge is the result of Russia's invasion of Ukraine. This section focuses on this third and (at the time of writing, August 2022) ongoing crisis, as it illustrates both the modern risks and opportunities differentiation entails. In doing so, we focus on both the 'deepening' and 'widening' dimensions of the process of European integration, as modern forms of differentiation impact both.

While the process of widening the European Union reached its peak in the mid-2000s with the so-called 'big bang enlargement' that saw 10 countries joining the Union, the enlargement process has stalled over the past decade. Before the war in Ukraine started, six countries were recognised as official candidate countries: Turkey (since 1999), North Macedonia (since 2005), Montenegro (since 2010), Serbia (since 2012), and Albania (since 2014). The lack of accession talks progress proved to be quite frustrating for some negotiating teams: while the European Union was in the midst of dealing with the polycrisis and rising Euroscepticism, there were fears among some member states that any pro-enlargement policies would benefit Eurosceptic and far-right parties that link enlargement to a rise in immigration (due to the freedom of movement) and sometimes a threat to national sovereignty. France, for instance, has become particularly passive and unwilling to push for further enlargement discussions, especially with countries from the Balkans (Wunsch 2017). In sum, and with the exception of Croatia's accession to the EU in 2013 (following eight years of negotiations), the 2010s did not provide fruitful grounds for enlargement prospects due to the socio-political consequences of the EU's polycrisis (see also Whitman & Juncos 2012).

The war in Ukraine radically changed this enlargement scepticism. Shortly after the beginning of Russia's invasion, Ukraine applied to join the European Union on 28 February 2022, promptly followed by Moldova and Georgia which tabled their applications on 3 March. While a decision regarding Georgia's application was deferred until specific reforms are conducted, both Ukraine and Moldova were granted formal candidate status on 23 June. In combination with the rounds of sanctions against Russia and material support given to Ukraine, Brussels sent a strong message to all three countries as well as the rest of the international com-

---

4 It is worth noting, however, that Hungary was an outlier as it opted to unilaterally purchase doses of the Sputnik V vaccine, even though this vaccine had not been approved by the European Medicines Agency.

munity: the European Union is ready to play a significant geopolitical role. This also signalled to all three countries but also existing candidates that the European Union and its member states are ready to end a period of 'enlargement drought', although some candidate countries expressed concerns over a sped-up procedure for Ukraine that would lead the country to skip the queue.

In practice, however, these new candidate countries face a significant wait before being (possibly) admitted into the Union. Historically, enlargement procedures have always taken years or even decades, to ensure that candidate countries are fully ready to be integrated. Naturally, instrumental differentiation can be used to progressively integrate new member states into specific policy areas, but all 35 chapters of the EU's *Acquis Communautaire* need to be negotiated ahead of accession. This makes any genuine fast-track enlargement option from candidacy to full-fledged admission highly unlikely. Similarly, accession to the European Economic Area would require substantial negotiations. As such, one could argue there is an institutional void that can be filled for EU candidate countries, beyond the scope of the European Neighbourhood Policy.

In what can be interpreted as an attempt to manage expectations regarding enlargement prospects in the short-term but also a way to fill this institutional void, Emmanuel Macron unexpectedly proposed the creation of a new political entity, the European Political Community, on 9 May 2022. In the French President's words, the European Political Community "would allow democratic European nations that subscribe to our shared core values to find a new space for political and security cooperation, cooperation in the energy sector, in transport, investments, infrastructures, the free movement of persons and in particular of our youth" (Macron 2022). This is not a new idea: three decades earlier, in the context of the fall of the Berlin Wall, then-French President François Mitterrand proposed the creation of a European Confederation which would include members of the (then) European Community and Central and Eastern European countries in order to foster cooperation in the areas of culture, communication, energy, the environment, and the freedom of movement. Initially, this initiative was seen as a step in the right direction to facilitate dialogue and cooperation with countries that would ultimately join the European Community and led to a meeting in Prague on 13 and 14 June to determine the next steps. However, this momentum did not last, most notably because Central and Eastern European countries saw the European Confederation as a step to slow down or even hinder their path toward accession to the European Union (Chopin et al. 2022).

The idea of setting up a European Political Community differs from Mitterrand's in several respects. Firstly, the context is significantly more sober: while the end of the Cold War paved the way for a transition towards liberal democracy for most Central and Eastern European countries, the war in Ukraine was driven by an external threat, namely Putin's regime, with the cost of living and energy crises deriving from this war. At the beginning of Fall 2022, the European Union was still attempting to muddle through these crises by coordinating their actions, for instance by introducing price caps on gas consumption. The energy crisis requires cooperation that goes beyond the borders of the European Union, and it is one of the core themes that are expected to be discussed within the framework of this new Political Community. Secondly, the relationship between the EU and the United Kingdom has been relatively frosty ever since the Brexit referendum. Withdrawal negotiations were particularly difficult for both sides, and successive Conservative governments have been accused of not negotiating with Brussels in good faith, as some British politicians have called for unilaterally scrapping the Northern Ireland Protocol that allows goods to be transported across the Irish border without the need for checks until they reach Northern Ireland's ports, effectively making Northern Ireland a trading 'buffer' between Great Britain and the European Single Market. As tense relations between both parties are suboptimal, the European Political Community could pave the way to rebuild a constructive collaboration between London and Brussels, away from the risks of politicization that would fuel the still lively Eurosceptic mood across the United Kingdom. Thirdly, the European Political Community has initially been branded as a forum for discussion, with loose institutional obligations and therefore limited expectations. This aims at appeasing voices in Moldova and most importantly Ukraine that the Political Community would slow down their accession process, as could have been the case with Mitterrand's European Confederation. In other words, the European Political Community can be conceived as a 'sandbox institution' that could lead to formal or informal cooperation between all or some of its 44 participating countries. As a result, differentiation (here again understood as an umbrella term) lies at its core.

The European Political Community's first meeting took place in Prague in October 2022. During this meeting, a series of political decisions involving non-member states of the EU were made. These included an agreement between Norway and the Union to establish joint tools to tackle the energy crisis, sending an EU civilian mission to Armenia and Azerbaijan in order to appease tension at the border between these two countries, and a series of bi- and trilateral talks between participating countries to establish policy initiatives within and beyond the scope of European integration. While most participating countries attended this initial meeting with some reluctance, the outcome was widely assessed as a positive one, and it was agreed that a subsequent meeting would be held in Moldova in early 2023, with a focus on Europe's key infrastructure and facilities. Although it is too early to tell whether the Political Community will succeed where the European Confederation failed, the idea of establishing thematic meetings is promising and may give more depth to subsequent discussions that would result in policy action. As a result, the European Political Community has the potential to both deepen and widen the process of European integration, by fostering policy development in key strategic areas and promoting cooperation with non-EU member states. The role the United Kingdom will play in this Community will be particularly interesting to follow, as the relationships between the UK and the EU remain tense.

The European Political Community is therefore a supply-driven model of differentiation that carries both risks and opportunities. An optimistic take can argue that this Community will fill an important institutional void and make cooperation between European countries smoother. A pessimistic take, however, would state that it complicates an already very complex picture, given the numerous overlapping institutions and policies that involve non-EU member states, and it could become an attractive option for Eurosceptic leaders in search of an alternative to EU membership. It cannot be ruled out that the European Political Community fails as the European Confederation project did three decades earlier. Yet, this attempt at setting up another institution is an important step in the history of differentiation in the European Union, and it will be worth analysing these efforts over the coming years.

Conclusion: Between integration and differentiation, where do we draw the line?

This chapter has focused on the dynamics behind differentiation, hereby understood as an umbrella term covering different modes and strategies of integration and disintegration in the European Union, and some of its most recent developments. Although scholars remain divided over its consequences for the future of European integration, differentiation has become a persistent and mainstream feature of the European Union. While transitional forms of differentiation that have a well-defined temporal dimension (such as instrumental differentiation) remain widely uncontroversial, permanent forms of differentiation, either de facto or de jure, can pose some challenges to the European Union.

Crises have shaped the use of differentiated mechanisms of integration and disintegration since the early 1990s. The recent Danish experience has proven that opt-outs can, under specific circumstances, be turned into opt-ins. Differentiation can be used as a strategy both within insider groups (as was the case in the context of an avoided Grexit) or by prospective outsiders wishing to divert from the mainstream integrationist trajectory, either by pushing for more or less integration. The prospects created by the European Political Community seem to indicate that differentiation will become even more prominent over the coming years, either in an experimental (hence the 'sandbox' analogy mentioned above) or in a more institutionalised form. One could argue that the European Union's capacity to 'muddle through' crises is, at least partially, driven by its capacity to accommodate different preferences and interests by allowing for a certain degree of differentiation to occur. In other words, working towards an 'Ever Closer Union' does not imply an 'ever more homogeneous' one.

This raises two fundamental and interconnected questions: what types of differentiation are adequate for the sustainability of European integration, and most importantly, where should one draw the line between homogeneity and differentiation? Answers to these questions are likely to have a normative dimension, as illustrated by lasting divergences of scholarly opinions over the risks and opportunities differentiation entails. As differentiation can also be shaped by short, medium, or long-term crises, answers may be context-specific and hard to extrapolate. However, the core EU values advocated by Jean-Claude Juncker in his 2017 State of the Union Address should indeed be 'unshakeable'. Over recent years, the rule of law has been challenged in both Hungary and Poland, leading European institutions to sanction these countries (albeit lightly). Yet, the absence of clear checks and balances regarding the respect of these core EU values means that member states remain, to date, free to test the waters and push boundaries when it comes to what is tolerated by European institutions. This carries a significant risk for the future of European integration and it could shake the Union at its core. In sum, differentiation has been and remains a useful tool to sustain the process of European integration, but demands for differentiation should not be accepted or tolerated 'at all costs', as tolerating moves away from core EU values would threaten the very nature of the European integration project and generate an existential crisis for the Union.

References

Bellamy, Richard & Kröger, Sandra (2021). 'Differentiated integration as a fair scheme of cooperation', *Review of Social Economy*, Online First.

Chopin, Thierry & Lequesne, Christian (2016): 'Differentiation as a Double-Edged Sword: Member States' Practices and Brexit', *International Affairs*, 92:3, 531–545.

Chopin, Thierry, Macek, Lukáš & Maillard, Sébastien (2022): 'The European Political Community: A new anchoring to the European Union', *Law & Institutions Policy Brief*, May 2022, Institut Jacques Delors.

European Commission (2003): *Commission Statement on the Swedish Referendum*, IP/03/1242, European Commission.

European Commission (2017): *White Paper on the Future of Europe*, European Commission.

Fossum, John Erik (2015): 'Democracy and Differentiation in Europe', *Journal of European Public Policy*, 22:6, 799–815.

Grant, Charles (2022): 'Macron is Serious about the "European Political Community"', *Centre for European Reform* [online] available at: https://www.cer.eu/insights/macron-serious-about-european-political-community [Accessed 22 September 2022].

Holzinger, Katharina & Schimmelfennig, Frank (2012): 'Differentiated Integration in the European Union: Many Concepts, Sparse Theory, Few Data', *Journal of European Public Policy*, 19:2, 292–305.

Hooghe, Liesbet & Marks, Gary (2005): 'Calculation, Community and Cues: Public Opinion on European Integration', *European Union Politics*, 6:4, 419–443.

Jones, Erik (2016): 'Why We Need a Theory of Disintegration' [online], Available at: https://erikjones.net/2016/11/12/why-we-need-a-theory-of-disintegration/ [Accessed 22 September 2022].

Juncker, Jean-Claude (2017): State of the Union Address 2017, European Commission.

Kelemen, R. Daniel (2021): 'Epilogue: A Note of Caution on Differentiated Integration', *Swiss Political Science Review*, 27:3, 672–681.

Kölliker, Alkuin (2001): 'Bringing Together or Driving Apart the Union? Towards a Theory of Differentiated Integration', *West European Politics*, 24:4, 125–151.

Kröger, Sandra & Loughran, Thomas (2021): 'The Risks and Benefits of Differentiated Integration in the European Union as Perceived by Academic Experts', *Journal of Common Market Studies*, 60:3, 702–720.

Kroll, Daniela A. & Leuffen, Dirk (2015): 'Enhanced Cooperation in Practice. An Analysis of Differentiated Integration in EU Secondary Law', *Journal of European Public Policy*, 22:3, 353–373.

Leruth, Benjamin (2021): 'Differentiation as a Response to Crises?', in Nathalie Brack & Seda Gürkan (eds.): *Theorising the Crises of the European Union*, Routledge, 226–245.

Leruth, Benjamin (2023): 'Experimental differentiation as an innovative form of cooperation in the European Union: Evidence from the Nordic Battlegroup', *Contemporary Security Policy*, 44:1, 125–149.

Leruth, Benjamin, Gänzle, Stefan & Trondal, Jarle (2019a): 'Differentiated Integration and Disintegration in the EU after Brexit: Risks versus Opportunities', *Journal of Common Market Studies*, 57:6, 1383–1394.

Leruth, Benjamin, Gänzle, Stefan & Trondal, Jarle (2019b): 'Exploring Differentiated Disintegration in a Post-Brexit European Union', *Journal of Common Market Studies*, 57:5, 1013–1030.

Leruth, Benjamin, Gänzle, Stefan & Trondal, Jarle (eds.) (2022): *The Routledge Handbook of Differentiation in the European Union*, Routledge.

Leruth, Benjamin & Lord, Christopher (2015): 'Differentiated Integration in the European Union: A Concept, a Process, a System or a Theory?', *Journal of European Public Policy*, 22:6, 754–763.

Leuffen, Dirk, Rittberger, Berthold & Schimmelfennig, Frank (2013): *Differentiated Integration: Explaining Variation in the European Union*, Palgrave Macmillan.

Macron, Emmanuel (2022): Speech by Emmanuel Macron at the closing ceremony of the Conference on the Future of Europe. https://presidence-francaise.consilium.europa.eu/en/news/speech-by-emmanuel-macron-at-the-closing-ceremony-of-the-conference-on-the-future-of-europe/ [Accessed 22 September 2022].

Matthijs, Matthias (2017): 'Europe After Brexit: A Less Perfect Union', *Foreign Affairs*, 96:1, 85–95.

Moland, Martin (2022): 'Constraining dissensus and permissive consensus: variations in support for core state powers', *West European Politics*, Online First.

Mucznik, Marta (2022): 'The European (geo)political community and enlargement reform: Two important but separate discussions', *European Policy Centre* [online] Available at: https://www.epc.eu/en/Publications/The-European-geopolitical-community-and-enlargement-reform~49e404 [Accessed 22 September 2022].

Nicolaïdis, Kalypso (2013): 'European Demoicracy and Its Crisis', *Journal of Common Market Studies*, 51:2, 351–369.

Oliver, Tim (2018): *Understanding Brexit: A Concise Introduction*, Policy Press.

Piris, Jean-Claude (2012): *The Future of Europe: Towards a Two-Speed EU?* Cambridge University Press.

Rosamond, Ben (2016): 'Brexit and the Problem of European Disintegration'. Journal of Contemporary European Research, 12:4, 865–871.

Schimmelfennig, Frank (2014): 'EU Enlargement and Differentiated Integration: Discrimination or Equal Treatment?' *Journal of European Public Policy*, 21(5), 681–698.

Schimmelfennig, Frank (2018): 'Brexit: Differentiated Disintegration in the European Union'. Journal of European Public Policy, 25:8, 1154–1173.

Schimmelfennig, Frank & Winzen, Thomas (2014): 'Instrumental and Constitutional Differentiation in the European Union', *Journal of Common Market Studies*, 52:2, 354–370.

Schneider, Christina (2007): 'Enlargement Processes and Distributional Conflict: The Politics of Discriminatory Membership in the European Union', *Public Choice*, 132, 85–102.

Stubb, Alexander (1996): 'A Categorisation of Differentiated Integration', *Journal of Common Market Studies*, 34:2, 283–295.

Taylor-Gooby, Peter, Leruth, Benjamin & Chung, Heejung (eds.) (2017): *After Austerity: Welfare State Transformation in Europe after the Great Recessio*n, Oxford University Press.

Tindemans, Léo (1975): 'European Union: Report by Mr Leo Tindemans, Prime Minister of Belgium, to the European Council', *Bulletin of the European Communities*, supplement 1/76, European Council.

Trondal, Jarle, Gänzle, Stefan & Leruth, Benjamin (2022): 'Differentiation in the European Union in Post-Brexit and -Pandemic Times: Macro-Level Developments with Meso-Level Consequences', *Journal of Common Market Studies*, Online First.

Vollaard, Hans (2014): 'Explaining European Disintegration', *Journal of Common Market Studies*, 52:5, 1142–1159.

Walker, Neil (1998): 'Sovereignty and Differentiated Integration in the European Union', *European Law Journal*, 4:4, 355–388.

Webber, Douglas (2014): 'How Likely is it that the European Union will Disintegrate? A Critical Analysis of Competing Theoretical Perspectives', *European Journal of International Relations*, 20:2, 341–365.

Whitman, Richard & Juncos, Ana E. (2012): 'The Arab Spring, the Eurozone Crisis and the Neighbourhood: A Region in Flux', *Journal of Common Market Studies*, 50:s2, 147–161.

Wunsch, Natasha (2017): 'Between indifference and hesitation: France and EU enlargement towards the Balkans', *Southeast European and Black Sea Studies*, 17:4, 541–554.

Zeitlin, Jonathan, Nicoli, Francesco & Laffan, Brigid (2019): 'Introduction: the European Union beyond the polycrisis? Integration and politicization in an age of shifting cleavages', *Journal of European Public Policy*, 26:7, 963–976.

Zielonka, Jan (2014): *Is the EU Doomed?* Polity Press.

Piotr Bogdanowicz

5 The difficulty of upholding the rule of law across the European Union: *The case of Poland as an illustration of problems the European Union is facing*

Abstract: This chapter identifies the most important means and institutions that are or might be responsible for the upholding of the rule of law in the European Union, either at the European Union or the national level, such as the Rule of Law Framework, Article 7 TEU procedure, and infringement proceedings under Article 258 TFEU. It also shows, in the case of Poland, some abusive actions that are taken by Member States to weaken the rule of law and the effectiveness of EU law. Poland and the persisting intra-EU tensions resulting from its insufficient implementation of the rule of law principle are shown as an exemplary illustration of a larger issue, demonstrating the Union's limited ability to enforce the rule of law, if the country concerned persists in challenging it. That said, this chapter concludes with some recommendations on how the European Commission can act in order to counter breaches of the rule of law even more effectively.

Keywords: European Union; Poland; rule of law; Commission, Court of Justice; enforcement

Introduction

The rule of law, which has become a focal aspect in the EU political and legal discourse over the last decade or two, is a fundamental value of the EU. It is enshrined in Article 2 of the Treaty of the European Union ("TEU"), according to which the EU is founded, among other things, on the rule of law as the value common to the Member States. However, recent years have not been easy for the rule of law in the EU. It is difficult to state when and where exactly the rule of law crisis[1] in the European Union started. Was it as early as 2000 when the far-right Freedom Party joined the Austrian government? In 2011 when Viktor Orbán com-

---

[1] Interestingly, the word 'crisis' is no longer used, only in colloquial language or in academic articles to describe the situation in Poland, but also appears in EU documents. See e.g. European Parliament resolution of 21 October 2021 on the rule of law crisis in Poland and the primacy of EU law (2021/2935(RSP)).

https://doi.org/10.1515/9783110790337-006

menced his reforms in Hungary? Or no earlier than in 2015 when the Law and Justice party seized power in Poland and started dismantling the major checks and balances by, among other things, subordinating courts to the will of the executive power? Without a doubt, however, all these potential starting points have a lot in common – they have triggered concern about the ability of the European Union to address challenges to the rule of law principle deriving from such situations. At the same time, the last few years have shown that some Member States continue to struggle with observing the rule of law in the European Union. Poland is a prime example of this. Few could have imagined that the whole situation would develop so dynamically when the European Commission launched a dialogue with Poland in January 2016, under the title "A new EU Framework to strengthen the Rule of Law" (Commission 2014). Six years later there are still ongoing proceedings against Poland, activated under Article 7(1) TEU (Commission 2017).[2] There have been numerous preliminary references[3] from Polish courts to the Court of Justice of the European Union ("Court" or "CJEU"),[4] including from the "high-level courts" such as the Supreme Court or the Supreme Administrative Court, concerning the EU requirements on the independence of the judiciary. Finally, there have been several infringement proceedings on the same subject, started against Poland by the European Commission under Article 258 TFEU.[5] In spite of that, the problem with the rule of law in Poland is still present.

Poland and the persisting intra-EU tensions resulting from its insufficient implementation of the rule of law principle have thus become an exemplary illustration of a larger issue, demonstrating the Union's limited ability to enforce the rule

---

2 Under Article 7(1) TEU, on a reasoned proposal by one-third of the Member States, by the European Parliament or by the European Commission, the Council, acting by a majority of four-fifths of its members after obtaining the consent of the European Parliament, may determine that there is a clear risk of a serious breach by a Member State of the values referred to in Article 2. Before making such a determination, the Council shall hear the Member State in question and may address recommendations to it, acting in accordance with the same procedure. The Council shall regularly verify that the grounds on which such a determination was made continue to apply. See further point II.2 below.

3 A procedure enshrined in Article 267 of the Treaty on the Functioning of the European Union (**"TFEU"**), used in cases where mainly the interpretation of an EU law is in question and where such interpretation is necessary for a national court to give judgment.

4 For instance, in 2020, approx. 70 % of preliminary references from Polish courts concerned the rule of law. See: https://prawo.gazetaprawna.pl/artykuly/1494903,tsue-wnioski-prejudycjalne-polskie-sady-praworzadnosc.html (last access: 16 October 2022).

5 See judgment of the Court dated 24 June 2019, Case C-619/18, *Commission v Poland*, ECLI:EU:C:2019:531; judgment of the Court dated 5 November 2019, Case C-192/18, *Commission v Poland (Indépendance des juridictions de droit commun)*, ECLI:EU:C:2019:924 and judgment of the Court dated 15 July 2021, Case C-791/19, *Commission v Poland (Régime disciplinaire des juges)*, ECLI:EU:C:2021:596.

of law, if the country concerned persists in challenging it. In 2013, i.e. before the Law and Justice party started dismantling the major checks and balances in Poland,[6] David Landau defined "abusive constitutionalism" as "the use of mechanisms of constitutional change in order to make a state significantly less democratic than it was before." (Landau 2013: 195). When writing these words, he was not thinking about Poland, but they accurately describe the recent situation in Poland.

To tell the truth, backsliding in respect of the rule of law has become a question of concern to the EU in recent times due to events that took place not only in Poland but also in Austria (entry of a far-right party into government), France (the threatened deportation of members of the Roma community), Hungary (many concerns regarding e.g. judicial independence or media freedom), Italy (control of broadcast and printed media by the executive) or Romania (government's refusal to obey constitutional court rulings) (Barrett 2018: 31). Having said that, except for Hungary and to a lesser extent Romania, we must be cautious in comparing situations in these Member States to the backsliding of the rule of law in Poland. The scale of violations in Poland is large and the problem with the rule of law is comprehensive.

This chapter is divided into three sub-chapters. The first section aims to identify the most important means and institutions that are or might be responsible for the upholding of the rule of law in the European Union, either at the EU or the national level. The second section shows, in the case of Poland, some abusive actions taken thereby to weaken the rule of law and effectiveness of EU law, and the context within which such processes unfold. Finally, I will present what actions were taken by the Commission and the Court to uphold the rule of law in Poland and will discuss to what extent at least some of them were taken too late or were insufficient. That said, the chapter concludes with some recommendations on how the Commission can act to counter breaches of the rule of law more effectively for the benefit of the European Union as a whole.

---

6 Under the guise of "reforms". For more on this see R.D. Kelemen and L. Pech who note that the changes adopted by the Polish authorities should not be called "reforms", but rather a set of unconstitutional measures whose main effect – if not the main goal – "has been to hamper the constitutionally protected principle of judicial independence" so as "to enable the legislative and executive branches to interfere with the administration of justice" (Kelemen & Pech 2018: 17).

Institutional mechanisms to uphold the rule of law in the EU

The EU needs its Member States to turn EU law and policy into a living reality, and this in turn requires that the EU values are enforced and that the rule of law is strongly adhered to in all Member States. The EU has several instruments to protect the rule of law therein. The following subsections discuss the core tools.

The rule of law framework

The Rule of Law Framework was created by the EU in 2014 to enable the Commission to find a solution with the Member State concerned to prevent the emergence of a systemic threat to the rule of law in that Member State that could develop into a "clear risk of a serious breach" within the meaning of Article 7 TEU (Commission 2014). In other words, the role of the Rule of Law Framework is to resolve future threats to the rule of law in Member States already before the conditions for activating the mechanisms foreseen in Article 7 TEU (discussed in the next subsection) would be met. This is done through dialogue with the EU country concerned. The Rule of Law Framework establishes a three-stage process. They are (i) the Commission's assessment, (ii) the Commission's recommendation, and (iii) monitoring of the EU country's follow-up to the Commission's recommendation. Interestingly, as described by Artur Nowak-Far, although the procedure foreseen in the Rule of Law Framework was meant to produce a legal and binding effect, the Rule of Law Framework rules were deprived of a binding force (Nowak-Far 2021: 321).

In a nutshell, in the first stage, the Commission collects and examines all the relevant information and assesses whether there are clear indications of a systemic threat to the rule of law as described above. If, as a result of this preliminary assessment, the Commission is of the opinion that there is indeed a situation of a systemic threat to the rule of law, it will initiate a dialogue with the Member State concerned, by sending a "rule of law opinion" and substantiating its concerns, giving the Member State concerned the possibility to respond. In the second stage, unless the matter has already been satisfactorily resolved in the meantime, the Commission issues a "rule of law recommendation" addressed to the Member State concerned, if it finds that there is objective evidence of a systemic threat and that the authorities of that Member State are not taking appropriate action to redress it. Where appropriate, the recommendation may include specific indications on ways and measures to resolve the situation. In the third stage, the Commission monitors the follow-up given by the Member State concerned to the recommendation addressed to it. If there is no satisfactory follow-up to the recommendation by the Member State concerned within the time limit set, the Commission shall assess the possibility of activating one of the mechanisms set out in Article 7 TEU.

Poland was the first ever, and the only one so far, Member State to be subject to the Rule of Law Framework with four recommendations issued by the Commission.[7]

Article 7 TEU procedure

Article 7 TEU has been characterised as a provision of unique, exceptional character aimed at the protection of the substance of the EU (Tichý 2018: 89). In fact, it incorporates three different procedures which further can be divided into two mechanisms: (i) a procedure to declare the existence of a "clear risk of a serious breach" of the values referred to in Article 2 TEU and the adoption of recommendations how to remedy the situation addressed to the Member State in breach (Article 7(1) TEU); (ii) a procedure to determine the existence of a serious and persistent breach of values (Article 7(2) TEU) – both procedures constitute a mechanism with the aim to prevent further breaches – and (iii) a sanctioning mechanism following the occurrence and recognition of a serious and persistent breach which allows the Council to suspend certain rights deriving from the application of the treaties to the Member State in question, including its voting rights in the Council (Kochenov 2021: 136). Importantly, the existence of a serious and persistent breach may only be determined by the European Council acting by unanimity (except for the respective country facing allegations regarding a breach of the rule-of-law value). This requirement of unanimity is considered the major hurdle in the process. Consequently, some authors suggest a possibility to initiate a joint Article 7 procedure against two or more states if the merits of the case are similar and offended values are identical. This would disqualify the member states that are feared to be the next in line from vetoing the European Council's decision (Dumbrovsky 2018: 205).

So far, the procedure has been initiated twice – against Poland (Commission 2017) and Hungary (European Parliament 2018).[8] In both cases, although several years have passed, proceedings are ongoing.

---

7 Commission Recommendations: (EU) 2016/1374 of 27 July 2016, (EU) 2017/146 of 21 December 2016, (EU) 2017/1520 of 26 July 2017 and (EU) 2018/103 of 20 December 2017.
8 Interestingly, this was made without the Rule of Law Framework having been used before.

Infringement proceedings

For many years it has been debated in the literature whether Article 7 TEU excludes the applicability of Article 258 TFEU on the Commission's options for action in case a Member State fails to fulfil its rule of law obligations as provided by the Treaty (Schmidt & Bogdanowicz 2018: 1069–1073). By its judgment in the case C-619/18 *Commission* v *Poland (Independence of the Supreme Court)*, in which the Court has held that Poland infringed the principle of judicial independence under Article 19(1)(2) TEU, the Court confirmed that Article 7 TEU and Article 258 TFEU are separate procedures and may be invoked at the same time (see also P. Bárd & A. Sledzinska-Simon 2020: 1555–1584; Bogdanowicz & Taborowski 2020: 306–327).

In a nutshell, the procedure under Article 258 TFEU works as follows. If the Commission considers that a given Member State may not be meeting its obligations arising from EU law, it sends a letter of formal notice to the Member State in question requesting further information. That State must send a detailed reply by a given deadline, usually two months. On the basis of this reply, the Commission may either issue a reasoned opinion (which may be understood as a formal request to comply with EU law, calling on the EU country in question to inform it of the measures taken to comply within a specified period, usually two months) or close the case. If the country concerned fails to comply with the Commission's opinion within the timetable given, the Commission may refer the case to the Court.

As aforementioned, the Commission has already carried out several infringement proceedings against Poland concerning its breach of rule of law obligations.

Other mechanisms

Whereas the three abovementioned mechanisms are arguably the most important means and institutions for upholding the rule of law in the European Union, they are not the only ones. For instance, the Cooperation and Verification Mechanism, set up by the Commission in 2007, is a transitional measure to assist specifically one member state – Romania – to remedy persisting shortcomings in the field of judicial reform. For assessing progress, the Commission set criteria (benchmarks) and reports progress thereon on a regular basis.[9]

---

9 In 2021, Romania still had 17 outstanding recommendations and had met no benchmarks. See question for written answer to the Commission raised by Traian Băsescu: https://www.europarl. europa.eu/doceo/document/E-9-2021-003380_EN.html#:~:text=The%20Cooperation%20and%20Ver ification%20Mechanism,Member%20States%20and%20the%20EU (last access: 12 December 2022).

Most recently, an additional instrument was introduced, seeking to allow for swifter and at the same time more effective counteraction than the above-mentioned mechanisms in case a Member State breaches the rule of law principle. Namely, Regulation 2020/2092 of the European Parliament and of the Council of 16 December 2020 on a general regime of conditionality for the protection of the Union budget ("Regulation 2092/2020") was adopted in order to protect the Union budget against breaches of the principles of the rule of law which may affect the sound financial management and the financial interests of the Union. Under this regulation, the Commission will propose appropriate and proportionate measures (such as a suspension of EU funds) to the Council in case rule of law breaches in a given Member State threaten the EU's financial interests. The Council will then take a final decision on the proposal of measures. Importantly, unless the decision adopting the measures provides otherwise, the imposition of these measures shall not affect the obligations which the concerned Member State's government entities have toward the final recipients or beneficiaries, including the obligation to make payments.

In February 2022, the Court dismissed the action for annulment of Regulation 2092/2020 lodged by Poland and Hungary (Judgment of the Court in Joined Cases C-156–157/21, *Hungary and Poland against European Parliament and Council of the European Union*). A few months later, the Commission proposed for the first time budget protection measures to the Council against Hungary (Commission 2022a). At the time of writing, it has not proposed any similar measures against Poland.

Actions against upholding the rule of law in the EU. The Polish case

In its annual report on the rule of law situation in the European Union, the Commission pointed out that Member States' constitutional courts play a key role in the system of checks and balances (Commission 2022b). Unfortunately, decisions taken by constitutional courts may sometimes raise concerns about the rule of law. It may be argued that the rule of law crisis in Poland started from the crisis around the Polish Constitutional Tribunal.[10] Poland's rule of law crisis – i. e. the governing

---

10 Another one would be a judiciary crisis (see point III.2 below). It must also be remembered, however, that there are other elements of an "illegal" war, as one Polish professor put it, against the Constitution of Poland carried out by the constitutional authorities, the Parliament, the President, and the government – namely the freedom of the media, the civil service, human rights and

party's attempts to undermine judicial independence in its pursuit of further power gains – became a challenge for the Union, which henceforth had to ensure that Member States respected the rule of law not only at the time of accession, but also afterwards, and to restore the rule of law when it was eroded in a Member State. Thus, to contribute to a better understanding of what the Union is up against, this section explains the evolution of Poland's rule of law situation, emanating from its constitutional crisis. This crisis has several dimensions, but I will focus on two. The first concerns the elections – held before the lower chamber of parliament, the "Sejm" – of new judges to the Constitutional Tribunal in November 2015.

The whole dispute started in October 2015, when the outgoing legislature, ahead of the general elections to the Sejm, nominated five individuals to be appointed as judges of the Constitutional Tribunal by the President of Poland. Three judges were to fill seats vacated during the mandate of the outgoing legislature, while two were to step into office during the term of the incoming legislature. However, in November 2015, the new Sejm annulled all five nominations by the previous legislature and, shortly thereafter, nominated five new judges. The President of Poland immediately (literally, in the middle of the night) swore in these new candidates, having consistently refused to swear in the previously appointed judges. In its following judgments of 3 December 2015 (Case K 34/15) and 9 December 2015 (Case K 35/15), the Constitutional Tribunal ruled, among other things, that the previous legislature of the Sejm had been entitled to nominate three judges, while it had not been entitled to elect the remaining two. Despite these judgments, the three judges nominated by the previous legislature have not been permitted to take up their posts on the Tribunal until today, and their oath has not been taken by the President (Wiącek 2021: 16–22).

In its recommendations adopted under the Rule of Law Framework, the Commission set out its concerns on the situation of the Constitutional Tribunal and recommended how these should be addressed. However, none of the recommended actions set out by the Commission have been implemented. Consequently, in its proposal for a Council decision on the determination of a clear risk of a serious breach by Poland of the rule of law, the Commission considered that the independence and legitimacy of the Constitutional Tribunal are seriously undermined, the constitutionality of Polish laws can no longer be effectively guaranteed, and judgments rendered by the Tribunal under these circumstances can no longer be considered as providing an effective constitutional review (Commission 2017).

---

freedoms including the guarantees of fundamental rights. See further Wyrzykowski 2019: 417–418. On the rule of law in the context of competition law see also Bernatt 2022.

Tomasz Tadeusz Koncewicz aptly noted that the Constitutional Tribunal "was targeted first [by the governing majority], because that would ensure that further phases [of the unconstitutional capture] would sail through without any scrutiny." (Koncewicz 2017) This leads to the second aspect of the constitutional crisis in Poland: the current practice of the Constitutional Tribunal, as this court was turned into "a defender and protector of the legislative majority" (Sadurski 2019: 84).

The current position of the Constitutional Tribunal was perhaps best summarised by the Polish Ombudsman in July 2018: *"in matters that are of systemic importance, matters in which there is a deep and political interest, one cannot count on the independence of the Tribunal."* (Flis 2018) Indeed, since 2017, i.e. the first full year of Julia Przyłębska's presidency of the Constitutional Tribunal, in all politically sensitive issues the panels have had a majority of PiS-elected judges (Sadurski 2019: 69). Given the outspoken nature of the Ombudsman, and his criticism of the situation, it should come as little surprise that one of those panels found a reason to remove him from office in 2021, by ruling that he cannot perform his duties after the end of his term, even in a situation when parliament has not yet elected a successor (Judgment of 15 April 2021, Case K 20/20). This draft judgment was prepared by Stanisław Piotrowicz, who was, until 2019, an active member of Law and Justice.

Having effectively taken over the Constitutional Tribunal, the governing majority was not shy in using it as a weapon to fight judicial independence in Poland. One of the illustrations of this fight was lowering the mandatory retirement age of Supreme Court judges from 70 to 65. This was subject to one of the EU infringement proceedings described in point II.3 above which eventually resulted in the judgment of the Court in favour of the Commission, demanding the abolition of the newly introduced retirement rule. Reducing the mandatory retirement age of Supreme Court judges in Poland from 70 to 65 was, to some extent, also adjudicated by the Court in Joined Cases C-585/18, C-624/18 and C-625/18, this time in preliminary reference procedure, in connection with the Law on the Supreme Court of 8 December 2017 entering into force (see also Leloup 2020: 145–169; Krajewski & Ziółkowski 2020, 1107–1038).[11]

---

11 It is worth mentioning that a few weeks after the preliminary references were made by the Supreme Court, on 5 October 2018, the Attorney General/Minister of Justice filed for the unconstitutionality of Article 267 TFEU, to the scope within which Article 267 TFEU allows a court to refer a question for a preliminary ruling, asking for interpretation of the Treaties or the validity or interpretation of acts of law adopted by institutions, authorities or organisational units of the Union in matters related to form of government, shape, and organization of the judiciary, as well as proceedings before the judicial authorities of a Member State of the European Union. In the view of the Attorney General/Minister of Justice, "the question referred in Case no. PO 7/18 consists *de facto*

The CJEU's judgment was of pivotal importance in the larger context of the rule of law crisis, beyond the detailed regulation of retirement conditions. Namely, among other things, the Court held that a body like the Polish National Council of the Judiciary (*Krajowa Rada Sądownictwa*), which takes part in the process of the appointment of judges, must be sufficiently independent of the legislative and executive authorities.[12] Through this assessment, the Court ruled that the circumstances in which members of the National Council of the Judiciary were elected, and the way in which it functions, may be evaluated from the point of view of EU law.

The importance of the judgment went well beyond the case in which references for preliminary rulings were made. The case itself concerned the Supreme Court's new Disciplinary Chamber, formed in 2017 by judges newly appointed by the President of the Republic of Poland on a proposal of the National Council of the Judiciary. However, the judgment should be read in a way that all courts whose judges were appointed with the involvement of the National Council of the Judiciary must meet the standards specified in the judgment. In particular, as the National Council of the Judiciary's potential lack of independence from the legislature and the executive was determined to have resulted in (in this specific judgment) a lack of independence and impartiality of the Disciplinary Chamber judges, the judgment furthermore established – to this extent – a lack of independence and impartiality of other judges appointed with the involvement of the National Council of the Judiciary.

The position of the CJEU led the Supreme Court to the general conclusion that its Disciplinary Chamber is not a court within the meaning of EU law, as stated in its Judgment of 5 December 2019 (Case III PO 7/18, para. 79). In practical terms, it opened the door to questioning panels in courts that include individuals appointed with the recommendation of the National Council of the Judiciary, and the judgments these panels issued.[13] However, the jurisprudence of the courts in such cases has been divergent.[14]

---

in obtaining CJEU's answer to the scope of compliance with EU law of the manner of appointing judges [...] as well as the status of the National Council of the Judiciary within the system of public authorities of the Republic of Poland." Although it has been for years, the case before the Constitutional Tribunal has not yet been decided (Case K 7/18).

12 See in particular paras. 140–145 of the judgment.

13 In this context see also judgment of the Court dated 6 October 2021, Case C-487/19, *WŻ*, ECLI:EU:C:2021:798. In this judgment the Court held that the second subparagraph of Article 19(1) TEU and the principle of the primacy of EU law must be interpreted as meaning that a national court must declare *null and void* an order of another national court on the ground that, in the light of the circumstances in which the appointment of the judges sitting in that court took place, the latter does not constitute an independent and impartial tribunal previously established by law, for the purpos-

Consequently, on 23 January 2020 a resolution of the combined Civil Chamber, Criminal Chamber, and Labour Law and Social Security Chamber of the Supreme Court[15] was issued in which it was held – contrary to the government's position – that the National Council of the Judiciary is not independent from legislative and executive power (Case BSA I-4110–1/20). As a consequence, three chambers pointed out a court formation is unduly appointed (unlawful) where the court formation includes a person appointed to the office of a judge of the Supreme Court upon application of the current National Council for the Judiciary. In the case of common courts, the conclusion was the same, save that the defective appointment causes, under specific circumstances, a breach of the standards of independence within the meaning of both the Polish Constitution, Charter of Fundamental Rights of the European Union, and the Convention for the Protection of Human Rights and Fundamental Freedoms.

The response from the Constitutional Tribunal was immediate. Only five days later (*sic!*) it decided to issue an interim measure and suspend the application of the resolution of the Supreme Court from the date of its issue (Order of the Constitutional Tribunal, 28 January 2020, Case Kp 1/20). The purpose of this measure was that the resolution would have no effect until the Constitutional Tribunal's final judgment in question. Finally, the Constitutional Tribunal held in an Order of 21 April 2020 (Case Kp 1/20) that "the Supreme Court – also in connection with an international court ruling – does not have the jurisdiction to provide *a law-making interpretation* of legal provisions that leads to modifications in the legal situation regarding the organisational structure of the judiciary, by adopting a resolution". In the April 2020 Order, it also ruled that the act of appointing judges constitutes the exclusive competence of the Polish President, which s/he exercises – at the request of the National Council of the Judiciary – in person, in an irrevocable way, and without any participation or interference on the part of the Supreme Court.

The decision of the Constitutional Tribunal clearly ran contrary to EU law. In fact, as Michał Ziółkowski noted, a careful reading of the Polish Constitution and

---

es of the second subparagraph of Article 19(1) TEU (emphasis added). For further discussion on this judgment see Mańko & Tacik 2022: 1169–1194.

14 See e.g. Resolution of the Extraordinary Control and Public Affairs Chamber of the Supreme Court dated 8 January 2020, Case I NOZP 3/19, para. 32, according to which the appointment of judges cannot be questioned before any court or any authority in Poland regardless of the nature and scope of violation of the law.

15 I.e. without the Disciplinary Chamber and Extraordinary Control and Public Affairs Chamber, i.e. another new Chamber of the Supreme Court that was created in 2018. Both Chambers would be acting as "judges in their own case".

the statute on the Supreme Court was sufficient to assert that the Tribunal did not have the power to question the Supreme Court's constitutional position and powers to interpret and apply the law (Ziółkowski 2020: 362) One of the former judges of the Polish Constitutional Tribunal (in 2007–2016), pointed out that, following the decision, the Tribunal's position degraded further (Granat 2021). Others even concluded that the Constitutional Tribunal, by issuing its decision, had crossed the EU Rubicon and indirectly nullified the judgment of the CJEU in Joined Cases C-585/18, C-624/18, and C-625/18, *AK, CP, and DO vs Sąd Najwyższy*, ECLI:EU:C:2019:982. Consequently, in the view of these authors, the situation around the Constitutional Tribunal became worse than ever (Pech et. al 2021: 8).

The worst, however, was yet to come.

Following a judgment of 2 March 2021 in Case C-824/18, *A.B. and Others (Nomination des juges à la Cour suprême – Recours)*, in which the Court held that the rules of national law, including even constitutional provisions, cannot be allowed to undermine the unity and effectiveness of EU law (see para. 148 of the judgment), the Polish Prime Minister applied in March 2021 to the Constitutional Tribunal to verify the compliance of Articles 2, 4(3) and 19(1) of the TEU with the provisions of the Polish Constitution (Case K 3/21). This request constitutes a key moment in Polish rule of law crisis and shows the scale of the challenge the Union is currently facing, as Poland's head of government questioned the fundamental supremacy of EU law over national (constitutional) law in the context of basic principles and values the Union is founded on. Suffice it to mention that in Article 4(3) TEU the principle of sincere cooperation is enshrined, whilst Article 19(1) TEU covers the principle of effective judicial control. In the Prime Minister's view, the provisions of the TEU that are not compliant with the Constitution are those that entitle or oblige the authorities applying the law to "derogate from applying the Constitution" where it does not comply with EU law, prescribe the application of the law in a way that is inconsistent with the Constitution, or which entitle courts to check the independence of judges appointed by the President of Poland and to verify the resolutions of the National Council of the Judiciary concerning a motion to the President to appoint judges.

In October 2021 the Constitutional Tribunal issued a ruling which was fundamentally convergent with the Prime Minister's motion: Art. 1 (1) and Art. 1 (2) in conjunction with Art. 4 (3) TEU, Art. 2 TEU and Art. 19 (1) (2) TEU, understood in a certain way,[16] are inconsistent with the Polish Constitution.

---

16 For instance, the Constitutional Tribunal held that Article 1 (1) and Article 1 (2) in conjunction with Article 4 (3) TEU are inconsistent with the Polish Constitution *"insofar as the European Union, established by equal and sovereign states, creates "an ever closer union among the peoples of Eu-*

The judgment of the Constitutional Tribunal represents a flagrant violation of European Union Law.[17] One should not be surprised, though. As pointed out by Taborowski, this is yet another link in the chain, intended to legalise the lawlessness and arbitrariness of the appointment of judges, alongside the operation of the new chambers in the Supreme Court, the "muzzle law"[18] and the abusive disciplinary and criminal proceedings against judges (Taborowski 2021).

Response from the EU

In October 2019, the European Commission brought proceedings against Poland on account of national measures establishing the new disciplinary regime for judges of the Supreme Court and the ordinary courts (Case C-791/19, *Commission v Poland (Régime disciplinaire des juges)*). Specifically, in the view of the Commission, Poland had infringed the second subparagraph of Article 19(1) TEU on four grounds: first, the treatment of the content of judicial decisions as a disciplinary offence; second, the lack of independence and impartiality of the Disciplinary Chamber of the Supreme Court; third, the discretionary power of the president of that chamber to designate the competent court, thereby preventing disciplinary cases from being decided by a court established by law; and, fourth, the failure to guarantee the ex-

---

rope", the integration of whom – happening on the basis of EU law and through the interpretation of EU law by the Court of Justice of the European Union – enters "a new stage" in which: a) the European Union authorities act outside the scope of the competences conferred upon them by the Republic of Poland in the Treaties; b) the Constitution is not the supreme law of the Republic of Poland, which takes precedence as regards its binding force and application; c) the Republic of Poland may not function as a sovereign and democratic state". Meanwhile, the binding interpretation of EU law is the CJEU's exclusive domain. Pursuant to Art. 19(3)(b) in connection with Art. 19(1)(2) TEU, it is the CJEU that ensures the legal interpretation of the Treaties by issuing preliminary rulings (Art. 267 TFEU) on the interpretation of EU law at the request of courts in Member States.
17 For a more detailed discussion of this judgment see P. Bogdanowicz, *Legal opinion on the legal consequences of the Constitutional Tribunal ruling in case K 3/21 on the incompatibility of the provisions of the Treaty on European Union with the Constitution of the Republic of Poland in light of European Union law,* available at: https://www.batory.org.pl/wp-content/uploads/2021/11/P.Bogdnanowicz_Legal.opinion.on_.the_.legal_.consequences.of_.the_.Polish.Constitutional.Tribunal.ruling.in_.caseK3_.21.pdf (last access: 12 December 2022). To tell the truth, in other Member States, some decisions taken by other constitutional courts, e.g. in Romania and Germany, have also raised concerns as regards the primacy of EU law. On the German decision see further e.g. Annunziata 2021: 123. On the Romanian case see further e.g. Selejan-Gutan 2022.
18 Formally speaking, this is the Act of 20 December 2019 amending the Act – Law on the System of Ordinary Courts, the Act on the Supreme Court and Certain Other Acts. The Act entered into force on 14 February 2020.

amination of disciplinary cases within a reasonable time and the rights of the accused judges to a defence, thus taking into account the rights enshrined in Articles 47 and 48 of the Charter of Fundamental Rights of the European Union. The Commission also claimed that Poland has infringed the second and third paragraphs of Article 267 TFEU, because the right of national courts to make a reference for a preliminary ruling is limited by the possible initiation of disciplinary proceedings against judges who exercise that right.

On 8 April 2020, the CJEU sided with the Commission and adopted interim measures (Case 791/19 R), pending the Court's final judgment, obliging Poland to suspend the provisions constituting the grounds for the Disciplinary Chamber ruling on disciplinary cases concerning judges, both at first instance and on appeal, and to refrain from referring cases pending before the Disciplinary Chamber before a panel whose composition does not meet the requirements of independence, as defined in the CJEU's case law (see also Pech 2020: 137–162).

It has been noted in the literature that the CJEU's order suffered from one key weakness, namely the Commission's incomprehensible failure to prevent the Disciplinary Chamber, acting hand in hand with Poland's National Prosecutor's Office, from using the national procedure to waive judicial immunity as a threat or weapon (Pech et. al 2021: 31). Few months after the CJEU's order, the National Prosecutor's Office motioned the Disciplinary Chamber to strip the immunity of those judges of common courts who are known for defending free, independent courts (Jałoszewski 2020), that is, the "old" judges of the Criminal Chamber of the Supreme Court (Woźnicki 2021).

However, I do not fully share this overly critical reading of the CJEU's order. From a legal point of view, the CJEU's order prevented the Disciplinary Chamber of the Supreme Court from adopting a resolution allowing a common court judge to be held criminally liable and suspending them from their duties. First, no composition of the Disciplinary Chamber satisfies the independence requirements arising from European Union law. Therefore, the Disciplinary Chamber should not be able to consider any cases that are pending before it until the Court judgment ending the proceedings in Case C-791/19 is issued. Regardless of the above, in its order, the CJEU ordered the suspension of the provisions of the Act on the Supreme Court whereby "the Supreme Court is divided into the following chambers: [...] 5) Disciplinary Chamber" and those that specify the jurisdiction of the Disciplinary Chamber. As a result, the Disciplinary Chamber should not be able to operate at all. The order implies no jurisdiction of the Disciplinary Chamber. In particular, the Disciplinary Chamber should not be permitted to take any action in which it acts as a disciplinary court for judges. Adjudicating on whether or not to allow a judge to be held criminally liable, which is the responsibility of the disciplinary court, constitutes acting in such a capacity.

Where I am critical is that in light of the above, the Commission should have returned to the CJEU and asked for a daily penalty payment to be imposed (Pech et al. 2021: 23) in line with the CJEU's earlier case law (see order of the Court, 20 November 2017, in Case C-441/17 R *Commission v Poland (Białowieża Forest)*). Instead, on 3 December 2020, the Commission sent an additional letter of formal notice to Poland, adding a new grievance to a previous infringement procedure started on 29 April 2020 and also concerning the "muzzle law".

The "muzzle law", among other things, broadens the notion of disciplinary offence and thereby increases the number of cases in which the content of judicial decisions can be qualified as a disciplinary offence. It grants the new Extraordinary Control and Public Affairs Chamber of the Supreme Court the sole competence to rule on issues regarding judicial independence and prevents Polish courts from assessing, in the context of cases pending before them, whether other judges had the power to adjudicate cases.

Here, once more, the Polish rule of law crisis fuelled further the Union's limited ability to enforce the rule of law as its institutions' – and notably, the Commission's – reaction proved insufficient in bringing the defecting Member State back to abiding by the rules. Basically, it might have been expected that the Commission would at least bring the "muzzle law" before the CJEU as quickly as possible. However, nothing could be further from the truth. The Commission's action, along with the request to order *interim measures* pending the delivery of the final judgment, was brought to the Court on 1 April 2021.[19] In other words, it took the Commission nearly 16 months to bring the "muzzle law" before the CJEU.

Two years later, the CJEU has not yet issued its judgment. At the same time, I note that the CJEU has eventually delivered its judgment in another of the cases referred to above, i.e., concerning the Disciplinary Chamber of the Supreme

---

19 On 14 July 2021, the Vice-President of the Court issued the order for interim measures in Case C-204/21 R *Commission v Poland*, ECLI:EU:C:2021:593. On 27 October 2021, another order was issued by the Vice-President of the Court: Poland was obliged to pay the Commission a periodic penalty payment of EUR 1 000 000 per day until Poland complies with the obligations arising from the previous, or, if it fails to do so, until the date of delivery of the judgment closing the proceedings in Case C-204/21 (ECLI:EU:C:2021:878). Since *Poland* refused to *pay* these penalties, starting from April 2022 the Commission has been deducting them from payments due to Poland under EU funds. Interestingly, on 14 July 2021, the Constitutional Tribunal held that Article 4(3), the second sentence, of the TEU in conjunction with Article 279 of the TFEU – "*insofar as the Court of the European Union ultra vires imposes obligations on the Republic of Poland as an EU Member State, by prescribing interim measures pertaining to the organisational structure and functioning of Polish courts and to the mode of proceedings before those courts*" (case P 7/20). This judgment is another flagrant breach of EU law by the Constitutional Tribunal.

Court.[20] Unsurprisingly, the Court held that Poland has failed to fulfil its obligations under the second subparagraph of Article 19(1) TEU and Article 267 TFEU. Surprisingly, it took the Court 21 months to do so. For the abolition of the Disciplinary Chamber of the Supreme Court, which was an obvious consequence of the CJEU's judgment, we had to wait another 12 months.[21] It is hard not to recall Penn's much-quoted phrase that "to delay justice is injustice" (Penn 1905: 86).

In this context, it should also be mentioned that in December 2021 the Commission launched another infringement procedure against Poland, here for violations of EU law by its Constitutional Tribunal (Commission 2021). However, it took the Commission more than one year to refer Poland to the CJEU for these violations (Commission 2023).

Conclusion

The European Union has a number of means and instruments to uphold the rule of law within the Union. However, when a given Member State is unwilling to respect the rule of law, the whole process of enforcement is much more difficult. Poland is a good example. In recent years, Poland has turned into a state where some institutions charged with the task of protecting democracy against distortions by a current majority – such as the Constitutional Tribunal – have become disabled and are then enlisted in service of the governing majority (Sadurski 2019: 243).

While appreciating the Commission's role in enforcing the rule of law in Poland – it brought the first case ever on the compatibility of national measures on the organisation of the judicial system in question with EU law in the context of an infringement action under Article 258 TFEU and made Poland undergo Article 7(1) TEU proceedings – one cannot shake off the feeling that the Commission did not do all it could against the development of the rule of law crisis in Poland. One can even argue that some of the Commission's delayed reaction, if any, to the Disciplinary Chamber ignoring the CJEU's order in Case C-791/19, or on the adoption of the infamous "muzzle law", led to the abusive actions that have been taken recently by Polish authorities with the use of the Constitutional Tribunal.

These actions constitute a further stage of the rule of law crisis in Poland. This crisis consists no longer only in passing unlawful laws or court-packing but of the systemic negation of European Union law, including the questioning of the princi-

---

20 See footnote 5.
21 However, illegally appointed judges of the Disciplinary Chamber were left in the Supreme Court which raises serious doubts about proper implementation of the CJEU's judgments.

ple of primacy, compliance with the rulings of the CJEU, or respect for the rule of law. All of this results in a sad conclusion that judicial independence must now be said to have been structurally disabled by Polish authorities (Pech et al. 2021: 41). This shows the scale of the challenge the Union is currently facing.

It seems that the Commission has a choice now: either take its job as guardian of the Treaties even more seriously or face the risk that there will not be anything left to guard. It is not yet too late but the Commission must at least act: more quickly (e.g. two months given to Member States to respond to a letter of formal notice or reasoned opinion is generally too long), more decisively (not to wait until the last minute), more consistently (not to be afraid to request the CJEU for a penalty payment if previous decisions are not implemented) and more boldly (i.e. launching infringement proceedings even in cases when there is not a 100% chance of winning in Luxembourg).

At the same time, it is submitted by some authors that enforcement of the rule of law per se is not a *panacea*. Under this view, the most mature answer to the problems should necessarily involve not merely the reform of the enforcement mechanisms but the reform of the Union as such (Kochenov, Bard 2019: 30). But that's a paper for another time.

References

Annunziata, Filippo (2021): 'Cannons over the EU legal order: The decision of the BVerfG (5 May 2020) in the *Weiss* case', *Maastricht Journal of European and Comparative Law*, 28:1, 123–142.

Bárd, Petra & Sledzińska-Simon, Anna (2020): 'On the principle of irremovability of judges beyond age discrimination: Commission v. Poland, Case C-619/18, Commission v. Poland, Judgment of the Court (Grand Chamber) of 24 June 2019, EU:C:2019:531', *Common Market Law Review*, 57:5, 1555–1584.

Barrett, Gavin (2018): 'Reflections on What the Rule of Law Means and its Significance at EU Level', in Armin Hatje & Luboš Tichý (eds.): *Liability of Member States for the Violation of Fundamental Values of the European Union*, Nomos, 23–37.

Bernatt, Maciej (2022): *Populism and Antitrust. The Illiberal Influence of Populist Government on the Competition Law System*, Cambridge University Press.

Bogdanowicz, Piotr & Taborowski Maciej (2020): 'How to Save a Supreme Court in a Rule of Law Crisis: the Polish Experience: ECJ (Grand Chamber) 24 June 2019, Case C-619/18, European Commission v Republic of Poland', *European Constitutional Law Review*, 2:16, 306–327.

Commission (2014): Communication from the Commission to the European Parliament and the Council. A new EU Framework to strengthen the Rule of Law /*COM/2014/0158 final.

Commission (2017): Proposal for a COUNCIL DECISION on the determination of a clear risk of a serious breach by the Republic of Poland of the rule of law COM/2017/0835 final – 2017/0360.

Commission (2021): Press release of the European Commission dated 22 December 2021: https://ec.europa.eu/commission/presscorner/api/files/document/print/en/ip_21_7070/IP_21_7070_EN.pdf (last access: 12 December 2022).

Commission (2022a): Proposal of 18 September 2022 for a COUNCIL IMPLEMENTING DECISION on measures for the protection of the Union budget against breaches of the principles of the rule of law in Hungary. COM(2022) 485 final.

Commission (2022b): Communication from the Commission to the European Parliament, the Council, the European Economic and Social Committee and the Committee of the Regions. 2022 Rule of Law Report: The rule of law situation in the European Union. COM/2022/500 final.

Commission (2023): Press release of the European Commission dated 15 February 2023: https://ec.europa.eu/commission/presscorner/detail/en/ip_23_842 (last access: 21 March 2023).

Dumbrovsky, Tomas (2018): 'Beyond Voting Rights Suspension. Tailored Sanctions as Democracy Catalyst under Article 7 TEU', in Armin Hatje & Luboš Tichý (eds.): *Liability of Member States for the Violation of Fundamental Values of the European Union*, Nomos, 203–228.

European Parliament (2018): Proposal for a COUNCIL DECISION on the determination of a clear risk of a serious breach by Hungary of the rule of law. 12266/1/18. REV 1 (European Parliament).

Flis Damian (2018): 'Bodnar w Sejmie: "Nie można liczyć na niezależność Trybunału". Piotrowicz: "Zamykam dyskusję", https://oko.press/bodnar-w-sejmie-nie-mozna-liczyc-na-niezaleznosc-trybunalu-piotrowicz-zamykam-dyskusje/, published on 18 July 2018 (last access: 12 December 2022).

Granat, Mirosław (2021): '*A Weapon the Government Can Control: Non-Final Final Judgments of the Polish Constitutional Court*', VerfBlog, 2021/1/25, https://verfassungsblog.de/a-weapon-the-government-can-control/ (last access: 12 December 2022).

Jałoszewski, Mariusz (2020): 'The Disciplinary Chamber goes to task on judges Morawiec and Tuleya', https://ruleoflaw.pl/the-disciplinary-chamber-goes-to-task-on-judges-morawiec-and-tuleya/, published on 27 September 2020 (last access: 29 October 2022).

Kelemen, Roger Daniel & Pech Laurent (2018): 'Why autocrats love constitutional identity and constitutional pluralism. Lessons from Hungary in Poland', *RECONNECT-Working Paper*, 2, 1–23.

Kochenov, Dimitry (2021): 'Article 7: A Commentary on a Much Talked-About 'Dead' Provision', in: Armin von Bogdandy, Piotr Bogdanowicz, Iris Canor, Christoph Grabenwarter, Maciej Taborowski & Matthias Schmidt (eds.), *Defending Checks and Balances in EU Member States. Taking Stock of Europe's Actions*, Springer, 127–154.

Kochenov, Dimitri & Bard, Petra (2019): 'The Last Soldier Standing? Courts vs Politicians and the Rule of Law Crisis in the New Member States of the EU', *University of Groningen Faculty of Law Research Paper Series*, 5, 1–39.

Koncewicz, Tomasz Tadeusz (2017): '*Farewell to the Separation of Powers – On the Judicial Purge and the Capture in the Heart of Europe*, VerfBlog, 2017/7/19, https://verfassungsblog.de/farewell-to-the-separation-of-powers-on-the-judicial-purge-and-the-capture-in-the-heart-of-europe/ (last access: 12 December 2022).

Krajewski, Michał & Ziółkowski, Michał (2020): 'Court of Justice EU judicial independence decentralized: A.K.', *Common Market Law Review* 57:4, 1107–1138

Landau, David (2013): 'Abusive Constitutionalism', *UC Davis Law Review*, 47:1, 189–260.

Leloup, Mathieu (2020): 'An Uncertain First Step in the Field of Judicial Selfgovernment. ECJ 19 November 2019, Joined Cases C-585/18, C-624/18 and C-625/18, A.K., CP and DO', *European Constitutional Law Review*, 16:1, 145–169.

Mańko, Rafał & Tacik, Przemysław (2022): 'Sententia non existens: A new remedy under EU law?: Waldemar Zurek (W. Z.)', *Common Market Law Review* 59:4 (2022), 1169–1194.

Nowak-Far, Artur (2021): 'The Rule of Law Framework in the European Union: Its Rationale, Origins, Role and International Ramifications', in Armin von Bogdandy, Piotr Bogdanowicz, Iris Canor,

Christoph Grabenwarter, Maciej Taborowski & Matthias Schmidt (eds.), *Defending Checks and Balances in EU Member States. Taking Stock of Europe's Actions*, Springer, 305–331.

Pech, Laurent (2020): 'Protecting Polish judges from Poland's Disciplinary "Star Chamber": Commission v. Poland (Interim Proceedings)', *Common Market Law Review*, 58:1, 137–162.

Pech, Laurent, Wachowiec, Patryk & Mazur, Dariusz (2021): 'Poland's Rule of Law Breakdown: A Five-Year Assessment of EU's (In)Action', *Hague Journal on the Rule of Law*, 13:1, 1–43.

Penn William (1905): *Some Fruits of Solitude*, Headley Brothers.

Sadurski, Wojciech (2019): *Poland's Constitutional Breakdown*, Oxford University Press.

Schmidt, Matthias & Bogdanowicz, Piotr (2018): 'The Infringement Procedure in the Rule of Law Crisis: How to Make Effective Use of Article 258 TFEU', *Common Market Law Review*, 55:4, 1061–1100.

Selejan-Gutan, Bianca (2022): 'Who's Afraid of the "Big Bad Court"?' https://verfassungsblog.de/whos-afraid-of-the-big-bad-court/.

Taborowski, Maciej (2021): 'On the PM Morawiecki motion to the Constitutional Tribunal regarding EU Treaties conformity with the Polish Constitution (case K 3/21)', https://ruleoflaw.pl/on-the-pm-morawiecki-motion-to-the-constitutional-tribunal-regarding-eu-treaties-conformity-with-the-polish-constitution-case-k-3-21/ (last access: 12 December 2022).

Tichý, Luboš (2018): 'The nature and requirements for liability of a Member State under Article 7 TEU', in Armin Hatje & Luboš Tichý (eds.): *Liability of Member States for the Violation of Fundamental Values of the European Union*, Nomos, 87–108.

Wiącek, Marcin (2021): 'Constitutional Crisis in Poland 2015–16 in the Light of the Rule of Law Principle', in Armin von Bogdandy, Piotr Bogdanowicz, Iris Canor, Christoph Grabenwarter, Maciej Taborowski & Matthias Schmidt (eds.), *Defending Checks and Balances in EU Member States. Taking Stock of Europe's Actions*, Springer, 15–32.

Woźnicki, Łukasz (2021): 'The public prosecutor's office is taking on the Supreme Court. It wants the immunity of three judges to be lifted', https://ruleoflaw.pl/the-public-prosecutors-office-is-taking-on-the-supreme-court-it-wants-the-immunity-of-three-judges-to-be-lifted/, published on 17 March 2021 (last access: 29 October 2022).

Wyrzykowski, Mirosław (2019): 'Experiencing the Unimaginable: the Collapse of the Rule of Law in Poland', *Hague Journal of the Rule of Law*, 11:2–3, 417–422.

Lucy Kinski

6 Representation in polycrisis: Towards a new research agenda for EU citizens

Abstract: In the last 15 years, crises have been plentiful in the European Union (EU): the Great Recession, the Eurozone crisis, the 'migration crisis', the climate crisis, the Brexit crisis, the rule of law crisis, the Covid-19 crisis, and the Russian war on Ukraine just to name the most prominent ones. This chapter argues that this constant state of polycrisis is actually connected to an underlying crisis of political representation in the EU and its member states. This crisis manifests itself in dwindling linkages between parties and voters, changing lines of political conflict along a multidimensional polycleavage and a growing tension between responsibility and responsiveness.

Following this argument, this chapter explores the questions of who represents whom, on what and how in the EU, both from a legal and political perspective. In doing so, it discusses conceptual and theoretical innovations to reframe political representation in the multilevel system of EU governance beyond the supranational – intergovernmental divide. It finds that the actual empirical practice of representation is much more multidimensional than expected and goes well beyond the artificial dichotomy of national vs. European interest representation. There is polyrepresentation in the polycrisis, in that we find patterns that cut across borders and institutional channels of representation.

The chapter concludes by proposing three innovative avenues for future research on representation in an EU under strain. Scholars should investigate: (1) polyrepresentation as a multidimensional phenomenon, (2) justification and communication alongside representation, and (3) the demand side of political representation, i.e. what kind of representation citizens want.

Keywords: European Union, polycrisis, representation, responsiveness, citizens.

The EU's polycrisis as a crisis of representation

For the last 15 years, the European Union (EU) seems to have been in a constant state of "polycrisis" (Juncker 2016). The global financial and economic crisis of 2008 quickly turned into the Eurozone crisis as an unprecedented sovereign debt crisis. In 2015, the EU struggled to respond collectively to refugee and migration surges and continues to struggle to this day. Shortly after, Brexit dramatically altered the image of an ever-growing union and the stability of the EU as a political

https://doi.org/10.1515/9783110790337-007

system. The Covid-19 pandemic and the Russian war on Ukraine are the most recent crises, while democratic backsliding in member states such as Hungary and Poland or the climate crisis have long been ongoing.

While these crises differ in their origins, nature, and consequences, they share a common feature: they are linked to a deeper *crisis of political representation in the European Union and its member states* (Mair 2009). The polycrisis and its management have revealed and fuelled contestation and polarization in European societies including the rise of anti-EU and radical right populist parties that have become endemic in the EU multilevel political system (Hobolt & de Vries 2016; Treib 2021). Questions of transnational solidarity (Cinalli et al. 2021; Grasso & Lahusen 2018; Schelkle 2017; Wallaschek 2020) are linked to questions on "who gets what", but increasingly so on "who is one of us?" (Hooghe & Marks 2009: 16; 2018). In that sense, the polycrisis has revealed what Zeitlin et al. (2019) term a "polycleavage" with multiple, interrelated conflict lines emerging from the various crises, their specific problems, and contexts. At the same time, these crises "feed each other, creating a sense of doubt and uncertainty in the minds of our people" (Juncker 2016).

This sense of doubt and uncertainty (sometimes anger and frustration) is linked to a crisis of representation in the EU and its member states that is both old and new. It is old because its characteristics have long been identified. It is new because specific crises have put these characteristics under the spotlight. According to Brause and Kinski (2022), the crisis of representation has three interrelated elements – *dwindling linkage, changing lines of political conflict, and the well-known tension between responsibility and responsiveness.*

With membership in political parties and organizations steadily in decline, 'catch-all' parties lose their *linkage* to society (Hagevi et al. 2022; Van Biezen et al. 2012; Van Biezen & Poguntke 2014). Also, this makes interest aggregation and responsiveness increasingly difficult because remedies focus on representing majorities to the detriment of other societal groups (Traber et al. 2022). Additionally, the diversification of societies and representative actors leads to new forms of representation outside of traditional political and organizational channels (Castiglione & Warren 2006; Kröger& Friedrich 2012). The problem is that these old and new channels of representation may rather 'collide' than 'cohere' in the EU multilevel system (Lord & Pollak 2010).

As a second element of the crisis of representation, political cleavages in European societies have long been shifting away from the traditional economic left-right cleavage with the emergence of a cultural cleavage between "cosmopolitans" and "communitarians" (Zürn & de Wilde 2016). These shifting cleavages are inextricably linked to the transnationalization of politics and societies (Hooghe & Marks 2018; Kriesi et al. 2006). Especially in the EU with its strong economic and political interdependence, and many political actors, decisions can have far-reaching (and asymmetric) consequences on EU citizens across national borders. With the European integration of so-called "core state powers" (Genschel & Jachtenfuchs 2014) linked to national sovereignty, territory and identity, European integration and cultural demarcation become increasingly contested.

Finally, elected representatives in the EU must manage the tension between responsibility and responsiveness in normal and especially in crisis times. They need to be responsive to their voters, but also responsible for their legal and political commitments in the EU context (and beyond) (Mair 2009). Scholars argue that the gap between responsibility and responsiveness is growing, while political actors are at the same time struggling more and more to close it in an interdependent EU and a globalized world (Bardi et al. 2014; Karremans & Lefkofridi 2020).

Arguably, the various crises have accentuated and fuelled these developments. For example, during the Great Recession, social democratic parties in Western Europe in fact supported strict budgetary discipline and austerity policies (although, they did move to the left on welfare state policies and opposition to economic liberalism) (Bremer 2018). High (youth) unemployment rates, especially in Southern European countries (di Napoli & Russo 2018), aggravated the perceived gap between responding to citizens' needs and 'saving the Euro'. "It is therefore a matter of nothing more and nothing less than preserving and proving the European idea. This is our historic task, because *if the euro fails, Europe fails*" (Merkel 2010: 4126 B).

At the same time, mainstream political parties are struggling to aggregate and represent citizens' interests on cultural issues and European integration (Lefkofridi 2014), a representative void that specifically right-wing populist (anti-EU) parties tend to capitalize on (see contributions in Hawkins et al. 2019). The Brexit vote pitted so-called 'losers of globalization' against its winners (Hobolt 2016), and while we saw a containment rather than contagion effect on EU public opinion with regard to exiting the EU (De Vries 2017; Hobolt et al. 2022), anti-EU, -immigration, and -establishment sentiments drove leave voters (Hobolt 2016). We know that attitudes towards the Covid-19 pandemic and climate crisis are related to anti-establishment sentiment, distrust in science, and conspiratorial thinking that are, in essence, inextricably linked to populist attitudes (Eberl et al., 2021; Huber et al. 2021). Ultimately, this crisis of representation is to a certain extent about (not) feeling represented (Vik, de Wilde 2021). Certain groups of the European population feel underrepresented, especially those with less formal education and members of the working class (Holmberg 2020).

While the polycrisis has been a challenge to representative democracy in the EU, the EU as a political system has been remarkably resilient in the face of all these crises, and we have even seen a deepening of integration as a result. Theories of European integration provide different, oftentimes contradictory explanations for these crisis-induced reforms (e.g. Niemann & Ioannou 2015; Schimmelfennig 2015, 2018), but three more general observations seem important to include from a crisis of representation perspective.

First, the EU's response to the polycrisis has been characterized as a "failing forward" (Jones et al. 2016; Scipioni 2018; see also contributions in Jones et al. 2021) where incomplete and incremental reforms are preferred over both far-reaching and absent reforms. With this kind of "'sticking plaster'" approach (Howarth & Quaglia 2021: 1556), integration moves forward, but oftentimes does not solve underlying causes of the crises, like asymmetries in the governance of the Economic and Monetary Union, for example. The downside of this approach is that it is detrimental to EU public support as it further fuels the perception of the EU in a constant state of crisis. It is one thing for immediate crisis management to be patchy, it is quite another for long-term reform.

Second, this retreat of the "permissive consensus" on EU integration (Lindberg & Scheingold 1971), that is citizens' benevolent ignorance of EU affairs, and the deeper crisis of representation, have important implications for how national governments (can) act at the EU level. The theory of postfunctionalism attests a "constraining dissensus" (Hooghe & Marks 2009), a growing public dissatisfaction with EU politics that hampers integration. The theory of new intergovernmentalism (Bickerton et al. 2015) is even more pessimistic in that "it sees divides between integrationist leaders and a sceptical public as fuelling a *destructive dissensus* that casts doubt on the future sustainability of the EU" (Hodson & Puetter 2019: 1154, emphasis added). New intergovernmentalists essentially argue that national executives struggle to balance responsibility with responsiveness. On the one hand, they move integration forward during crises, often through summit diplomacy and informal channels. On the other hand, they are aware of the representative crisis at home. Their claim is that "national executives in Europe often seem to identify more with one another than with their own populations" (Bickerton et al. 2015: 710–11).

In a version of her famous argument, Schmidt (2019) argues that we have seen "politics without policy" at the national level and "policy without politics" at the EU level before the polycrisis. We now even witness what she calls "politics *against* policy" and even "politics *against* polity" both by national and EU level actors who act destructively (see also Ripoll Servent 2019; Ripoll Servent & Panning 2019). Now all this sounds rather pessimistic, but a more optimistic take follows when we investigate the actual practice of political representation in the EU multilevel system in times of polycrisis.

Polycrisis, polycleavage ... polyrepresentation?

Before we can discuss what is *new* in political representation in the EU, we need to define what political representation is. According to the well-known classic by Pitkin (1967), it has four distinct, yet connected elements. *Formal representation* refers to institutional mechanisms of authorization and accountability. How do we elect our representatives and how can we hold them accountable? *Descriptive* and *symbolic representation* are what Pitkin calls representation as "standing for" the represented (Pitkin 1967: 59). It tells us what the representatives must be like in order to represent. Descriptive representatives share certain characteristics and life experiences with those they represent, e. g., women, ethnic minorities or minorities of sexual orientation. In symbolic representation, politicians use symbols, political rhetoric or style to create a representative connection and the *feeling* of being represented. Finally, *substantive representation* as "acting for" (Pitkin 1967 59) refers to what representatives actually *do* to represent, e. g., policy output and its congruence with citizens' demands.

The so-called "standard account of political representation" (Castiglione & Warren 2006) has a straightforward answer to the questions of who can be a representative, whom they represent, and how this representation takes place. An electorate defined by territory and citizenship democratically elects a representative who is then accountable and responsive to their interests and preferences. This view is very much state- and election-centred, but agnostic towards alternative forms of representation beyond the nation-state and beyond elections.

Formally, the EU is a mixed representative system between a federal state and a confederation of states whose "functioning (...) shall be founded on *representative democracy*" (Article 10.1 TEU, emphasis added). The supranational channel of representation in which "Citizens are directly represented at Union level in the European Parliament" is supplemented by the intergovernmental channel of representation in which "Member States are represented in the European Council by their Heads of State or Government and in the Council by their governments, themselves democratically accountable either to their national Parliaments, or to their citizens." (Article 10.2 TEU).

At first glance, this suggests a clear division of labour as to who represents whom: *National citizens* are represented at EU level through their national governments, which, in turn, are accountable to their national parliaments. The Lisbon Treaty saw an upgrade of national parliaments becoming formal players at the EU level both individually and collectively (Auel & Neuhold 2017). For the first time, they were explicitly acknowledged as key institutions within the main body of the Treaty on the European Union (TEU) with the task to "contribute actively to the *good functioning* of the Union" (Article 12 TEU, emphasis added). *European citizens* are directly represented at the EU level through elections to the European Parliament (EP), whose constant empowerment as co-legislator has led scholars to conclude that it has, in fact, become quite a "normal parliament in a polity of a different kind" (Ripoll Servent & Roederer-Rynning 2018: 1).

When we look at the EU institutions, the Treaties are again rather explicit on whom and how they should represent. Article 17.1 TEU, for example, stipulates that the "Commission shall promote the general interest of the Union." Article 17.3 continues that the members of the Commission "shall be chosen on the ground of their general competence and European commitment from persons whose independence is beyond doubt. (...) the members of the Commission shall neither seek nor take instructions from any Government or other institution, body, office or entity."

Empirical research into whom and how Commissioners represent paints a much more nuanced picture. This representation includes national alongside European interests, portfolio and party as well as institutional interests (Egeberg 2006; Mérand 2021). What is more, the Commission pays attention to what citizens find important (Koop et al. 2022). It even increasingly seeks public opinion through commissioning Special Eurobarometers on many issues (Haverland et al. 2018), and picks up election pledges of the Europarties (Kostadinova & Giurcanu 2018), the European umbrella organizations of national parties outside the European Parliament (European Parliament 2014; on recent reforms, see Díaz Crego 2022). They work closely together with their related political groups formed by the members of the EP (EUR-Lex 2022).

Formally, the Council of the EU (Article 16 TEU) is an intergovernmental institution in which we expect national governments to be responsive to what their citizens at home want. Research again shows that the empirical practice of representation is more complex. We find different "modes of responsiveness" towards national citizens (Wratil 2018). Governments respond to public opinion when European integration is domestically salient (Hobolt & Wratil 2020; Hagemann et al. 2017), while ministers' party affiliations also influence their voting behaviour in the Council (Mühlböck & Tosun 2018).

In the EU's polycrisis, many have argued that the European Council (EUCO) (Article 15 TEU) has become the main decision-maker, moving away from its treaty-mandated role as the agenda setter. Intergovernmental co-ordination in response to the Eurozone crises, for example, sidelined both Commission and EP. Traditional legislative channels were avoided and "de novo" bodies such as the European Central Bank (ECB) received more executive power (Bickerton et al. 2015: 705). New leadership approaches to crisis governance contradict this narrative of EUCO power, highlighting how the Commission slowly reinterpreted existing rules to empower itself with regard to banking supervision and the Covid Recovery Fund (Smeets & Beach 2022). Such research urges us to switch perspective from the high-level "control room" of the European Council to the "machine room" (Smeets & Beech 2022: 4) in which crisis solutions are forged and protected against intergovernmental interference.

The European Parliament (Article 14 TEU) is directly elected based on national lists, and members of the EP (MEPs) organize in transnational EP party groups along a left-right conflict line. This means they have two principals: their national party, which puts them up for election, and their European party, which controls offices in the EP (Mühlböck 2012). We see voting behaviour in EP party groups with clear and coherent policy alternatives along left-right and pro-anti-EU conflict lines (Lefkofridi & Katsanidou 2018). Increasing polarization and fragmentation in the EP (Fenzl et al. 2022; Ripoll Servent & Costa 2022), including the steady rise of Eurosceptic voices (Treib 2021), has made it increasingly difficult for the EP to play out its powerful position as co-legislator in most policy areas to represent European citizens' interests. While the EP has been effectively sidelined during the Eurozone crisis (Rittberger 2014), the Covid-19 crisis has seen slow gain in power of the EP in Economic and Monetary governance (Fromage & Markakis 2022). When looking at the patterns of debate in the EP, we see that MEPs represent a diverse set of national and European citizens and groups, for example, on climate policy ambitions or the Covid-19 recovery fund (Kinski & Ripoll Servent 2022; Gianna et al. 2022).

Being fought on national grounds and less visibly, EP elections are still considered 'second-order' compared to national electoral contests, albeit to a lesser extent than in the past (Schmitt, Toygür 2016). The second-order thesis presumes that the turnout in EP elections is lower than in national elections. It also holds that there is no clear choice for citizens because they do not elect an EU government. The campaign focus is primarily on national rather than European issues. The *Spitzenkandidaten* process was introduced in 2014 to establish a more direct connection between EP elections and a 'European government'. In this procedure, European political parties appoint lead candidates for Commission President ahead of the EP elections. According to Article 17.7 TEU, the European Council is proposes a candidate to parliament "[t]aking into account the elections to the European Parliament" which elects this candidate by majority. While Jean-Claude Juncker, *Spitzenkandidat* of the European People's Party (EPP), was elected Commission President in 2014, the process failed in 2019 with Ursula von der Leyen, a non-*Spitzenkandidat*, becoming Commission President (Crum 2022).

The procedure had differing yet limited effects on visibility, turnout, and vote (Gattermann & de Vreese 2020; Gattermann & Marquart 2020; Hobolt 2014; Schmitt et al. 2015). As the transnational umbrella organisations at the European level, Europarties are to "contribute to forming European political awareness and to expressing the will of citizens of the Union" (Article 10.4 TEU). While they are becoming better at realising this transnational partisan potential to represent EU citizens, they are not full-fledged parties in a system of transnational party competition (Kinski 2022; Pittoors 2022).

Finally, scholars have turned to national parliaments as a promising representative connection between national citizens and EU politics, establishing ownership and communicating EU affairs to their national electorates (Auel & Christiansen 2015; Auel & Höing 2015; Auel et al. 2016, 2018). Notably, members of national parliaments (MPs) represent not only national citizens in EU affairs but also national citizens from other EU member states (transnational representation), and an overarching European citizenry (supranational representation) (Kinski 2021; Kinski & Crum 2020). Contrary to the dominant narrative of national representation, these new representative linkages across and beyond national borders are especially prevalent during the Eurozone crisis. MPs combine national with non-national representative modes, in fact, narrowing the gap between responsiveness and responsibility.

Overall, we can conclude that there are many traces of polyrepresentation in the EU. We need to investigate actor behaviour beyond formal representation, and representation beyond policy congruence to see beyond entrenched representative paths. This allows us to move beyond artificial dichotomies between national and European representation or intergovernmental and supranational policy-making in the EU.

Conclusion: A new research agenda on polyrepresentation in the EU

Nowadays, both political theory and empirical practice have long outrun the narrow understanding of representation displayed in the aforementioned 'standard account' (e.g. Brito Vieira 2019; Castiglione & Pollak 2019; Mansbridge 2003; Saward 2010) focused on electoral representation and the nation-state. Surprisingly, when scholars and politicians think about responses to the polycrisis in the EU, they oftentimes stay within this standard account. There only seems to be a choice between two options for representation to work in the EU – it is either re-nationalising or supranationalising competencies. In his State of the Union speech (2017), then Commission President Jean-Claude Juncker said, "We only had two choices. Either come together around a positive European agenda or each retreat to our own corners." In this view, for representation to work democratically in the EU, it is either reverting back to national sovereignty and guarding core state powers or strengthening the Community Method.

There are many well-known proposals on how to narrow the representation and democracy gaps in the EU by means of strengthening input, throughput and output legitimacy (for an overview see Neuhold 2020; Weiler 2012; for the different legitimacy types Schmidt 2013). These include participatory and deliberative formats, such as the recent Conference on the Future of Europe (Puntscher Riekmann 2022), which aim to foster input legitimacy as government *by* the people. Throughput legitimacy refers to procedural mechanisms of accountability, transparency, and inclusiveness (Schmidt & Wood 2019), such as empowering the European as well as national parliaments (Bellamy & Kröger 2014; Goetze & Rittberger 2010). Output legitimacy is the effectiveness of governance outcomes and performance *for* the people (Lindgren & Persson 2010; Toshkov 2011). This section will not re-iterate these proposals but instead offer a new research agenda for scholars researching representation in the EU and also policymakers who represent citizens in the EU. I make three distinct proposals for future research:

1. Investigate polyrepresentation as a multidimensional phenomenon: As we have seen, representative patterns are more diverse than the 'standard account' would have us believe. Members of national parliaments represent transnational constituencies with whom they do not have an electoral connection. European Commissioners define 'the European interest' in various ways depending on their portfolio or national interests. MEPs go far beyond the national vs. European interest representation and claim to represent future generations, different social groups and business interests. We cannot simply assume a political actor's representative behaviour to follow a representative mandate, merely because she is a member of a specific institution. At the same time, we know virtually nothing about the representative patterns in institutions that do not primarily have a representative mandate, for example, the European Central Bank (ECB) or the European Court of Justice (CJEU). How do they navigate the tension between responsibility and responsiveness in the EU in a time of increasing politicization (Blauberger & Martinsen 2020; Blauberger et al. 2018)? Essentially, who represents whom, on what, how and why in the EU?

To tackle all these questions, we need to refute the perception of these institutions as unitary actors in EU governance, and instead focus on the actor-level of political representation. Who do these actors (claim to) represent, how do they reconcile tensions between different constituencies and their interests in the multilevel EU system, and why do they choose to represent the way they do? The actor-level focus naturally includes institutional contexts and diverse types of actors, from parties to unelected representatives, and beyond. Party and representation scholars share the diagnosis of a crisis of representation and investigate similar questions surrounding it, while the literatures are oftentimes surprisingly disconnected. When we zoom in to the actual empirical practice of representation in the EU, we see that multiple actors establish new representative linkages, reconcile multiple cleavages and may, in fact, narrow the gap between responsibility and responsiveness in crisis times. In addition to such empirical investigations, this also signals for an update to our conceptual and theoretical toolkit beyond the standard account and the two go-to options in EU politics (Kinski 2021; Wolkenstein & Wratil 2021).

2. Investigate justification and communication alongside representation: Pitkin already notes that representatives must always communicate and justify their decisions, especially when there is a conflict between what representatives do and what citizens want. Representatives "must not be found persistently at odds with the wishes of the represented without *good reason* in terms of their interest, without *good explanation* of why their wishes are not in accord with their interest" (1967: 209–10, emphasis added). Democratic representation needs to be visible and representatives need to be publicly accountable for their actions. The longstanding focus on formal representation and substantive representation as preference or policy congruence has clouded our views from the communicative dimension of representation. How do political actors frame, justify and explain their representative efforts vis-à-vis their peers and those they represent (Lord 2013)? Such discursive justifications were significantly important in the context of the EU's polycrisis, in which decisions were frequently at odds with many EU citizens' wishes. Here, we can use manual content analysis methods (De Wilde 2020; Wendler 2016) alongside recent advances in quantitative text analysis to capture crisis communication (Eisele et al. 2021). These methods use the many texts that are by-products of the political process and allow us to investigate the communicative dimension of representation in the EU, which is especially important during crises.

3. Investigate the demand side of political representation: Finally, the focus has so far been on the supply side of representation, and we have neglected its demand side (for a notable exception see Werner 2019a, 2019b). There are, of course, many comparative surveys asking citizens about their ideological positions, voting preferences, and party affiliations, but there is very little public opinion research on their actual *representative preferences.* What qualities do they expect of their representatives? Do they prefer a certain style of representation? Do they recognize the tensions between responsibility and responsiveness? Do they want their representatives to stick to their election pledges or respond effectively to crises? Under which conditions do they feel represented (Vik & de Wilde 2021)? Focusing on these questions is essential to filling in our blind spot towards what EU citizens expect of their representatives in a multilevel system. It helps narrow gaps in representation from the side of the citizen .

As we have seen, the constant state of polycrisis in the EU is linked to an underlying crisis of political representation in the European Union and its member states with dwindling linkages between parties and citizens, changing lines of political conflict, and a growing tension between responsibility and responsiveness. At the same time, we see innovative representative linkages across the polycleavage and beyond the intergovernmental and supranational channels, narrowing the gap between responsibility and responsiveness. Scholars must seize that opportunity and explore this polyrepresentation in an EU under strain.

References

Auel, Katrin & Christiansen, Thomas (2015): 'After Lisbon: National Parliaments in the European Union', *West European Politics*, 38:2, 261–281.

Auel, Katrin, Eisele, Olga & Kinski, Lucy (2016): 'From Constraining to Catalysing Dissensus? The Impact of Political Contestation on Parliamentary Communication in EU Affairs', *Comparative European Politics*, 14:2, 154–176.

Auel, Katrin, Eisele, Olga & Kinski, Lucy (2018): 'What Happens in Parliament Stays in Parliament? Newspaper Coverage of National Parliaments in EU Affairs: Parliamentary EU Affairs in the Media', *Journal of Common Market Studies*, 56:3, 628–645.

Auel, Katrin & Höing; Oliver (2015): 'National Parliaments and the Eurozone Crisis: Taking Ownership in Difficult Times?', *West European Politics*, 38:2, 375–395.

Auel, Katrin & Neuhold; Christine (2017): 'Multi-Arena Players in the Making? Conceptualizing the Role of National Parliaments since the Lisbon Treaty', *Journal of European Public Policy*, 24:10, 1547–1561.

Bardi, Luciano, Bartolini, Stefano & Trechsel, Alexander H. (2014): 'Responsive and Responsible? The Role of Parties in Twenty-First Century Politics', *West European Politics*, 37:2, 235–252.

Bellamy, Richard & Kröger, Sandra (2014): 'Domesticating the Democratic Deficit? The Role of National Parliaments and Parties in the EU's System of Governance', *Parliamentary Affairs*, 67:2, 437–457.

Bickerton, Christopher J., Hodson, Dermot & Puetter, Uwe (2015): 'The New Intergovernmentalism: European Integration in the Post-Maastricht Era: The New Intergovernmentalism', *Journal of Common Market Studies*, 53:4, 703–722.

Blauberger, Michael, Heindlmaier, Anita, Kramer, Dion, Sindbjerg Martinsen, Dorte, Sampson Thierry, Jessica, Schenk, Angelika & Werner, Benjamin (2018): 'ECJ Judges Read the Morning Papers. Explaining the Turnaround of European Citizenship Jurisprudence', *Journal of European Public Policy*, 25:10, 1422–1441.

Blauberger, Michael & Sindbjerg Martinsen, Dorte (2020): 'The Court of Justice in Times of Politicization: "Law as a Mask and Shield" Revisited', *Journal of European Public Policy*, 27:3, 382–399.

Brause, Simon & Kinski, Lucy (2022): 'Mainstream party agenda-responsiveness and the electoral success of right-wing populist parties in Europe', *Journal of European Public Policy*, online first: 1–29. https://doi.org/10.1080/13501763.2022.2155214.

Bremer, Björn (2018): 'The Missing Left? Economic Crisis and the Programmatic Response of Social Democratic Parties in Europe', *Party Politics* 24:1, 23–38.

Brito Vieira, Mónica (ed.) (2019): *Reclaiming Representation: Contemporary Advances in the Theory of Political Representation*, Routledge.

Castiglione, Dario & Pollak, Johannes (eds.) (2019): *Creating Political Presence: The New Politics of Democratic Representation*, University of Chicago Press.

Castiglione, Dario & Warren, Mark E. (2006): 'Rethinking Democratic Representation: Eight Theoretical Issues', *Workshop Rethinking Democratic Representation*, University of British Columbia https://citeseerx.ist.psu.edu/viewdoc/download?doi=10.1.1.565.9652&rep=rep1&type=pdf (last accessed: 11 December 2022).

Cinalli, Manlio, Trenz, Hans-Jörg, Brändle, Verena K., Eisele, Olga & Lahusen, Christian (2021): *Solidarity in the Media and Public Contention over Refugees in Europe*, Routledge.

Crum, Ben (2022): 'Why the European Parliament Lost the *Spitzenkandidaten*-Process'. *Journal of European Public Policy*, online first: 1–21. https://doi.org/10.1080/13501763.2022.2032285.

De Vries, Catherine E. (2017): 'Benchmarking Brexit: How the British Decision to Leave Shapes EU Public Opinion', *Journal of Common Market Studies*, 55:S1, 38–53.

De Wilde, Pieter (2020): 'The Quality of Representative Claims: Uncovering a Weakness in the Defence of the Liberal World Order', *Political Studies* 68:2, 271–292.

Díaz Crego, María (2022): 'Recasting the Rules Applicable to European Political Parties and Foundations'. PE 733.620. AT A GLANCE – Plenary. *European Parliamentary Research Service*, https://www.europarl.europa.eu/RegData/etudes/ATAG/2022/733620/EPRS_ATA(2022)733620_EN.pdf (last accessed: 11 December 2022).

Eberl, Jakob-Moritz. Huber, Robert A. & Greussing, Esther (2021): 'From Populism to the "Plandemic": Why Populists Believe in COVID-19 Conspiracies', *Journal of Elections, Public Opinion and Parties*, 31:S1, 272–284.

Egeberg, Morten (2006): 'Executive Politics as Usual: Role Behaviour and Conflict Dimensions in the College of European Commissioners', *Journal of European Public Policy*, 13:1, 1–15.

Eisele, Olga, Tolochko, Petro & Boomgaarden, Hajo G. (2021): 'How Do Executives Communicate about Crises? A Framework for Comparative Analysis', *European Journal of Political Research*, online first: 1–21. https://doi.org/10.1111/1475-6765.12504.

EUR-Lex (2022): 'European Political Parties'. Glossary of Summaries. https://eur-lex.europa.eu/EN/legal-content/glossary/european-political-parties.html (last accessed: 11 December 2022).

European Parliament (2014): 'European Political Parties'. European Parliament. https://www.europarl.europa.eu/politicalparties/index_en.xml (last accessed: 11 December 2022).

Fenzl, Michele, Slapin, Jonathan B. & Wilhelm, Samuel (2022): 'From Polarization of the Public to Polarization of the Electorate: European Parliament Elections as the Preferred Race for Ideologues', *European Union Politics*, online first: 1–22. https://doi.org/10.1177/14651165221098501.

Fromage, Diane & Markakis, Menelaos (2022): 'The European Parliament in the Economic and Monetary Union after COVID: Towards a Slow Empowerment?', *The Journal of Legislative Studies*, online first: 1–17. https://doi.org/10.1080/13572334.2022.2107811.

Gattermann, Katjana & Marquart, Franziska (2020): 'Do *Spitzenkandidaten* Really Make a Difference? An Experiment on the Effectiveness of Personalized European Parliament Election Campaigns', *European Union Politics*, 21:4, 612–633.

Gattermann, Katjana & de Vreese, Claes (2020): 'Awareness of *Spitzenkandidaten* in the 2019 European Elections: The Effects of News Exposure in Domestic Campaign Contexts', *Research & Politics* 7:2, 1–8. https://doi.org/10.1177/2053168020915332.

Genschel, Philipp & Jachtenfuchs, Markus (eds.) (2014): *Beyond the Regulatory Polity? The European Integration of Core State Powers*, Oxford University Press.

Gianna, Ermela, Kinski, Lucy & Ripoll Servent, Ariadna (2022): 'Recovery, Resilience… and Fragmentation? The European Parliament and Coalition Dynamics in Covid-19 Pandemic Debates', *ECPR General Conference*. Innsbruck, 22–26 August.

Goetze, Stefan & Rittberger, Berthold (2010): 'A Matter of Habit? The Sociological Foundations of Empowering the European Parliament', *Comparative European Politics*, 8:1, 37–54.

Grasso, Maria T. & Lahusen, Christian (eds.) (2018): *Solidarity in Europe: Citizens' Responses in Times of Crisis*, Springer; Palgrave Macmillan.

Hagemann, Sara, Hobolt, Sara B. & Wratil, Christopher (2017): 'Government Responsiveness in the European Union: Evidence From Council Voting', *Comparative Political Studies*, 50:6, 850–876.

Hagevi, Magnus, Blombäck, Sofie, Demker, Marie, Hinnfors, Jonas & Loxbo, Karl (2022): *Party Realignment in Western Europe: Electoral Drivers and Global Constraints*, Edward Elgar Publishing.

Haverland, Markus, de Ruiter, Minou & Van de Walle, Steven (2018): 'Agenda-Setting by the European Commission. Seeking Public Opinion?', *Journal of European Public Policy*, 25:3, 327–345.

Hawkins, Kirk A., Carlin, Ryan E., Littvay, Levente & Rovira Kaltwasser, Cristóbal (eds.) (2019): *The Ideational Approach to Populism: Concept, Theory, and Analysis*, Routledge.

Hobolt, Sara B. (2014): 'A Vote for the President? The Role of *Spitzenkandidaten* in the 2014 European Parliament Elections', *Journal of European Public Policy*, 21:10, 1528–1540.

Hobolt, Sara B. (2016): 'The Brexit Vote: A Divided Nation, a Divided Continent'. *Journal of European Public Policy* 23:9, 1259–1277.

Hobolt, Sara B., Popa, Sebastian A., Van der Brug, Wouter & Schmitt, Hermann (2022): 'The Brexit Deterrent? How Member State Exit Shapes Public Support for the European Union', *European Union Politics*, 23:1, 100–119.

Hobolt, Sara B. & de Vries, Catherine E. (2016): 'Public Support for European Integration', *Annual Review of Political Science*, 19:1, 413–432.

Hobolt, Sara B. & Wratil, Christopher (2020): 'Contestation and Responsiveness in EU Council Deliberations', *Journal of European Public Policy*, 27:3, 362–381.

Hodson, Dermot & Puetter, Uwe (2019): 'The European Union in Disequilibrium: New Intergovernmentalism, Postfunctionalism and Integration Theory in the Post-Maastricht Period', *Journal of European Public Policy*, 26:8, 1153–1171.

Holmberg, Sören (2020): 'Feeling Represented', in Robert Rohrschneider; Jacques Thomassen (eds.): *The Oxford Handbook of Political Representation in Liberal Democracies*, Oxford University Press, 412–431. https://doi.org/10.1093/oxfordhb/9780198825081.013.21.

Hooghe, Liesbet & Marks; Gary (2009): 'A Postfunctionalist Theory of European Integration: From Permissive Consensus to Constraining Dissensus'. *British Journal of Political Science*, 39:1, 1–23.

Hooghe, Liesbet & Marks, Gary (2018): 'Cleavage Theory Meets Europe's Crises: Lipset, Rokkan, and the Transnational Cleavage', *Journal of European Public Policy*, 25:1, 109–135.

Howarth, David & Quaglia, Lucia (2021): 'Failing Forward in Economic and Monetary Union: Explaining Weak Eurozone Financial Support Mechanisms', *Journal of European Public Policy*, 28:10, 1555–1572.

Huber, Robert A., Greussing, Esther & Eberl, Jakob-Moritz (2021): 'From Populism to Climate Scepticism: The Role of Institutional Trust and Attitudes towards Science', *Environmental Politics*, online first: 1–24. https://doi.org/10.1080/09644016.2021.1978200.

Jones, Erik, Kelemen, Daniel R. & Meunier, Sophie (2016): 'Failing Forward? The Euro Crisis and the Incomplete Nature of European Integration', *Comparative Political Studies*, 49:7, 1010–1034.

Jones, Erik, Kelemen, Daniel R. & Meunier, Sophie (2021): 'Failing Forward? Crises and Patterns of European Integration', *Journal of European Public Policy*, 28:10, 1519–1536.

Juncker, Jean-Claude (2016): 'Speech at the Annual General Meeting of the Hellenic Federation of Enterprises'. June 21. http://europa.eu/rapid/press-release_SPEECH-16-2293_en.htm (last accessed: 11 December 2022).

Juncker, Jean-Claude (2017): 'State of the Union Address 2017'. September 13. https://ec.europa.eu/commission/presscorner/detail/en/SPEECH_17_3165 (last accessed: 11 December 2022).

Karremans, Johannes & Lefkofridi, Zoe (2020): 'Responsive versus Responsible? Party Democracy in Times of Crisis', *Party Politics*, 26:3, 271–279.

Kinski, Lucy (2021): *European Representation in EU National Parliaments*. Palgrave Macmillan.

Kinski, Lucy (2022): 'Transnational Partisanship in the EU: Opportunities, Incentives and Obstacles', in *Transforming the Political Union*, Foundation for European Progressive Studies (FEPS). Brussels.

Kinski, Lucy & Crum, Ben (2020): 'Transnational Representation in EU National Parliaments: Concept, Case Study, Research Agenda', *Political Studies*, 68:2, 370–388.

Kinski, Lucy & Ripoll Servent, Ariadna (2022): 'Framing Climate Policy Ambition in the European Parliament', *Politics and Governance* 10:3.

Koop, Christel, Reh, Christine & Bressanelli, Edoardo (2022): 'Agenda-setting under Pressure: Does Domestic Politics Influence the European Commission?', *European Journal of Political Research*, 61:1, 46–66.

Kostadinova, Petia & Giurcanu, Magda (2018): 'Capturing the Legislative Priorities of Transnational Europarties and the European Commission: A Pledge Approach', *European Union Politics*, 19:2, 363–379.

Kriesi, Hanspeter, Grande, Edgar, Lachat, Romain, Dolezal, Martin, Bornschier, Simon & Frey, Timotheos (2006): 'Globalization and the Transformation of the National Political Space: Six European Countries Compared', *European Journal of Political Research*, 45:6, 921–956.

Kröger, Sandra & Friedrich, Dawid (eds.) (2012): *The Challenge of Democratic Representation in the European Union*. Palgrave Macmillan.

Lefkofridi, Zoe & Katsanidou, Alexia (2018): 'A Step Closer to a Transnational Party System? Competition and Coherence in the 2009 and 2014 European Parliament: A Transnational Party System?', *Journal of Common Market Studies*, 56:6, 1462–1482.

Lefkofridi, Zoe, Wagner, Markus & Willmann, Johanna E. (2014): 'Left-Authoritarians and Policy Representation in Western Europe: Electoral Choice across Ideological Dimensions', *West European Politics*, 37:1, 65–90.

Lindberg, Leon & Scheingold, Stuart (eds.) (1971): *Regional Integration: Theory and Research*, Harvard University Press.

Lindgren, Karl-Oskar & Persson, Thomas (2010): 'Input and Output Legitimacy: Synergy or Trade-off? Empirical Evidence from an EU Survey', *Journal of European Public Policy*, 17:4, 449–467.

Lord, Christopher (2013): 'No Representation without Justification? Appraising Standards of Justification in European Parliament Debates', *Journal of European Public Policy*, 20:2, 243–259.

Lord, Christopher & Pollak, Johannes (2010): 'The EU's Many Representative Modes: Colliding? Cohering?', *Journal of European Public Policy*, 17:1, 117–136.

Mair, Peter (2009): 'Representative versus Responsible Government', MPIfG Working Paper, No. 09/8. https://www.econstor.eu/bitstream/10419/41673/1/615284884.pdf (last accessed: 11 December 2022).

Mansbridge, Jane (2003): 'Rethinking Representation', *American Political Science Review*, 97:4, 515–528.

Mérand, Frédéric (2021): *The Political Commissioner: A European Ethnography.* Oxford University Press.

Merkel, Angela (2010): 'Speech by Chancellor Angela Merkel in the German Bundestag', Plenary Protocol 17/24, 19 May. https://dserver.bundestag.de/btp/17/17042.pdf (last accessed: 11 December 2022).

Mühlböck, Monika (2012): 'National versus European: Party Control over Members of the European Parliament', *West European Politics*, 35:3, 607–631.

Mühlböck, Monika & Tosun, Jale (2018): 'Responsiveness to Different National Interests: Voting Behaviour on Genetically Modified Organisms in the Council of the European Union: Responsiveness to National Interests', *Journal of Common Market Studies*, 56:2, 385–402.

Di Napoli, Ester & Russo; Deborah (2018): 'Solidarity in the European Union in Times of Crisis: Towards "European Solidarity"?', in Veronica Federico & Christian Lahusen (eds.): *Solidarity as a Public Virtue?: Law and Public Policies in the European Union*, Nomos, 195–248.

Neuhold, Christine (2020): 'Democratic Deficit in the European Union', in *Oxford Research Encyclopedia of Politics*, Oxford University Press. https://doi.org/10.1093/acrefore/9780190228637.013.1141.

Niemann, Arne & Ioannou; Demosthenes (2015): 'European Economic Integration in Times of Crisis: A Case of Neofunctionalism?', *Journal of European Public Policy*, 22:2, 196–218.

Pitkin, Hanna F. (1967): *The Concept of Representation.* University of California Press.

Pittoors, Gilles (2022): 'National Parties as Multilevel Organizations in the EU. A Comparative Case Study of Flanders, Denmark and the Netherlands', *Journal of Common Market Studies*, online first: 1–18. https://doi.org/10.1111/jcms.13379.

Puntscher Riekmann, Sonja (2022): 'The European Representation Conundrum: Can the Conference on the Future of Europe Resolve It?', in Göran von Sydow; Valentin Kreilinger (eds.): *Making EU Representative Democracy Fit for the Future*, Sieps 2022:2op, 33–44. https://www.sieps.se/global assets/publikationer/2022/sieps-2022_2op-eng-webb.pdf? (last accessed: 11 December 2022).

Ripoll Servent, Ariadna (2019): 'The European Parliament after the 2019 Elections: Testing the Boundaries of the "Cordon Sanitaire"', *Journal of Contemporary European Research*, 15:4, 331–342.

Ripoll Servent, Ariadna & Costa, Olivier (2022): 'Chapter 6: The European Parliament: Powerful but Fragmented', in Dermot Hodson, Uwe Puetter, John Peterson & Sabine Saurugger (eds.): *The Institutions of the European Union*, Oxford University Press, 128–148.

Ripoll Servent, Ariadna & Panning, Lara (2019): 'Eurosceptics in Trilogue Settings: Interest Formation and Contestation in the European Parliament', *West European Politics*, 42:4, 755–775.

Ripoll Servent, Ariadna & Roederer-Rynning, Christilla (2018): 'The European Parliament: A Normal Parliament in a Polity of a Different Kind', in *Oxford Research Encyclopedia of Politics*, Oxford University Press. https://doi.org/10.1093/acrefore/9780190228637.013.152.

Rittberger, Berthold (2014): 'Integration without Representation? The European Parliament and the Reform of Economic Governance in the EU', *Journal of Common Market Studies*, 52:6, 1174–1183.

Saward, Michael (2010): *The Representative Claim.* Oxford University Press.

Schelkle, Waltraud (2017): *The Political Economy of Monetary Solidarity: Understanding the Euro Experiment.* Oxford University Press.

Schimmelfennig, Frank (2015): 'Liberal Intergovernmentalism and the Euro Area Crisis', *Journal of European Public Policy*, 22:2, 177–195. https://doi.org/10.1080/13501763.2014.994020.

Schimmelfennig, Frank (2018): 'Liberal Intergovernmentalism and the Crises of the European Union: LI and the EU Crises', *Journal of Common Market Studies*, 56:7, 1578–1594.

Schmidt, Vivien A. (2013): 'Democracy and Legitimacy in the European Union Revisited: Input, Output and "Throughput"', *Political Studies*, 61:1, 2–22.

Schmidt, Vivien A. (2019): 'Politicization in the EU: Between National Politics and EU Political Dynamics', *Journal of European Public Policy*, 26:7, 1018–1036.

Schmidt, Vivien A. & Wood, Matthew (2019): 'Conceptualizing Throughput Legitimacy: Procedural Mechanisms of Accountability, Transparency, Inclusiveness and Openness in EU Governance', *Public Administration*, 97:4, 727–740.

Schmitt, Hermann, Hobolt, Sara B. & Popa, Sebastian A. (2015): 'Does Personalization Increase Turnout? *Spitzenkandidaten* in the 2014 European Parliament Elections', *European Union Politics*, 16:3, 347–368.

Schmitt, Hermann & Toygür, Ilke (2016): 'European Parliament Elections of May 2014: Driven by National Politics or EU Policy Making?', *Politics and Governance*, 4:1, 167–181.

Scipioni, Marco (2018): 'Failing Forward in EU Migration Policy? EU Integration after the 2015 Asylum and Migration Crisis', *Journal of European Public Policy*, 25:9, 1357–1375.

Smeets, Sandrino & Beach, Derek (2022): 'New Institutional Leadership Goes Viral EU Crisis Reforms and the Coming about of the Covid Recovery Fund', *European Journal of Political Research*, online first: 1–20. https://doi.org/10.1111/1475-6765.12508.

Toshkov, Dimiter (2011): 'Public Opinion and Policy Output in the European Union: A Lost Relationship', *European Union Politics*, 12:2. 169–191.

Traber, Denise, Hänni, Miriam, Giger, Nathalie & Breunig, Christian (2022): 'Social Status, Political Priorities and Unequal Representation', *European Journal of Political Research*, 61:2, 351–373.

Treib, Oliver (2021): 'Euroscepticism Is Here to Stay: What Cleavage Theory Can Teach Us about the 2019 European Parliament Elections', *Journal of European Public Policy*, 28:2, 174–189.

Van Biezen, Ingrid, Mair, Peter & Poguntke, Thomas (2012): 'Going, Going, . . . Gone? The Decline of Party Membership in Contemporary Europe', *European Journal of Political Research*, 51:1, 24–56.

Van Biezen, Ingrid & Poguntke, Thomas (2014): 'The Decline of Membership-Based Politics', *Party Politics*, 20:2, 205–216.

Vik, Andrea & de Wilde, Pieter (2021): 'Feeling Represented: A New Approach to Measure How Citizens Feel Represented Through Representative Claims', *ECPR General Conference*. Innsbruck, 22–26 August.

Wallaschek, Stefan (2020): 'Contested Solidarity in the Euro Crisis and Europe's Migration Crisis: A Discourse Network Analysis', *Journal of European Public Policy*, 27:7, 1034–1053.

Weiler, Joseph H. H. (2012): 'In the Face of Crisis: Input Legitimacy, Output Legitimacy and the Political Messianism of European Integration', *Journal of European Integration*, 34:7, 825–841.

Wendler, Frank (2016): *Debating Europe in National Parliaments: Public Justification and Political Polarization*. Palgrave Macmillan.

Werner, Annika (2019a): 'What Voters Want from Their Parties: Testing the Promise-Keeping Assumption', *Electoral Studies*, 57, 186–195.

Werner, Annika (2019b): 'Voters' Preferences for Party Representation: Promise-Keeping, Responsiveness to Public Opinion or Enacting the Common Good', *International Political Science Review*, 40:4, 486–501.

Wolkenstein, Fabio & Wratil, Christopher (2021): 'Multidimensional Representation', *American Journal of Political Science,* 65:4: 862–876.

Wratil, Christopher (2018): 'Modes of Government Responsiveness in the European Union: Evidence from Council Negotiation Positions', *European Union Politics,* 19:1, 52–74.

Zeitlin, Jonathan, Nicoli, Francesco & Laffan, Brigid (2019): 'Introduction: The European Union beyond the Polycrisis? Integration and Politicization in an Age of Shifting Cleavages', *Journal of European Public Policy,* 26:7, 963–976.

Zürn, Michael & de Wilde, Pieter (2016): 'Debating Globalization: Cosmopolitanism and Communitarianism as Political Ideologies', *Journal of Political Ideologies,* 21:3, 280–301.

Part III: **The EU in a changing world**

Michael Smith

7 After the deluge: Europe, the European Union and crisis in the world arena

Abstract: This chapter sets out to re-assess a number of arguments made in the past twenty years about the relationships between Europe, the EU and international order in the light of recent and current changes and crises within the world arena. Specifically, it starts from the emergence of an apparently new international and European order after the end of the Cold War, based on new forms of institutions, rules, negotiation and boundary-making and on new roles for key actors, including states and the European Union. It goes on to examine the key mechanisms underpinning this order, including the interactions between markets, hierarchies and networks and the impact of the EU as a 'realist power', a 'market power,' an 'institutional power,' and a 'normative power'. The chapter then explores the challenges to this conception of European order in the early 21st century, emerging from power shifts at the domestic and European levels, the impact of economic crisis, the fragility of existing boundaries and the emergence of a multipolar or 'interpolar' world arena. Finally, it assesses the capacity of European actors, and, specifically, the EU, to absorb, divert or capitalise upon the 'deluge' of multiple crises that emerged during the period 2019–2022, and explores alternative future courses for the EU's engagement with European and world order.

Keywords: European Union; European order; international order; realist power; market power; institutional power; normative power.

Introduction

Since the end of the Cold War and the accompanying transformations of the 1990s and beyond, there has been a consistent focus on thinking about the generation of international order with specific reference to Europe and the European Union (see for example Carlsnaes & Smith 1994; Keohane, Nye & Hoffmann 1993; M. Smith 1996, 2006, 2008; Niblett & Wallace 2001; Elgström & Smith 2000; Carlsnaes et al. 2004; K. Smith 2004, 2014; Duke 2018; Biscop 2019). Whilst there is natural dis-

Note: This chapter is an expanded and much-revised version of a commentary published in the *Journal of Contemporary European Research*, 14(4), December 2018, 296–302, and a paper presented at the European Union Studies Association Conference in Denver, May 2019.

https://doi.org/10.1515/9783110790337-008

agreement among commentators about both explanation and prescription, a number of key aspects run through the debates. One aspect has concerned the relationship between old states, new states and the European order: how far have the changes since the early 1990s revived or transformed the role of states in generating and maintaining order? A second aspect has related to the links between order and stability: how far have new mechanisms of order created stable boundaries and institutions, both in Europe and beyond? A third aspect gives a central role to the place of negotiation and the establishment of negotiated order: how far have negotiations provided a robust foundation for the accommodation of change and challenges, and what role has diplomacy played in consolidating and developing order? A final aspect centres on the role(s) played by the European Union in generating, consolidating and developing order: to what extent has the EU become the centre of a stable European order, and how has this related to the challenge of change both inside and outside the continent?

This chapter focuses on the four questions set out above, in the context of this volume's concern with 'Europe under strain'. Specifically, it starts from the emergence of an apparently new international and European order after the end of the Cold War, based on new forms of institutions, rules, negotiation, and boundary-making and new roles for key actors, including states and the European Union. It goes on to examine the key mechanisms underpinning this order, including the interactions between power structures, market structures, institutional structures, and normative structures and the impact of the EU as a 'realist power', a 'market power', an 'institutional power', and a 'normative power'. The chapter then explores the challenges to this conception of European and international order that emerged in the early 21st century, reflecting power shifts at the domestic and European levels, the impact of economic crisis, the contestability of existing institutions and norms, and the resulting emergence of a multipolar or 'interpolar' world arena, and evaluates the EU's attempts to respond to them. Finally, it assesses the capacity of European actors, and specifically the EU, to absorb, divert or capitalise upon the intensified and interconnected challenges that emerged between 2019 and 2022 – in both the European and the world arenas – particularly those arising from Brexit and political divergence in the EU, economic, energy and environmental turbulence, and the impact of renewed conflict in eastern Europe. The Conclusions explore the implications of three scenarios: first, the emergence of a pluralistic yet resilient European and international order in which a reformed EU would be a central component; second, the emergence of a polarised European and world order in which the EU would be re-absorbed into a renewed 'western alliance'; and third, the development of a fragmented order in which the EU might be paralyzed or marginalised.

Order after the Cold War

The emergence of a new European order after the end of the Cold War was a confusing and seemingly paradoxical process. The collapse of the multinational empire centred on the Soviet Union and the emergence of a number of new, often fragile states in central and eastern Europe raised fundamental questions about the nature of statehood and the 'system of states'. The notion of a 'neo-medieval' system in which competing and overlapping centres of power enjoyed a conditional form of sovereignty, producing a 'mosaic' of economic, diplomatic, and military organizations at national, international, and sometimes subnational levels conveyed a powerful sense of the unstable and contingent nature of order (Zielonka 2006). The creation of the European Union with the Maastricht Treaty, which entered into force in 1993, provided at least a partial anchor, specifically through the prospect of membership for a wider range of states and the creation of multiple dialogues that engaged most of the 'new' states (K. Smith 2004; Weber et al. 2007). The tension between the desire for independence and the drive to become part of an integrated Europe was evident in countries such as Poland or the Baltic states. However, it was either finessed or suppressed in the process of enlargement – a process which contributed to the generation of a new form of multilateral negotiated order in Europe (M. Smith 2000; Niblett & Wallace 2001).

In this context, the roles played by the EU were central, and to a certain extent, contradictory. The Union became indispensable to the creation of a form of multilateral negotiated order, but there remained pivotal questions about who or what should belong to such an order – in other words, about whether the Union represented a politics of inclusion or exclusion (M. Smith 1996). By developing a process of managed accession, the EU reflected and refracted divisions both among its existing member states and those 'outsiders' who wished to enjoy the benefits of membership. By emphasizing the importance of institutional density among insiders and the application of rules in a 'community of law', the Union automatically created new divisions and raised the stakes surrounding processes of accession and non-accession. It became a key venue – but not the only venue – for the development of new forms of negotiated order. Yet, at the same time, there was an underlying tension between negotiations as a form of inclusion or exclusion. Whilst the emerging post-Cold War European order came to centre quite largely on the Union, there were also clear tensions with other institutions such as NATO, the OSCE, and the United Nations in arenas such as those created by conflict in former Yugoslavia or the former Soviet empire in eastern Europe and central Asia (Keohane et al. 1993). A key question concerned the extent to which the EU could 'internalise' European order, or whether it would remain a part of a broader continental order – and this linked to questions about the nature of the global arena and global order to which the EU could contribute, but not control (M. Smith 2007).

The EU and order

The EU has had a foundational relationship with issues of European and international order since the end of the Cold War. But how does this help us to think about the resources that the EU brings to those issues and the extent to which the Union can hope to exercise leverage over them? I argue that ideas of international order rely on four central structural attributes: power structure, market structure, institutional structure, and normative structure. Each of these is important in its own right, but the linkages and balances between the different pillars add complexity to the creation and maintenance of order. Also, equally important are the implications of these components for the roles that might be played by the EU, particularly concerning the strains created by conflicts and crises.

In the first place, power structure relies upon the balance of material capabilities (for example, economic strength, military capacity and diplomatic resources), and the ability to apply these in specific contexts. The end of the Cold War led to major shifts in the balance of material capabilities, both inside and outside Europe – but these shifts were not unidirectional, cumulative, or permanent. In the case of Europe, they had the effect of highlighting the centrality of the EU, but also of drawing attention to the fact that the Union simply did not possess the classical instruments of 'hard power', such as military strength. In a sense, the period since 1990 has been one for the Union of successive attempts to equip itself with more instruments of 'hard power' and to become a 'realist power' (Ross Smith 2015; Rynning 2011; Zimmerman 2007), in the face of resistance among some member states, competition from other bodies such as NATO, and the resurgence in Europe of former powers, especially Russia. In Europe itself, it is to some extent appropriate to see the EU as exercising structural power through its centrality to the European economy and its institutional strength, even without the key components of 'hard power', but this remains an issue, especially where crises and conflicts occur.

Second, the importance of market structure privileges the EU's role as a 'market power' (Damro 2012, 2014, 2015), driven by market imperatives and seeking both economic security and economic leverage in a world of 'competitive interdependence' (Sbragia 2010). There is no doubt that in this domain, the EU exercises both structural power and power in specific policy domains, not only in Europe but also beyond. But this simple statement raises questions about how market power is exercised by and through the Union. As a 'trading state', the EU centres its international activity on multilateral rules and institutions, but is itself a dense 'community of law' centred on the generation of economic benefits for its member states and citizens (Rosecrance 1986, 1993; M. Smith 2004). Not surprisingly, the internal distribution of these benefits, and the external response to the EU's search for appropriate mechanisms of stability and growth, create tensions and contradictions. Most obviously, the internal prosperity of the Union and the need for multilateral cooperation to create stable and open trading conditions can come into conflict.

Third, the maintenance and consolidation of the international order, both at European and global levels, has come to rely upon the generation of institutional density and the production of forms of multilevel governance in the European and world arenas. As noted above, the EU is at the same time an example of a dense system of rules and institutional processes, and a distinctive sub-system in the broader arena (Hill et al. 2023, chapters 1 and 20). This is not just a question of the key EU institutions based in Brussels, though – the EU generates and encompasses transnational, transgovernmental, and intergovernmental networks that add to the robustness – and some would say, the impenetrability – of its internal order. This in turn provides the basis for claims of legitimacy in multilateral institutions at the global and continental levels, in some cases superseding the claims of EU member states themselves (Laatikainen & Smith 2006; Jørgensen & Laatikainen 2013: Part VI). There is of course a contradiction between the generation of ever-increasing institutional density at the EU level and the residual claims of member states and others to autonomy, and this in turn is linked to the ways in which EU institutions in the broadest sense are seen as providing collective and more specific goods – economic, political and normative.

Finally, the normative structure of the European and broader world orders demands consideration, shaping as it does the ideational contexts and challenges faced not only by the EU but also by a host of other internationally acting bodies. The 'reigning ideas' of European and international order are strongly linked to the notion of 'normative power Europe' (Manners 2002; Sjursen 2006; Gerrits 2009; Whitman 2010) and the associated assumption that the EU is a 'force for good' in the world arena because of the ideas that it encompasses. This reflects, in part, the search during the immediate post-Cold War period for forms of European identity and normative order at a time of normative confusion and contention. The EU has represented for many a central repository of ideas associated with liberal international order and a key expression of those ideas. Not only this, but the ideas themselves – rule of law, good governance, human rights and others – have been given concrete expression in a host of the EU's international agreements and institutional engagements. A central issue in this area, inevitably, is the extent to which these normative commitments can survive engagement with material, political, security and economic imperatives – and with the emergence of competing normative orders in the global arena (Hyde-Price 2006; Youngs 2004, 2010).

In the context described above, the production of the EU's first Global Strategy in 2016 (EEAS 2015; EU 2016; K. Smith 2017; Tocci 2017) could be interpreted as an attempt to bring together the four strands of European and international order and to devise criteria for the mobilisation of EU resources in pursuit of such order. Significantly, the Strategy was intended to be 'global' in two senses: first, in having a global reach and in placing the EU's neighbourhood within a broader global order, and second, in bringing together the institutions and resources of the Union in a 'joined up' system of external action. In other words, in terms of the argument here, the Strategy responded to the need for action in all four of the domains outlined in this chapter: power, market, institutions, and norms. In pursuit of this synthesis, the Strategy also attempted to square the circle of material power and normative power, by committing the Union to the pursuit of 'principled pragmatism' as a guide to action. Further, the Strategy committed the Union to pursue three key elements in furthering its global role: 'strategic autonomy,' 'resilience,' and a coherent 'comprehensive approach'. Each of these elements raised important questions about the nature and direction of EU external action, but in the context of the argument here, they can be seen as a systematic attempt by the Union to define its approach to questions of European and international order. Importantly, this approach was to be pursued in a European and broader international arena that was, by the Union's admission 'complex, connected and contested' and thus posed major challenges to those who would attempt to shape it.

Challenges of the early 21st century

It is clear that there were major if not fundamental challenges in the first two decades of the 21st century to each and all of the components of European and international order as outlined above. Not only this, but there were major challenges to the EU itself as a form and focus of international order – a potent combination. Whilst it may be convenient to lump together the period since 1990 as the 'post-Cold War era', international order has moved through several phases over the past twenty-five or more years, and each of them has posed challenges and opportunities for the EU.

In terms of the power structure, we have already seen that the EU's position in Europe changed markedly over the period since 1990. But alongside this change, the broader international arena arguably changed more profoundly and continued to change in fundamental ways in the early 21st century (Alcaro et al. 2016; Brown 2017). From a period in which US hegemony appeared not only complete but also assured for the foreseeable future, there emerged major and persistent challenges from both inside and outside of the USA. The power shift in the world arena was incomplete and certainly inconclusive, but it also played into a US domestic context in which a curious mixture of 'declinism', victimhood, and the desire to still dominate permeated US politics. This was not an unusual combination, but was given a new and radical twist by the politics of the Trump administration, the effects of which were still being felt at the time of writing in 2022. From a European perspective, the US remained the continent's most significant other, but the combination of Trumpism and its legacy with Russian revanchism under Vladimir Putin (not to mention a more assertive Chinese stance on world order issues) proved a mercurial and disruptive set of forces (see for example Cohen 2018; Glasser 2018; M. Smith 2018b; Stokes 2018; Nye 2019). When this was combined further with challenges to the existing power structure within the EU, both at the Brussels level and in national contexts, the level of uncertainty and potential division only increased.

At the same time, there were persistent and pervasive challenges in the area of market structure – the core, some would argue, of the EU's engagement with issues of European and world order. The impact of the financial and sovereign debt crises from 2008 onwards was corrosive at a number of levels. In the global arena, it created conditions in which the existing structures of market power were partly if not largely overturned – linked to the emergence of 'rising powers' and especially China in the global political economy, it subverted expectations about the future shape of the world economy and the viability of international economic institutions (Alcaro et al. 2016; Brown 2017; Riddervold & Rosén 2018; M. Smith 2013). This subversion was compounded by the actions of the Trump administration in either ignoring or confronting the rules-based order in trade and related areas, and it was transmitted broadly in the global economy by the persistence of high levels of economic interdependence (Rachman 2018). The emergence of an 'interpolar' world (Grevi 2009), in which the rise of new centres of power combined with persistently high levels of interdependence, was nowhere better illustrated than in the turmoil surrounding world trade and multilateral commercial institutions. Whilst trade was at the centre of challenges, the global financial structure and areas such as the economics of development bore witness to continued turmoil and the potential for further disruption.

All of this implies that the institutional structure that nurtured the liberal world order – and indeed, the EU itself – for decades was and remains open to question as never before (Ikenberry 2018). This could be conceptualised as a chronic crisis of multilateralism, both as an idea and a set of institutional commitments (Bouchard et al. 2014; Rachman 2018; M. Smith 2018a). At the global level, the extent of commitment to multilateral institutions by several leading players was contested, as were the detailed commitments themselves in the case of trade (for example, by the Trump administration's use of national security rationales for the declaration of trade wars and the imposition of unilateral measures, or the use of energy supplies as a weapon by Vladimir Putin's Russia). Different versions of multilateralism competed, at the same time as bilateral and regional agreements proliferated, and the fluid nature of commitments and undertakings led to opportunistic and disruptive behaviour (M. Smith 2018c). Within Europe broadly defined, the use of economic instruments to subvert or disrupt political institutions (for example through oil and gas supplies) became more frequent, with uncertain consequences. Equally, whilst the institutions of European integration might be attacked and challenged from without, they were also challenged from within, by the rise of neo-nationalist politics within member states such as Poland and Hungary and by the processes surrounding the departure of the United Kingdom from the EU.

Finally, the normative order underpinning conventional conceptions of European and international order was challenged. The crisis of multilateralism noted above was not merely a crisis of institutions – it was a crisis of normative order, in which the 'reigning ideas' associated with open processes of international commercial and financial exchange were contested (M. Smith 2018a). These ideas are foundational for the EU (although some would argue they have never been perfectly reflected in EU policies) and thus this was an area in which external and internal challenges combined to produce a kind of multiplier effect. The neo-nationalist political movements that became prominent in many EU member states drew not only on European roots but also on varieties of 'transnational nationalism' reflected most obviously in the Trump administration, and also in other radical right-wing movements (Glasser 2018). The emphasis on 'sovereignist' politics that characterised many neo-nationalist groupings challenged not only the external but also the internal order of the Union, and thus raised questions about the EU's roles in both the European and the broader international order.

Responses: Before the deluge

Throughout the early years of the 21st century, and thus well before the 'deluge' of the period 2019–2022, there were debates about the relationship between the EU and international order. At their centre was a simple but challenging question: How should Europe and the EU in particular respond to the set of early 21st-century challenges outlined above, and how did they do so? After 2010 there were a number of proposals for the extension and/or reform of the Union's institutions, and also the working through of the Lisbon Treaty provisions establishing an EU diplomatic structure centred on the External Action Service and the High Representative for Foreign Affairs and Security Policy. But there was also a resurgence of 'domesticism', effectively giving priority to the treatment of internal problems (both at the EU and the member state level) above the projection of EU power, interests, or values. One symptom of this tension might be the idea of 'foreign policy as anti-dote' (Gnesotto et al. 2005; Juncker 2018) – the idea that a more activist and extend-ed set of external actions could defuse some of the internal tensions – but this was in a sense a circular argument since the internal tensions were precisely what might set strict limits for an extension of EU external activism, and thus lead to processes of 'de-Europeanisation' (Müller et al. 2021; M. Smith 2021a). Prior to the multiple crises of 2019–2022, the EU was at a potential turning point or sticking point in its relationship with European or international order, in which the stakes were heightened but the internal constraints on external activism were simulta-neously reinforced – partly because the stakes and potential risks were more sali-ent. As Erik Jones and Anand Menon argued (2019), the gap between the 'dream' of European unity and the reality of division and fragmentation was at a historic turning point – one that had implications for the role of Europe, and the EU in par-ticular, in broader international order.

One way of developing these arguments is to go back to the four elements of international order sketched in the previous sections of this chapter and to ask what resources (actual and potential) the EU deployed in attempting to shore them up prior to 2019. In the first place, the Union still found itself in an ambigu-ous position concerning international power structures, although it took some sig-nificant initiatives between 2016 and 2019 with collective defence planning and structured cooperation (M. Smith 2023). In principle, more resources were made available, but there were still important constraints on the perceived legitimacy of action in 'high politics' beyond diplomatic engagement. When it came to market structure, the EU continued to occupy a prominent position as a leading commer-cial actor, and continued to develop a range of tools to exercise leverage through the deployment of its economic power in such areas as development cooperation in the global arena – but there were new and potent competitors in such domains, most notably China. At the European level, the EU showed an inclination to engage with geo-economic issues but encountered severe problems when geo-economics and geopolitics became closely linked, as in the case of the Ukraine crisis of 2013–2014 (Haukkala 2016).

The Union continued to occupy a leading position in the institutional power structures of Europe and the world arena, but the undermining of institutions in key areas of the global political economy (trade, environment) meant that the EU suffered a loss of leverage in the multilateral system, allied to the losses arising from its own internal economic and institutional contradictions. Again, in this area, a distinction should be made between engagement in Europe, despite the set-backs that arose there, and engagement in the world arena; in the former, the EU retained significant structural power and the 'power of attraction', whilst in the latter, its position was increasingly open to challenge. Finally, the credentials of the EU as a key pillar of the European and global normative structure were challenged both by internal developments and by the growth of competing normative 'poles' with different interpretations of what it means to be a 'force for good' and with resources to back them up.

Another – and complementary – way of exploring the ways in which challenges to European and world order were met by the EU before 2019 is to return to the four aspects of international order identified at the beginning of this chapter: statehood, stability, negotiated order, and the legitimacy and centrality of the EU itself. It seems clear that in the 21st century, the tension between statehood and the search for forms of order across or among states and other actors became more rather than less severe, and therefore could be discerned in many of the EU's internal and external activities. At the same time, linked to this tension, the search for stability in Europe and beyond through the consolidation or the transformation of boundaries became more fraught, with issues such as migration highlighting the imperfect nature of cross-national consensus on what the boundaries of Europe and the EU should or could be (Hill 2023). As a result, the tension between a politics of inclusion and a politics of exclusion remained severe and persistent, with new symptoms and stresses arising from the old roots. Not surprisingly, the nature and extent of negotiated order in Europe and the wider world arena were questioned and in important respects constrained: whilst modest gains might still be made in the extension of the EU order through accession, the Union's neighbourhood had become more rather than less contested and likely to remain so. In this context, as noted above, the EU's credentials as a supplier of order, both within the wider Europe and beyond, came into question, and the extension of its external actions and ambitions was, at least to some extent, curtailed, despite the apparent ambition of the Global Strategy. What the Strategy labelled 'principled pragmatism' may well have been an appropriate response to the circumscription of its resources and potential leverage, but it was a far cry from the heyday of the EU as a 'force for good' at the European and global levels.

The deluge: Crisis and disorder in Europe and the world since 2019

The chapter so far has effectively presented the 'past as prelude', arguing that important components of strain and challenge faced the EU's external action and engagement in the period surrounding the Lisbon Treaty, the Global Strategy, and their implementation. There is no doubt, in this context, that the period 2019–2022 represented a step towards change in the intensity and scope of the challenges faced by the EU, and by extension the threats to European and world order. Given the EU's foundational investment in international order, what can we say about the nature of the challenge, its impact on the EU's external engagement, and its implications for the EU's role in future international order? In order to explore this question, the chapter focuses on three sets of cases to provide brief surveys of evidence and implications.

The first set of cases deals with two sets of linked challenges: those of Brexit and the intensification of 'new nationalisms' in the EU itself. Both of these have been challenges to the legitimacy and effectiveness of the EU order itself, either through defection (in the case of Brexit) or through the increasing tensions between Eurosceptic regimes in the Union and the EU's institutions (for example in the cases of Hungary and Poland). Both of them are also linked to more distant external pressures, particularly the rise of 'Trumpism' in the USA and its attempts at undermining the EU's international credentials (M. Smith 2021b). In each case, there were important implications for the internal coherence of the Union, reflecting on the one hand the Brexit challenge to the solidarity of the institutions and between member states, and on the other hand, the 'new nationalist' challenge to the legitimacy of the EU as a 'community of law' and a normative order.

One feature of the EU's response to these linked challenges was an impressive capacity to maintain solidarity, despite efforts by the UK government to detach certain member states through bilateral initiatives and despite the open challenges to the EU's legal order by governments in both Poland and Hungary. In the case of Brexit, solidarity was put in question not only by the process of negotiation but also by the UK government's attempts to modify or renegotiate key areas of the Trade and Cooperation Agreement, including the Northern Ireland Protocol, after formal negotiations were concluded in early 2020. In addition, London's aspiration to conduct a new form of global foreign and security policy meant that relations between the EU and NATO (a key focus of UK policy in the absence of formal cooperation in the EU context) were subject to new strains. At the bilateral level, the UK's participation in the AUKUS pact with the USA and Australia, which derailed French attempts to build a partnership with the Australian government, created an atmosphere of crisis and recrimination in 2021. Within the EU itself, attempts by the Polish and Hungarian governments to 'de-Europeanise' in key areas of foreign and security policy, whilst not carried through into formal defection in the short term, presented new rhetorical strains and needs for internal negotiation (M. Smith 2021a).

Whilst it might be argued that during 2020 and 2021 the strains imposed by Brexit and the 'new nationalism' of certain member states did not fundamentally shake the solidarity on which the EU's contribution to international order relies, the same cannot be argued in the case of the second set of issues addressed here:

those relating to the economy, the environment, and energy. Since 2008, there has been effectively a continuous series of economic crises in and around the EU, challenging not only specific lines of policy but also the institutional capacity of the Union itself. There has also been a gradual shift in the orientation of the EU's external action within the global political economy, linked to the broader crisis of multilateralism and the liberal world order identified earlier in the chapter. This had led to the adoption of 'open strategic autonomy' as a key element of the Union's external economic policies, and especially trade policies (Gehrke 2021). As noted earlier, such a strategic position was challenged by a series of trends within the global political economy, bringing together environmental, energy, and financial considerations, and posing a challenge to the EU's ambitions in environmental policy.

The period between 2019–2022 saw a confluence of these trends which, combined with a series of unanticipated challenges, created a perfect economic storm, from which the EU has yet to emerge. The Covid-19 crisis was at the same time a fundamental challenge to governance within the EU, and a challenge to the EU's position in the global political economy; whilst a surprising degree of solidarity was maintained among member states and the EU's institutions during 2020–2022, and indeed significant innovation in financial and other policy instruments, the effects on national economies and divergence among member states were also considerable. At the same time, the legacy of the Trump Administration and the economic challenges it posed had to be worked through, even given the more propitious US policies adopted by the Biden Administration. The US-China confrontation continued to create spin-off effects that were felt directly in the EU. But then the sharpening of tensions and eventually the outbreak of war precipitated by the Russian invasion of Ukraine in February 2022 gave another sharp twist to the dilemmas faced by the EU in the global political economy: an escalation of energy prices and the challenges to energy and food security were accompanied by divergent economic responses within the EU, the spillover of war in the shape of millions of refugees, the contrasting economic impacts on member states, and by the consequent strains in the framing and conduct of economic policy at the Union level (Bruyninckx 2022; Chazan et al. 2022; Sheppard 2022).

From this, it is clear that the third element in the exploration of the multiple crises that confronted the EU – conflict, and security – is important not only in itself but also through its role as a catalyst for a number of longer-standing trends and policy challenges. Since 2014, the war in Ukraine had in some ways been a constant feature of European politics, with the Russian annexation of Crimea and their sponsorship of client regimes in Donetsk and Luhansk. But the invasion of February 2022 and the onset of the largest territorial conflict in Europe since 1945 constituted a fundamental challenge both to European order and the central organising principles of EU external action – in other words, to the idea that in some ways European order had become 'civilianised' since the end of the Cold War. The challenge was not entirely new – since the Global Strategy had been adopted, the Union had been working towards a more muscular set of security policies to reflect the altered European and global security environments, and in 2021 it had formalised its work towards adopting a 'strategic compass' with pathways for implementation of new mechanisms for innovation and investment in 'hard' security resources (Fiott 2020, 2021; European Union 2022; Smith 2023). But coming as it did in the midst of an economic crisis and the threat of fragmentation within the Union and between the Union and the UK, it became subject to an acute 'omni-crisis' both for EU policy-makers and for European and international order, which threatened to render it irrelevant (Whitney 2022).

At the time of writing, the extent and implications of this crisis have yet to be fully recognised. However, the combination of strains in (at least) three registers could be seen as almost an existential challenge to the EU and its leadership. The primary challenge, it might be argued, was the notion of solidarity – a fundamental element to the European project (Chassany 2022; Chazan et al. 2022). As we have seen, this was threatened by several political and economic forces from 2008 onwards. However, the Ukraine crisis attacked it in a concentrated and sustained way, particularly through connections to energy security (and consequently to the cost of living, and national economic management in member states), and through the impact of renewed and large-scale flows of involuntary migration, this time from within the eastern neighbourhood (Seibel 2023). A second challenge was economic performance, a basis for much if not all of the EU's weight in the world order: in the context already outlined, it was no surprise that the Euro experienced a major decline in the Summer of 2022, especially against the US Dollar, reaching a position of parity which evoked arguments reminiscent of the early 2000s about the status and sustainability of the Eurozone. A third challenge was the notion of the EU as a 'power' in the European and global security orders. Whilst the 'hardening' of EU external security policy had proceeded gradually over some decades, spurred on by crises such as those over Georgia in 2008 and Ukraine in 2014, the war of 2022 posed the most acute of dilemmas: would (could) the EU become a central player in a newly confrontational European order, or would it once again experience the self-limiting effects of internal fragmentation and a persistent legacy of 'civilian power'? The initial hardening of EU responses, with not only comprehensive sanctions but also the financing of military assistance to Ukraine, was persistently countered with resistance among member states, either on the basis of national policies (for example, Hungary) or domestic political and economic constraints (for example, Germany). This ambivalence reflected once again the foundational contradictions of the European project – on the one hand, a way of 'sneaking up on sovereignty' and establishing the Union as a 'power', but on the other hand, a set of delegated powers subject to control by member states.

Conclusion: Three scenarios for the future

What kind of future for the EU and European order, in a global context, can be deduced from this argument? Three alternatives can be proposed, each of them reflecting the impact of the challenges and constraints outlined above. The first might be labelled 'A reformed Union in a pluralist European and world order'. In this alternative, the EU overcomes its internal tensions and the geopolitical challenges of a conflicted continent to create new institutional and material resources and succeeds in deploying them within Europe and beyond. But both the European order and broader global order in the mid-21st century will require action within a more pluralistic context, with new alignments of forces at the transnational, transgovernmental, and intergovernmental levels. The challenge for the EU will be to develop and deploy new instruments, but above all to adapt them to shifting constellations of power, markets, institutions, and norms both internally and externally. The pursuit of a leading role in international order carries with it – as it always has – potential costs and risks that are multiplied in a more pluralistic arena, and the EU will have to both identify and respond to these costs and risks both in the short and in the longer term. Such a process demands legitimacy and leadership in areas that are currently questioned both within and outside the Union – and such legitimacy and leadership cannot be generated simply by institutional reforms.

A second alternative future can be labelled 're-absorption of the EU into a polarised European and international order'. Here, the logic of polarization crystallised by the Russian assault on Ukraine and by the challenge of China both at the global level and in the Indo-Pacific would lead to a re-consolidation of alignments reminiscent of (but not the same as) the Cold War period. This process would underline the primacy of the USA in the 'west' and its responsibility for leadership of a revived Euro-Atlantic coalition, reflecting the ways in which Washington led the response to the invasion of Ukraine and in which both the USA and the UK assumed leading roles in NATO to shape its response to the conflict. There are important potential barriers to this process, including the development of politics in the USA itself, reflecting the resurgence of 'America First' attitudes and the possibility of a recapture of the White House in 2024 either by Donald Trump or by a Trumpian candidate emerging from the Republican Party during the primary campaign. But if the process takes place, the position of the EU would become a key focus for contention and contestation. Would the Union be re-absorbed into a reinvigorated Atlantic Alliance, as argued by Wolfgang Streeck (2022), where its position would essentially be subordinate to that of the USA and NATO, and where 'civilian power' might once again be the currency of its status? This would entail a frontal assault on the ideas of 'strategic autonomy' and the 'strategic compass', not only from outside the EU but also potentially from some member states, either because of their links to Russia and China or because of their anxiety to restrict the risks and the costs inherent in the role of the EU as a 'power' in a polarised European and world order.

The third alternative future might be labelled 'A paralyzed EU in a fragmented European and world order'. In this version, fragmentation would take place both within the Union and outside, with the two tendencies reinforcing each other. Reform of the EU institutions and practices would be obstructed from within and challenged from outside, whilst order and stability would become commodities in short supply. Such a situation would be self-reinforcing, in the sense that problems within the Union would be compounded and fed by challenges from new constellations of actors, pursuing partial aims and a materialist agenda focused on short-term gains. In some ways, as can be seen from the argument above, this is a more concentrated and dysfunctional version of the tensions inherent in the first and second potential futures. As a result, the EU's retreat to 'conditional multilateralism' or 'contingent multilateralism' would be accelerated, and this in turn would reinforce tendencies towards fragmentation in the broader field of global or regional governance. A further effect of this set of processes would be to re-nationalise key areas of policy within the Union, especially foreign, security and defence policy but also central areas of commercial and financial action. The EU would not be destroyed, at least in the short term, but would be eroded, bypassed, and ignored in an expanding range of issues and situations.

None of these scenarios is likely to come about in an unalloyed form, but each of them can be inferred from current tendencies – and recent events in the 'deluge' between 2019 and 2022 have shifted the emphasis away from the first and towards either the second or the third. Each of the scenarios reflects major changes in the opportunities and risks facing the EU, both in Europe and beyond, through a combination of shifts in power, market, institutional, and normative structures; as a result, the role(s) of the EU and its ability to operate as a 'power' in Europe and beyond are open to debate in new and challenging ways.

References

Alcaro, Ricardo, Peterson, John & Greco, Ettori (eds.) (2016): *The West and the Global Power Shift: transatlantic relations and global governance*, Palgrave Macmillan.
Biscop, Sven (2019): *European Strategy in the 21st Century: new future for old power*, Routledge.

Bouchard, Caroline, Peterson, John & Tocci, Nathalie (eds.) (2014): *Multilateralism in the 21st Century: Europe's quest for effectiveness*, Routledge.

Brown, Scott (2017): *Power, Perception and Foreign Policymaking: US and EU responses to the rise of China*, Routledge.

Bruyninckx, Hans (2022): 'Summer 2022: living in a state of multiple crises', *EEA Newsletter*, September, European Environment Agency.

Carlsnaes, Walter & Smith, Steve (eds.) (1994): *European Foreign Policy: the EU and changing perspectives in Europe*, SAGE.

Carlsnaes, Walter, Sjursen, Helene & White, Brian (eds.) (2004): *Contemporary European Foreign Policy:* SAGE.

Chassany, Anne (2022): 'Age of 'permacrisis' shows EU that solidarity is tough, but worth it', *Financial Times*, 5 August 2022, 4.

Chazan, Guy, Fleming, Sam & Kazmin, Amy (2022): 'Can Europe's unity hold?' *Financial Times*. 30/31 July 2022, 8.

Cohen, Eliot (2018): 'Trump's Lucky Year: why the chaos can't last', *Foreign Affairs*, 97:2, 2–9.

Damro, Chad (2012): 'Market Power Europe', *Journal of European Public Policy*, 19:5, 682–699.

Damro, Chad (2014): 'Market Power Europe: externalization and multilateralism', in Caroline Bouchard, John Peterson & Nathalie Tocci (eds.): *Multilateralism in the 21st Century: Europe's quest for effectiveness*, Routledge, 116–134.

Damro, Chad (2015): 'Market Power Europe: exploring a dynamic conceptual framework', *Journal of European Public Policy*, 22:9, 1336–1354.

Duke, Simon (2018): *Europe as a Stronger Global Actor: challenges and strategic responses*, Palgrave Macmillan.

Elgström, Ole & Smith, Michael (eds.) (2000): *Journal of European Public Policy*, Special Issue on 'Negotiation and Policy-making in the European Union', 7:5, December 2000.

European External Action Service (2015): *The European Union in a Changing Global Environment: A more connected, contested and complex world*, EEAS.

European Union (2016): *Shared Vision, Common Action: A Stronger Europe. A Global Strategy for the EU's Common Foreign and Security Policy*, June.

European Union (2022): *A Strategic Compass for Security and Defence: for a European Union that protects its citizens, values and interests and contributes to international peace and security*, 22 March.

Fiott, Daniel (2020): *Uncharted Territory? Towards a common threat analysis and a Strategic Compass for European security and defence*, ISS Brief 16, European Union Institute for Security Studies, July.

Fiott, Daniel (2021): *The EU's Strategic Compass for Security and Defence: what kind of ambition is the needle pointing to?*, CSDS Policy Brief 2021/2, Centre for Security, Diplomacy and Strategy, 9 March.

Gehrke, Tobias (2021): 'Threading the trade needle on Open Strategic Autonomy', in Niklas Helwig (ed.): *Strategic Autonomy and the Transformation of the EU: new agendas for security, diplomacy, trade and technology*, FIIA Report 67, Finnish Institute for International Affairs, April, 87–105.

Gerrits, André (ed.) (2009): *Normative Power Europe in a Changing World: a discussion*, Clingendael Institute of International Relations.

Glasser, Susan (2018): 'An Ocean Apart: How Trump made war on Angela Merkel and Europe', *The New Yorker*, 24 December 2018, 46–53.

Gnesotto, Nicole, Grevi, Giovanni & Ortega, Manuel (2005): 'La PESC en antidote', *Bulletin No. 16*, EU Institute for Security Studies, 1 October.

Grevi, Giovanni (2010): *The Interpolar World: a new scenario*, Occasional Paper 79, EU Institute for Security Studies, June.

Haukkala, Hiski (2016): 'The perfect storm: or what went wrong and what went right for the EU in Ukraine', *Europe-Asia Studies*, 68:4, 653–664.

Hill, Christopher (2023): 'Migration: the dilemmas of external relations', in Christopher Hill, Michael Smith & Sophie Vanhoonacker (eds.): *International Relations and the European Union*, 4th edition, Oxford University Press.

Hill, Christopher, Smith, Michael & Vanhoonacker, Sophie (eds.) (2023): *International Relations and the European Union*, 4th edition, Oxford University Press.

Hyde-Price, Adrian (2006): '"Normative" Power Europe: A Realist critique', *Journal of European Public Policy*, 13:2, 217–234.

Ikenberry, John (2018): 'The end of liberal international order?', *International Affairs*, 94:1, 7–23.

Jones, Erik & Menon, Anand (2019): 'Europe: between dream and reality?', *International Affairs*, 95:1, 161–180.

Jørgensen, Knud Erik & Laatikainen, Katie (eds.) (2013): *Routledge Handbook on the European Union and International Institutions: performance, policy, power*, Routledge.

Juncker, Jean-Claude (2018): State of the Union Speech, Strasbourg, 12 September 2018. Found at https://ec.europa.eu/commission/presscorner/detail/en/SPEECH_18_5808 (last access: 8 March 2023).

Keohane, Robert, Nye, Joseph & Hoffmann, Stanley (eds.) (1993): *After the Cold War: international institutions and state strategies in Europe, 1989-1991*, Harvard University Press.

Laatikainen, Katie & Smith, Karen (eds.) (2006): *The European Union at the United Nations: intersecting multilateralisms*, Palgrave Macmillan.

Manners, Ian (2002): 'Normative Power Europe: a contradiction in terms?', *Journal of Common Market Studies*, 40:2, 234–258.

Manners, Ian (2005): 'Normative Power Europe Reconsidered', *Journal of European Public Policy*, 12:6, 182–199.

Müller, Patrick, Pomorska, Karolina & Tonra, Ben (2021): 'The Domestic Challenge to EU Foreign Policy-Making: from Europeanisation to de-Europeanisation?', *Journal of European Integration*, 43:5, 519–534.

Niblett, Robin & Wallace, William (eds.) (2001): *Rethinking European Order: West European responses, 1989-1997*, Cambridge University Press.

Nye, Joseph (2019): 'The rise and fall of American hegemony from Wilson to Trump', *International Affairs*, 95:1, 63–80.

Rachman, Gideon (2018): 'From leader to lone ranger', *Financial Times*, 12/13 May 2018, 7.

Riddervold, Marianne & Rosén, Guri (2018): 'Unified in response to rising powers? China, Russia and EU-US relations', *Journal of European Integration*, 40:5, 555–570.

Rosecrance, Richard (1986): *The Rise of the Trading State*, Basic Books.

Rosecrance, Richard (1993): 'Trading states in a new Concert of Europe', in Helga Haftendorn & Christian Tuschhoff (eds.): *America and Europe in an Era of Change*, Westview Press, 127–146.

Ross Smith, Nicholas (2015): 'The EU under a Realist Scope: employing a neoclassical realist framework for the analysis of the EU's Deep and Comprehensive Free Trade Agreement offer to Ukraine', *International Relations*, 30:1, 29–48.

Rynning, Sten (2011): 'Realism and the Common Security and Defence Policy', *Journal of Common Market Studies*, 49:4, 23–42.

Seibel, Walter (2023): 'The Ukraine Crisis: Russia, the European Union and the unstable East' in Neill Nugent, Willie Paterson & Mark Rhinard (eds.): *The European Union: crises and challenges*, Bloomsbury.

Sheppard, David (2022): 'EU confronts worst fears over gas as Russia puts squeeze on supplies', *Financial Times*, 18/19 June, 6.

Sjursen, Helene (2004): 'The EU as a "normative" power: how can this be?', *Journal of European Public Policy*, 13:2, 235–251.

Smith, Karen (2004): *The Making of European Union Foreign Policy: the case of Eastern Europe*, 2nd edition, Palgrave Macmillan.

Smith, Karen (2014): *European Union Foreign Policy in a Changing World*, 3rd edition, Polity.

Smith, Karen (2017):'European Union Global Strategy for a Changing World', *International Politics*, 54, 503–518.

Smith, Michael (1996): 'The European Union in a Changing Europe: establishing the boundaries of order', *Journal of Common Market Studies*, 34:1, 5–28.

Smith, Michael (2000): 'Negotiating New Europes: the roles of the European Union', *Journal of European Public Policy*, Special Issue on 'Negotiation and Policy-making in the European Union', 7:5, 806–822.

Smith, Michael (2004): 'Between Two Worlds? The European Union, the United States and World Order', *International Politics*, 41:1, 95–117.

Smith, Michael (2006): 'The Shock of the Real? Trends in European Foreign and Security Policy Since September 2001', *Studia Diplomatica*, LIX:1, 27–44.

Smith, Michael (2007): 'The European Union and International Order: European and Global Dimensions', *European Foreign Affairs Review*, 12:1, 437–456.

Smith, Michael (2013): 'Beyond the comfort zone: internal crisis and external challenge in the European Union's response to rising powers', *International Affairs*, 89:3, 653–672.

Smith, Michael (2018a): 'The European Union, the United States and the Crisis of Contemporary Multilateralism', *Journal of European Integration*, 40:5, 539–553.

Smith, Michael (2018b): 'Contestation and Crisis in EU-US Relations: The Trump Challenge in Perspective', paper presented at the International Studies Annual Convention, San Francisco, April 2018, and at the UACES Annual Conference, University of Bath, September 2018.

Smith, Michael (2018c): 'Rules, Institutions and Power in the Global Political Economy: China, the EU and the US compared', paper presented at the International Studies Annual Convention, San Francisco, April 2018.

Smith, Michael (2021a): 'De-Europeanisation and European Foreign Policy: assessing an exploratory research agenda', *Journal of European Integration*, 43:5, 637–649.

Smith, Michael (2021b): 'European Union Diplomacy and the Trump Administration: multilateral diplomacy in a transactional world?', in Roberta Haar, Thomas Christiansen, Sabina Lange & Sophie Vanhoonacker (eds.): *The Making of European Security Policy: between institutional dynamics and global challenges*, Routledge, 179–197.

Smith, Michael (2023): 'The External Challenge: crises and the EU's quest for strategic autonomy', in Neill Nugent, Willie Paterson & Mark Rhinard (eds.): *The European Union: crises and challenges*, Bloomsbury.

Stokes, Doug (2018): 'Trump, American hegemony and the future of the international liberal order', *International Affairs*, 94:1, 133–150.

Streeck, Wolfgang (2022): 'The EU after Ukraine', *American Affairs* VI:2, 107–124.

Tocci, Nathalie (2017): *Framing the EU Global Strategy: a stronger Europe in a fragile world*, Palgrave Macmillan.

Weber, Katja, Smith, Michael E. & Baun, Michael (eds.) (2007): *Governing Europe's Neighbourhood: partners or periphery?*, Manchester University Press.

Whitman, Richard (ed.) (2010): *Normative Power Europe: empirical and conceptual perspectives*, Palgrave Macmillan.

Whitney, Nick (2022): *The EU's Strategic Compass: brand new, already obsolete*, European Council on Foreign Relations Commentary, 31 March 2022.

Youngs, Richard (2004): 'Normative Dynamics and Strategic Interests in the EU's External Identity', *Journal of Common Market Studies*, 42:2, 415–435.

Youngs, Richard (2010): *The EU's Place in World Politics: a retreat from liberal internationalism*, Routledge.

Zielonka, Jan (2006): *Europe as Empire: the nature of the enlarged European Union*, Oxford University Press.

Zimmerman, Hubert (2007): 'Realist Power Europe? The EU in the negotiations about China's and Russia's WTO accession', *Journal of Common Market Studies*, 45:4, 813–837.

Sören Keil & Bernhard Stahl

8 EU enlargement in times of crisis: Strategic enlargement, the conditionality principle and the future of the "Ever-Closer Union"

Abstract: The European Union's (EU) enlargement policy has been an integral part of its historical development since the Treaty of Rome in 1957. Several enlargement rounds have ensured that the EU has grown to include a majority of the countries of the European continent. Yet, enlargement has never been a straightforward process and has been characterised by compromises, concessions, and strategic considerations. However, recent developments in Hungary and Poland have questioned the ability of the EU to ensure democratic governance amongst its members, and a lack of progress in the integration of the Western Balkan states also questions the EU's willingness to enlarge any further at this point in time. Enlargement fatigue has been carrying the day since the big bang enlargement and increases the likelihood of mere 'strategic accession' in the future. However, the Russian intervention in Ukraine in February 2022, and the subsequent awarding of candidate status for EU membership for Ukraine and Moldova in June 2022 have highlighted the importance of a clear enlargement strategy and membership perspective for EU crisis management in its near neighbourhood.

Keywords: EU enlargement, Western Balkans, conditionality, enlargement fatigue, strategic accession

Introduction

In many respects, enlargement policy is one of the biggest success stories of the European Union (EU). Increasing its membership and integrating new states has enabled the EU to expand its Single Market, so it would become one of the largest common economic spaces in the world. It has also united the European continent, and ensured peace, first in Western Europe by contributing to the reconciliation between (West-) Germany and France, and later by integrating, stabilising, and supporting the young democracies in Southern Europe (Spain, Portugal, and Greece), as well as the newly independent and newly democratic countries of the former Warsaw Pact in 2004 and 2007 (and 2013, when Croatia joined to become the then 28th member of the EU). EU integration, therefore, has been about

https://doi.org/10.1515/9783110790337-009

reconciliation, democratisation, and the creation of a new political union, which provides economic opportunities for its members, as well as a security community, and a union of norms and values (Stahl 1998). As pointed out by Desmond Dinan in his well-known discussion of the history of the EU, enlargement went hand in hand with the 'deepening' of the Union – as more members joined, its institutional framework had to adjust and further integration became possible (Dinan 2004). 'Widening' and 'Deepening' – in other words, together formed the integration process, which included institutional integration and territorial expansion through accession simultaneously.

However, in the post-Cold War period, enlargement has also become a reaction to crises and opportunities. The break-up of the Soviet Union and the opportunities given by the democratization of countries in Central and Eastern Europe (CEE) allowed for the EU to engage in the largest expansion in its history in 2004 and 2007 when altogether twelve new Member States joined the Union, followed by Croatia in 2013. This triumphant moment of European unification, which now enabled the EU to cover most of the European continent, expanding its union of peace, democracy, and economic prosperity was seen by many as a unique opportunity to bring Europe's East and West together on the basis of a common normative and institutional framework (Davies 2007).

Today, however, this period of enlargement is criticised as being rushed, overburdening the EU, and highlighting how different the old EU-15 countries were from the new members that joined after 2000.[1] Indeed, much of the current talk about 'enlargement fatigue'[2] goes back to the consequences of the so-called big-bang enlargement of 2004 and 2007, which has left the EU weakened in its institutional capacity on the one side, and produced increased opposition to any future enlargement on the other.

This contribution will look at EU enlargement in its current state. Based on the crises of EU enlargement policy after the 2004 and 2007 rounds of enlargement, we will demonstrate how the current enlargement framework, the Stabilisation and Association Process towards the Western Balkans, is not fit for purpose anymore. There is a deep division amongst EU Member States, with some, such as France pushing for deeper institutional reform (Wunsch 2017), including addressing the

---

1 As examples for this kind of criticism it is worth mentioning that former European Commission President Jean-Claude Juncker announced immediately when coming into office in 2014, that there would be no further enlargement in the near future. The sentiment was shared by other members of the European Commission. See for example: Alexe 2014.

2 Enlargement fatigue is an analytical term which denotes a widespread feeling of discontent with the policy outcomes of enlargement. It leads to a lack of political will to support and push for further enlargement.

problems of democracy and the rule of law amongst EU Members before any future enlargement can be considered. Others, such as Austria, Slovenia, and Croatia continue to support and push for further enlargement towards the countries of the former Yugoslavia. This internal conflict has had a profound impact not only on the half-hearted commitments of EU officials towards future enlargement (Ker-Lindsay et al. 2017), but also on the candidate and potential candidate countries in the former Yugoslavia (Serbia, Montenegro, North Macedonia, Albania, and most recently Ukraine and Moldova, are candidate countries, while Bosnia and Herzegovina and Kosovo are potential candidate countries). The Russian invasion of Ukraine in February 2022, and the subsequent awarding of candidate status to Ukraine and Moldova has deepened both the internal divisions amongst EU Member States and the crises of EU enlargement, the future of which has become ever-more uncertain, particularly towards the Western Balkans.

This contribution will tackle the issue in three sections. In the first section, we discuss the framework of EU enlargement policy historically and how it has changed after the end of the Cold War. In the second section, we look at the Stabilisation and Association Framework for the Western Balkans to discuss how it was designed as a specific response to the crisis linked to the break-up of Yugoslavia. Finally, the third section looks at the increasing narrative around 'enlargement fatigue' on the one side and the revival of the 'Strategic Enlargement' narrative in the wake of Russia's intervention in Ukraine on the other. By doing so, it discusses how this newly-found focus on enlargement does not mean that the EU has overcome its enlargement fatigue, nor that the deep crisis of the EU in terms of engaging with countries in its near neighbourhood is over.

EU enlargement and the symbiosis of widening and deepening

EU enlargement has been an integral part of the overall integration process of the Union since its foundation in 1957. It is no wonder that the Treaty of Rome already provided for expansion and a process for the integration of additional Member States – what started with six countries at the beginning was therefore always designed to grow and enlarge over time. Of course, this commitment to the evolution of what is today the European Union goes back to the very foundational ideas of Jean Monnet, who famously declared that

> The contribution which an organized and living Europe can bring to civilization is indispensable to the maintenance of peaceful relations. [...] Europe will not be made all at once, or according to a single plan. It will be built through concrete achievements which first create a de facto

solidarity [...] With this aim in view, the French Government proposes that action be taken im-
mediately on one limited but decisive point. It proposes that Franco-German production of coal
and steel as a whole be placed under a common High Authority, within the framework of an
organization open to the participation of the other countries of Europe (Schuman Declaration
9th May 1950).

As this excerpt from the Schuman Declaration highlights, the EU was born out of
crisis (i.e. the Second World War and the destruction it caused), it was designed to
overcome the generation-long conflict between Germany and France (Smeekens
and Keil 2022), and it was designed to be open for others to join. Enlargement,
therefore, was already foreseen before even the first Treaty for the European Economic Community had been signed. Over time, the European Community's (EC,
and after 1993 EU) ability to use enlargement as a tool to overcome other crises
became ever more important. In the 1970s, Ireland, the UK, and Denmark joined
the EC, partly as a response of these countries to the effects of ongoing global economic crises. When Greece (prematurely) joined the EC in 1981 and Portugal and
Spain in 1986, enlargement was proposed as a tool to support the democratization
of these countries that had only recently transformed from dictatorships. Enlargement, at this point, became a tool to support regime change toward liberal democracy, in addition to expanding the internal market of the Union (Juncos & Perez-
Solorzano Borragan 2018).

As the EU expanded, it also reformed. The unity of 'widening' – i.e. expanding
the Union – and 'deepening' it by reforming its institutional architecture towards
more democratic decision-making and strengthening supranational institutions
should not be neglected in the process of integration (Jachtenfuchs 2005). Even
the Treaty on European Union (1993 – sometimes also referred to as Maastricht
Treaty) was designed to prepare the EU for the membership of Austria, Finland,
and Sweden, which joined in 1995, and to pave the way for the Union to play a bigger role in a post-Cold War era, hence the focus on a new foreign and security policy. When the big-bang enlargement of 2004 and 2007 occurred, the EU had under-
gone numerous further reforms through treaty revisions (Treaty of Amsterdam,
1999, Treaty of Nice 2003), and the Treaty of Lisbon in 2009 was also designed to
make the Union more efficient and ensure its ability to function with soon-to-be
28 Member States (by then, the accession of Croatia was already agreed, though
a date was not yet set). However, Eastern enlargement proved to be a much
more challenging task than foreseen by many, and in hindsight, it is often seen
as the moment when EU absorption capacity reached its limits, and countries
such as Romania and Bulgaria were accepted without necessarily fulfilling all
the membership requirements properly (Icener & Phinnemore 2015). What many
characterised as a complex process of Europeanisation, namely the transformation

of previously Communist, one-party regimes into multiparty democracies, that would embrace liberal market economies, has been an initial success, but over time became much more contested and not fully sustainable in numerous new Member States (Zhelyazkova et.al 2019).

EU enlargement, as a result, became a much more contested issue. This was not just the case because of the growing recognition that the political transformation in Central and Eastern European countries was not as linear and as sustainable as previously predicted. But it was also a direct consequence of growing economic imbalances in the newly enlarged Union – new Member States were mainly economically weak and saw EU integration as a way to get access to substantial Regional Development Funds. At the same time, there was also a growing economic imbalance within older Member States – of course, most visible in Germany where the much poorer East joined West Germany, but also observable in growing economic inequalities in the UK (for example between London and the Southeast, and the rest of the country), in France (where areas in Northern France were economically left behind by Paris and the South) and Italy (where there was a growing diversity between the North and the South). This stronger focus on economic development, social welfare policies, and their link to overall institutional reforms would become an important feature for any further discussions on enlargement rounds (Bartlett 2008).

The completion of the big-bang enlargement rounds of 2004 and 2007 collided with another important development in the EU: The financial and economic crisis that followed shortly afterward shook the Union to its core. Particularly the financial crisis in Greece and several other European countries threatened to not only end the currency union and the achievements of monetary integration, but they re-opened old conflict lines between different Member States. Germany and France focused on stronger reforms and fiscal discipline, while other countries such as Spain, Portugal, and Italy initially highlighted the need to respond more directly with state interventions and additional spending to the crisis. In the end, the EU saw a substantial amount of integration, through the Banking Union, the new powers of the European Central Bank, and the ability of the European Commission to oversee Member States' budgets, investment, and economic development plans (Violi 2021). However, the economic crisis also had several repercussions for the EU's enlargement policy. First, it ensured that enlargement was taken off the agenda as a priority. In the EU, the years after 2009 were mainly focused on dealing with the economic and political fallout from the financial crisis, while the 2015 migration crisis already loomed on the horizon. Enlargement, therefore, was taken off the agenda for EU leaders. Second, fiscal and economic stability became key ingredients in the discussion on enlargement. Countries such as Germany but also Sweden, which have previously strongly supported enlargement, now requested that any new members would be able to economically contribute and be able to cope with any major crisis (Töglhofer & Adebahr 2017). Third, the need for further internal reforms became obvious. France became a champion of those voices that asked for a delay of any future enlargement until further internal reforms had improved the functioning and crisis resilience of the Union. However, the countries of the Western Balkans, which were affected by the different crises as well, remained engaged in the enlargement process, whilst actual membership became ever-more difficult to achieve.

EU enlargement towards the Western Balkans

The EU's engagement in the Western Balkans begins as a story of failure. While the EU had economic and political ties to Socialist Yugoslavia, it was unable to provide an economic and political alternative to the growing nationalist rhetoric and political conflicts within Yugoslavia and therefore, prevent the violent dissolution of the state in the early 1990s (Keil & Stahl 2015). This was particularly problematic, as the EU had become the main negotiator during the Yugoslav crisis (Silber and Little, 1996). In 1991, when it became obvious that the Yugoslav state was dissolving and Slovenia and Croatia were preparing for independence, the Chairman of the European Council of Ministers Jacques Poos famously stated 'This is the hour of Europe, not the hour of the Americans' – highlighting the EU's commitment to dealing with the evolving crisis (Glaurdic 2011). However, the EU's diplomacy and conflict resolution mechanisms failed to prevent and later end the violence in the region. The EU was seen as neither able nor willing to enforce its ultimatums and underline its policy proposals with hard power (Holbrooke 1999; Glenny 1996; Baker 2015).

The war in Croatia and later in Bosnia and Herzegovina (BiH) ended because the US administration under the leadership of President Bill Clinton eventually shifted its focus and became more involved. The Dayton Peace Conference and the subsequent Peace Accords enforced Pax Americana and thereby secured the dominance of the US as the sole superpower in the post-Cold War period (Daalder 2000). The EU had to rethink its foreign policy approach and overall structures. As Ana Juncos (2013) has demonstrated, what followed after 1995 was the evolution of important foreign and security mechanisms in the EU, as well as a new framework for engagement with the Western Balkan countries. The "Return to Europe" discourse played a major role at the time, as the EU was not only preparing for enlargement towards the former Communist countries in Central and Eastern Europe but the expansion towards the post-Yugoslav states was seen as an important element of the wider unification of the European continent.

The war in Kosovo heavily influenced the evolving relationship between the EU and the Western Balkans. This is for three reasons. First, the involvement of NATO and the US demonstrated an important lesson learned for the EU in its engagement in the region – any political and diplomatic efforts to uphold international law needed to be backed by a credible threat to use force if necessary. Second, the Kosovo war finalised the link between European and Atlantic integration and involvement in the region – NATO and the US would become the main security providers (as was the case after 1995 in Bosnia), while the EU would become the main driver for political and economic reforms – i.e.. democratisation and state-building in the countries. Third, the war in Kosovo shifted discourses in the EU; it became obvious that a simple application of previous enlargement frameworks, including the policies used in Central and Eastern Europe, would not be enough to deal with the post-Yugoslav states. As a consequence, the EU Head of States and Governments extended the 'great promise' of membership at the 2003 Thessaloniki Summit to South Eastern Europe (SEE):

> The EU reiterates its unequivocal support to the European perspective of the Western Balkan countries. The future of the Balkans is within the European Union. The ongoing enlargement and the signing of the Treaty of Athens in April 2003 inspire and encourage the countries of the Western Balkans to follow the same successful path. Preparation for integration into European structures and ultimate membership into the European Union, through adoption of European standards, is now the big challenge ahead [...] The speed of movement ahead lies in the hands of the countries of the region. The countries of the region fully share the objectives of economic and political union and look forward to joining an EU that is stronger in the pursuit of its essential objectives and more present in the world (European Commission 2003).

Categorizing all post-Yugoslav countries as future EU Member States and the EU's commitment to their integration also followed important democratic changes in Serbia and Croatia in 2000, as well as more active engagement of the EU in Bosnia. Indeed, the EU became heavily involved in state-building, the promotion of power-sharing arrangements, and substantial reform efforts in a variety of countries in the former Yugoslavia (Cooley 2019). The EU's approach fundamentally shifted, enlargement became about more than membership preparation adopting EU law, it became linked to wider state-building and democratisation as well as security sector reform, refugee return, economic recovery after conflict, and extensive EU presence in countries that were severely affected by the conflicts between 1991 and 2000 (Keil 2013; Belloni 2020). At the same time, elites in the Western Balkans clearly committed to EU and NATO membership (with the exception of Serbia, which did not commit to membership in NATO) (Keil & Stahl 2015). As Rupnik (2011) has argued, this was another moment for the "Hour of Europe" in the region – a new commitment to political, social, and economic integration, that linked European integration of the region with a commitment to overcoming the results of the conflicts of the 1990s and early 2000s as well as committing to extensive European-driven state-building in countries such as Bosnia, Kosovo and North Macedonia (Keil & Arkan 2015).

The EU's enlargement framework towards the Western Balkans

The EU's enlargement policy is distinctly different from traditional foreign policy, as it aims to turn 'foreign policy' into 'domestic affairs' through the process of enlargement – aimed at the eventual accession of the candidate country. Hence, the EU expanded its policy portfolio for the Western Balkans to adapt to the challenges of the region, including conflict legacies, weak states, and ongoing neighbourly tensions. At times there were three EU Special Representatives (for Bosnia, North Macedonia, and Kosovo), a police mission in Bosnia (EUPM), an ongoing military mission in Bosnia (EUFOR), as well as a previous military mission in Macedonia, and the EU's largest civilian mission, the ongoing EU Rule of Law Mission in Kosovo (EULEX), which first launched in 2008. The EU's engagement in the region expanded further after 2009 when the Treaty of Lisbon strengthened the EU's foreign policy capabilities and the newly created European External Action Service took over many of the representations of the EU in the region.

The EU's enlargement policy, like its foreign policy more generally, is characterized by different frameworks, actors, and priorities, which are shifting over time. The framework for enlargement has evolved throughout the years from a more ad hoc approach for the first rounds of enlargement in the 1970s to a more complex and coordinated approach after the Treaty of Maastricht and the evolving enlargement framework in the context of the Copenhagen criteria for membership in the EU. The Copenhagen criteria define what conditions future member states of the EU must meet before they will be able to join. These are:

- political criteria: stability of institutions guaranteeing democracy, the rule of law, human rights, and respect for and protection of minorities;
- economic criteria: a functioning market economy and the capacity to cope with competition and market forces;
- administrative and institutional capacity to effectively implement the *acquis* and ability to take on the obligations of membership.

For the Western Balkans, the EU developed additional tools after 1999 in the Stabilization and Association Process as a result of a new Enlargement Strategy. This is defined by the EU as:

> The Stabilisation and Association Process is the European Union's policy towards the Western Balkans, established with the aim of eventual EU membership. Western Balkan countries are involved in a progressive partnership with a view of stabilising the region and establishing a free-trade area. The SAP sets out common political and economic goals although progress evaluation is based on countries' own merits. The SAP was launched in June 1999 and strengthened at the Thessaloniki Summit in June 2003 taking over elements of the accession process. (European Commission 2016).

The SAP builds on the EU's previous experience with enlargement and combines two main elements – stabilisation through engagement on the one side, and enlargement through economic and political reforms ensuring deeper integration on the other (Keil 2013). The new focus on post-conflict reconstruction and state-building has meant that the EU became much more active and directly involved in the Western Balkan countries. The current enlargement framework links financial incentives, trade preferences, and closer political cooperation with conditionality around the EU's own legal framework (the *acquis communautaire*), as well as additional conditionality in the areas of regional reconciliation, rule of law implementation and the commitment to international law and justice (Gordon 2009). The EU's motivation for enlargement is therefore also clearly articulated in the SAP – it links its own desire for a safe and secure neighbourhood with its foreign policy focus on stabilisation and regional integration in the post-Yugoslav states (Keil & Stahl 2022b).

The SAP treats each country in the region differently, and progress has been mixed. While Croatia was able to join in July 2013, Serbia and Montenegro are currently candidate countries negotiating their membership with the EU. North Macedonia and Albania are also candidate countries and have recently been given the green light for membership negotiations, although no official start for negotiations has been determined (as of November 2022). Bosnia became an official candidate for EU membership in 2022, while Kosovo remains a potential candidate. Both countries have signed a Stabilisation- and Association Agreement (SAA) with the EU, which formally binds them to the current enlargement framework.

The EU's Stabilisation and Association framework was initially seen as a useful policy guide to engage with a region that was characterised by state weakness and violent conflict in the 1990s. The combination of stabilising fragile states (and democracies) and integrating them into the EU was seen as the solution to the ongoing tensions and conflicts in the region. Yet, after 2009 more criticism of the Union's approach emerged as the EU's enlargement framework was contradicted by the policies of individual EU Member States (Dzankic et. al. 2019). The negotiations on the future of Kosovo in 2007 already demonstrated a split among EU Member States, and the complex accession of Croatia in 2013 as well as ongoing negotiations since then have demonstrated that the EU, despite its detailed enlargement framework, is often unable to speak with one voice. European policy in the post-Yugoslav states has instead been characterised by internal divisions and the Europeanisation of bilateral problems. Greece's name dispute with Macedonia, which hindered the country's progress towards EU membership after 2013, as well as Croatia's current unwillingness to support any further progress for Serbia due to historical tensions, and the fact that five EU member states have not recognized Kosovo's independence are all examples for the divisions within the EU over its approach in the region (Keil & Arkan 2015b, Blockmans 2007). The different interests of EU member states (both the large and influential ones such as Germany and France, which focus more strongly on EU internal reform, as well as smaller ones like Croatia and Slovenia, which continue to support further enlargement as it is in their geopolitical interests) are additionally problematic because they allow different elites in the post-Yugoslav states to exploit European disunity. For example, Serbian President Aleksandar Vucic has been criticized by the European Parliament for his authoritarian style of government but has consistently received support from certain EU member states, mainly from the Visegrad countries, who have celebrated him as a committed and strong leader with a pro-EU discourse. In addition, actors such as Russia have become major players in some countries in the region, exploiting European disunity and the lack of progress for their own interests (Bechev 2020).

Enlargement fatigue and a new focus on strategic accession?

The developments away from democratic governance within the region, a series of internal crises within the EU, and a shifting geopolitical framework in Southeastern Europe all explain the crisis of EU enlargement and growing enlargement fatigue. This enlargement fatigue is a more recent phenomenon of European integration literature and denotes an analytical term for the observation that a feeling of frustration with the process and the result of enlargement becomes more and more widespread. As an analytical observation, it could only appear some years after the Big Bang 2004 when the biggest enlargement ever was prestigiously celebrated on the lawns of Dublin castle. What is more, on the iconic media event of the Thessaloniki summit one year before, the European Union had promised the remaining Western Balkan states that they are entitled to join the club – the concrete accession date being only a matter of timing. Yet, after these huge political successes, a certain uneasiness crept into the process since the Croatian accession turned out to be rocky while burdened with the war criminal affair of Ante Gotovina and border issues with Slovenia. Furthermore, Romania and Bulgaria, not part of the Big Bang due to domestic reform problems, demanded favorable treatment and succeeded in getting a definite entry date (2007) without having accomplished the *acquis communitaire*. It was in the 2010s then when the progress reports of the European Commission increasingly revealed stagnation and even backlashes of democratic reforms in the Union's newest member states (Wunsch and Olszewska 2022). Further accessions looked so unlikely and far away that the formerly powerful job of the EU Commissioner for Enlargement was merged with responsibilities for the EU's neighbourhood policies. The portfolios were merged – despite the fact that the EU has always been stressing the strict co-existence of two separate political instruments of the EU's external relations.[3]

In the following, we will sketch an analytical model of enlargement fatigue which makes a social-constructivist argument fed with liberal elements. Interestingly, while enlargement fatigue is widely used as a descriptive term in the academic literature, it has so far not been properly conceptualised within a political science framework (see for example Economides 2020, O'Brennan 2014). Enlargement fatigue is understood here as a widespread feeling of discontent with the policy outcomes of the enlargement process. Reference point is the three-level ontology of enlargement which consists of the people in the Western Balkan states (level 1), the governments and their supporting elites in the Western Balkan states (level 2), and the Brussels actors – the Commission, Parliament, and EU Member States (level 3). In an ideal world, Brussels supports the Western Balkan governments in adopting the Copenhagen criteria while the governments transform the political systems to become liberal democracies. As a consequence, compliance with the criteria becomes credible and sustainable. The populations in the Western Balkans engage in a more and more lively civil society, make use of their participation chances, and vote for reformist pro-EU, liberal political parties. In this ideal type world, enlargement fatigue has hardly any place. The win-win-win game would only produce winners since the people can already reap the benefits of the ongoing process, be it cheap credit, selective access to the internal market, and visa liber-

---

3 Even on the website of DG NEAR – as it is called now (standing for European Neighbourhood Policy and Enlargement Negotiations), these two are strictly linked. See further: https://neigh bourhood-enlargement.ec.europa.eu/index_en

alizations. Now, how does enlargement fatigue come into play, and how does it link to the perception of crisis?

First, there is a natural delay factor based on the steadily growing gap between the increasing *acquis communautaire* on the one hand and the condition of weak states' bureaucracies on the other. When the first Northern enlargement occurred, there were only four years between the announcement and the actual accession (1969–1973). Before the Big Bang, the gap widened to around 10 years. For the Western Balkan states, 20 years already looked like wishful thinking. One could reasonably argue that extensive time frames over 20 years irritate the calculation of entire age cohorts in the Western Balkans societies since they would not be able to make EU accession a part of their personal career. Frustration comes as a natural consequence, and this has consequences in the attitudes towards the EU, the willingness to accept EU-oriented reforms, and in the electoral behavior of citizens of the Western Balkan countries.

Second, the role of governments in the Western Balkans and their supporting elites deserve attention. As Vachudová (2005: 15–16) has pointed out, in many East European countries post-Soviet elites carried the day after 1991 which show no intrinsic motivation for reforming their societies. Instead, they are interested in staying in power and pursuing their own interests, including access to financial and human resources for their benefit. Nationalist and partly anti-Western rhetoric divert from their political deeds putting the blame on Brussels, Berlin, or Paris for their alleged arbitrary acts and hypocrisy. By doing so, they inhibit idealist-minded and pro-European contenders in the domestic realm, while feeding the historical victimization discourse of the populations. Their nationalist rhetoric is often mixed with clear practices of state capture and authoritarian governance (Bieber 2020, Keil and Perry 2018). Vis-à-vis Brussels, though, they play a double game employing doublespeak: They pretend their pro-European attitudes, point to the rigour and depth of their reformative agenda, applaud the help from Brussels and demand more. Gergana Noutcheva (2012) uses the term "fake compliance" to describe this behavior – pretending to implement key reforms towards the EU while avoiding a commitment to fundamental change that would threaten the position of these elites at home. In these cases, the EU is often seen from two perspectives. On the one side, Brussels, Washington, and other external forces are often blamed for internal developments, conspiracies, and for political interference (Blanusa et.al 2021), while on the other side, the EU is seen as an important source of financial revenues and as a paymaster (Bretherton & Vogler 2006: 20), providing additional rents for their entourage and their cronies. The idealist implications of EU integration – democracy, peace, reconciliation, permanent conflict management, care for European common values– do not bother them much: They are the promoters and profiteers of enlargement fatigue. The crisis of EU enlargement is therefore also a crisis of governance in the Western Balkans – the lack of commitment by the EU to integrate these countries in a reasonable timeframe has enabled authoritarian elites to capture these states and use EU integration for their own purposes (Bieber 2018)

Third, the Brussels actors experience a growing unease as far as the validity and purpose of the Western Balkans enlargement are concerned. Here, enlargement fatigue means frustration with the stagnation of political processes in the region, be it democratic reforms, compliance with the Copenhagen criteria, or regional conflict resolution. Hence, since democratization takes so long and the region may degenerate into turmoil, democracy and stability may look like a trade-off: The EU, such a reading goes, must choose between unstable democratic regimes and stable undemocratic ones: the latter, "stabilocracy" has become the buzzword in the Brussels sphere. One more threat adds to this rationale. The "weakening pull of integration" triggers inference from outside. Regional and great powers beyond the West (Russia, China, Turkey, and the Gulf states) feel tempted to exploit the alleged emerging "power vacuum" in the Western Balkans (Keil & Stahl 2022, Bieber & Tzifakis 2020). They come up with political and economic incentives and motivate the Western Balkan governments for cooperation. In the eyes of EU elites, these incentives may go beyond usual cooperation for everyone's benefit. Rather, they are apt to deepen the autocratic tendencies in the region, weaken the "transformative power" (Grabbe 2006) of the EU and further dilute peace-building efforts.

Overall, these trends on all three levels contribute to the abandoning of the core principle of enlargement, the conditionality principle: It was meant to make the acceding states similar to the EU i.e.. "Europeanise" them. "Europeanise" means a *"process of constriction, diffusion and institutionalization of formal and informal rules, procedures, policy paradigms, styles, 'ways of doing things' and shared beliefs and norms"* (Radaelli 2003: 10). Recalling the EU relations with Serbia one has to acknowledge on the one hand to what extent the conditionality principle has been overburdened. It was used to hunt war criminals, bargain on Kosovo, and support seemingly pro-European politicians in election campaigns (Mladenov & Stahl 2015). On the other hand, the conditionality principle was extended and flanked considering the launch of an additional instrument for the Western Balkans before the candidate status within the Stabilisation and Association Process. Yet all of this, as outlined above, takes time and de facto increases the delay factor. This is why the EU now tends to dilute conditionality and sacrifice it for short-term stability gains pleasing Western Balkan population claims and signaling progress to EU publics. By doing so, the overall enlargement turns to "strategic accession" (Stahl 2013). This is a historical pattern of the enlargement process which made countries accede to the EU without having incorporated the *acquis* and without

having accepted the ideals of European integration (democracy, peace and reconciliation, solidarity). As a quick look at the historical patterns of such strategic accessions already reveals, the policy outcomes may be problematic and sometimes
disastrous. The partial idealisation of Denmark's membership in the EC as part of
the expansion in the 1970s led to the invention of treaty opt-outs in the 1990s as
part of the Maastricht Treaty to accommodate growing Euroscepticism in Denmark, while the normative glorification of British membership in the 1970s resulted in consistent conflicts between the UK and other Member States, as well as finally resulting in Brexit. Greece's non-compliance with the *acquis* at least
contributed to its de-facto bankruptcy causing the most severe integration crisis
in 2010, when the common currency union around the Euro was close to collapsing
and failing (Pisani-Ferry 2011). Cyprus' accession despite territorial non-saturation
led to diplomatic clashes with Turkey and the latter's turn away from Europe. Romania's and Bulgaria's premature entry motivates ongoing surveillance of the
Commission regarding their defects in democratization.

Despite ongoing enlargement fatigue in many European Member States, a new
turn to 'Strategic Enlargement' emerged in the wake of Russia's invasion of Ukraine. While there is no genuine willingness amongst EU Members to enlarge
and adopt, not least a country the size of Ukraine, the new geopolitical reality,
and the EU's commitment to supporting Ukraine in light of the aggression, resulted
in the EU awarding Ukraine the status as a candidate country. Hence, the EU declared Ukraine and Moldova candidates of the Union despite the fact that it had
refused to do so in peaceful times and had oftentimes criticised the deplorable
state of democratic reforms in both countries. Suffice it to say that candidacy status was most evidently granted for geopolitical, strategic reasons, and with no real
intention to integrate the countries any time soon. This hypocrisy will trigger negative effects on the Western Balkans since the turn to strategic accessions taught
the regional governments how to proceed: when the security situation deterio-
rates, the EU will be forced to grant new rewards (Stahl 2011). Moreover, countries
such as North Macedonia and Albania that have been waiting for membership
talks for several years now, and Bosnia, which had its application for candidate status rejected in 2019, will wonder how Ukraine and Moldova, without any progress
in political and economic reforms, have now levelled up with them in terms of EU
progress (or in Kosovo's case, even overtaken it). In the end, the conditionality
principle runs the risk of being reversed and thus "perverted" (ibid.): Only if the
EU delivers new incentives will the Western Balkans remain on the European
track. Yet some EU actors will not be willing to import further instability and autocratic structures via enlargement in the EU. This tension between strict conditionality and strategic accession will accompany future political debates on Western
Balkan enlargement.

Conclusion

EU enlargement is a story of success for a long time, but it is, as highlighted, also a story of crisis. A story of an external crisis that the EU reacted to, be it economic such as in the case of the UK and Ireland; democracy support as was the case in Spain, Portugal, and Greece or geopolitical as occurred with the "Big Bang" enlargement in 2004 and 2007. The most recent crises during the Yugoslav wars in the 1990s and the current war in Ukraine highlight how the EU enlargement framework has adapted over time to accommodate the challenges that these new potential EU Member States pose.

Whilst these adaption capabilities of the EU and its institutions should be recognised, it is also important to highlight that in recent years, the "Widening" and "Deepening" of the Union have both failed to substantially progress and the EU, as it is at the moment, is not ready to accommodate its current members and deal with challenges from within, including the serious threats to democracy and the rule of law in Member States such as Poland and Hungary (Bogdanowicz in Chapter 5; Bernhard 2021). Increasing Member State disunity over the progress of integration both through internal reform and external accession has also paralysed the Union in recent years. There is general agreement amongst the academic community and policymakers alike that the current enlargement framework through the Stabilisation and Association Process is not working anymore, however, a credible alternative that can bridge the divides within the EU has so far not emerged. Instead, the war in Ukraine, the deteriorating political situation in Bosnia and Herzegovina, and increased tensions between Serbia and Kosovo have all resulted in increased calls for strategic accession, less focused on the EU as a Union of norms and values such as human rights and democracy, and more centred around the idea that the EU needs to compete with other global powers in an increasingly hostile geopolitical environment. What this will mean for the actual process of enlargement remains to be seen, but it can easily be foreseen that it will have severe consequences for the EU as a Union as well as for its candidate countries.

References

Alexe, Dan (2014): 'The Juncker Commission: No Further EU Enlargement', in: *The New Europe*, 10 September 2014, available at: https://www.neweurope.eu/article/juncker-commission-no-further-eu-enlargement/ [Accessed: 12.12.2022].

Baker, Catherine (2015): *The Yugoslav Wars of the 1990s*, Palgrave MacMillan.

Bartlett, William (2008): *Europe's Troubled Region – Economic Development, Institutional Reform and Social Welfare in the Western Balkans*, Routledge.

Bechev, Dimitar (2020): 'Russia: Playing a Weak Hand Well?', in Florian Bieber & Nikos Tzifakis (eds.): *The Western Balkans in the World – Linkages and Relations with non-Western Countries.* Routledge, 187–204.

Belloni, Roberto (2020): *The Rise and Fall of Peacebuilding in the Balkans*, Palgrave MacMillan.

Bernhard, Michael (2021): 'Democratic Backsliding in Poland and Hungary', *Slavic Review*, 80:2, 685–607.

Bieber, Florian (2020): *The Rise of Authoritarianism in the Western Balkans*, Palgrave MacMillan.

Bieber, Florian (2018): 'Patterns of Competitive Authoritarianism in the Western Balkans', *East European Politics*, 34:3, 337–354.

Bieber, Florian & Tzifakis, Nikolaos (eds.) (2020): *The Western Balkans in the World – Linkages and Relations with Non-Western Countries*, Routledge.

Blanuch, Nebojsa, Denkovski, Ognjan, Fidanovski Kristijan & Gjoneska, Bilijana (2021): 'EU-Related Conspiracy Theory in the Western Balkans – Gravitating between rejecting and embracing Europe through Eurovilification and Eurofundamentalism', in Anders Önnerfors & Andre Krouwel (eds.): *Europe: Continent of Conspiracies – Conspiracy Theories in and about Europe*, Routledge, 185–213.

Blockmans, Steven (2007): *Tough Love: The European Union's Relations with the Western Balkans*, T.M.C. Asser Press.

Bretherton, Charlotte & John Vogler (2006): *The European Union as a Global Actor,* 2nd edition. Routledge, 2006.

Cooley, Laurence (2019): *The European Union's Approach to Conflict Resolution – Transformation or Regulation the Western Balkans*, Routledge.

Daalder, Ivo (2000): *Getting to Dayton – The Making of America's Bosnia Policy*, Brookings Institution Press.

Davies, Norman (2007): *Europe – East & West*, Pimlico.

Dinan, Desmond (2004): *Europe Recast – A History of European Union*, Palgrave MacMillan.

Dzankic, Jelena, Keil, Soeren & Kmezic, Marko (2019): 'Introduction: The Europeanisation of the Western Balkans', in Jelena Dzankic, Soeren Keil & Marko Kmezic (eds.): *The Europeanisation of the Western Balkans – A Failure of EU Conditionality?*, Palgrave MacMillan, 1–14.

Economides, Spyros (2020): 'From Fatigue to Resistance: EU enlargement and the Western Balkans', in: *The Dahrendorf Forum Working Paper No. 17*, Berlin. Available at: http://eprints.lse.ac.uk/104393/ [Accessed: 12.12.2022].

European Commission (2016)_ 'Stabilisation and Association Process' [online]. Available at: https://neighbourhood-enlargement.ec.europa.eu/enlargement-policy/glossary/stabilisation-and-association-process_en [Accessed: 01.12.2022].

European Commission (2003): 'Eu-Western Balkans Summit Thessaloniki' [online]. Available at: https://ec.europa.eu/commission/presscorner/detail/en/PRES_03_163 [Accessed: 20.11.2022].

Glenny, Misha (1996): *The Fall of Yugoslavia*, 3rd edition, Penguin Books.

Gordon, Claire (2009): 'The Stabilization and Association Process in the Western Balkans: An Effective Instrument of Post-conflict Management?', *Ethnopolitics*, 8:3–4, 325–340.

Grabbe, Heather (2006): *The EU's Transformative Power. Europeanization through Conditionality in Central and Eastern Europe*, Palgrave/Macmillan.

Holbrooke, Richard (1999): *To End a War,* The Modern Library.

Icener, Erhan & Phinnemore, David (2015): 'Building on Experience? EU enlargement and the Western Balkans', in Soeren Keil & Zeynep Arkan (eds.): *The EU and Member State Building – European Foreign Policy in the Western Balkans*, Routledge, 32–54.

Jachtenfuchs, Markus (2005): 'Deepening and Widening Integration Theory', in Frank Schimmelfennig & Ulrich Sedelmeier (eds.): *The Politics of European Union Enlargement – Theoretical Approaches*, Routledge, 279–286.

Juncos, Ana (2013): *EU Foreign and Security Policy in Bosnia – The Politics of Coherence and Effectiveness*, Manchester University Press.

Juncos, Ana & Perez-Solorzano Borragan, Nieves (2018): 'Enlargement', in Michelle Cini & Nieves Perez-Solorzano Borragan (eds.): *European Union Politics*, 6th edition, Oxford University Press, 166–180.

Ker-Lindsey, James, Armakolas, Ioannis, Balfour, Rosa & Stratulat, Corina (2017): 'The national politics of EU enlargement in the Western Balkans' *Southeast European and Black Sea Studies*, 17:4, 511–522.

Keil, Soeren (2013): 'Europeanization, State-Building and Democratization in the Western Balkans', *Nationalities Papers*, 41:3, 343–353.

Keil, Soeren & Arkan, Zeynep (2015): 'The Limits of Normative Power? EU Member State Building in the Western Balkans', in Soeren Keil & Zeynep Arkan (eds.): *The EU and Member State Building – European Foreign Policy in the Western Balkans*, Routledge, 15–31.

Keil, Soeren & Arkan, Zeynep (2015b): 'Theory and Practice of EU Member State Building in the Western Balkans', in Soeren Keil & Zeynep Arkan (eds.): *The EU and Member State Building – European Foreign Policy in the Western Balkans*, Routledge, 235–239.

Keil, Soeren & Perry, Valery (2018): 'The Business of State Capture in the Western Balkans: An Introduction', *Southeastern Europe*, 42:1, 1–14.

Keil, Soeren & Stahl, Bernhard (2015). 'Introduction: The Foreign Policies of Post-Yugoslav States', in Soeren Keil & Bernhard Stahl (eds.): *The Foreign Policies of the Post-Yugoslav States – From Yugoslavia to Europe*, Palgrave MacMillan, 3–17.

Keil, Soeren & Stahl, Bernhard (eds.) (2022): *A New Eastern Question? The Great Powers and the Post-Yugoslav States*, Ibidem.

Keil, Soeren & Stahl, Bernhard (2022b): 'The European Union and the Post-Yugoslav States – From Negligence to Dominance and Back?', in Soeren Keil & Bernhard Stahl (eds.): *A New Eastern Question? The Great Powers and the Post-Yugoslav States*, Ibidem, 83–104.

Mladenov, Mladen & Stahl, Bernhard (2015): 'Signaling right and turning left. The Response to EU conditionality in Serbia', in: Soeren Keil & Zeynep Arkan (eds.): *The EU and Member State Building. European Foreign Policy in the Western Balkans*, Routledge, 122–139.

Noutcheva, Gergana (2012): *European Foreign Policy and the Challenges of Balkan Accession – Conditionality, Legitimacy and Compliance*, Routledge.

O'Brennan, John (2014): 'On the Slow Train to Nowhere? The European Union, 'Enlargement Fatigue' and the Western Balkans', *European Foreign Affairs Review*, 19:4, 221–241.

Pisani-Ferry, Jean (2011): *The Euro Crisis and Its Aftermath*, Oxford University Press.

Radaelli, Claudio (2003): 'Europeanization of Public Policy', in Kevin Featherstone & Claudio Radelli (eds.): *The Politics of Europeanization*, Oxford University Press, 27–56.

Schuman Declaration, 9 May 1950, full text available at: https://european-union.europa.eu/principles-countries-history/history-eu/1945-59/schuman-declaration-may-1950_en [Accessed 12.12.2022].

Smeekens, Daan & Keil, Soeren (2022): 'Revisiting European Integration as a Federal Peacebuilding Project', in Carlos Fernacisco Molina del Pozo & Virginia Sladana Ortega (eds.): *Hacia La Contruccion De un Verdadero Proyecto Federal Para La Union Europa*, Colex, 177–197.

Silber, Laura & Little, Alan (1996): *The Death of Yugoslavia*, Penguin Books.

Stahl, Bernhard (1998): *Warum gibt es die EU und die ASEAN? Faktoren Weltpolitischer Institutionalisierung in Vergleichender Analyse*, Nomos.

Stahl, Bernhard (2011): 'Perverted conditionality – the Stabilisation and Association Agreement between the European Union and Serbia', *European Foreign Affairs Review*, 4:16, 465–487.

Stahl, Bernhard (2013): 'Another "strategic accession"? The EU and Serbia (2000–2010)', *Nationalities Papers* 41:3, 447–468.

Töglhofer, Thresia & Adelbahr, Cornelius (2017): 'Germany's two-pronged approach to EU enlargement in the Western Balkans', *Southeast European and Black Sea Studies*, 17:4, 523–539.

Vachudova, Milada Anna (2005): *Europe undivided. Democracy, leverage, and integration after Communism*, Oxford University Press.

Violi, Francesco (2021): *New Paths of Asymmetrical Federalism in the EU: The Eurozone as a Federal System*, PhD Thesis unpublished – Canterbury Christ Church University.

Wunsch, Natasha (2017): 'Between Indifference and Hesitation: France and EU Enlargement towards the Balkans', *Southeast European and Black Sea Studies*, 17:4, 541–554.

Wunsch, Natasha & Olszewska, Nicole (2022): 'From Projection to Introspection: Enlargement Discourses since the "Big Bang" Accession', *Journal of European Integration*, 44:7, 919–939.

Zhelyazkova, Asya, Damjanovski, Ivan, Nechev, Zoran & Schimmelfennig, Frank (2019): European Union Conditionality in the Western Balkans: External Incentives and Europeanisation', in Jelena Dzankic, Soeren Keil & Marko Kmezic (eds.): *The Europeanisation of the Western Balkans – A Failure of Conditionality?* Palgrave MacMillan, 15–38.

Simon Usherwood

9 The EU after Brexit: EU-UK relations and the latent crisis of withdrawal

Abstract: The UK represents an ambiguous object in the EU's near neighbourhood: simultaneously a major partner, closely aligned on many matters of policy and knowledgeable in how the EU works, and a persistent source of significant difficulties, railing against any stabilisation of a new relationship post-withdrawal. As much as the EU was able to rapidly produce a strong and coherent response to the UK's decision, and so turn a crisis into something much more manageable, this does not mean that the crisis aspects have been banished for good. Instead, the UK has carved out a new path for other member states, lowering the barriers to future withdrawals and establishing precedents of process and preference that might come to be used against the EU down the line. Moreover, the operationalisation of withdrawal also creates a moral hazard insofar as current member states will recognise that the EU cannot afford to lose another member this way, so increasing the leverage of any state seeking renegotiations of the terms of that membership. In this way, Brexit seems to provide two perspectives on crisis: the lived experience of a seemingly successful defence of core values with its containment and management of the UK, but also a pathway to a future crisis where such success cannot be guaranteed.

Introduction

In comparison to most of the other chapters in this volume, the issue of Brexit would appear to stand apart. While undoubtedly an unprecedented and highly significant event, the decision of a (large) member state to withdraw from the European Union (EU) was undertaken within a legal framework previously established by the foundational treaties, in line with relevant national and international obligations and has resulted in a new set of formal relations between the parties. Certainly, the process was longer, more difficult, and more acrimonious than might have been predicted, and equally, we have to note the range of outstanding questions on and around the EU-United Kingdom (UK) relationship. However, difficult politics and antagonistic relations are hardly the monopolies of this particular pairing, so why consider it here?

The answer to this is two-fold. Firstly, the opening phases of the process – from the 2015 British general election to late 2018 – saw a number of crisis-like features

https://doi.org/10.1515/9783110790337-010

in play for the EU. By announcing and then following through on a referendum on continuing membership, the British government challenged one of the core teleological norms of the system, namely that convergence and normalisation of membership grow over time: it was a crystallisation of the hitherto nebulous fears about the persistent democratic deficit in the EU's structures. The need to simultaneously handle the UK's withdrawal and to avoid any other state making the same decision placed the Union's central institutions in a critical and existential situation. As much as this initial crisis was closed off by a mixture of a positive reaffirmation of the value of membership by the remaining 27 members (hereafter EU27) and the self-sabotaging behaviour of the departing British, it is worth considering how this played out.

Secondly, and more significantly, Brexit matters because it has refigured the political landscape of European integration. However painfully and imperfectly it did it, and however many ongoing obligations it still faces, the UK still managed to navigate a way out of formal membership, turning the Article 50 TEU provision from a nominal right to withdraw into a substantive one, with process, procedure and benchmarked expectations. In so doing, the precedent has been set and so lowers the bar for it to happen again. Should that occur, the EU will find itself in even more of a crisis than it ever was over Brexit in 2016: as Oscar Wilde almost certainly would have put it, to lose one member state is a misfortune but to lose another is an unravelling of the system. As such, the greater significance of Brexit-as-crisis is in its potential, rather than its actuality.

With these points in mind, this chapter will briefly review how the UK came to leave the EU, before describing in more depth the contemporary relationship between the two, identifying those elements that will be most salient for the future development of this crisis space. It concludes with a discussion of the ways in which Brexit has and hasn't fitted into the language and action of crisis, both to make more sense of what is happening and to cast light on the wider questions raised by this volume.

Brief timeline of Brexit

Detailed histories of how the UK came to withdraw from the EU are plentiful, covering every aspect from the long run of the relationship (Wall 2020, Gowland 2016, MacShane 2016, Geddes 2013), to the strategy and tactics of eurosceptics, to engineer a referendum (Vasilopoulou 2016), to the comparative performance of the two campaigns (Glynn & Menon 2018, Evans & Menon 2017, Farrell & Goldsmith 2017) and the role of assorted individuals (Shipman 2016, Banks 2016). Rather than rehash all of this, the intention here is to draw out a number of important aspects that speak to the more general question of how and why a member state might come to decide, revisit – and then reject – membership. In this, three elements stand out: entanglement, self-image, and contingency.

Membership of the EU differs from any other international organisation in the breadth of its effects. The European Union is both wide and deep in penetration of member states' polities, politics, and policies; reaching into almost every aspect of the public sphere and – exceptionally – into significant parts of the private realm too. This is a function of its incremental expansion over time, as members decide that the multi-purpose constitutional and institutional frameworks are useful mechanisms for further collaborations, even if this has not been the automatic process of spillover that neo-functionalism once proclaimed, whereby integration in one area would create incentives to integrate into related areas (Niemann 2021, Rosamond 2005). The legal innovations of primacy (EU law coming before national provisions) and direct effect (citizens, rather than just member states, being able to use EU law) also created a channel of popular involvement and individual rights-holding. Scharpf's notion of entanglement (1988, 2006) was initially conceived as a way of explaining blockages to policy development, but it rested on the prior interconnection of national and European systems. In Laffan et al.'s (2013) phrase, nation states become member states, recasting their territory, function and identity along the way.

Much eurosceptic campaigning in the UK from the 1990s onwards was about the ways in which 'Brussels' was stealthily shaping domestic decisions and options, creeping beyond the 'Common Market' that those campaigners argued had been originally signed up to (Vasilopoulou 2013). The frequent trope of being 'shackled to the EU' not only presented the latter as a deadweight, holding the UK back but also captured the sense of being held firmly by the bonds of membership (Daddow 2019). In the absence of a strong governmental education (or even promotion) of the nature of membership, such narratives were able to take hold and frame the long-term debate about the UK's position within the EU system, notably through the persistent print media criticism both of 'Europe' and of successive British governments' efforts. More generically, feelings of disconnection and disenfranchisement in a remote system are found across the Union (e,g, Kratochvil & Svchara 2019, Hooghe & Marks 2009, Kohler-Koch & Rittberger 2007).

Paradoxically, it has been in Brexit that the depth of that entanglement has been fully exposed, albeit not in the way that the previous debate had proposed. The latent benefits of regulatory alignment for traders, policymakers and citizens only really came to the fore as that alignment was lost: the diffuse gains that came from no border controls with other EU member states, or from stable regulatory requirements for public procurement, or from no roaming charges on mobile telephony, all only gained public traction and support after 2016 (Curtice 2018, but also note Sorace & Hobolt 2021). This is relevant more broadly because it shows the potentially structural imbalance facing all member states in trying to convince citizens that the changes that come with membership are worth paying for the political and economic efficiencies that they create.

This brings us to the second key element of self-image. Undoubtedly, the UK was the archetype of an 'othered' member state, seeing itself as apart from the EU even as it participated (and also sought to lead (George 1998)). Even if the objective foundations of that otherness are highly debatable – all member states have some form of uniqueness about their histories or geographies or cultures – where the UK did stand apart was in the extent to which such narratives formed a central part of political and public discourse: Young's (1999) excellent history sets out this Arthurian-Shakespearian-Churchillian complex in ways that still feel very familiar, despite being written long before Brexit was a glint in most campaigners' eyes.

Otherness matters here because it lays the foundations for a political discussion about being outside the EU: the logic is no more complex than that the UK was once great, but hasn't been great while it's been inside the EU, so leaving is the pathway to regaining greatness (e. g. Hannan 2016). This is a classic populist refrain – paradise regained – but no less evocative for it: the role of the Second World War and how Britain won it [sic] plays a key part in the political imaginarium (Stratton 2019, Beaumont 2017). It also helps to explain the strong/weak paradox of much Brexit rhetoric; the way in which the UK was under the thumb of the EU, made to do whatever the faceless 'eurocrats' wanted, but by leaving the organisation those same oppressors would suddenly be forced to accept the will of the British, who would now be able to get whatever concessions they liked from an EU that would be only too glad to comply. This political equivalent of the internet's 'one weird trick' obviously failed to account for the power that the UK always held to exercise its right to withdraw, but such logical inconsistencies counted for little in this creation of a vision of a viable alternative outside of the EU.

But such visions count for little without opportunity and contingent events. To make the obvious point, as much as the UK was the home of euroscepticism in the 1990s and 2000s, the notion of a project to secure British withdrawal from the EU was a marginal one, as attention focused primarily on avoiding membership of the single currency and on reform to limit political integration (Tournier-Sol 2016, Spiering 2004). The shift in the mid-2000s to calling for a referendum on membership was a function of the Constitutional Treaty ratification process and a recognition of the rhetorical value of democracy as a way to overcome the weight of the status quo (Usherwood 2005). Likewise, David Cameron's commitment to hold a vote, made in 2013, was done at a point when it looked unlikely to be followed through, hedged as it was with various conditions (Daddow 2015). As for the role of political opportunists, who saw the 2016 referendum as a means to advance their own agendas and careers, much has been written elsewhere (Shipman 2016, Ryan 2016).

In summary, membership in the EU is not the one-way trip that it is typically seen as. As Neunreither (1998) puts it, European integration is a system of governance without opposition: while it is very good at building a broad and flexible consensus, it is not very good at allowing those outside the consensus a way back inside. Over time, that means that there is an accumulation of individuals and groups who feel not only poorly served on particular points but also excluded from the process as a whole, turning their critiques and criticisms into something more structural. The entanglement that membership produces is therefore consequential, especially in terms of national and European political management of popular engagement: the case has to be made actively, particularly if other narratives about alternative paths exist. As the British case has demonstrated, there is not a straight path to withdrawal, but rather a continuous set of decision points that might produce – more accidentally than intentionally – a situation where withdrawal is both possible and desirable. Consequently, it is critical here to note that Brexit was at least as much about the nature of the EU as it was about the nature of the UK.

The key features of the contemporary EU-UK relationship

In many ways, Brexit is a salutary tale for the EU. From being a generally engaged member state (albeit with regular noises off) in 2015, the UK became an antagonistic third country five years later, unwilling to even confirm its willingness to stand by its international treaty obligations. Such a rapid decline in relations is made all the more remarkable by the nominal maintenance of liberal democracy in the UK: the corrosion of standards in political life over the post-referendum period has not been nearly so marked as in any number of other EU neighbours (or even some of its current member states, for that matter).

This poor state of affairs has much of its source in the UK. More particularly, it is a manifestation of the persistent British failure to identify or action a comprehensive and constructive European policy: arguably no post-war British government has been able to devise an approach towards its continental neighbours that goes beyond crisis management (Usherwood 2015). Just as Cameron's offer of a referendum on membership was driven by the needs of party-political management, so too has the leitmotif of the negotiations of both the Withdrawal Agreement (WA) and the Trade & Cooperation Agreement (TCA) been one of the ways the

UK tries to avoid problems (Usherwood 2021, Gifford 2020). Theresa May's decision ahead of the WA negotiations to not seek participation in either the EU's single market or its customs union made sense in reaffirming her credentials with back-bench MPs worried about her ideological commitment, but it closed down a wide range of options that might have made other questions – such as Northern Ireland's status, or maintenance of trading access – less problematic (Figueira & Martill 2021, Schnapper 2021). Indeed, the belated recognition of Northern Ireland's particular problems and the unwillingness to accept the logic required by the assorted legal obligations of the Belfast/Good Friday Agreement, the EU's constitutional treaties, the World Trade Organization and others should only further highlight the absence of either planning or flexibility in Whitehall (Hayward 2021, Phinnemore 2020).

The negative definition of British objectives has also tended to privilege a mode of interaction that focuses on the non-resolution of problems rather than practical and equitable solutions. Since there is an understanding within the British government of the consequences of any particular form of resolution and there is also a political calculation that it is politically more expedient to continue blaming the EU as the source of difficulties than it is to try to win over public opinion to any settled model, it, therefore, makes (internal) sense to keep the points of conflict alive rather than close them down. This high-tension model of semi-permanent instability is seen in the various pushes to enact domestic legislation – the Internal Market Bill, the Northern Ireland Protocol Bill – to disapply parts of the Protocol and in the non-implementation of in-coming border checks on goods from the EU (Fabbrini 2022), as well as in the persistent and inflammatory rhetoric for senior government figures from (successive) Prime Ministers downwards. While the instability never raises to the level of a flat-out crisis – mainly because the British government always serves at the last minute – this does not mean future conflicts will be actively avoided. That this model is intrinsically unstable and liable to produce bigger problems over time is beside the point: the intention is simply not to be the one to have to be responsible for shouldering the various costs of the situation.

Understandably, this chaotic British approach has strongly shaped the EU's policy. This latter has been highly defensive, focused on protecting essential interests, ensuring effective enforcement mechanisms and leaving the door open for future cooperation, but only on strict terms. The rapid formation of a formal EU position on the UK's withdrawal – underpinned by a declaration from the Union's presidents the day after the 2016 vote (European Council 2016) – stands in stark contrast to the British uncertainty about the purpose of it all. This partly reflects the much better preparation that the EU had undertaken, but even more, it was a function of the existential threat that withdrawal created: as outlined above if one member state could decide to leave, then so could others (Jacobs 2018).

The chopping-up of the process into withdrawal issues – those areas that needed to be resolved before the UK left – and future relationship issues – what might be done after it had departed – was an early and key EU demand; one that appears increasingly justified with time, albeit not entirely to the EU's satisfaction. The questions of citizens' rights, financial liabilities and the Irish/Northern Irish border stood apart from whether the UK might want to continue economic or political co-operation and so they formed the heart of the very limited agenda in the Article 50 process, even if that also exposed Theresa May to a ratification process for the WA that ultimately brought her down (Schnapper 2021). Similarly, while the British went for a very minimal line in requests for the TCA negotiations, the EU still sought to create an institutional framework that could accommodate further work together, as well as an enhanced set of dispute settlement mechanisms that crosslinked with the WA (Usherwood 2021). More informally, the EU has also blocked the UK's full participation in the Horizon Europe programme of research funding, as a sign of its concerns over the challenges to the Northern Ireland Protocol, reflecting its interconnected view of the WA and TCAtreaties (see Gibney 2020 for wider implications for UK researchers).

Crucially, the EU has also devoted much attention to trying to manage the internal effects of Brexit. Recognising that the pressures within the UK that contributed to the Leave vote were not unique to that country, the EU27 Bratislava summit in September 2016 focused on ways in which popular engagement and trust could be enhanced (Jacobs 2018). While this led to the Conference on the Future of Europe, the unwillingness in 2022 to translate its findings into a concrete plan of reforms (including treaty amendments) rather weakened the effect (see Kinski's chapter). Likewise, the renewed focus on the Rule of Law can also be understood as a way of reaffirming the value of membership, albeit with question marks about how far it is willing to push sanctions under Article 7 TEU (see Bogdanowicz's chapter). Part of the explanation for the non-follow-through on these initiatives lies in the highly visible knots that the UK tied itself into from 2017 onwards: eurosceptics in other member states who had held up the referendum result as a model for their own country's exit rapidly disowned an option that even the most generous observer would struggle to describe as easy or beneficial to the UK. In that sense, the critique that the EU's negotiators sought to 'punish' the UK for leaving – both as a penalty on the British themselves and as a warning to other potential withdrawers – is wide of the mark: the punishment was first and foremost one that was self-inflicted (Beaumont 2019).

The upshot of these two stances is that trust either way is very low. With the significant contraction of points of contact between the two sides, now that the UK is no longer structurally participating in EU business and the WA/TCA institutions are only operating at a minimal frequency (Foster 2022), the opportunities to rebuild that trust look few and far between. Indeed, even if there was a desire to actively build trust, that would require the UK to unambiguously step back from its efforts to disapply the Protocol and then to unambiguously implement all provisions of the WA and TCA in a persistent and durable way that would make the EU confident about British willingness to accept obligations under international law: this seems unlikely under any Conservative government at present, regardless of leader. Even where circumstance has generated opportunities for cooperation – notably over Ukraine (Blockmans 2022) – neither side has been willing to build on that positive experience, especially on the British side. As such, the prognosis for future relations looks relatively bleak, especially if there is no change of party in government. Even if a Labour government were to be returned in a general election in 2023/4, it is not clear that things would be significantly better in material terms, given the unwillingness of the Labour leadership under Keir Starmer to seek closer ties, for fear of being accused of trying to 'undo' Brexit (Hayton 2022).

Brexit as a crisis?

The picture painted above is not a positive one: there are significant and persistent problems at play that do not appear to be readily resolvable. However, this is not the same as saying this is a crisis. As outlined above, it is perhaps more useful to think of Brexit as a two-fold case of how crises can emerge for the EU: one contingently, the other more structural.

The argument set out above is that Brexit was not inevitable, but rather a product of particular circumstances. Those circumstances were more readily realised in the British case, but neither necessarily so nor only possibly in the UK. The second step of this is that the outcome – withdrawal – contains key features of crisis within it. The rest of this section will explore these elements.

The EU exists as a function of its members. As much as integration theory has argued over this question for decades, the effect of interlinking national and European organisational structures and of switching from the Monnet method to a more regulatory model has been that the EU level still necessarily requires the presence of member states to provide a key source of legitimacy, to make and implement key decisions and to supply resources (Moravcsik 2013 is a starting point).[1]

---

1 The Monnet method – named for Jean Monnet, one of the key figures in post-war moves to integrate – aimed to produce deep, but narrow integration, moving competences from national to European bodies (the Common Agricultural Policy is the main contemporary example). While producing deep connections, it was also rather unwieldy and inflexible, hence the move towards

Put differently, the removal of member states from the EU would leave a non-existent organisation, legally or politically.

Throughout its history, the Union has been in a position where European states have overwhelmingly wanted to become members. This was true in its initial Cold War phase where it rapidly became the logical destination for those Western European states not bound by their relations with the Soviet Union; it was also true after 1989 when it gained status as a symbol of modernity and democracy for post-Communist societies (Mattli & Plümper 2002). Those that did join almost universally took their membership as a permanent choice: the compromises and concessions made to achieve accession were to be managed away as members of the club, with all the new benefits that membership conferred, economic and political. Even the case of Greenland, exiting the then-European Economic Community in 1983, was an extreme outlier, given the very limited participation it had in joint policies (Harhoff 1983). Much more typical is the situation in 2022, with Ukraine, Moldova, and Georgia pushing hard to join the queue to accede by simultaneously affirming their liberal democratic and free-market credentials and securing protection against (very active) Russian aggression.

In this sense, losing members was never a real concern of the EU, despite the obvious existential crisis that such an event would create. As discussed above when considering entanglement, a key reason for this was that for most politicians the weight of the status quo was enough to ensure that the question of withdrawal was never that viable: the implications of trying to unpick all of the ways in which membership reshaped national structures, processes, and preferences were seen as evidence enough that they required no real justification. Moreover, with time the expansion of EU competences meant that leaving the organisation would simply result in a state finding itself subject to the 'Brussels effect': in order to access the highly desirable EU market, non-member states would align their regulation and practices to the EU's, thus making any notion of 'taking back control' (to use an obvious phrase) illusory (Bradford 2020).

Brexit has changed that, permanently. The introduction of Article 50 TEU in the Lisbon Treaty was intended to underline the non-coercive nature of membership, rather than to be an invitation to leave that anyone would genuinely take up (see Anthanassiou 2016). Its provisions turned out to be less than completely clear to all involved speaking to the rhetorical function for which it was intended (Frantziou & Eeckhout 2017). However, those lacunae have now been swept away by the operationalisation required to complete the UK's withdrawal. Leaving is no longer a no-

---

focusing on creating broad frameworks of sharing rules and regulations, within which member states could find approaches that met their needs.

tional right that member states have, but a concretised process (Usherwood *et al.* 2017).

Importantly, the realisation of withdrawal-in-practice has meant two key things. Firstly, it has established the precedent. No matter how difficult and painful Brexit might have been, the UK ultimately was able to secure its policy of withdrawal. In so doing, it swept away a lot of the uncertainty about how this would work in practice, which in turn lowers the barriers to other states making the same decision in the future, all things being equal. The model of the process and the roles of the various parties is now established, and member states can better evaluate how that might work in their individual cases: that the UK did not try to do (and was clearly not that interested in even trying to do so) is irrelevant in this context, since it is the creation of a template of action that matters.

Similarly, the case of Brexit has also established the baseline expectations of the European Union and its member states. This marking out of preferences and red lines is necessarily case-specific (no other member state would have an equivalent situation like Northern Ireland), but in terms of much of the content, there is an obvious carry-over. As with the precedent over process, the establishment of preferences also lowers the barriers for future cases, since it makes it harder for the EU to introduce new requirements either in the withdrawal negotiations or the negotiations for a future relationship, especially if the departing state has developed a more coherent plan for post-membership relations than existed (and exists) in the UK, which is both logically and politically highly likely.

The reduction in barriers to future withdrawals means that this sets up the potential for a future crisis. Despite the firm efforts of the EU to not portray the UK's withdrawal as being a reflection of the particular British relationship with 'Europe', it is possible to place that country in a separate category, not least by virtue of its numerous opt-outs from various common policies while inside. Its geographical location at the edge of the continent and its extensive global presence also gives some objective weight to the exceptionalist rhetoric that drove the campaigning in 2016. But it is precisely because of those particularities that if another member state were to leave then the existential challenge would be that much greater. None of the EU27 has that same combination of opt-outs, location, and global ambition: consider how Sweden, often held up as the next most likely member to leave, has sought to pull itself closer into international organisations with its move to join NATO (Alberque & Schreer 2022).

Others have considered the matter of who else might be in line to leave next (Gastinger 2019): more importantly, it is worth underlining how another withdrawal might be much more problematic for the EU. The next to go might well be a participant in the Schengen area or the Eurozone or both. In the former case, this will complicate post-membership economic arrangements if the state does not want to be maintaining full single-market access. In the latter, removing a state from the Euro would be both hugely complex and would establish a precedent and a mechanism for others to follow: any re-run of the Eurozone crisis might play out very differently in those circumstances, as the pressures to eject members would now have a pathway to being achieved.

This structural crisis may be latent, but it still has practical effects now. The analysis of EU leaders in 2016 – that this was significantly about the way member states react to being members – is reflected in much of the analysis of the challenges of legitimacy, accountability, and democracy (see Kinski's chapter). The highly problematic efforts to address those issues are equally clear, hindered as they are by the difficult balancing act of interests that characterises the EU's governance (Tsebelis & Garrett 2001). The easing of withdrawal outlined above reinforces the need to make further, reinforced attempts to draw citizens into the process and move beyond a simple output legitimacy model.

To make the obvious point, this is a crisis-to-be with a ticking clock. In the run-up to the 2016 referendum and its immediate aftermath, it was evident that the withdrawalist strand of Eurosceptic rhetoric had taken some root beyond the UK. This was a notable departure from earlier points, where even the most ardent critics of European integration in other member states had spoken of the need for structural reform of the EU rather than of leaving if that were impossible (Brack & Startin 2015). The political advance of the UK Independence Party (UKIP) as a force in British politics from the late 2000s, with its central anti-membership message, probably played a contributory factor in encouraging others such as Marine Le Pen and the Sweden Democrats to adopt a more overt framing of withdrawal in campaign messages (Persson *et al.* 2019, Ivaldi 2018). That encouragement ended abruptly in late 2016, as the scale of the task, the rapid emergence of British confusion about next the steps, and the strength of pro-membership reaction across the UK and the EU27 made it seem a much less attractive option.

However, the collapse of withdrawalist rhetoric does not mean that it will not return. With the UK now out of the EU and with no clarity about the extent of the economic costs, it is simple to imagine a point in the relatively near future where campaigners in the EU27 return to withdrawal as an option. The UK might have been damaged economically and politically by its choice, but it has not collapsed, and it is easy enough to paint a picture of various relative successes for the country (much as British politicians have been doing). The Covid pandemic of 2020–21 provided a much bigger economic shock to all economies and made it very hard to identify any clear signals about the effects of Brexit on its own: the very selective use of data on the speed of securing access to vaccines or on relative levels of Covid infections by British politicians also was tied into claims about the beneficial flexibilities produced by withdrawal. More generally, any negative news (either absolute or merely relative to the UK) about the EU or its member states has been seized upon as evidence of why the country was right to vote to leave: witness how a British trade deal with Australia was pushed through rapidly to allow a comparison to much slower EU-Australian talks, even if the terms of the latter are likely to be much less favourable to Australian preferences (House of Commons Library 2022). The inference that such successes were only possible because of Brexit will be made, even where this is evidently not the case, even as the costs and inconveniences of membership remain. Those pushing once more for their state's withdrawal will make the argument that they can navigate Article 50 TEU much more smoothly and with far fewer costs than the UK: partly because of the lower barriers mentioned above and also that these campaigners will claim to have a clear vision of what they seek, unlike the British. Moreover, they will count on the support of the British themselves, who will welcome the affirmation of their choice.

Such a scenario should not stretch the imagination too much. In a context of continuing low popular knowledge about the nature and operation of the EU, and little active work by national politicians to sell the advantages of membership, the weight of the status quo is probably less than most imagine. In this, Brexit reflects the more general weaknesses of the EU's system, in that the entanglement of many parties in joint policy-making and dense interaction also creates an impression that breaking out of such ties is neither desirable nor possible and so there is no great need to make an active case for why integration is a worthwhile activity. With most citizens much more deeply attached to their national political orders, the disconnection of elites and the public grows wider – especially when populist critics use the gap to stoke resentment – setting up the conditions for future tensions and crises (see Taylor 2007 and Mair 2013 for less-optimistic views on how this plays out). Paradoxically, the actual Brexit crisis of 2016 might have contributed to this situation.

23 June 2016 was undoubtedly a crisis for the EU: it went against the dominant logic of integration, namely that being in a club is better than being out. It also required strong, rapid, and coherent action from the collective institutions of the organisation, both European and national. As already mentioned, it got exactly that, from the morning after the vote through to the present. The level of cooperation and cohesion among institutions and member states in both the WA and TCA negotiations has been exceptional, by any measure (Chopin & Lequesne 2021, Schuette 2021, Jensen & Kelstrup 2019): with the sole (and very brief) exception of Spain raising Gibraltar's status in 2018, there has been no occasion where a member state has worked against the central line adopted in late June 2016 (Fabbrini 2020). Even critical members such as Hungary and Poland have used the matter as an opportunity to say nice things about the EU and the way it works (Brusen-

bauch Meislová 2021, Csehi & Kaniok 2021). The strong consensus around the value of membership and the need to protect it has endured even into the post-withdrawal phase, where national interests might have been expected to pull in different directions: none of the EU27 have ever questioned the need to make exceptional efforts to protect Irish interests in Northern Ireland nor tried to bypass the Commission in making bilateral deals with London.

Such a strong and unified response was undoubtedly a factor in turning the crisis into a problem, albeit not as big a factor as British aimlessness. But it also raises a form of moral hazard for the future. If protecting membership is such a strong norm, and avoiding another withdrawal is imperative, then it might also be expected that member states will be more willing to make concessions to stop a member state from heading for the door. A much-overlooked part of the Brexit story was Cameron's effort to secure commitments from other member states that would head off the need for withdrawal (Vasilopoulou & Keith 2019, Smith 2016). Poor expectation management on his part meant that this renegotiation was always likely to fail, but Cameron was right to see that the EU was more likely to bend for a member trying to stay in than it would be for one already on its way out. Other member states might take the lesson of this to be that a more careful selection of demands and/or threats to initiate moves to withdrawal might be effective in gaining what they want.

Conclusions

In the context of this present volume, Brexit is an instructive case for conceptualising crisis. It is simultaneously a model of how to handle and contain a crisis situation, an example of how crises can emerge unexpectedly, and a harbinger of troubles to come. Importantly, it highlights the role of contingent factors in crisis formation and resolution: structural issues might point in a general direction, but they do not automatically produce situations, which instead result from much more localised and unpredictable actions. As a result, a necessary corollary is that the EU needs to be proactive in managing and forestalling those situations which might potentially produce future crises; and this is more than is the case for other political systems, because of the underlying weaknesses in its legitimacy.

In a sense, the EU was fortunate to have the UK be the first member state to withdraw. The lack of strategic intent, the chaos of its politics, and the apparent desire of some British politicians to distance themselves from anything involving the word 'Europe' all made it easier to place the UK as an 'other' in the long and difficult negotiations between 2017 and 2020. The egregious attempts to break with the basic precepts of international law in order to wriggle out of commitments made only raised more general questions about the UK as a good faith actor. Such behaviour facilitated internal EU cohesion and burnished its image with the public as a responsible and valuable body. But such distancing will not be nearly so simple with another withdrawal, especially if that country's leadership plays a more subtle game of talking up commonalities rather than differences.

Part of what makes a crisis is how it is understood and received. The strength and depth of response by the EU in 2016 were central in managing it down into something less critical: the contrast with the UK's response should only magnify this point. But that EU response was not a given and it is likely that should withdrawal raise itself as an option in the future it will not take the same form as it did with the UK. Many lessons were drawn from this experience, but there is little evidence that lasting ways of addressing root causes have taken hold, much less had an effect. Brexit overturned some of the basic assumptions about integration, which should invite the EU's leaders and stakeholders to consider what else they take for granted, the better that they might be able to protect what they value.

References

Alberque, William & Benjamin Schreer (2022): 'Finland, Sweden and NATO Membership', *Survival*, 64:3, 67–72.

Athanassiou, Phoebus L. (2016): 'Reflections on the interpretation, scope and practical application of Article 50 TEU.', in Allen Franklin, Elena Carletti, Joanna Gray & Mitu Gulati (eds.): *Filling the Gaps in Governance*, European University Institute, 89–106.

Banks, Arron (2016): *The bad boys of Brexit: tales of Mischief, Mayhem & Guerrilla Warfare in the EU referendum campaign*, Biteback Publishing,

Beaumont, Paul (2019): 'Brexit and EU Legitimation: Unwitting Martyr for the cause?', *New Perspectives*, 27:3, 15–36.

Beaumont, Paul (2017): 'Brexit, Retrotopia and the perils of post-colonial delusions', *Global Affairs*, 3:4/5, 379–390.

Blockmans, Steven (2022): 'Why the Ukraine crisis should push the UK and EU into a tighter embrace on security policy', CEPS Policy Contribution, February 2022, available at: http://aei.pitt. edu/103818/1/CEPS-PB2022-03_Why-the-Ukraine-crisis-should-push-the-UK-and-EU-into-a-tighter-embrace-on-security-policy.pdf, accessed 24 August 2022.

Brack, Nathalie & Nicholas Startin (2015): 'Introduction: Euroscepticism, from the margins to the mainstream', *International political science review*, 36:3, 239–249.

Bradford, Anu (2020): *The Brussels effect: How the European Union rules the world*, Oxford University Press.

Brusenbauch Meislová, Monika & Balázs Szent-Iványi (2021): 'Exploitation opportunities for distant crises: Political framings of Brexit in the Czech Republic and Hungary', *Problems of Post-Communism*, early access.

Chopin, Thierry & Christian Lequesne (2021): 'Disintegration reversed: Brexit and the cohesiveness of the EU27', *Journal of Contemporary European Studies*, 29–3, 419–431.

Csehi, Robert I. & Petr Kaniok (2021): 'Does politicization matter? Small states in East-Central Europe and the Brexit negotiations', *East European Politics and Societies,* 35:1, 136–155.

Curtice, John (2018): 'Buyer's Remorse: Has Britain Changed Its Mind on Brexit?', *Political Insight* 9:1, 12–15.

Daddow, Oliver (2019): 'GlobalBritain™: the discursive construction of Britain's post-Brexit world role', *Global Affairs,* 5:1, 5–22.

Daddow, Oliver (2015): 'Strategising European Policy: David Cameron's Referendum Gamble', *The RUSI Journal,* 160:5, 4–10.

European Council (2016): 'Statement by the EU leaders and the Netherlands Presidency on the outcome of the UK referendum', press release, 24 June 2016, available at: https://www.con silium.europa.eu/en/press/press-releases/2016/06/24/joint-statement-uk-referendum/, accessed 24 August 2022.

Evans, Geoffrey & Anand Menon (2017): *Brexit and British politics,* John Wiley & Sons.

Fabbrini, Federico, ed. (2022): *The Law and Politics of Brexit Volume IV: The Protocol on Ireland/Northern Ireland,* Oxford University Press.

Fabbrini, Federico, ed. (2020): *The Law & Politics of Brexit: Volume II: The Withdrawal Agreement,* Oxford University Press.

Farrell, Jason & Goldsmith, Paul (2017): *How to lose a referendum: The definitive story of why the UK voted for Brexit,* Biteback Publishing.

Figueira, Filipa & Benjamin Martill (2021): 'Bounded rationality and the Brexit negotiations: why Britain failed to understand the EU', *Journal of European Public Policy,* 28:12, 1871–1889.

Foster, Peter (2022): 'Business groups frustrated at UK-EU gridlock on post-Brexit trade', Financial Times, 17 July 2022.

Frantziou, Eleni & Piet Eeckhout (2017): 'Brexit and Article 50 TEU: A constitutionalist reading', *Common Market Law Review,* 54:3, 695–733.

Gastinger, Markus (2019): 'Brexit! Grexit? Frexit? Considerations on how to explain and measure the propensities of member states to leave the European Union', Robert Schuman Centre for Advanced Studies Research Paper No. RSCAS 2019/85, available at https://papers.ssrn.com/sol3/papers.cfm?abstract_id=3489132, accessed 24 August 2022.

Geddes, Andrew (2013): *Britain and the European Union,* Bloomsbury Publishing.

George, Stephen (1998): *An awkward partner: Britain in the European Community,* Oxford University Press.

Gibney, Elizabeth (2020): 'Brexit is happening: what does it mean for science?', *Nature,* 577:7792: 608–609.

Gifford, Chris (2020): *The making of Eurosceptic Britain: Identity and economy in a post-imperial state,* Routledge.

Glynn, Jack & Anand Menon (2018): 'Brexit', in Philip Cowley & Dennis Kavanagh (eds.) (2018): *The British General Election of 2017,* Palgrave Macmillan, 21–40.

Gowland, David (2016): *Britain and the European Union,* Routledge.

Hannan, Daniel (2016): *What Next: How to get the best from Brexit,* Head of Zeus.

Harhoff, Frederik (1983): 'Greenland's withdrawal from the European Communities', *Common Market L. Rev.* 20, 13–33.

Hayward, Katy (2021): 'The new trading 'relationship' between Great Britain and Northern Ireland: Why, what and how', *The Political Quarterly,* 92:2, 360–364.

Hayton, Richard (2022): 'Brexit and party change: The Conservatives and Labour at Westminster', *International Political Science Review,* 43:3, 345–358.

Hooghe, Liesbet & Gary Marks (2009): 'A postfunctionalist theory of European integration: From permissive consensus to constraining dissensus', *British journal of political science*, 39:1, 1–23.

House of Commons Library (2022): 'UK-Australia Free Trade Agreement', Research Briefing, 15 July 2022, available at: https://commonslibrary.parliament.uk/research-briefings/cbp-9484/, accessed 24 August 2022.

Ivaldi, Gilles (2018): 'Contesting the EU in times of crisis: The Front National and politics of Euroscepticism in France', *Politics*, 38:3, 278–294.

Jacobs, Francis B. (2018): *The EU after Brexit: Institutional and policy implications*. Springer.

Jensen, Mads Dagnis & Jesper Dahl Kelstrup (2019): 'House united, house divided: explaining the EU's unity in the Brexit negotiations', *Journal of Common Market Studies*, 57:S1, 28–39.

Kohler-Koch, Beate & Berthold Rittberger (eds.) (2007): *Debating the democratic legitimacy of the European Union*, Rowman & Littlefield.

Kratochvíl, Petr & Zdeněk Sychra (2019): 'The end of democracy in the EU? The Eurozone crisis and the EU's democratic deficit', *Journal of European Integration*, 41:2, 169–185.

Laffan, Brigid, O'Donnell, Rory & Smith, Michael (2013): *Europe's experimental union: Rethinking integration*, Routledge.

MacShane, Denis, (2016): *Brexit: How Britain Left Europe*, Bloomsbury Publishing.

Mair, Peter (2013): *Ruling the void: The hollowing of Western democracy*, Verso books.

Mattli, Walter & Thomas Plümper (2002): 'The demand-side politics of EU enlargement: democracy and the application for EU membership', *Journal of European Public Policy*, 9:4, 550–574.

Moravcsik, Andrew (2013): *The choice for Europe: Social purpose and state power from Messina to Maastricht*, Routledge.

Neunreither, Karlheinz (1998): 'Governance without opposition: the case of the European Union', *Government and Opposition*, 33:4, 419–441.

Niemann, Arne (2021): 'Neofunctionalism', in Marianne Riddervold, Jarle Trondal & Akasemi (eds.) Newsome (2021): *The Palgrave Handbook of EU Crises*, Palgrave Macmillan, 115–133.

Persson, Thomas, Mårtensson, Moa & Karlsson, Christer (2019): 'Eurosceptic Challenger Parties and Political Opposition in European Union Politics: Part of the Problem or Part of the Solution?', *Scandinavian Political Studies*, 42:3–4, 245–269.

Phinnemore, David (2020): 'Northern Ireland: A 'Place Between' in UK–EU Relations?'. *European Foreign Affairs Review*, 25:4, 631–650.

Rosamond, Ben (2005): 'The uniting of Europe and the foundation of EU studies: revisiting the neofunctionalism of Ernst B. Haas', *Journal of European public policy*, 12:2, 237–254.

Ryan, Cillian (2016): 'Where does one start to make sense of Brexit?', *International Economics and Economic Policy*, 13:4, 531–537.

Scharpf, Fritz W. (2006): 'The joint-decision trap revisited', *JCMS: Journal of Common Market Studies*, 44:4, 845–864.

Scharpf, Fritz W. (1988): 'The joint-decision trap: lessons from German federalism and European integration', *Public administration*, 66:3, 239–278.

Schnapper, Pauline (2021): 'Theresa May, the Brexit negotiations and the two-level game, 2017–2019', *Journal of Contemporary European Studies*, 29:3, 368–379.

Schuette, Leonard August (2021): 'Forging unity: European Commission leadership in the Brexit negotiations', *JCMS: Journal of Common Market Studies*, 59:5, 1142–1159.

Shipman, Tim (2016): *All out war: the full story of how Brexit sank Britain's political class*, William Collins.

Smith, Julie (2016): 'David Cameron's EU renegotiation and referendum pledge: A case of déjà vu?', *British Politics*, 11:3, 324–346.

Sorace, Miriam & Sara Binzer Hobolt (2021): 'A tale of two peoples: motivated reasoning in the aftermath of the Brexit Vote', *Political Science Research and Methods*, 9:4, 675–692.

Spiering, Menno (2004): *Euroscepticism*, Brill.

Stratton, Jon (2019): 'The language of leaving: Brexit, the second world war and cultural trauma', *Journal for Cultural Research*, 23:3, 225–251.

Taylor, Paul (2007): *The end of European integration: Anti-Europeanism examined*, Routledge.

Tournier-Sol, Karine (2016): *The UK challenge to Europeanization: the persistence of British Euroscepticism*, Springer.

Tsebelis, George & Geoffrey Garrett (2001): 'The institutional foundations of intergovernmentalism and supranationalism in the European Union', *International organization*, 55:2, 357–390.

Usherwood, Simon (2021): "Our European Friends and Partners'? Negotiating the Trade and Cooperation Agreement', *JCMS: Journal of Common Market Studies*, 59:S1, 115–123.

Usherwood, Simon (2015): 'Britain and Europe: a model of permanent crisis?', in Kyriakos Demetriou (ed.) (2015): *The European Union in Crisis*, Springer, 3–14.

Usherwood, Simon (2005): 'Realists, sceptics and opponents: opposition to the EU's Constitutional Treaty' *Journal of Contemporary European Research*, 1:2, 4–12.

Usherwood, Simon, Leruth, Benjamin & Startin, Nicholas (2017) 'Conclusion: Euroscepticism and European (dis) integration in the age of Brexit', in Benjamin Leruth, Nicholas Startin & Simon Usherwood (eds.) (2017): *The Routledge Handbook of Euroscepticism*, Routledge, 468–477.

Vasilopoulou, Sofia (2016): 'UK Euroscepticism and the Brexit referendum', *The Political Quarterly*, 87:2, 219–227.

Vasilopoulou, Sofia (2013): 'Continuity and Change in the Study of Euroscepticism: Plus ça change?' *JCMS: Journal of Common Market Studies*, 51:1, 153–168.

Vasilopoulou, Sofia & Dan Keith (2019): 'Renegotiation versus Brexit: the question of the UK's constitutional relationship with the EU' *JCMS: Journal of Common Market Studies*, 57:3, 486–501.

Wall, Stephen (2020): *Reluctant European: Britain and the European Union from 1945 to Brexit*, Oxford University Press.

Young, Hugo (1999): *This blessed plot: Britain and Europe from Churchill to Blair*, Overlook Books.

Daniel Schade

10 A strained partnership? A typology of tensions in the EU-US transatlantic relationship

Abstract: This chapter considers recent developments in the transatlantic relationship between the European Union (EU) and the United States of America (USA) as an example of how multiple kinds of simultaneous crises can affect an area of EU activity at once. In so doing it disentangles the effects of certain short-term and prominent inflection points, such as the election of Donald Trump as US president, or Russia's full-scale invasion of Ukraine from more long-term and background elements of strain affecting the overall trajectory of the transatlantic relationship. This focus on different types of crises also allows for the chapter to consider both tensions arising from within the transatlantic relationship, as well as those which are technically exogenous to it, yet which have spillover effects into the state of transatlantic ties. Overall, the chapter concludes that while prominent and sudden developments have a significant impact on the state of transatlantic relations in the short term, it is the more long-term and less prominent gradual divergence of the underlying preferences of both actors which is likely going to have a more lasting and drastic impact overall.

Keywords: Transatlantic relations, United States, NATO, trade war, overlapping crises

Introduction

When then US president Donald Trump announced on 14 July 2020 at a press conference held in the White House Rose Garden that "[t]he European Union was formed in order to take advantage of the United States" (Trump 2020) transatlantic relations, defined here as the bilateral relationship between the United States and the European Union, had reached an absolute low. While the state of the transatlantic relationship has trended much closer to its historical, relatively cordial state since the election of Joe Biden as Trump's successor, the Trump era has still demonstrated how easily it can be strained and receive long-term damage. This is particularly problematic given the diverse composition of both partners in terms of their relative size, their democratic foundations, as well as their joint long-term interests concerning issues such as free trade, a rules-based international system, or

https://doi.org/10.1515/9783110790337-011

the promotion of democracy (with none of the two partners being a perfect proponent of either of these issues, however). Symbolically the importance of this partnership has been emphasized on numerous occasions, with the European Union considering the United States as one of its ten long-term so-called strategic partners with which it wants to maintain particularly close ties.[1]

While the developments of the Trump era have already shown that long-standing European assumptions about the United States as a key promoter of European integration since the EU's humble beginnings (Rappaport 1981) cannot be seen as natural constants, this episode nonetheless raises further questions as to the state and trajectory of the transatlantic relationship. In particular, it is unclear whether the Trump presidency serves as a temporary exception during which the interests of both parties were merely politically out of sync, or whether those developments foreshadowed genuinely diverging interests between both parties, thus hurting the overall relationship in a more structural sense. This chapter attempts to answer this question by considering different types of strain that have and continue to affect the transatlantic relationship, as well as how their effects vary by type. This allows for distinguishing between the kind of negative short-term impact that the Trump presidency has mainly represented, as well as wider and often less prominent long-term trends which stand to affect the transatlantic relationship on a more permanent basis. Overall, the chapter argues that while different types of short-term crises can serve to illustrate both the fragilities and strengths of the transatlantic relationship, it is more profound shifts in interests, underlying conditions, and positions on both sides of the Atlantic which represent the bigger long-term risk for bilateral ties.

By disentangling different kinds of strain, the chapter illustrates how their respective impact differs, as well as how the overall state of the transatlantic relationship is the result of multiple elements of strain occurring in parallel. Discussing distinct types of crises also allows us to distinguish between strain arising from within the transatlantic relationship itself, and that which is technically exogenous in nature yet affects the overall state of the transatlantic relationship regardless. In the latter case, it is important to note that such crises can ultimately have a positive, rather than overall negative impact on the state of the transatlantic ties.

This introduction is followed by a brief discussion of existing research on the state and recent evolution of the transatlantic relationship. Based on these perspectives, the remainder of the chapter then focuses on individual crises which have shap-

---

1 The other original "strategic partners" are Brazil, Canada, China, India, Mexico, Japan, Russia, South Korea, and South Africa. However, China has since also been considered as both a "competitor" and "systemic rival" (European Commission 2019, 1), with Russia's status also in doubt not least since the country's reinvasion of Ukraine since the spring of 2022.

ed transatlantic relations in recent years. While these are considered in separate sections, most of these are necessarily interrelated, with the chapter pointing to such linkages whenever necessary. Furthermore, it is important to point out that the chapter does not attempt to capture all elements of strain affecting the transatlantic relationship, but instead highlights particular crises as an illustration of how strain can affect the relationship. The examples chosen are not only the most prominently discussed ones but also represent a cross-section of the kinds of strain affecting transatlantic ties. In the order that they are discussed, these are 1.) the dominant yet relatively short-term crisis in transatlantic relations induced by the Trump presidency; 2.) domestic issues affecting both partners alike, and which have contributed to both parties' introspection; 3.) fundamental long-term shifts affecting the foundations of the transatlantic relationship; and 4.) Russia's full-scale invasion of Ukraine as an example of an external crisis having had a positive effect on transatlantic ties.

The state of the transatlantic relationship in context

It is difficult to overstate the importance of the transatlantic relationship in its larger dimension, bringing together the United States on the one side, the EU and its 27 member states on the other, and even further countries when including additional institutional contexts such as NATO membership. This has led scholars to argue that said relationship lies at the heart of the global liberal order (Hofmann 2021: 150). Furthermore, "[i]n terms of values and interests, economic interactions and human bonds, the United States and the European Union are closer to one another than either is to any other major international actor." (Hamilton 2014: 25).

While the said relationship is thus central to both parties involved in it, it is also very complex given the different nature of both actors. The United States is arguably the most powerful sovereign state in the world, while the European Union's status as an ultimately confederal entity with only some of the powers of sovereign states, and the continued parallel existence of its 27 member states, make this a particularly complex relationship defined by its multi-layered nature (Hamilton 2014: 25). It is this underlying asymmetry in the relationship (Polyakova & Haddad 2019: 109) which has, on the one hand, enabled the United States to play a role supportive of European integration underlying the EU project, while enabling the EU to develop on its own regardless of Europe's geopolitical position. On the other hand, it has enabled the United States to shape global order by leading a coalition of largely like-minded countries throughout the Cold War and beyond.

Identifying the strength and evolution of this relationship is thus relevant far beyond the confines of transatlantic ties itself, as it has the potential to affect geo-politics. Recent analyses have both raised concerns and given hope to the status of this relationship going forward. While, during the Trump presidency, Riddervold and Newsome argued that "the transatlantic relationship is under more pressure today than in any other period since its establishment after the Second World War" (2018: 518), only a few years later they then made the case that Russia's full-scale invasion of Ukraine meant that "relations between the European Union (EU) and the United States (US) seem more robust than ever" (2022: 128). According to these analyses, the state of the relationship is thus subject to relatively short-term swings dependent on developments internal and external to it.

When taking a more long-term perspective, such back-and-forth developments are not entirely unexpected, as the "relations are beset by competitive impulses, underlying questions of trust, and mutual doubts about relative commitment and capacity" (Hamilton 2014: 25). At the same time, the duration of the partner-ship, and said swings within it, are often also seen as evidence for its robustness, with the relationship being able to bounce back (Hofmann 2021), and the swings in public rhetoric hiding underlying structural issues attesting the transatlantic rela-tionship's strength (Olsen 2022).

The Trump-era transatlantic breakdown: A template of things to come?

The Trump presidency and its all-encompassing political claim of putting 'America first' were perhaps the most visible recent instance of significant short-term strain being introduced in the transatlantic relationship. The prominence of this partic-ular episode in the partnership can ultimately be attributed to the underlying sym-bolism of some of President Trump's actions, such as his public statements oppos-ing the EU, or a decision to downgrade the status of the EU's representation in Washington, D.C. in 2019 (Borger 2019a).

What turned the Trump presidency into a more significant actual strain on the transatlantic relationship, however, were some underlying political decisions that also affected its foundations. For most of these issues, responsibility lies directly and unequivocally with the Trump administration. However, some instances of transatlantic tension illustrate how the EU's and its member states' sometimes naïve approach toward global and transatlantic issues has facilitated the negative fallout of the Trump administration's choices.

Given the centrality of economic issues for the European Union, it was some of the protectionist measures introduced by the Trump administration which have added the most significant strain to the transatlantic relationship. Here, it was Trump's view of the EU as an economic competitor and rival (much like China), and Germany, in particular (Larres 2020: 106), which informed several economic policy measures alienating the European Union.

The most significant of these measures was the 2018 introduction of tariffs on US imports of steel and aluminium products. While these tariffs were chiefly aimed at China, with the United States initially granting certain exemptions to EU imports, they ultimately hurt EU-US trade and led the EU to retaliate by imposing tariffs of its own (Larres 2020: 121). Trump's anger over an ongoing trade deficit between the US and the EU, and the US and Germany, in particular, also led his administration to threaten additional tariffs on the importation of automobiles by European carmakers. While such an escalation was avoided by a trip of the then European Commission president Jean-Claude Juncker for negotiations with Trump in Washington (Larres 2020: 122–23), the damage in trust between the EU and its member states on the one side, and the Trump administration, on the other, was hard to reverse. Tensions were not eased by the fact that while Trump eventually buried the hatchet in an escalation of trade tensions, he continued to be an outspoken supporter of Brexit, the principal issue affecting the EU internally at the time.

These tensions were made worse by certain decisions of the Trump administration affecting global order including, but also going beyond, the realm of trade. Here, the Trump administration's assault on the global trading system was rendered worse by also attacking the WTO and essentially rendering its dispute settlement mechanism ineffective (Hopewell 2021). To make matters worse, it is this body that is tasked with mediating trade conflicts of the sort initiated by the Trump administration. Beyond the realm of trade, the United States' decision to withdraw from the World Health Organization (WHO) (Rogers & Mandavilli 2020) also critically weakened an institution which at the time played a central role in managing the fallout of the Covid-19 pandemic.

Beyond this, the Trump administration also threatened the EU's role in global governance more directly. One such example was the United States' withdrawal from the Joint Comprehensive Plan of Action (JCPOA), also known as the Iran nuclear deal, and the introduction of economic sanctions against the country. JCPOA was initially reached through the central mediating role played by the EU, thus illustrating its novel importance in foreign policy since the institutional changes introduced with the Lisbon Treaty. The departure of the United States from the agreement led the EU to actively counter this development by attempting to uphold JCPOA's terms on its own. Given the central role played by the United States and its currency for international finance, it even led the EU to develop a mechanism that would allow Iran to participate in international commerce despite the economic sanctions of the United States (Immenkamp 2020: 9–10).

Another field in which the Trump administration not only snubbed the international community, but the EU in particular, was by withdrawing from the Paris climate agreement (Pavone 2018) given the EU's (perceived) leadership on this issue not just within the transatlantic relationship (Cross 2018). Ultimately, the sum total of such decisions by the Trump administration not only hurt the transatlantic partnership internally but also had external consequences, with the EU having to partly rebalance its international outlook in the affected issues away from the United States and often towards cooperating more closely with China. In the realm of international trade, this led both the EU and China to collectively challenge Trump's protectionist policies at the WTO (Larres 2020: 121–22), while both also collaborated more closely on tackling climate change (Boffey & Neslen 2017), thus further antagonizing the Trump administration amidst its critical stance towards China.

Another core area in which the Trump administration's actions significantly worsened the transatlantic relationship is in the realm of security. While transatlantic security cooperation continues to be the principal remit of NATO, rather than the EU, the overlap in membership between both organisations, as well as the EU's modest integration steps in the realm of security and defence meant that the transatlantic relationship would also be affected in its US-EU dimension. Here, it was the Trump administration's threat for the United States to leave NATO which represented the most significant risk to transatlantic ties.

However, short of implementing this extreme decision, the relationship was nonetheless strained anyway by the United States' decision to withdraw from the Open Skies Treaty, which had previously allowed unarmed surveillance activities to ease East-West tensions, as well as the announcement of a withdrawal of US troops from Germany (Hofmann 2021: 154). While it was yet again the decisions of the Trump administration which ultimately sparked this dimension of the crisis in transatlantic relations, this was enabled by decades of underinvestment in defence capabilities by many EU countries. As explored below, it was this long-term imbalance in the transatlantic security relationship which led to the Trump administration taking and threatening the decisions outlined above. Lastly, and affecting security cooperation outside of NATO's own territory, the Trump administration also weakened transatlantic ties by increasingly taking unilateral decisions such as withdrawing US troops from Afghanistan without consulting major allies.

While the Trump administration principally contributed to a crisis within the transatlantic relationship itself, it also increased strain within the EU as some EU countries advocated for different kinds of reactions to certain decisions taken by the United States. Overall, this did not lead to EU unity over central issues in the transatlantic relationship or topics such as Brexit being threatened but instead became visible in the margins of other areas of EU activity. For instance, Donald Trump's decision to relocate the US embassy in Israel to Jerusalem in 2018 led to a weakening of a previously held EU position over the status of the city. Here, the Czech Republic, Hungary, and Romania blocked EU statements condemning the embassy's move, with representatives of the three countries as well as Austria also attending the embassy's opening ceremony (Aggestam & Bicchi 2019: 526).

While the immediate crisis in transatlantic relations caused by the Trump presidency was resolved due to Joe Biden's election as US president, as well as the Biden administration's underlying measures to repair the damage that had been done, this episode has nonetheless had a lasting effect on transatlantic ties. While, on the one hand, the rhetoric and many actions by the Biden administration helped to assuage the EU and its member states (Olsen 2022: 157), a complete policy reversal to a status quo before the Trump administration did not happen. Here, some damage simply could not be undone in the short term, such as the weakening of the WTO. The Biden administration also took relatively long – in part deliberately – to reverse certain other Trump-era policies, and did not alter some at all, as illustrated by the hasty withdrawal from Afghanistan during the summer of 2021 (Olsen 2022: 154).

Lastly, while the Trump years illustrate the fragility of the transatlantic relationship to short-term internal shocks, there is also some evidence for its built-in resilience. This can be seen when considering Donald Trump's support for Brexit and the UK government's attempts at weakening certain parts of their agreement with the EU when it came to the status of Northern Ireland. Here, the Trump administration promised the quick conclusion of a UK-US trade agreement as a near-term benefit of Brexit. This would have directly contravened the EU's efforts to hold the UK to the promises made in its EU withdrawal agreement, and particularly to preserve the precarious status quo in Northern Ireland. These promises were contravened, however, by checks and balances built into the US system of government, with key members of the United States Congress threatening to block any potential trade agreement should the UK's approach to relations with the EU affect the status quo in Northern Ireland (Borger 2019b).

Domestic political strain on both sides of the Atlantic: United in crisis?

While the election of Donald Trump as US president marked an immediate crisis in transatlantic relations, the political dynamics that led to his success are not unique to the United States. Instead, the success of political figures like Trump is illustrative of a wider trend of the rise of populist and far-right political movements on both sides of the Atlantic. While this trend affects both partners alike, ironically it is this similarity that has contributed to a weakening of their ties (Aggestam & Hyde-Price 2019: 118). The drastic change in foreign policy positions of the Trump administration aside, this is mainly due to these domestic challenges to the established political order that have led both the United States and the EU in becoming more self-centred and inward-looking to deal with said challenges.

In the EU this is best illustrated by the political developments which contributed to the Brexit campaign in the United Kingdom. Brexit itself has been the foremost factor leading to the EU's introspection in the aftermath of the UK's referendum on the matter (see the chapter by Usherwood) and has reduced the EU's overall international clout (see the chapter by Smith). With Brexit negotiations underway not only were large parts of the EU's bureaucracy preoccupied with managing the actual dissolution process and its fallout, but this also contributed to the EU deliberately focusing on discussing potential domestic reforms (e.g. European Commission 2017). Central political figures such as French president Emmanuel Macron have also used Brexit and associated issues to argue that the EU would need to look inward before focusing again on key foreign policies such as enlargement (Chrisafis & Rankin 2019).

Political developments similar to those which led to Brexit have also introduced additional strain on the EU's internal coherence by empowering far-right political parties and empowering some Trump-like political figures within the EU. The latter dynamic has, so far, principally remained limited to certain domestic contexts such as Janez Janša's premiership in Slovenia between 2020 and 2022, or former Czech Prime Minister Andrej Babis (whose government supported the Trump administration's decision to move the US embassy to Jerusalem). However, far-right and often Eurosceptic parties have also seen a general rise across much of the EU (Rump 2022) independent of Trumpian rhetoric, thereby threatening overall European unity. In certain country contexts, such as Hungary, a similar trend has also come to the fore, albeit not through the rise of novel political movements, but the gradual transformation of the existing Fidesz party under prime minister Viktor Orbán into a populist and largely anti-European political outfit (Fabry 2019).

Given the set-up of the EU's political system, the impact of the rise of such political movements has so far been relatively limited at large. Even though far-right anti-EU political parties have managed to increase their number of seats in the European Parliament over several electoral cycles, they have so far remained marginalized at the EU level. However, the impact of increasing fragmentation of the EU can instead be seen in areas of EU activity where unanimity voting requirements apply, thus giving individual countries large leeway in blocking EU decision-making and requiring extensive negotiations over underlying trade-offs. Such issues of EU unity are likely going to be tested even further with additional far-right parties entering EU member state governments.

While the EU's capacity to fruitfully engage in a renewed transatlantic relationship has thus been limited both by Brexit and the impact of the rise of far-right and populist political movements, the fallout beyond the Trump administration has been somewhat similar in the US. Here, the fundamental weakening of the country's political system amidst the questioning of the electoral process by Trump and his allies has contributed to the country's inward focus even into the Biden administration. As some developments ahead of the November 2022 mid-term elections have shown, this tendency has continued well into the term of the Biden presidency (Pilkington 2022).

What's more, with Trump having been supported by many traditionally Democratic voting parts of the electorate, such as blue-collar workers, efforts to block the success of Trump or similar political figures in the future will necessarily contribute to the country continuing to focus on domestic economic and social policies, which, as the next section illustrates, may run counter to common interests such as free trade in the wider transatlantic dimension. Such developments then ultimately create the foundations for a transatlantic alliance that has been eroded by its constituent parts being weakened domestically.

The gradual erosion of the transatlantic alliance's foundations

While the presidency of Donald Trump, based on underlying political dynamics playing out on both sides of the Atlantic, has demonstrated the potential for immediate disruption in the transatlantic relationship, the excesses of the Trump presidency are ultimately but a symptom of wider geopolitical trends which lead to a gradual erosion of the long-term common basis of transatlantic ties. These developments occur irrespective of this recent episode, as "[a]lthough it is tempting to attribute the deterioration in transatlantic relations to one specific factor [...] the problems besetting transatlantic relations are deeper and more multifaceted than that" (Aggestam & Hyde-Price 2019: 114). Indeed, an increasing overall divergence between both partners has already been noted for quite some time (Riddervold & Newsome 2018).

On the one hand, this increasing divergence reflects structural shifts in the wider international system, which contribute to the weakening of the transatlantic partnership over time. This, in turn, is a product of the rise in relevance of certain international actors such as China but also results from the kind of domestic trends (Smith 2022) which were outlined above. With both parties changing preferences and having to reorientate their positions in response to these developments it is ultimately possible to observe a weakening commitment to collective values shared by both, which in turn negatively affects the strength of the overall bilateral relationship (Smith 2018: 550–51).

While the prior alignment of values and goals also served to hide any underlying structural deficiencies in the partnership beforehand, the diverging positions now highlight problems related to how the transatlantic relationship operates. Here, it is important to remember that the interaction between both sides cannot be regarded as one of equals. The EU's limited capacity to engage in international relations has led to interactions between the EU and the US to remain relatively technocratic in nature, to focus on processes rather than outcomes, as well as approaching many issues in an ad hoc rather than strategic manner (Hamilton 2014: 25).

Such technical constraints on the EU's side are made worse by an underlying power asymmetry in the broader transatlantic alliance which also includes NATO and the individual positions of EU member states. Here, the divergence on security issues between the United States and European parties is at the heart of one of the developing rifts (Polyakova & Haddad 2019: 109).

While president Trump merely highlighted such asymmetries in the context of NATO, European countries' reluctance to invest in their own security amidst the security umbrella provided by the United States has contributed to more long-term strain affecting the relationship. The long-term importance of this issue can be illustrated by the fact that Trump was not the first US president to prominently criticize Europe's under-investment in its own defence. Instead, the Obama administration issued similar warnings against European free-riding on security issues (Szabo 2018: 541). What made matters worse was that a significant shortfall in defence capabilities could even be observed for the EU's (then) largest defence spenders, France and the UK, who faced significant difficulties amidst the NATO intervention in Libya in 2011 (Aggestam & Hyde-Price 2019: 116).

While these ongoing warnings by two US presidents have had a small positive impact on European defence spending, the underlying asymmetry has remained even as the United States entered the Biden era. As a result, many European countries delayed further significant defence investment, which could have moderated the positions of the Trump administration, and instead hedged on a win by Biden in the 2020 presidential election and an eventual return to normal in the transatlantic security relationship (Hofmann 2021: 156–57). This has only changed more recently amidst Russia's war against Ukraine.

Difficulties due to the existing power asymmetry of both actors aside, there is also potential for further long-term strain in the relationship when considering a gradual divergence of both parties' positions when it comes to their geopolitical outlook. Here, it is particularly the observation of an ongoing geographic shift in the United States' political attention, often described as a 'pivot to Asia', and the EU's increasing focus to develop what has been described as 'strategic autonomy' which can serve to illustrate the ongoing erosion of a common basis for the transatlantic relationship.

With NATO and EU enlargement in the 2000s radically altering the political set-up of the European continent in the aftermath of the Cold War, the attention of the United States increasingly began to move elsewhere. This could first be observed under the Obama administration which initiated the United States' first significant pivot towards Asia (Szabo 2018: 541). With the increasing relevance of the latter continent amidst the world's growth patterns, as well as the potential for conflict due to the rise of China, this pivot has only continued since then (Aggestam & Hyde-Price 2019: 117) and is likely to continue progressing going forward.

Aside from reinforcing the need for the EU to become a more autonomous actor on its own continent (see below), this development also serves to underline the potentially distinct perspectives of both the EU and the US on the wider Asian sphere. Here, the increasingly hostile position of the United States towards China, which began to become apparent during the Trump presidency and has since continued into Joe Biden's term in office (Olsen 2022: 154), has the potential for additional policy divergence between both partners. This came to the fore, in particular, amidst the announcement of a military alliance between Australia, the United States, and the United Kingdom (AUKUS), which would include providing Australia with nuclear-powered submarines. This was seen as an affront in France and the EU, as it coincided with Australia reneging on an advanced military procurement contract that would have provided the country with submarines of a French design (Olsen 2022: 158).

This attempt to strengthen the United States' ties to a key partner in the Pacific region thus ultimately had the indirect effect of alienating (parts of) the EU, thus further weakening the potential for transatlantic collaboration in the Asia-Pacific region. This is unfortunate as the EU and an increasing number of its member states have similarly started to become worried about the rise of China and its policies. However, this is a much more gradual development in the European case as many EU countries are more highly intertwined with China than the US, and central EU members such as Germany particularly so (Bergsen et al. 2022: 5–6). Here, the United States more rapid turn towards Asia and the lack of coordination with its European allies may have thus fundamentally damaged the potential for developing a collective view of the region within the transatlantic partnership.

Key European countries such as France have seen this as an element to justify a European approach that would explicitly be distinct from that of the United States – a view that was already reinforced by key policy choices of the Trump administration (Larres 2020: 119–24). This is ultimately related to increasing calls to develop greater European 'strategic autonomy' (Szewczyk 2022) amidst the US withdrawal from Europe and emerging divergence of positions, where "discussions in Europe on attaining strategic autonomy are often held not so much with China in mind, but the US" (Bergsen et al. 2022: 19). Underlying such initiatives is the realization that "Europe will never be as central to the United States as it once was and will have to focus on ensuring the survival of its own model before claiming global ambitions." (Polyakova & Haddad 2019: 119). At the same time, prior to Russia's full-scale invasion of Ukraine, it was also assumed that "Europe is now no longer as reliant on US security guarantees as it was during the East-West conflict" (Aggestam & Hyde-Price 2019: 117), thus allowing (if not forcing) it to develop a more independent perspective on pressing international issues.

The United States' ongoing pivot to Asia is thus a parallel yet interrelated development to calls for the EU and its member states to become more independent in their geopolitical outlook. After all, while the desire by the US for its European partners to invest more heavily in their own security necessarily contributes to an increasing European foreign and security policy autonomy, so can the EU's desire to become more independent only be realized when emerging from the security umbrella provided by the United States (Polyakova & Haddad 2019: 110). The contrary developments of the United States pivot to Asia, as well as increasing calls for a more autonomous EU position thus have the potential for further eroding the basis of transatlantic ties going forward, irrespective of the short-term political developments observed above.

The economic dimension of the transatlantic partnership would seem to offer a more positive outlook on its foundations at first sight. Here, both partners had attempted to negotiate the world's largest bilateral trade agreement, the so-called Transatlantic Trade and Investment Partnership (TTIP) prior to the Trump presidency. Despite underlying difficulties at the time, the mere existence of said negotiations is thus a testament to both parties' desire to strengthen this element of their relationship. However, here again, it was a decision by the Trump administration preceding the protectionist measures outlined above which brought the project to a halt.

While one could once again conclude that this represents a mere short-term disruption, developments since the end of the Trump presidency have also hinted at a more long-term shift affecting trade and economic ties as a foundational aspect of the transatlantic relationship. Here, the Biden administration has been quite reluctant to return the economic dimension of transatlantic relations to the status quo prior to Trump entering office. While the lack of a resumption of trade talks between both parties is one of the clearest indicators of this, it can also be seen in how the Biden administration has undone some of the more extreme trade policy measures introduced by Trump.

While a certain détente in transatlantic trade relations was already reached by June of 2021, six months into Biden's term in office, by ending a long-lasting dispute over subsidies for Boeing and Airbus respectively (Brundsen et al. 2021), it took until October of 2021 to end the escalating trade war over punitive tariffs. Here, ahead of the EU taking further retaliatory measures against US tariffs the Biden administration announced in the margins of a G20 meeting in Rome that most of the Trump-era tariffs on European steel and aluminium goods would be rolled back (Swanson & Rogers 2021). This did not amount to a full-scale removal of said tariffs, with some protections remaining in place given constraints fuelled by the domestic political developments in the United States outlined in the previous section.

Rather than further reducing trade tensions over the ensuing period, these have only escalated again amidst US plans to overhaul and expand subsidies for the onshoring of production in critical sectors necessary for the energy transition and future technologies, which would put the European economy at a disadvantage (von der Burchard & Leali 2022). While one could thus have expected that EU-US trade ties would return to normal after the end of the Trump presidency, the developments since then point to a similar erosion of the common basis which had enabled both parties relatively cordial economic relationship in the past.

The impact of external shocks: Temporary transatlantic unity amidst Russia's war against Ukraine

The above sections have principally considered strain emanating from within the transatlantic relationship, including parallel challenges at the domestic level. To complete this picture through yet another perspective, this section considers Russia's full-scale war against Ukraine since 24 February 2022 as a crisis external to the transatlantic relationship which has, however, had a largely positive impact on it – at least in the security domain. While many of the crises outlined above have served to underscore the immediate and long-term negative effects on the existing transatlantic relationship, the transatlantic response to Russia's war against Ukraine instead serves to illustrate that transatlantic ties continue to have a significant potential, which can re-emerge when existing difficulties within the transatlantic relationship are dwarfed by larger geopolitical developments. This renewed unity was expressed, on the one hand, through the extensive need for transatlantic coordination to make measures such as economic sanctions as effective as possible, and secondly, the renewed relevance of the transatlantic security community to ensure the safety of the wider European area (and beyond) against military threats.

Here, Russia's full-scale invasion of Ukraine ultimately served as an external shock which, while affecting the EU in a much more immediate manner, has focused minds on both sides of the Atlantic given its geopolitical repercussions. With both the United States and the European Union ultimately defending similar interests when it comes to this conflict, analysts have considered that "[t]he war in Ukraine has reinvigorated transatlantic unity" (Wright & Cooley 2022). Others have compared the effects of the Russia-Ukraine war to a vaccination, representing a positive "shot in the arm to the transatlantic relationship" (Bouchet 2022). This conflict has thus served to make the existing transatlantic tensions fade into the background of this much more immediate and threatening largely external crisis, while also bringing common transatlantic values, such as a commitment to a rules-based international order or the support of democracy back to the fore.

What has led to this external crisis having a direct effect on the transatlantic relationship is ultimately its intensity. While Russia had already violated Ukraine's territorial integrity through its annexation of Crimea and by waging war against Ukraine in a more restrained manner since 2014, the underlying conflict and its potential repercussions were never perceived as relevant enough to have a lasting impact on the wider dynamics of transatlantic ties. There were also some differences in how the parties on both sides of the Atlantic perceived the sequence of events following 2014 (Stahl et al. 2016). Regardless, the rather weak cornerstones of the failed attempts to contain Russia's expansionism were transatlantic in nature. Here, the Obama administration coordinated its policy response closely with EU partners, and Germany, in particular (Szabo 2018: 543–44), all while never turning into a central aspect of the transatlantic partnership at the time.

It was the failure of this policy, as well as the larger geopolitical implications of Russia's full-scale invasion of Ukraine which then made this crisis the centre of transatlantic relations since 24 February 2022. Unlike before, however, there was also a shift of leadership within the EU. Here, central European countries such as the Baltic countries, Czechia, Slovakia, and Poland have been proven right in their long-standing hostile attitude towards Russia. In turn, these countries have been at the forefront of EU aid towards Ukraine (Antezza et al. 2022), their own military reorganization (Karnitschnig & Kość 2022), as well as calls for tough EU sanctions on Russia and Belarus.

The reinvigoration of the transatlantic relationship occurred in many areas. One of these central issues has been the need for coordinating the United States' and the EU's non-military response to the conflict. With sanctions policy being at the heart of Western efforts to impose costs on Russia amidst its war against Ukraine, extensive coordination had to be undertaken between the partners to ensure the largest possible effectiveness of the overall Western sanctions regime. Consequently, certain trade sanctions imposed by only, say, the United States, but not the EU would ultimately allow Russia to simply shift the origin and destination of its trade in sanctioned goods elsewhere. This is also one of the most central areas of direct cooperation between the EU and the United States since EU sanctions policy is an exclusive competence of the European Union with member states no longer being able to maintain sanctions of their own.

Throughout all of 2022, the gradual increase of sanctions against Russia has been coordinated amongst Western partners, with the US and the EU at the heart of such efforts. What's more, such coordination – despite not reaching absolute synchronicity in the overall sanctions package – has been at the centre of communication efforts to demonstrate transatlantic and Western unity (e.g. The White House 2022). Such coordination only became more extensive as the conflict intensified and further sanctions measures increased in complexity. Although a ban on the transport, insurance, and facilitation of trade in Russian oil sold above a certain price threshold, it was the EU that ultimately set the suggested price cap for itself and all G7 countries alike (Kijewski & Cooper 2022). This represents an instance in which the G7 partners of the EU, including the United States, were willing to concede some of their own scope of action in light of the higher European exposure to the negative side effects of such sanction efforts.

The consequences of Russia's full-scale invasion of Ukraine are also likely going to reduce another long-standing element of strain in the transatlantic relationship, namely the mismatch in membership between the EU and NATO on the European side, which has previously rendered cooperation between both organizations difficult. Prior to the developments of 2022, there were six EU members not simultaneously part of NATO. Two of these, Finland and Sweden, have since also applied for NATO membership (Reuters 2022), with only Austria, Ireland, Malta, and Cyprus currently committed to remaining outside of the security alliance.

Lastly, Russia's full-scale invasion of Ukraine has also served to bury one long-standing issue in transatlantic relations in the form of the Nord Stream 2 natural gas pipeline between Russia and Germany. While the project had long faced criticism from other EU member states and the United States alike, Germany had nonetheless continued to support the pipeline project which was completed but not yet operational by the end of 2021. The transatlantic conflict (or more precisely principally a conflict between the United States and Germany) over the construction of the pipeline had been long-lasting but ultimately peaked during the Trump administration (Olsen 2022, 159–60) which even introduced economic sanctions against the project (de Jong 2022). The conflict surrounding this pipeline was ultimately resolved when the German government announced its suspension already immediately before Russia's full-scale invasion of Ukraine (Marsh & Chambers 2022) when an escalation on the part of Russia had already become all but certain. This decision then also eliminated the need for the EU to continue to discuss retaliatory measures against the US which were also highly controversial internally (de Jong 2022: 227).

While the effects of Russia's full-scale invasion of Ukraine on the transatlantic relationship have thus so far been positive overall, this ongoing crisis nonetheless has the potential to introduce renewed strain into the relationship going forward. As a result, the outward political unity of both partners cannot hide the continued underlying imbalance of contributions to the solution of this security crisis. Much like the earlier debate about Europe's contributions to NATO's collective defence, EU (countries) security support for Ukraine has fallen short of that provided by the United States (Shapiro 2022). This has even extended to a security-adjacent domain with the United States playing a bigger role in ensuring the continued liquidity of the Ukrainian state than the EU.

While some predict that this will bring the transatlantic security burden-sharing debate back to the fore in the short term (Shapiro 2022), others believe that this will only occur after the war has ended (Engelbrekt 2022), thus once more revealing the underlying transatlantic structural tensions. In short, while Russia's reinvasion of Ukraine has shown the strength and potential of transatlantic relations amidst a major crisis, it is not a given that this will have a fundamental structural effect going forward.

Conclusion

As this chapter has shown, the state of transatlantic relations has been affected by multiple prominent tensions in recent years. Whereas an all-time low in the bilateral relationship had been reached during the Trump presidency, Russia's full-scale invasion of Ukraine has since led the relationship to a novel high. The swing in both directions has demonstrated the fragility and resilience of the transatlantic relationship in response to both an internal crisis and one external to the relationship. However, these swings are likely not the best indicator to assess long-term strain present within the transatlantic relationship, or its likely trajectory going forward.

Instead, a better indicator of the overall tensions affecting the relationship can be found when assessing the less prominent foundations of transatlantic ties. Here, both parties have been negatively affected by similar kinds of domestic strain which have led each to turn inwards. Similarly, while the long-term goals and values of both the US and the EU had largely aligned in the past on issues such as a rules-based international trading system, there is growing evidence that both are increasingly diverging from one another.

Overall, the transatlantic relationship is subject to various kinds of tensions that intersect in multiple ways, and which have contributed to this relationship, thus adding to the different elements of crisis with which the EU has to deal with amidst its polycrisis. The insights presented in this chapter ultimately caution that an analysis of crises in the EU needs to consider not just short-term effects but distinct perspectives in longer-term horizons so as to gain a better overview of political strain, its evolution, consequences, and underlying determinants.

References

Aggestam, Lisbeth & Bicchi, Federica (2019): 'New Directions in EU Foreign Policy Governance: Cross-Loading, Leadership and Informal Groupings', *Journal of Common Market Studies*, 57:3, 515–32.

Aggestam, Lisbeth & Hyde-Price, Adrian (2019): 'Double Trouble: Trump, Transatlantic Relations and European Strategic Autonomy', *Journal of Common Market Studies*, 57:S1, 114–27.

Antezza, Arianna, Frank, André, Frank, Pascal, Franz, Lukas & Kharitonov, Ivan (2022): *The Ukraine Support Tracker: Which Countries Help Ukraine and How?*, Kiel Institute for the World Economy, Kiel Working Paper 2218. https://www.ifw-kiel.de/fileadmin/Dateiverwaltung/IfW-Publications/-ifw/Kiel_Working_Paper/2022/KWP_2218_Which_countries_help_Ukraine_and_how_/KWP_2218_Version5.pdf (Last access: 5 December 2022).

Bergsen, Pepijn, Froggatt, Antony, Nouwens, Veerle & Pantucci, Raffaello (2022): *China and the Transatlantic Relationship: Obstacles to Deeper European-US Cooperation*, Chatham House, Briefing Paper.

Boffey, Daniel & Neslen, Arthus (2017): 'China and EU Strengthen Promise to Paris Deal with US Poised to Step Away', *The Guardian*, 31 May 2017. https://www.theguardian.com/environment/2017/may/31/china-eu-climate-lead-paris-agreement (Last access: 4 December 2022).

Borger, Julian (2019a): 'Trump Administration Downgrades EU's Status in US, without Informing Brussels', *The Guardian*, 8 January 2019. https://www.theguardian.com/us-news/2019/jan/08/trump-administration-downgrades-european-union-status (Last access: 4 December 2022).

Borger, Julian (2019b): 'We'll Block Trade Deal If Brexit Imperils Open Irish Border, Say US Politicians', *The Guardian*, 31 July 2019. https://www.theguardian.com/politics/2019/jul/31/brexit-mess-with-good-friday-and-well-block-uk-trade-deal-us-politicians-warn (Last access: 4 December 2022).

Bouchet, Nicholas (2022): *How the War Could Reinforce the Transatlantic Relationship*, Italian Institute for International Political Studies, Commentary. https://www.ispionline.it/en/pubblicazione/how-war-could-reinforce-transatlantic-relationship-34855 (Last access: 4 December 2022).

Brundsen, Jim, Fleming, Sam, Williams, Aime & Politi, James (2021): 'EU and US End Airbus-Boeing Trade Dispute after 17 Years', *Financial Times*, 15 June 2021. https://www.ft.com/content/985ae1d6-89eb-46d6-b06c-8299ba70c588 (Last access: 5 December 2022).

von der Burchard, Hans & Leali, Giorgio (2022): 'Germany and France Join Forces against Biden in Subsidy Battle', *Politico EU*, 22 November 2022. https://www.politico.eu/article/germany-france-biden-green-subsidy-inflation-reduction-act-robert-habeck-bruno-le-maire/ (Last access: 5 December 2022).

Chrisafis, Angelique & Rankin, Jennifer (2019): 'EU Must Learn from Brexit and Reform, Says Emmanuel Macron'. *The Guardian*, 4 March 2019. https://www.theguardian.com/world/2019/mar/04/eu-must-learn-from-brexit-and-reform-says-emmanuel-macron (Last access: 5 December 2022).

Cross, Mai'a K. Davis (2018): 'Partners at Paris? Climate Negotiations and Transatlantic Relations', *Journal of European Integration*, 40:5, 571–86.

Engelbrekt, Kjell (2022): 'Beyond Burdensharing and European Strategic Autonomy: Rebuilding Transatlantic Security After the Ukraine War', *European Foreign Affairs Review*, 27:3, 383–400.

European Commission (2017): *White Paper on the Future of Europe*, European Commission. https://ec.europa.eu/info/sites/default/files/white_paper_on_the_future_of_europe_en.pdf (Last access: 6 December 2022).

European Commission (2019): *EU-China – A Strategic Outlook*, European Commission, Communication. https://ec.europa.eu/commission/presscorner/api/files/attachment/858891/communication-eu-china-a-strategic-outlook.pdf.pdf (Last access: 5 December 2022).

Fabry, Adam (2019): 'Neoliberalism, Crisis and Authoritarian–Ethnicist Reaction: The Ascendancy of the Orbán Regime', *Competition & Change*, 23:2, 165–91.

Hamilton, Daniel S. (2014): 'Transatlantic Challenges: Ukraine, TTIP and the Struggle to Be Strategic', *Journal of Common Market Studies*, 52:S1, 25–39.

Hofmann, Stephanie C. (2021): 'Elastic Relations: Looking to Both Sides of the Atlantic in the 2020 US Presidential Election Year', *Journal of Common Market Studies*, 59(S1), 150–61.

Hopewell, Kristen (2021): 'When the Hegemon Goes Rogue: Leadership amid the US Assault on the Liberal Trading Order', *International Affairs*, 97:4, 1025–43.

Immenkamp, Beatrix (2020): *EU-Iran: The Way Forward. Can the JCPOA Survive the Trump Presidency?*, European Parliament Research Service, Briefing PE 652.001. https://www.europarl.europa.eu/RegData/etudes/BRIE/2020/652001/EPRS_BRI(2020)652001_EN.pdf (Last access: 5 December 2022).

de Jong, Moniek (2022): 'Too Little, Too Late? US Sanctions against Nord Stream 2 and the Transatlantic Relationship', *Journal of Transatlantic Studies*, 20:2, 213–29.

Karnitschnig, Matthew & Kość, Wojciech (2022): 'Meet Europe's Coming Military Superpower: Poland', *Politico EU*, 21 November 2022. https://www.politico.eu/article/europe-military-super power-poland-army/ (Last access: 6 December 2022).

Kijewski, Leonie & Cooper, Charlie (2022): 'EU Agrees $60 Price Cap on Russian Oil'. *Politico EU*, 2 December 2022. https://www.politico.eu/article/eu-agrees-russian-oil-price-cap-after-poland-backs-plan/ (Last access: 6 December 2022).

Larres, Klaus (2020): 'Trump's Trade Wars: America, China, Europe, and Global Disorder', *Journal of Transatlantic Studies*, 18:1, 103–29.

Marsh, Sarah & Chambers, Madeline (2022): 'Germany Freezes Nord Stream 2 Gas Project as Ukraine Crisis Deepens', *Reuters, 22 February 2022*. https://www.reuters.com/business/energy/germanys-scholz-halts-nord-stream-2-certification-2022-02-22/ (Last access: 6 December 2022).

Olsen, Gorm Rye (2022): '"America Is Back" or "America First" and the Transatlantic Relationship', *Politics and Governance*, 10:2, 154–64.

Pavone, Ilja Richard (2018): 'The Paris Agreement and the Trump Administration: Road to Nowhere?', *Journal of International Studies*, 11:1, 34–49.

Pilkington, Ed (2022): '"The Trump Playbook": Republicans Hint They Will Deny Election Results', *The Guardian*, 2 November 2022. https://www.theguardian.com/us-news/2022/nov/02/trump-play book-us-midterms-republicans-election-denial (Last access: 6 December 2022).

Polyakova, Alina & Haddad, Benjamin (2019): 'Europe Alone: What Comes after the Transatlantic Alliance?', *Foreign Affairs*, 98: July/August, 109–20.

Rappaport, Armin (1981): 'The United States and European Integration: The First Phase', *Diplomatic History*, 5:2, 121–50.

Reuters (2022): 'Finland, Sweden Promise to Join NATO Together in United Front to Turkey', *Reuters*, 28 October 2022. https://www.reuters.com/world/europe/finnish-swedish-pms-assure-commit ment-join-nato-together-2022-10-28/ (Last access: 5 December 2022).

Riddervold, Marianne & Newsome, Akasemi (2018): 'Transatlantic Relations in Times of Uncertainty: Crises and EU-US Relations', *Journal of European Integration*, 40:5, 505–21.

Riddervold, Marianne & Newsome, Akasemi (2022): 'Introduction: Out With the Old, In With the New? Explaining Changing EU–US Relations', *Politics and Governance*, 10:2, 128–33.

Rogers, Katie & Mandavilli, Apoorva (2020): 'Trump Administration Signals Formal Withdrawal From W.H.O.' *New York Times*, 7 July 2020. https://www.nytimes.com/2020/07/07/us/politics/coronavi rus-trump-who.html (Last access: 5 December 2022).

Rump, Maike (2022): 'Voting for Eurosceptic Parties and Societal Polarization in the Aftermath of the European Sovereign Debt Crisis', *Statistics, Politics and Policy*, 13:2, 145–62.

Shapiro, Jeremy (2022): *The Coming Transatlantic Rift over Ukraine*, European Council on Foreign Relations, Commentary. https://ecfr.eu/article/the-coming-transatlantic-rift-over-ukraine/ (Last access: 5 December 2022).

Smith, Michael (2022): 'How Much of a New Agenda? International Structures, Agency, and Transatlantic Order', *Politics and Governance*, 10:2, 219–28.

Smith, Mike (2018): 'The EU, the US and the Crisis of Contemporary Multilateralism', *Journal of European Integration*, 40:5, 539–53.

Stahl, Bernhard, Lucke, Robin & Felfeli, Anna (2016): 'Comeback of the Transatlantic Security Community? Comparative Securitization in the Crimea Crisis', *East European Politics*, 32:4, 525–46.

Swanson, Ana & Rogers, Katie (2021): 'U.S. Agrees to Roll Back European Steel and Aluminum Tariffs', *New York Times*, 30 October 2021. https://www.nytimes.com/2021/10/30/business/econo my/biden-steel-tariffs-europe.html (Last access: 5 December 2022).

Szabo, Stephen F. (2018): 'Partners in Leadership? American Views of the New German Role', *German Politics*, 27:4, 539–54.

Szewczyk, Bart M. J. (2022): 'Macron's Vision for European Autonomy Crashed and Burned in Ukraine', *Foreign Policy*, 8 April 2022. https://foreignpolicy.com/2022/04/08/macron-putin-france-russia-ukraine-europe-sovereignty-strategy/ (Last access: 6 December 2022).

The White House (2022): *United States, G7 and EU Impose Severe and Immediate Costs on Russia*, The White House, Fact Sheet. https://www.whitehouse.gov/briefing-room/statements-releases/2022/ 04/06/fact-sheet-united-states-g7-and-eu-impose-severe-and-immediate-costs-on-russia/ (Last access: 5 December 2022).

Trump, Donald J. (2020): *Remarks by President Trump in Press Conference*, The White House. https:// trumpwhitehouse.archives.gov/briefings-statements/remarks-president-trump-press-conference-071420/ (Last access: 5 December 2022).

Wright, Georgina & Cooley, Alexander (2022): *The Ukraine Moment in Transatlantic Relations… and Then What?*, Institut Montaigne, Analysis. https://www.institutmontaigne.org/en/analysis/ukraine-moment-transatlantic-relations-and-then-what (Last aceess: 5 December 2022).

Part IV: **European policy fields shaped by crisis**

Alexandra Bousiou & Linnea Schleyer

11 Consolidating the fortress Europe: Conceptualizations of solidarity in the EU Asylum System governance post-2015

Abstract: Over the last decade, the construction of a crisis narrative has continued consolidating the idea of a "fortress Europe" at the expense of access and the right to asylum in the EU. In this chapter, we embark on an analysis of how a series of crises and their management has been affecting EU asylum policies, and more specifically how the discursive construction of solidarity, a cornerstone of the Treaty on the Functioning of the EU and a core value of international asylum law, has been evolving within these policies. Our analysis demonstrates how the governance of asylum in the EU has shifted towards more restriction and less solidarity both with refugees and amongst Member States in the context of emergency management. We focus on the shifting perspectives on solidarity between 2015 and 2022 and trace how the concept of solidarity continues to evolve in the European governance of asylum. The analysis culminates in a discussion of the Temporary Protection Directive, the recent activation of which has once more shed light on different EU actors' and member states' answers to the question of who deserves solidarity in the EU and for how long, illuminating important aspects of racial discrimination and temporariness.

Keywords: Asylum, solidarity, refugee crisis, CEAS, fortress Europe

Introduction

Contemporary international asylum law was born in the aftermath of the Second World War and has thus moulded into crisis management. In the EU context, asylum policy has been developing through a series of crises or perceived crises and emergencies. In this chapter, we embark on an analysis of how this series of crises and their management has been affecting EU asylum policies in recent years, and more specifically how the discursive construction of solidarity, a cornerstone of the Treaty on the Functioning of the EU and a core value of international asylum law, has been evolving within these policies. We contribute to this volume by offering a better understanding of the relationship and patterns of action between crises and EU policy responses in the area of asylum, with a specific focus on solidarity.

https://doi.org/10.1515/9783110790337-012

Refugee protection as part of the international human rights regime has always been connected to shifts in global politics, as well as solidarity towards people fleeing persecution and responsibility-sharing between states. In 2015, when more than a million refugees, mostly Syrian, crossed the European borders, the perceived crisis in the EU was so extreme that President of the European Commission Jean-Claude Juncker stated it "shook … [the] very foundation of the European integration project" (Lavenex 2018). The image of Ukrainian refugees crossing the European Union (EU) borders under the Temporary Protection Directive[1] (Council Directive, 2001) in 2022 can be interpreted as a further paradigm shift in European asylum policy (Carrera et al. 2022; Rasche 2022). EU governance in the area took a significant turn from the closure of internal borders and the humanitarian emergency in Greece and Italy in 2015 to the Temporary Protection Directive (Council Directive 2001) in 2022, under which refugees from the Russian invasion of Ukraine have been freely crossing EU borders.

In this chapter, we conduct a framing analysis of the main policy documents of the EU in the area of asylum policy, to demonstrate how perceptions of solidarity in the EU have shifted under the guise of "emergency". Part of our inquiry concerns the recent events in Ukraine and the activation of the Temporary Protection Directive (Council Directive 2001). We see these policy developments connected to the securitization of migration (Huysmans 2006), which is historically and deeply embedded in the idea of "fortress Europe" (Geddes 2008; Levy 2010): a fortress which is keeping the external EU borders sealed in order to facilitate the internal freedom of movement (Geddes 2008; Levy 2010; Tsianos & Karakayali 2010). The idea of a fortressed Europe is inherently contradictive considering the EU's aim of reuniting the European nations after the Second World War. As Engelbert et al. (2019) stated this is due to two ideas: that freedom in Europe is inherently vulnerable and therefore it should be treated as a security matter, and that some people and their access to freedom are particularly risk-prone.

"Crises" and the Common European Asylum System

The large-scale movement of refugees fleeing from conflicts as a result of the dissolution of the former Yugoslavia put the issue of creating common European pol-

---

[1] The Temporary protection is an exceptional measure to provide immediate and temporary protection in the event of a mass influx or imminent mass influx of displaced persons from non-EU countries who are unable to return to their country of origin.

icies for the management of asylum in this and potential similar crises on the EU table (Moreno-Lax 2017). Consequently, the increased numbers of asylum seekers crossing the EU Member States' borders and applying for international protection triggered the creation of a Common European Asylum System. The problem which was labelled 'asylum shopping'[2] induced the idea of an EU-wide asylum system that would include a mechanism of allocating responsibility among Member States for each asylum application in a way that would promote what has since then been called 'burden sharing'.

The creation of a regional refugee protection system within the EU in the 1990s is not self-evident (Guild 2006). The direct connection of the Area of Freedom, Security and Justice to migration policies indicates that the main objective driving the creation of a European asylum regime was first and foremost the effective regulation of border management (Chetail 2016; Guild 2016). Therefore, a more careful reading of the evolution of the European asylum regime, as well as the discourse surrounding asylum such as 'asylum shopping', 'burden sharing', 'migrant and refugee flows' and 'migration/asylum crisis'", point to a clear connection between internal security and border control emergency management , in addition to anticipated crises.

More recently, the framing of the increase of refugee arrivals in Europe in 2015 as 'migration' crisis has been contested from within and outside the migration research community. As it has been noted, notions of crisis should reflect on the questions for whom and where crisis conditions would be met. Moreover, the crisis should be discussed as regards the root causes of the displacement, in this case: notably the Syrian civil war (Jeandesboz & Pallister-Wilkins 2016). Researchers studying the 2015 events and their consequences for and within the EU have considered it as a crisis of governance (Börzel 2016; Sahin-Mencutek et al. 2022) with severe humanitarian implications at the external borders (Afouxenidis et al. 2017). Rather than considering the high number of asylum seekers as a crisis in itself, Chamberlain (2020) argues that the member state governments' actions generated the crisis, turning it into a moral crisis shaped by Europe's failure to take responsibility for what took place at its external borders. Moreover, the crisis narrative was certainly influenced by unprecedented numbers of migrant deaths at sea (McMahon & Sigona 2021). Overall, there is consensus amongst researchers that the 2015 events and their aftermath constituted a crisis of political solidarity (Crawley 2016). Although the framing of a crisis is generally seen as an opportunity

---

2 The term "asylum-shopping" is not a formal legal term but it is used in different EU documents and communications and it has a rather negative connotation. It implies an abuse of the asylum procedure through the lodging of more than one application for international protection in different EU Member States.

for policy development (Baumgartner & Jones 2002: 293; Geddes 2018), some argue that the predominant reading of the situation in 2015 as a humanitarian emergency did not fundamentally alter the principle tenets of EU policy (Guiraudon 2018; Servent 2020).

EU institutional responses to the "migration crisis"

In order to understand how European asylum governance was, and is, affected by crises, and the way it is somewhat crisis-producing, it is important to understand the responses from key EU institutions to instances of strain and (perceived) emergency. Following the 2015 'crisis', the EU was strongly criticized for not being able to provide adequate access to asylum for people fleeing persecution and for not properly addressing the unequal distribution of asylum applications between the Member States (Thielemann 2018). In the context of the emerging crisis, the Commission sought to reform the CEAS whilst simultaneously lacking the time to properly evaluate already existing asylum legislation or to monitor the impact of new legislative proposals. It has therefore been argued that the crisis was to some extent exacerbated by the lack of strong enforcement, weak monitoring, and low harmonisation of EU law (Cornelisse & Reneman 2020). At the same time, and partly as a result, political leaders of various member states shifted towards more nationalistic approaches in migration governance, rather than towards calls for more solidarity, responsibility sharing, or Europeanisation, leading to more restrictive and illiberal migration policies across the EU.

Since an extension of its competences through the Treaties of Amsterdam and, notably, of Lisbon, the European Commission has assumed an increasingly influential role in the traditionally intergovernmental area of asylum governance. Especially during the last decade, the EC has taken on a more political, value-based role in its pursuit of building a system that normalizes migration in a long-term perspective, and that is fully grounded in European values (Fassi & Lucarelli 2021). The so-called "migration crisis" of 2015 led to a renewed struggle for competence between the EC and the Member States: as high pressure was placed on national asylum systems, member states' perception of urgently required action clashed with the EC's more long-term political agenda. This struggle contributed to an increasing politicization of the Commission's role in EU asylum governance. This shift towards a more political role can be explained by the EC's desire to retain agency in a political area where Member States show growing resistance towards European integration and where the policies are increasingly framed as an emergency or a crisis (Cornelisse & Reneman 2020). Collectively, the Commission's increasingly politicized role in asylum governance, the crisis narrative dominating policy responses, and the Commission's effort to retain authority in its policies resulted in measures primarily focused on efficiency and effectiveness (Cornelisse & Reneman 2020), as well as on enhanced border controls and policies seeking to deter irregular migrants.

Moreover, the larger dynamic of politicization of migration (Entzinger & Scholten 2019), which is directly connected to its construction as a security threat, has set the stage for political debate between Member States in the area. The latter are reluctant to revise a common asylum system which is evidently failing both in allocating responsibility and creating decent conditions for asylum seekers. According to the Dublin Regulation,[3] the country the applicants enter first is the country responsible for the asylum process. The Dublin Regulation has been the cornerstone of the CEAS and also the center of its contestation.

After the increase in refugee arrivals, this contestation intensified. Due to their geography, some member states such as Italy and Greece were forced to take on responsibility for a large part of the asylum seekers who reached the EU's external borders. Other member states with advanced asylum systems and strong economies that were desirable destinations for asylum seekers, such as Germany and Sweden, took responsibility initially by granting the largest numbers of refugee protection. Last, there were member states who strongly refused to share any sort of responsibility, such as Hungary, Slovakia, and Poland. This unequal sharing of responsibility enabled finger-pointing and scapegoating between the member states. Member states started blaming each other for the "crisis", leading to conflicts both internally within the EU and externally with third countries (Crawley 2016).

Thus, it becomes clear that any perception of emergency concerning asylum management in the EU is inseparable from ideas about fair sharing of responsibility. Consequently, the principle of solidarity as a way of sharing the responsibility for refugees within the CEAS is key in understanding the policy developments.

---

3 Regulation (EU) No 604/2013 of the European Parliament and of the Council of 26 June 2013 establishing the criteria and mechanisms for determining the Member State responsible for examining an application for international protection lodged in one of the Member States by a third-country national or stateless person (recast), [2013] OJ L180/31.

Conceptualizing solidarity in the EU

The lack of solidarity in European migration policies is clearly reflected in the protectionism that shaped the CEAS, as well as in the more nationalist agendas and conflicts among the Member States, and also between them and the Commission, during the crisis (Lavenex 2018). Wallaschek (2020) argues: "The solidarity debate underpins the high degree of potential conflict around the migration issue in the EU", and further explains that political solidarity in the area is contested by security-oriented framings of migration. Most scholars agree that solidarity is key to developing a more effective common European asylum system (Thielemann 2018).

More recently, the current events in Ukraine have shown a new side of European solidarity. The swift activation, for the first time since it was adopted, of the Temporary Protection Directive (Council Directive 2001) in 2022, and the unanimity among Member States in receiving Ukrainian refugees in a way that is bypassing the Dublin Regulation raises the question of whether there has been a fundamental change with the European asylum regime and its framing of solidarity. Yet, this solidarity has been extended only to a delimited group of recipients, namely to persons from one specific country, fleeing one concrete conflict which is also to an increasing extent perceived as a direct threat to the rest of Europe. This delimitation of solidarity, and its absence vis-à-vis with other groups of forced migrants, calls for a systematic conceptualisation of solidarity, which is necessary to understand European action – or inaction – in response to situations of strain, crisis, and emergency in the area of migration and asylum.

One conceptualization of solidarity separates state-refugee solidarity and interstate solidarity. The former refers to the solidarity shown towards individuals in need of protection, from states who are legally obliged to protect the individual in question. The latter describes the type of solidarity states show towards each other by, for instance, sharing the responsibilities of refugees' allocation. Both dimensions are encouraged by the EU and can be difficult to distinguish. Nevertheless, both dimensions were not sufficiently developed either in the CEAS or in the Member States during the migration crisis (Karageorgiou 2016).

The second conceptualization of solidarity has to do with the fair sharing of responsibility according to Article 80 TFEU, which states:

> *The policies of the Union set out in this Chapter and their implementation shall be governed by the principle of solidarity and fair sharing of responsibility, including its financial implications, between the Member States.*

The implementation measures for this fair sharing of responsibility have, however, been less evident. Fair sharing of responsibility in terms of solidarity has typically been emergency-driven and is built on the assumption that in order to deserve solidarity, Member States must first implement other obligations. Following this approach, if the border states, for instance, would have shown greater responsibility, in the sense of managing the situation with their own means, they would not have needed exceptional solidarity from the other member states (Tsourdi 2017). This creates a paradox where solidarity and fair sharing of responsibility cannot exist apart from each other since you need one of them to receive the other; yet once one is achieved, the other would technically no longer be required (Karageorgiou 2019). To this end, it has been argued that if Article 80 TFEU was reformed in a way that obliged the Member States to fair sharing of responsibility in advance of an emergency rather than after, an asymmetrical burden-sharing – as is currently the case – would not exist (Tsourdi 2017).

In practical terms, solidarity has been operationalised through allocation, relocation, and burden-sharing (Mitsilegas 2014). An allocation mechanism is expected to make member states share protection responsibilities. As long as the main allocation mechanism is the Dublin Regulation, allocation in the EU will continue to place heavy burdens on certain Member States instead of strategizing for fair distribution of responsibility (Karageorgiou 2016). Relocation is viewed as a corrective mechanism, and it entails the relocation of asylum seekers from one member state to another with the aim of sharing achieving fair sharing of responsibility. It is focused on the financial and logistical aspects of sharing asylum seekers, which makes it problematic since the responsibility for fair sharing between the member states is not clearly defined. In consequence, relocation is often merely an emergency-driven response after the allocation mechanism has failed and has proven no long-term sustainable solution. Connected to this is the burden-sharing narrative of distributing the financial and administrative effort of receiving and incorporating asylum seekers in equal shares among member states that have frequently been invoked by politicians during the crisis. The problem with burden-sharing is that it takes away the focus from the right to seek asylum and the people fleeing persecution and shifts it to the member states' situation as host/reception counties. The humanitarian perspective is thus easily overlooked when the discourse revolves around burden sharing. After all, what is fair for the member states is not necessarily fair for the affected people seeking asylum (Karageorgiou 2019).

We will be using these different interpretations of the solidarity concept as policy frames to identify the ways in which solidarity has been understood and used in EU policy documents within the above-mentioned contexts of emergency-driven policy responses. This allows us to illustrate how the framing of solidarity has been affected by crises and how the larger area of EU (forced) migration governance has evolved and either developed policies based on a crisis or been part of producing/exacerbating a crisis based on existing or adapted policies.

Framing analysis of the solidarity conceptualization

To trace the evolution of solidarity in the CEAS in recent years, we will conduct a framing analysis of the key documents that the EC has produced since 2015. Framing analyses seek to understand the discursive processes which construct policy problems and to explain how these problem constructions affect the subsequent reactions to the identified problem (Zito 2011). In consideration of the increased politicization of asylum and the complex policy-making processes and competence shifts/claims in the area of EU asylum governance, we are applying the framing analysis approach to untangle the conflicting problem definitions of solidarity and their impact on EU asylum governance.

The level of contestation in the framing of migration and asylum indicates that it is an "intractable problem" (Rein and Schön 1994). Unlike other types of policy conflicts that can in principle be settled by recourse to facts and established rules, Rein and Schön (1994) define this type of policy controversy as conflicts that can only be overcome when participants 'reflect on the frame-conflicts implicit in their controversies and explore the potentials for their resolution'. As described above, asylum policies are interlinked with multiple perspectives on the concept of crisis, as demonstrated in the case of the 2015 events and their aftermath – the crisis dimension of which has been identified as lying first and foremost in the Syrian civil war, in the humanitarian emergency at the EU's borders, or in the governance crisis resulting from the lack of consensus among EU member states. This case exemplifies how conflicting perspectives on what kind of crisis the EU is facing can produce different policy responses.

In the following analysis, we focus on the assignment of institutional responsibility allocation and the ways this allocation changed over time. Following the different conceptualisation approaches of solidarity outlined above, we trace the following policy frames in the analysed documents;
– interstate- and state-refugee solidarity,
– solidarity understood as the fair sharing of responsibility and burden-sharing,
– solidarity in allocation and relocation, and finally
– solidarity as an emergency-driven response.

The material analysed consists of the Commission's Agenda on Migration (2015), the New Pact on Migration and Asylum (2020), and the Temporary Protection Directive (2001, activated 2022), along with accompanying policy documents. The analysis demonstrates how the framing of solidarity has evolved under the impression of two major phases of a (perceived) crisis.

Interstate solidarity and state-refugee solidarity

In the context of the two above-mentioned crises, one major finding emerging from the analysis of Commission documents on asylum governance is a general absence of references to state-refugee solidarity. Among the few exceptions the analysis could trace, solidarity from the EU and Member States towards refugees can be spotted in the Agenda on Migration from 2015. Solidarity is framed as an issue in which more work needs to be done by the Member States to provide a safe haven for those fleeing persecution (COM (2015) 240: 2). The Agenda contains an overall strong humanitarian focus and an emphasis on fundamental human rights (COM(2015) 240). However, even here, the actual word solidarity is never used in this context.

In terms of interstate solidarity, member states are repeatedly urged to show solidarity towards each other to deal with the challenges of migration flows, for instance in funding Frontex (COM(2015) 240: 3), or relocation in which member states "... will need to show solidarity" to assist countries at the EU's external borders (COM(2015) 240: 4). Later on, solidarity is defined as something that needs to be balanced with responsibility; states are obliged to show support towards the most pressured among themselves, whilst emphasising that such solidarity would by no means reduce the responsibility of the border states (COM(2015) 490: 3). In a Commission communication on the Delivery of the Agenda on Migration from 2017, an increased use of interstate solidarity is visible, mostly concerning relocation and responsibility sharing, emphasising a strong moral dimension of the need for member states' ability to trust each other (COM(2017) 558).

In accordance with an increasingly dominant distinction between 'deserving' and 'undeserving' migrants in various European states' asylum policies, state-refugee solidarity can be traced to an effective return system for those who stay in Europe without legal documents. According to this argument, effective returns are the only way for the EU to show solidarity with refugees "in real need of protection." (COM(2017) 558: 20). The argument is based on the notion that the EU would have very limited resources to attend to refugees and therefore returning anyone who has no grounds for seeking international protection would allow the use of these scarce resources for those in 'real' need. This framing is echoing the "fortress Europe" narrative, where protecting the borders from irregular migration is claimed to be related to an efficient asylum policy. This is highly controversial given the fact that refugees have no other regular paths of applying for international protection except by crossing EU borders.

The most distinct disparity in the Pact, compared to the Agenda, is the more operational explanation of how interstate solidarity should be achieved. Instead of understanding solidarity as fairly shared funding and relocation, the Pact focuses on more common screening systems, a common EU system for returns, and suggested actions for rules determining which Member State is responsible for asylum applications (COM(2020) 609). Solidarity is defined as a concept that implies that all Member States should contribute (COM(2020) 609: 5) and consistently address the issue of migration in solidarity even after the crisis has ended (COM(2020) 609).

Finally, it is difficult to find any evidence of solidarity being framed in the state-refugee perspective in the Pact. It is merely argued that the EU must do more to protect refugees and that assisting those in need is an obligation under international law, a moral duty, and "a key element of the European integrated border management" (COM(2020) 609). However, solidarity is never mentioned, only the requirement of Member States to assist one another.

The Temporary Protection Directive (Council Directive 2001) is even more grounded than the other documents in the idea of inter-state solidarity. In chapter VI, which bears 'solidarity' in its title, it is clearly stated that "Member States shall receive persons who are eligible for temporary protection in a spirit of Community solidarity." In the Directive, the rationale of solidarity is for preventing a situation where a few Member States must deal with mass arrivals of refugees and the potential consequences for their respective asylum systems. The framing of state-refugee solidarity is implied through the framing of limited reception capacities which can result in national emergencies. The Directive recognizes that in case there are mass arrivals, the principle of solidarity could be used to balance the reception capacities of states exposed to particularly high numbers of arrivals. This framing, albeit including a humanitarian perspective, is not grounded in the individuals' right to protection or the responsibility of the state to provide it.

The EC proposal for the activation of the Directive (COM (2022) 91) and the Council Implementing Decision (2022), emerging more than twenty years after the Directive following Russia's invasion of Ukraine and the thereby triggered massive migration movement of persons fleeing the conflict, directly discuss the Ukrainian people as those in need of protection. Still, the framing analysis of solidarity points heavily to interstate solidarity. In particular, the Temporary Protection Directive "[..]the provisions under the Temporary Protection Directive promote a balance of efforts between the Member States." (COM (2022) 91). It further elaborates that the facilitation of the implementation of the Directive can be "done through a 'Solidarity Platform' whereby Member States exchange information regarding their reception capacities and the number of persons enjoying temporary protection on their territories." (COM (2022) 91). This is an important finding, as the basis of interstate solidarity relies more on ideas of effective management than the international protection regime which is focused on each individual's right to seek protection from persecution. Interestingly the unusually open response to Ukrainian refugees was not primarily driven by altruistic motives but first and foremost by the motive of preventing a system overload.

Fair sharing of responsibility and burden sharing

As indicated above, we can see that the framing of solidarity is increasingly connected to the framing of responsibility (Tsourdi 2017). This has blurred the lines between fair sharing of responsibility and burden sharing (Karageorgiou 2019). The Agenda emphasizes the need for Member States to act in solidarity and demonstrate the fair sharing of responsibility to address migration, for instance through a permanent system for responsibility-sharing for large numbers of asylum seekers (COM(2015) 240: 4). Responsibility-sharing is frequently mentioned in the migration crisis, where the Agenda emphasizes the need for both Member States and the EU to take on greater responsibility to help the states on the frontline of migration arrivals (COM(2015) 240: 6). In relation to the crisis, the burden narrative appears, where the failure of the Dublin Regulation is acknowledged as having led certain Member States to stand alone in "difficulties" (COM(2015) 240: 6). In a proposal from the Commission in 2016 for a regulation on the responsibility distribution for incoming asylum seekers among member states, it is stated that particularly strained Member States should be "relieved of some of the burden", and that extreme migration flows would need to be met by all Member States showing responsibility (COM(2016) 270: 5), clearly demonstrating the link between responsibility-sharing and burden-sharing.

This trend continues in the New Pact on Migration and Asylum, in which the Commission seeks to operationalise solidarity by introducing technical aspects of the responsibility-sharing mechanism, such as return sponsorships and rules for return responsibility (COM(2020) 609). Under the new solidarity mechanism, it is stated that Member States must provide those states facing a particularly high burden with the necessary support to return those who are not allowed to stay and share responsibility if a return is not carried out on time (COM(2020) 609: 5). This suggests that the Member State with the capacity to take responsibility and assist pressured Member States is also the one that must show solidarity.

A Proposal on Asylum and Migration Management from 2020 states that the only time Member States were obliged to show solidarity during the migration crisis was in terms of relocation. It mentions the burdens that the Dublin Regulation has imposed on some Member States in terms of fair sharing of responsibility, and proposes new actions to be taken in order to balance solidarity and burden-sharing more efficiently (COM(2020) 610). However, it also acknowledges a lack of political willingness to revise the Dublin Regulation, since it still states that the responsibility criterion related to first entry will remain in place (COM(2020) 610: 12). Furthermore, it reflects the general tendency in EU asylum governance to deal with short-term solutions to a crisis rather than considering long-term consequences. This is partially explained by the political contestation around asylum and migration. And it also indicates the EU's inability to cope with the migration crises compared to other policy areas where the union recently succeeded in adapting and sometimes developing new policies in response to crises (Riddervold et al. 2021).

The activation of the Temporary Protection Directive directly challenges the logic behind the Dublin Regulation, since it does not foresee a rule of seeking protection at the Member State of first entry. On the contrary, the EC proposal for the activation of the Directive (COM(2022) 91) states that Ukrainians can travel through the EU without a visa. This is framed under a logic of burden-sharing which is very different from the Dublin Regulation, and it shows that under different types of emergencies and political alignments highly politicised policies such as the Dublin Regulation can be challenged (in this case, of course, only as a temporary measure, although it should be kept in mind that many temporary solutions have gradually become a permanent rule in the EU's history, notably when adopted in response to a crisis). In the case of the Directive, the emergency at hand was viewed as a result of a conflict in Europe and thus requiring the involvement of European actors such as the EU. Consequently, there is less resistance to framing a European solution that diverges from the previously established principles of the CEAS.

Allocation and relocation

The Agenda on Migration puts a notable focus on the establishment of EU relocation mechanisms. It presents a relocation scheme with a focus on shared responsibility and a proposal for a permanent common relocation system for emergency situations (COM(2015) 240: 6), clearly suggesting that a well-functioning relocation system may constitute a solution for future emergencies. The most outstanding finding from the perspective of this framing analysis is that relocation is repeatedly framed in the Agenda as a solution to the migration crisis, but never explicitly as a strategy to achieve more solidarity – neither vis-à-vis forced migrants nor at the interstate level.

This framing, however, is not dominant in Commission documents of that time – to the contrary: in a Commission communication on "immediate operational, budgetary and legal measures under the European Agenda on Migration" from the same year, relocation is framed as proof of solidarity between Member States (COM(2015) 490), suggesting that the two concepts are considered as interconnected. This can further be corroborated in later documents where the relocation and protection of refugees is framed as a way for Member States to show solidarity towards affected member states (COM(2016) 165), and as a sign that (interstate) solidarity can work in practise (COM(2017) 558).

Interestingly, relocation and allocation are framed as acts, or in a context, of solidarity when immediate crisis (re-)action is discussed, rather than in proposals for general, more long-term relocation strategies. Moreover, discussions around relocation repeatedly refer to the failure of certain member states to contribute. Namely, members such as Hungary and Slovakia are singled out as having failed to implement the relocation plans (COM(2016) 165). Some states are named as not having relocated a single person, and the Commission urges all Member States to show (intrastate) solidarity by taking over relocations to answer the need for help in Greece and Italy (COM(2017) 405: 10).

In reports from 2018 and 2019, the relocation measures that were implemented during the crisis are equally presented as proof of intrastate solidarity. A similar framing strategy can be traced in the New Pact which presents a new solidarity mechanism with a primary focus on relocation or return sponsorship[4] (COM(2020) 609: 5). Although these long-term relocation measures seem contradictory to the approach of relocation as crisis management, they can be explained in the light of the strong contestation regarding the allocation mechanism of Dublin Regulation. In other words, as the EC acknowledges that the Dublin Regulation will not be revised any time soon, relocation becomes a solution for "enforcing" solidarity.

Up until the activation of the Temporary Protection Directive, allocation and relocation as solidarity framings have never included the notion of refugee agency. On the contrary, refugees' agency in the form of secondary movements, i.e. moving to another Member State to apply for asylum instead of applying in the Member State of first entry, according to Dublin Regulation, are considered by the EU and the Member States as a security threat and a threat to the CEAS. In the EC proposal for the activation of the Directive, the possibility of Ukrainian refugees moving under the temporarily introduce visa-free regime and choosing for themselves where to apply for asylum is viewed as a facilitator for the asylum systems of the Member States (COM(2022) 91: 11). This is a very interesting framing, as it points to what is possible within a common European asylum regime. Crisis management concerning asylum policies often portrays refugees as a risk in the sense that high numbers of arrivals can destabilise asylum systems, or that the irregular and uncontrolled movement of asylum seekers can trigger security concerns. In

---

4 Under the return sponsorship a member state would undertake the cost of returning

the Directive, however, refugees' agency is not viewed as a risk or a security threat. In contrast, in 2015, refugees from the Middle East and North African countries who due to aspects such as culture and religion were not seen as European, triggered many debates on (intrastate vs. state-refugee) solidarity and security when crossing the EU borders. Therefore, the activation of the Temporary Protection Directive reaffirms the fact that solidarity in the CEAS is not implemented in an equal and non-discriminatory manner (Carrera et al. 2022; Franck et al. 2022).

Emergency-driven responses

This final part of the analysis will focus on solidarity framings as a response to emergencies, rather than being an integral part of the EU asylum system. The Agenda on Migration was written as a response to the 2015 'migration crisis', and therefore presents several measures and actions framed as a response to the crisis. It demands more solidarity from the Member States, which should, however, last first and foremost for as long as the extreme migration flows persist (COM(2015) 240: 2). Solidarity is thus framed as a measure to solve a crisis, and a dimension that grows in importance during times of elevated strain and emergencies.

In a later document, emergency is mentioned in the discussions on relocation, where it is stated that Member States should take part in emergency relocation processes in the spirit of solidarity. Member States are furthermore urged to take the emergency situation on the ground into account when deciding on their allocation quota (COM(2016) 165: 13). Interstate solidarity is thus continuously framed as a solution to the emergency facing the EU, and the Commission purposefully uses an emergency framing in this sense in order to attribute high importance and urgency to the suggested solidarity measures. In the years after the immediate crisis context, however, solidarity gradually disappears from the Commission's discourse on emergency measures: whilst still containing proposals on better crisis management, the 2018 and 2019 documents do not contain a similarly clear connection between solidarity and emergency assistance (COM(2018) 250 & COM(2019) 481).

By the time of the New Pact's presentation in 2020, solidarity is framed as a constant concept of EU asylum policy rather than as a mere element of emergency response (COM(2020) 609), indicating that the crisis led the EC to adapt its long-term migration policies. Indeed, the Commission calls for solidarity to become a permanent feature in EU asylum governance, to make the EU constantly prepared for emergencies, and to avoid the need for emergency-driven responses in the future (COM(2020) 609: 3).

Yet, the year 2022 produced a noteworthy reappearance of emergency-driven solidarity. The whole idea behind the Temporary Protection Directive relates to emergency-driven solidarity, as it can only be activated when there is a case of "mass influx of displaced persons who cannot return to their country of origin" (Council Directive 2001: 212). The main novelty in the Commission's proposal for the Directive's activation (COM(2022) 91), compared to previous documents, is that the proposed action seeks to answer a crisis context proactively rather than retroactively, in that it seeks to prevent the consequences of the emergency at hand. Compared to 2015, when EU action was always running behind the escalating humanitarian emergency at its borders, we see here a call to solidarity already prior to a full-blown crisis of reception.

Arguably, this pre-emptive call for solidarity before the asylum systems of the Member States are overwhelmed, creating a reception crisis, could not have been achieved without a clear and uniform political will. Hungary, Slovakia, and Poland, all of which share borders with Ukraine, are member states which usually oppose any measures in the area of asylum policy, notably in the name of both interstate and state-refugee solidarity. The fact that they are located at the frontline of the emergency, however, as well as the notion of Ukrainians as fellow Europeans, seems to have shifted (at least temporarily) their political positioning. This demonstrates that the shared perception of an internal crisis was not sufficient in itself, but had to be combined with a wide political agreement among member states, to produce responses to the emergency which before this point in time did not find the necessary support at the EU level, albeit existing as a theoretical option – after all, the Temporary Protection Directive lay ready to be applied in European drawers ever since its adoption in 2001. Many scholars expressed their surprise in 2015 when the Temporary Protection Directive was not activated (Genç & Şirin Öner 2019; Ineli-Ciger 2016). One explanation which we see by looking at the framings of solidarity in 2015, is that there was strong resistance from certain member states to accept that the increase of Syrian refugees would constitute a European emergency, requiring a European solution in a spirit of solidarity. Notably, these same countries which rejected responsibility-sharing under the principle of solidarity then are the ones who are sharing borders with Ukraine.

Discussion and conclusion

Our goal in this chapter was to explore how two crises and their management have been affecting European asylum policies under the influence of different and evolving discursive constructions of solidarity. Compared to other EU policy areas, asylum policy has largely evolved around crises. Indeed, it might be considered synonymous with crisis management. Despite the Commission's efforts in the New Pact on Migration and Asylum in 2020 to have a more sustainable approach to solidarity in the area, the documents leading to the activation of the Temporary Protection Directive imply that developments in asylum policy continue to take place in the EU context as part of crisis management.

By looking more specifically at the shifting perceptions of solidarity in the EU and the name of the "emergency" since 2015, and more recently with the activation of the Temporary Protection Directive, our analysis has shown that solidarity is key in understanding the relationship between crisis and asylum policies. In particular, we see that solidarity under the impression or imminent threat of an emergency has been used in ways that consolidate the "fortress Europe" (Geddes 2008; Levy 2010), as it is used first and foremost in the sense of interstate rather than state-refugee solidarity, and with a focus first and foremost on member states rather than third countries. Indeed, in all the documents we have analysed, solidarity has been framed predominantly as a matter of interstate relations. The interstate framing of solidarity has multiple consequences. First, it renders the refugees invisible, who are conceived as a burden that needs to be shared, rather than as persons in need of protection, calling on states to act on – legal as well as moral – demands of (shared) responsibility. Second, the interstate framing creates a context in which Member States negotiate – and often enough disagree, as the post-2015 phase of EU asylum governance has shown – on how to share the "burden" of refugees without consideration of the principles of international law, human rights and, more specifically, the right to seek asylum. These negotiations disclose a notable degree of tension in differing perceptions of interstate solidarity, both between the Commission and member states and among member states themselves (Karageorgiou 2016). Namely, the Commission strives to claim authority and agency in the area of asylum governance by framing such solidarity as a collective responsibility. In the context of the 2015 crisis, a number of member states, however – most notably Slovakia, Poland, and Hungary – argued conversely that problems arising from a lack of EU-level interstate solidarity would not be affecting them, and that a common approach of shared solidary action would hence not be required from their point of view. Yet, when the number of arrivals at their borders sharply increased in 2022, these states' positioning changed fundamentally, opening the way for the activation of the Temporary Protection Directive.

Finally, the analysis has shown how notably the Commission's framing of solidarity has changed over time to accommodate more restrictive and reluctant member states. Namely, while in 2015 solidarity has been framed as a solution to the increased refugee arrivals, later documents applied a more retroactive and negative frame in the sense that Member States have failed to act in solidarity. In 2020, the New Pact attempted to reframe solidarity once more in a more proactive way and as a long-term solution rather than mere crisis management, in that it introduced a solidarity mechanism of relocation and presents a series of concrete operational proposals for its implementation. The documents surrounding the activation of the Temporary Protection Directive in 2022 have shown, however, that the EU-level framing of migration-related solidarity remains dependent on the respective context and the (perceived) needs for action it produces. Namely, the analysis of these documents demonstrates that solidarity in the area of asylum and migration is a principle that Member States are willing to follow when the crisis and the refugees are seen as intra-European, which stands in stark contrast to member states' reaction to a crisis perceived as external. It is very hard to argue that the situation in 2015 could not have qualified as a "mass influx", according to the terminology of the Temporary Protection Directive. It is also very hard to argue that the protection criteria of the directive are non-discriminatory when asylum seekers and non-Ukrainian people fleeing Russia's war in Ukraine regardless of their legal status have been excluded. Indeed, there is credible evidence that the Temporary Protection Directive was implemented at the external EU borders in a racist and discriminatory way, prohibiting people who looked insufficiently "European" to cross the borders (Franck et al. 2022). Therefore, although the activation of the Temporary Protection Directive provides a ray of hope for real solidarity in the area of asylum in the EU, it also shows that the CEAS is not fortified against racist and generally discriminatory practices which are incompatible with the general idea of solidarity.

References

Afouxenidis, Alex, Petrou, Michalis, Kandylis, George, Tramountanis, Angelo & Giannaki, Dora (2017): 'Dealing with a Humanitarian Crisis: Refugees on the Eastern EU Border of the Island of Lesvos', *Journal of Applied Security Research*, 12:1, 7–39.

Baumgartner, Frank R. & Jones, Bryan D. (2002): 'Positive and negative feedback in politics', in Frank R. Baumgartner & Jones Bryan D. (eds.): *Policy Dynamics*, University of Chicago Press, 3–28.

Börzel, Tanja A. (2016): "From EU governance of crisis to crisis of EU governance: Regulatory failure, redistributive conflict and Eurosceptic publics." *Journal of Common Market Studies*, 54, 8–31.

Carrera, Sergio, Ineli Ciger, Meltem Vosyliute, Lina & Brumat, Leiza (2022): 'THE EU GRANTS TEMPORARY PROTECTION FOR PEOPLE FLEEING WAR IN UKRAINE: Time to rethink unequal solidarity in EU asylum policy The EU grants temporary protection for people fleeing war in Ukraine', *CEPS Policy Insights*, 2022/09.

Chetail, Vincent (2016): 'Looking beyond the rhetoric of the refugee crisis: the failed reform of the common European asylum system', *European Journal of Human Rights*, 584–602.

Cornelisse, Galina & Reneman, Marcelle (2020): 'Border procedures in the Commission's New Pact on Migration and Asylum: A case of politics outplaying rationality?', *European Law Journal*, 26:3–4, 181–198.

Crawley, Heather (2016): 'Managing the Unmanageable? Understanding Europe's Response to the Migration 'Crisis'', *Human Geography*, 9:2, 13–23.

Engelbert, Jiska, Awad, Isabel & van Sterkenburg, Jacco (2019): 'Everyday practices and the (un) making of 'Fortress Europe': Introduction to the special issue', *European Journal of Cultural Studies*, 22:2, 133–143.

Entzinger, Han & Scholten, Peter (2019): 'Policy Dialogues on Migrant Integration in Europe. Bridging the Gaps: Linking Research to Public Debates and Policy Making on Migration and Integration', in Martin Ruhs, Kristof Tamas & Joakim Palme (eds.): *Bridging the Gaps*, Oxford University Press, 34–49.

Fassi, Enrico & Lucarelli, Sonia (2021): 'EU foreign policy and migration: A political and normative assessment', in Michela Ceccorulli & Enrico Fassi (eds.): *The EU's External Governance of Migration*, Routledge, 169–191.

Franck, Anja. K., Bousiou, Alexandra, Lindberg, Anika, Jern, Jessie, Azis, Avie & Anderson, Joseph (2022): 'Who Deserves to Be a Refugee? Ukraine, Racialization, and "Grievable" Lives', *School of Blogal Studies*, https://www.blogalstudies.com/post/who-deserves-to-be-a-refugee-ukraine-racialization-and-grievable-lives. Accessed on 29 November 2022.

Geddes, Andrew (2008): *Immigration and European integration: beyond fortress Europe*, Manchester University Press.

Geddes, Andrew (2018): 'The Politics of European Union Migration Governance', *JCMS: Journal of Common Market Studies*, 56, 120–130.

Genç, Deniz H. & Şirin Öner, Asli N. (2019): 'Why not Activated? The Temporary Protection Directive and the Mystery of Temporary Protection in the European Union', *International Journal of Political Science & Urban Studies*, 1–18.

Guild, Elspeth (2006): 'The Europeanisation of Europe's asylum policy', *International Journal of Refugee Law*, 18:3–4, 630–651.

Guild, Elspeth (2016): 'Does the EU Need a European Migration and Protection Agency?', *International Journal of Refugee Law*, 28:4, 585–600.

Guiraudon, Virginie (2018): 'The 2015 refugee crisis was not a turning point: Explaining policy inertia in EU border control', *European Political Science*, 17:1, 151–160.

Huysmans, Jef (2006): *The politics of insecurity: Fear, migration and asylum in the EU*, Routledge.

Ineli-Ciger, Meltem (2016): 'Time to activate the temporary protection directive: Why the directive can play a key role in solving the migration crisis in Europe', *European Journal of Migration and Law*, 18:1, 1–33.

Jeandesboz, Julien & Pallister-Wilkins, Polly (2016): 'Crisis, Routine, Consolidation: The Politics of the Mediterranean Migration Crisis', *Mediterranean Politics*, 21:2, 316–320.

Karageorgiou, Eleni (2016): 'Solidarity and sharing in the Common European Asylum System: The case of Syrian refugees', *European Politics and Society*, 17:2, 196–214.

Lavenex, Sandra (2018): 'Failing Forward' Towards Which Europe? Organized Hypocrisy in the Common European Asylum System', *Journal of Common Market Studies*, 56:5, 1195–1212.

Levy, Carl (2010): 'Refugees, Europe, camps/state of exception: "Into the zone", the European Union and extraterritorial processing of migrants, refugees, and asylum-seekers (theories and practice)', *Refugee Survey Quarterly*, 29:1, 92–119.

McMahon, Simon & Sigona, Nando (2021): 'Death and Migration: Migrant Journeys and the Governance of Migration During Europe's "Migration Crisis"', *International Migration Review*, 55:2, 605–628.

Mitsilegas, Valsamis (2014): 'Solidarity and Trust in the Common European Asylum System', *Comparative Migration Studies*, 2:2, 181–202.

Moreno-Lax, Violeta (2017): *Accessing asylum in Europe: extraterritorial border controls and refugee rights under EU Law*, Oxford University Press.

Rasche, Lucas (2022): 'Ukraine ' s refugee plight A paradigm shift for the EU 's asylum policy?', *Policy Brief*, March 2022, Hertie School of Governance, Jacques Delors Centre.

Rein, Martin & Schön, Donal (1994): *Frame reflection: Toward the resolution of intractable policy controversies*, Basic Book.

Ripoll Servent, Ariadna (2020): 'Failing under the 'shadow of hierarchy': Explaining the role of the European Parliament in the EU's 'asylum crisis'', in Edoardo Bressanelli & Nicola Chelotti (eds.): *The European Parliament in the Contested Union*, Routledge, 29–46.

Sahin-Mencutek, Zeynep, Barthoma, Soner, Gökalp-Aras, N. Ela & Triandafyllidou, Anna (2022): 'A crisis mode in migration governance: comparative and analytical insights', *Comparative Migration Studies*, 10:1.

Tsianos, Vassilis & Karakayali, Sehrat (2010): 'Transnational migration and the emergence of the European border regime: An ethnographic analysis', *European Journal of Social Theory*, 13:3, 373–387.

Tsourdi, E. Lilian (2017): 'Solidarity at Work? The Prevalence of Emergency-driven Solidarity in the Administrative Governance of the Common European Asylum System', *Maastricht Journal of European and Comparative Law*, 24:5, 667–686.

Wallaschek, Stefan (2020): 'The discursive construction of solidarity: Analysing public claims in Europe's migration crisis', *Political Studies*, 68:1, 74–92.

Zito, Anthony (2011): 'Policy framing', in Bertrand Badie, Dirk Berg-Schlosser & Leonardo A. Morlino (eds.): *International encyclopaedia of political science*, Sage London, 1924–1927.

Legislation and Policy Documents

Council Directive 2001/55/EC of 20 July 2001 on minimum standards for giving temporary protection in the event of a mass influx of displaced persons and on measures promoting a balance of efforts between Member States in receiving such persons and bearing the consequences thereof. OJ L 212, 7.8.2001, p. 12–23.

Council Implementing Decision (EU) 2022/382 of 4 March 2022 establishing the existence of a mass influx of displaced persons from Ukraine within the meaning of Article 5 of Directive 2001/55/EC, and having the effect of introducing temporary protection. ST/6846/2022/INIT OJ L 71, 4.3.2022, p. 1–6.

COM(2015) 240, Communication from the Commission – A European Agenda on Migration. Available at: https://eur-lex.europa.eu/legal-content/EN/TXT/PDF/?uri=CELEX:52015DC0240&from=EN Accessed on 29 November 2022.

COM(2015) 490, Communication from the Commission – Managing the refugee crisis: immediate operational, budgetary and legal measures under the European Agenda on Migration. Available at: https://eur-lex.europa.eu/legal-content/GA/TXT/?uri=CELEX:52015DC0490.

COM(2016) 165, Communication from the Commission – First report on relocation and resettlement. Available at: https://eur-lex.europa.eu/legalcontent/EN/TXT/?qid=1485252989182&uri=CELEX:52016DC0165. Accessed on 29 November 2022.

COM(2016) 270, Proposal for a new regulation – establishing the criteria and mechanisms for determining the Member State responsible for examining an application for international protection lodged in one of the Member States by a third-country national or a stateless person (recast). Available at: https://eur-lex.europa.eu/legal-content/EN/ALL/?uri=CELEX% 3A52016PC0270. Accessed on 29 November 2022.

COM(2017) 558, Communication from the Commission – on the Delivery of the European Agenda on Migration. Available at: https://home-affairs.ec.europa.eu/system/files/2020-09/20170927_commu nication_on_the_delivery_of_the_eam_en.pdf. Accessed on 29 November 2022.

COM(2017) 405, Report from the Commission – Fourteenth report on relocation and resettlement. Available at: https://eur-lex.europa.eu/legal-content/en/TXT/?uri=CELEX:52017DC0405. Accessed on 29 November 2022.

COM(2018) 250, Communication from the Commission – Progress report on the Implementation of the European Agenda on Migration. Available at: https://eur-lex.europa.eu/legal-content/en/TXT/ ?uri=CELEX:52018DC0250. Accessed on 29 November 2022.

COM(2019) 481, Communication from the Commission – Progress report on the Implementation of the European Agenda on Migration. Available at: https://eur-lex.europa.eu/legal-content/EN/ TXT/?uri=CELEX%3A52019DC0481. Accessed on 29 November 2022.

COM(2020) 609, Communication from the Commission – on a New Pact on Migration andAsylum. Available at: https://eur-lex.europa.eu/legal-content/EN/TXT/?uri=COM%3A2020%3A609%3AFIN. Accessed on 29 November 2022.

COM(2020) 610, Proposal for a Regulation – on asylum and migration management and amending Council Directive (EC)2003/109 and the proposed Regulation (EU)XXX/XXX [Asylum and Migration Fund]. Available at: https://eur-lex.europa.eu/legal-content/EN/TXT/?uri= COM:2020:610:FIN. Accessed on 29 November 2022.

COM(2022) 91, Proposal for a COUNCIL IMPLEMENTING DECISION establishing the existence of a mass influx of displaced persons from Ukraine within the meaning of Article 5 of Council Directive 2001/55/EC of 20 July 2001, and having the effect of introducing temporary protection. Available at: https://eur-lex.europa.eu/legal-content/EN/TXT/?uri=CELEX% 3A52022PC0091. Accessed on 29 November 2022.

Paulette Kurzer

12 EU Health: From pandemic crisis management to a European Health Union?

Abstract: The COVID-19 pandemic called for a coordinated European response to address the unprecedented global threat to Europe's health. The European Union in the past fifteen years designed multiple measures and programmes to prepare for such an event. It took action in a range of policy areas such as setting up the Centre for Disease Control and Prevention, establishing rules for the joint procurement of medical countermeasures, and strengthening intergovernmental committees to facilitate improved coordination and consultation. Yet when the pandemic struck, many elements of the health security governance regime did not function effectively. In retrospect, the Union's numerous measures and decisions were non-binding and were overly reliant on non-mandatory cooperation and coordination. In the early phase of the pandemic, most member states focused on protecting their citizens and ignored collective preparedness and response capacity. This chapter reviews the evolution of EU public health and examines the measures taken to protect the member states from cross-border threats to health. The chapter concludes by exploring the possibilities of creating a genuine European health union in the aftermath of the COVID-19 global health emergency.

Keywords: COVID-19, European Centre for Disease Control, European Health Union, Article 168 TFEU, politics

Introduction

In a world where people and goods move across borders in high numbers, the circulation of viruses and bacteria poses a clear health threat, something that the European Union has widely acknowledged. Since the early 2000s, the European Commission and the member states have invested ever greater resources in reinforcing Europe's approach to early detection and containment of contagious diseases, by monitoring and collecting epidemiological intelligence and by communicating these threats to other relevant agencies. In 2001, member states agreed to set up an intergovernmental Health Security Committee, bringing together national health ministry officials and Commission officials to assess health threats and to facilitate policy coordination. In 2004, the EU established the European Centre

https://doi.org/10.1515/9783110790337-013

for Disease Control and Prevention (ECDC), which provides technical collaboration during crises and is supposed 'to identify, assess and communicate current and emerging threats to human health from communicable diseases' (Regulation (EC) No. 851/2004). The EU also introduced the Early Warning and Response System (EWRS) in 2005, a database managed by the ECDC, with restricted access for monitoring public health threats in the EU.

In general, however, the member states hold primary responsibility for organising and delivering health services and medical care. EU health policy, therefore, serves to complement national policies, to ensure health protection in all EU policies, and to work towards a stronger Health Union. However, the space for EU activities in health is confined because the EU has no competence to formulate health policies directly (Naumann 2022). The focus of the EU has been on public health, which in contrast to health care delivery to individual patients, seeks to improve the health of the population by protecting it from external threats to health. It is a broad field and includes health promotion and disease prevention, health emergencies, health education, health information systems, and health disparities. But health care itself remains the sole responsibility of the member states. National governments do not want to relinquish control over health care because health spending in aging societies is one of the largest budget items. Moreover, health policy and healthcare systems emerged over decades of welfare state-building and possess distinctive features and priorities that are embedded in the collectivist expression of the nation-state (Greer et al. 2022). In contrast to health care, the EU has the mandate to combat cross-border health threats before, during, and after a crisis.

During a global health scare, the chain of command would be for the EWRS to issue an alert, which leads the staff of the ECDC to assess risks and notify the members of the Health Security Committee. In turn, the Health Security Committee would subsequently coordinate exchanges of information and countermeasures among each other and with the Commission. In short, the EU and the member states have constructed a health security framework, which consists of surveillance, preparedness plans, early warning and response protocols, as well as consultation tools (Bengtsson & Rhinard 2019).

Yet when the 'big one' landed in 2020, the EU was unprepared (as were most other countries!) and the member states pursued their own policy responses, ignoring the recommendations of the ECDC and disregarding existing coordination procedures. In this chapter, I will explain why intergovernmental decisions and supranational programmes, in preparing the EU for a global pandemic, failed to supply the kind of pan-European response that we could have expected given the creation of the ECDC and European procedures. The answer, in short, for why the health governance system functioned less than optimal is that the European

Union cannot pursue an autonomous health policy since the member states retain full control over this policy area. Treaty articles, therefore, stipulate that Union activities should consist of supporting, coordinating, and complementary measures. Various crises over time propelled the EU to go further and commit to deeper integration, but such decisions were not always supported by commitments to increase investments in administrative capacity and policy competence.

This chapter unfolds as follows: the first part reviews the evolution of European public health and emphasizes the role of 'crisis' or 'scandal' that played in fostering closer collaboration and integration. The second part introduces the efforts to improve EU resilience against manmade or natural threats to health and points out that member states are protective of their decision-making autonomy. The third section highlights the EU's shortcomings in mitigating and containing the spread of the coronavirus. The final section reviews the likelihood that the European Union will be better prepared to handle a future pandemic. The conclusion summarizes the main findings.

Evolution of public health

Article 168 in the 2009 Treaty of Lisbon (also referred to as the Treaty on the European Union (TEU)) elaborates on the powers of the EU in health. It states that 'a high level of human health protection shall be ensured in the definition and implementation of all Union policies and activities. Union action, which shall complement national policies, shall be directed towards improving public health, preventing physical and mental illness and diseases, and obviating sources of danger to physical and mental health.' [1] Thus, the relevant paragraph commended the Commission to coordinate with member states and initiate action in which collaboration would be useful and productive (Hervey & McHale 2015; Greer & Kurzer 2013).

Although the EU's involvement in health policy is modest by design, it has nonetheless succeeded in making its mark on European public health. In the examples provided below, common challenges and pressures to preserve the functioning of the single market, on top of blatant failures to protect Europe's population from health threats, account for why tentative steps towards harmonisation of health standards emerged.

There are three areas in which EU legislation encourages the integration of health standards. The three areas are: safety standards for organs and plasma

---

[1] For full language see, https://lexparency.org/eu/TFEU/ART_168/ [Accessed 7 September 2022].

and tissue substances, veterinary and phytosanitary measures aiming to protect public health, and safety standards for medicinal products and devices.

All three areas are bound up with the effective functioning of the single market, which is based on the removal of trade barriers through mutual recognition of different member states' standards. At the same time, all three areas emerged in the wake of a crisis or scandal that undermined public trust and confidence in EU institutions.

In 1991/92, it was discovered that French patients were given blood transfusions contaminated with the human immunodeficiency virus (HIV) and many patients eventually died of AIDS. An investigation by the French government justly accused the French ministry of health of this regretful situation, as the ministry had refused to acknowledge that blood donors recruited from prisons constituted a high-risk population even though many were suspected drug addicts and were likely HIV carriers. In other countries, this method of collection was off-limits and blood collection services routinely treated the collected plasma with heat to kill the virus. In addition, by 1985, commercial tests to detect HIV in blood samples were available, but the French government refused to import these U.S.-developed tests so that French laboratories had the space to develop their own testing kits (BMJ, 1998). The French blood scandals uncovered in the early 1990s destroyed the European market for plasma products, and Art. 168(4)(a) in the Treaty of Lisbon re-affirmed the Union's role in safeguarding the quality and safety of such products (Farrell 2009; Steffen 1999). Member states are required to set up risk assessment and monitoring institutions, and to collect and share information. Owing to the new European rules, a substantial market in blood and blood products exists within the EU.[2]

The EU also adopted common veterinary and phytosanitary measures in response to a spate of food scares in the 1980s and 1990s. By far the most sensational scandal was the bovine spongiform encephalopathy (BSE) crisis or mad cow disease, which emerged in the UK in the 1980s. The origins of this disease can be traced to infected cows, who had been fed ground-up meat and bone meal from sheep carrying this brain disease. Though British officials ordered the killing of millions of cows to prevent the spread of the disease, a human variant of BSE was diagnosed in people in 1993. The news of the presence of a fatal human brain disease, Creutzfeldt-Jakob disease (CJD), linked to the consumption of infected beef, led to calls for strengthening the EU system of risk regulation (Ansell & Vogel 2006). In 1999, the Council and European Parliament agreed to establish

2 Article 168 can be found here: https://eur-lex.europa.eu/legal-content/EN/TXT/?uri=CELEX%3A12008E168. [Accessed 7 September 2022].

the European Food Safety Authority (EFSA) to regulate the food supply chain by collaborating with member state regulatory bodies. It defined the problem as cross-border pan-European, which required a European solution (Buonanno 2006).

Likewise, the economic logic of the single market combined with pressures to protect the safety of medical devices and pharmaceuticals convinced member states to set up the European Medicines Agency (EMA) in 1995 to regulate the safety standards for medicinal products and devices for sale in the EU.

These case studies demonstrate the major failures in regulatory and risk governance that spurred collective action and the creation of standardized pan-European rules. One major prerequisite for public health common standards, however, is that member states must converge on a particular approach to address a common problem since sharp disagreements undermine collective action. In the absence of consensus, not much happens in the Council of Ministers. In the three policy areas above, intensive media coverage and widespread public criticism forged agreements to draft new pan-European rules to protect the functioning of the single market and restore consumer confidence.

Successful institutionalisation of common health standards also requires the full participation of the European Commission. The latter is formally in charge of initiating policy proposals. Whether the Commission is on board or not, depends in part on the priorities of the Commission's leadership. Jean-Claude Juncker, president of the Commission from 2014 to 2019, repeatedly declared that the European Union should go 'big on the big things and small on the small things.' [3] Health was considered a 'small thing.' His attitude towards health partly reflected the modest achievements of the past years. Crucially, moreover, the Juncker Commission made a conscious choice to focus on issues that mattered to European citizens such as overcoming the euro crisis and returning Europe to growth and financial stability. Commission leadership reasoned that it could not be involved in everything and that its energy should be spent on existential matters that dealt with current challenges. Infectious disease control and non-communicable diseases (like cancer or cardio-vascular diseases) were not regarded as 'existential' challenges of this time (Nugent & Rhinard 2019).

The Commission's political or administrative aversion towards public health had enormous ramifications for the EU during the years preceding the pandemic. For example, the Directorate General (policy department in the Commission) in which Health was housed until 2014, was called DG SANCO, and included the fol-

---

3 See for example, the summary statement of five years of Juncker leadership, *Better regulation: big on the big things and small on the small things* (May 2019). https://ec.europa.eu/info/sites/default/files/euco-sibiu-better-regulation_en_2.pdf [Accessed 15 July 2022].

lowing portfolios: health, medicine, and consumer protection. On the one hand, this made DG SANCO a substantial administrative unit in the Commission. On the other, each of the three policy sectors was governed by a distinct legal base, catered to dissimilar audiences and generated different political dynamics. DG SANCO lacked unity and coherence. Its sprawling or confusing organisation made it an easy target for restructuring when former Commission president Juncker expressed his desire to create a more hierarchical Commission, with stronger central leadership. Juncker suggested at some point that the health portfolio be removed from the Commission's competence in order to turn DG SANCO into a more uniform entity, representing only medicine and consumer protection. An enormous outcry prevented Juncker from purging public health from the Commission's portfolio, but the newly organized DG SANTE is small, located in Luxembourg (instead of Brussels), and is in charge of health and food safety. Not surprisingly, considering the Juncker Commission indifference towards public health, it also downgraded the EU health agenda. An earlier Commission led by José Manuel Barroso (2004–2014), launched *Together for Health*, which sought to bring together the different programs in health and give them extra funding and consistency.[4] However, in 2014, the Juncker Commission did not renew the *Together for Health* programme because it claimed that the same goals were included in the *Europe 2020* package, which in fact was a programme to improve competitiveness in the EU. Thus, EU public health was demoted and sidelined, both administratively and politically (Greer & Jarman 2021).

Fortuitously, Commission President Ursula von der Leyen (2019–2024), who has a medical background, decided to resurrect EU Health and announced a set of more ambitious goals for the DG SANTE. She asked the new Health Commissioner, Stella Kyriakides, installed in late 2019 to promote action on medicine affordability, stronger regulation of medical devices, e-health, vaccination, antimicrobial resistance, and cancer, among other things (Guagliardo 2020). Of course, this renewed attention came too late to prepare Europe for a global pandemic.

The rise of European communicable disease control

Although the EU has limited competence in health, one area in which considerable action has been taken is infectious disease control. From the 1990s on, various pub-

---

4 *Together for Health – A Strategic Approach for the EU, 2008–2013* (October 2007). https://ec.eu ropa.eu/commission/presscorner/detail/en/IP_07_1571 [Accessed 16 September 2022].

lic health crises – HIV/AIDS (1980s), bovine spongiform encephalopathy (1993), SARS (2003), and influenza pandemics (2005 and 2009), Ebola virus in Western Africa (2014), Zika (2016) – underscored Europe's vulnerability to manmade and natural disasters (Greer et al. 2022). These health scares worried epidemiological experts and highlighted the need to invest in effective preparedness and coordinated action before, during, and after a crisis. Yet, crises alone failed to enhance and expand the EU's capacity to respond to cross-border threats to health.

In this section, I will trace the rise of infectious disease control in the EU and the political obstacles faced by EU actors who favor a coordinated European response to pandemics. I show that, despite a number of important steps to improve joint action in countering the possible spread of infectious diseases, national governments were mostly reluctant to cede authority over infectious disease control to a European agency. While the EU passed new legislation to build a cross-border health security regime, member states insisted on retaining authority over risk management, data gathering, and participation in pan-European initiatives. Moreover, the years of the Juncker commission (2014–2019) were damaging to EU public health for the reason that the Commission expressed little interest in fostering greater coordination and collaboration in public health.

Communicable disease control requires vast coordination across a wide variety of people, positions, and territories, and can only function if member states routinely share infectious disease information and adhere to consultation protocols. Here, the EU could play a valuable and indispensable role by monitoring the emergence of new diseases and viruses in animal stock or people, alerting respective national agencies of possible health threats, and providing up-to-date risk assessments while recommending appropriate responses.

Historically, the fight against viruses and bacteria was one of the first tasks that the modern state undertook. Sanitation, childhood immunization, and foodborne diseases were the principal focus in the early phases of modern state formation (Baldwin 2005). Accordingly, states across Europe developed varying levels of institutional capacity and resources in the field of infectious disease control. By the late 1970s, it was believed that infectious diseases no longer posed a threat to health in advanced industrialized countries thanks to childhood immunizations, modern sanitation, reduction in environmental pollution, and so forth. In the 1980s, however, the HIV/AIDS crisis broke out and put this assumption once again into question and encouraged deeper scientific cooperation across the EU. The accession of ten Central and East European countries, scheduled for 2004, emphasized the need to institutionalise exchanges of information because the single market guaranteed the free movement of people. It was predicted that a large flow of poor migrants, coming from countries with weak health care capacity and underdeveloped vaccine programmes, would move westward once enlargement was completed. This highly mobile and marginalized pool of workers could boost the spread of infectious diseases and pose a threat to the health of the more prosperous member states (Steffen 2012). At the same time as enlargement loomed, the world faced a potential new pandemic in the form of SARS (severe acute respiratory syndrome), which had a relatively high fatality rate. The combination of enlargement and a new contagious coronavirus outbreak, first identified in China in 2002, convinced the member states to formalise cross-border cooperation on disease control.

The Commission proposed the creation of a Centre for Disease Control and Prevention, thereby bringing together the member states' different epidemiological and scientific networks into a single agency. Modelled after the U.S. Centre for Disease Control, the European Centre for Disease Control and Prevention was established in 2004 and opened its doors in Stockholm in 2005. Although its name is evocative of the U.S. Centre for Disease Control (CDC vs ECDC), the European agency was a modest outfit, with a budget of €60 million and a staff of 286 people, in contrast to the US CDC which had a budget of $6 billion and approximately 20,000 employees in 2020.

European Centre for Disease Control and Prevention

The ECDC is not a regulatory agency that exercises legislative, executive, and judicial authority (Elliott et al. 2012). Rather, it gathers information and is designed to serve as a point of contact for infectious disease control networks. Accordingly, it functions very differently from the American CDC and its responsibilities are centred on monitoring and surveillance, and to some extent capacity building and research. For the most part, the ECDC performs risk assessment with limited duties concerning risk communication and bears no responsibility for risk management. The agency runs the Epidemiological Surveillance Network (ESN) and the Early Warning and Response System (EWRS), which contains epidemiological data submitted by national agencies of disease control.

The ECDC statutes clearly point out that national public health agencies in the member states do retain control over the actual response to pandemics (Greer & Löblová 2017). To ensure that it will not compete with national disease control agencies, the ECDC's management board is composed of national officials from the member states who define its duties and responsibilities. Because the ECDC staff does not possess the tools or capabilities to collect its own epidemic statistics, it is reliant on its national partners to submit this data to its websites. Consistent with its mandate, the ECDC budget is small.

In the end, the creation of the ECDC did not effectively shift authority to the EU because its main objective is to collect information from the member states and subsequently share this data with its epidemiological networks. It does not have its own resources and relies on government and academic scientists as well as international organisations for data. Certainly, the ECDC has not become an autonomous European agency in the same way as the Centre for Disease Control and Prevention (CDC) has in the United States (Greer et al. 2022). Member states were unwilling to Europeanise the fight against cross-border health threats. They were reluctant to relinquish autonomy or authority in this field, in particular, because disease control has existed in many countries since the earliest phase of modern state building, and each country has its own infrastructure and procedures. Moreover, risk management involves health service delivery, hospitalization, and medical care all of which loom large in national budgets and are excluded from EU competence.

Moreover, after 2010, the EU experienced repeated crises, sapping the political will to finance and enhance European-wide infectious disease control. First, the eurozone crisis (2010–2014) ushered in years of budget retrenchment and austerity measures. During those years, public health was neglected, and austerity measures reduced national public health budgets. In this climate, it would have been impossible to convince member states to spend money on European disease control and European-level pandemic preparedness (Rechel 2019; OECD 2015). In 2015, the migration crisis, bringing more than a million asylum seekers to Europe, provoked both intense domestic and European conflicts, which made European governments reluctant to propose more integration in fields that seem irrelevant to the crisis at hand. Brexit followed in 2016, which raised hard questions about the principles behind European integration. All in all, the long-term corollaries of the polycrisis were to undermine European-wide coordination and cooperation in public health, which was in any event an inconsequential policy area for the Commission, which downplayed the need for stronger pan-European structures to prepare cross-border health threats. In addition, the crises also fueled disenchantment with the EU, legitimizing the diffusion of harsh anti-EU rhetoric and giving rise to Euro-hostile political parties that questioned pan-European solidarity and collective action.[5] Not surprisingly, both European and national pandemic preparedness languished.

---

5 For more detail, see Lucy Kinski (Chapter 6 in this volume).

The Big One

When the COVID-19 pandemic arrived in 2020, the response in Europe illustrated all of the limitations on the EU's public health capacities outlined above. The first months of the pandemic were a period of intense national chauvinism and a lack of coordination and cooperation.[6] As member states struggled to control the spread of the coronavirus, they adopted their own public health measures without much coordination and collaboration with the EU or other member states. Nearly all EU member states closed their borders and imposed restrictions on the free movement of people, challenging the core foundation of the single market. Governments also hunted for scarce PPE and competed against each other to acquire testing kits, ventilators, medicine, and face masks in order to protect their own citizens. The European Commission was paralyzed in the face of this lack of solidarity and fierce competition (Sabbati & Dumbrava 2020). The ECDC's role during the pandemic was greatly constrained by the fact that it lacked legal powers to intervene. In fact, the ECDC even struggled to obtain up-to-date information about the trajectory of the virus, because national infectious disease agencies did not submit their epidemiological and virological data in a timely fashion and a consistent format (Deruelle & Engeli 2021). In retrospect, the EU health governance framework revealed important shortcomings: early warning and prevention strategies were not sufficiently integrated with responses. Whereas the ECDC was established to issue risk assessments, it was prohibited from issuing recommendations on how to contain or mitigate those risks. It could not advise member states on how to control the spread of the coronavirus resulting in national experts designing an anti-pandemic response. Member states adopted their policy measures to fight COVID-19 in isolation of what their neighbors were choosing to prioritise.

Especially in the first few months of the COVID-19 epidemic, member states initially operated on their own and pursued their own mitigation and containment measures. In addition to the ECDC, the European Union had adopted a decision in 2013 to improve consultation and preparedness in the face of a future pandemic. Decision No 1082/2013/EU on Serious Cross-border Threats to Health[7] urged mutual

---

6 For a detailed timeline of the EU action, see Timeline of EU Action. https://ec.europa.eu/info/live-work-travel-eu/coronavirus-response/timeline-eu-action [Accessed 7 July 2022].

7 European Parliament and the Council of the European Union. *Decision 1082/2013/EU of the European Parliament and of the Council of 22 October 2013 on serious cross-border threats to health and repealing Decision 2119/98/EC.* https://eur-lex.europa.eu/legal-content/EN/TXT/?uri=celex%3A3 2013D1082 [Accessed 20 July 2022].

consultation to strengthen preparedness, sharing best practices while promoting the interoperability of national preparedness planning. It strengthened the position of the Health Security Committee (established in 2001 in light of the anthrax attacks in the US) which was tasked with the coordination of responses to health crises. However, coordination and cooperation were non-binding, and health officials, preoccupied with their national COVID-19 challenges, disregarded the existence of the intergovernmental Health Security Committee and met infrequently during the first months (Beaussier & Cabane 2020).

Thus, during the first months of the pandemic, member states remained protective of their authority over public health and were unwilling to delegate oversight and competencies to the ECDC or the Health Security Committee. While cooperation improved by May 2020, national officials continued to issue their own rules concerning face masks, social distancing, lockdowns, or test requirements for international visitors. Eventually, however, the Commission succeeded in reasserting itself and pressed for better organization in order to formulate a more coherent coronavirus response (Vila Maior & Camisão 2021). It mostly succeeded by bringing together the Health Security Committee, which represents health officials from the member states (Brooks et al. 2021).

There were several areas where the Commission was able to act on behalf of its member states. It was able to use the Joint Procurement provision, granted by the 2013 Decision on Cross-Border threats, to purchase pharmaceuticals and vaccines.[8] Though the measure was voluntary, by 2019 just about all member states had joined the agreement (Greer et al. 2022). From the start, the agreement allowed member states to procure their own medicine or medical devices alongside the joint procurement. The Commission negotiated the purchase of COVID vaccines through an advance purchase agreement in June 2020, though member states also negotiated the purchase of vaccines directly with the drug companies. On the one hand, the dual track of joint and national purchase agreements stirred controversy, but on the other, it assuaged large member states who could still negotiate their own vaccine procurement agreement with pharmaceutical companies. Eventually, the EU used €2.7b of pooled funding to vaccinate about 70 percent of the EU adult population. Mostly, the vaccine procurement initiative succeeded because powerful member states supported the joint provisioning of vaccines as it did not prevent them from negotiating with drug companies directly on behalf

---

8 Art. 2(a) in 2013 Decision on Cross Border Threats, "Joint Procurement Agreement to Procure Medical Countermeasures," can be found here: https://ec.europa.eu/health/sites/health/files/preparedness_response/docs/jpa_agreement_medicalcountermeasures_en.pdf [Accessed 10 July 2022].

of their own citizens, while small members lacked the leverage to compete in the global race for vaccines (Deters & Zardo 2022; Fortuna 2021).

Another area in which the Commission succeeded was in introducing the EU Digital COVID Certificate that guaranteed free movement of people during the pandemic.[9] The COVID Certificate shows proof of vaccination, recovery, or a negative PCR test for EU citizens. It was first proposed in March 2021 and came into force in the summer of 2021. Eventually, all member states signed up for the digital pass, and citizens in other countries also downloaded the COVID pass. This proposal passed because it protected the free movement of people, especially for member states that were highly reliant on tourism (e.g. Greece, Italy, Spain, France) and it appealed to European citizens of northern member states (e.g. the Netherlands, Germany, Sweden) who liked to travel during the summer. The Commission succeeded in passing the digital COVID certificate because it solved a collective problem and was a technical regulatory solution that did not require spending, while individual member states could still design their own vaccination pass (Goldner Lang 2021).

In conclusion, the EU started the pandemic in chaos and disorganization, which diminished over time as member states realized that competing against each other was counter-productive, especially since the Trump administration expressed support for vaccine nationalism during the global race for vaccines (Bucher 2022). In view of this, the member states opted for greater coordination and cooperation in the joint procurement of vaccines. The EU was also able to protect the free movement of people, after the haphazard closure of borders in the wake of the spread of the coronavirus in March 2020, by adopting the digital vaccine certificate. Nevertheless, responses to COVID-19 followed different patterns in the EU, especially as the highly contagious Omicron variant spread in early 2022 which led to a scrambling of new rules. Some countries were ready to ease rules while others introduced more restrictions. In short, coordination action took place in two important areas: vaccine procurement and free movement of people. Otherwise, some member states demanded proof of vaccination when entering bars, restaurants, and cafes while others did not. Some required negative tests (or evidence of recent COVID infection) for travelers from third countries, some required masks in public spaces, some closed schools (again), and other member states did not. Institutional context, administrative culture, public acceptance of precautionary measures, problem-solving strategies, and governance

---

9 See more about the digital COVID certificate, https://ec.europa.eu/info/live-work-travel-eu/coronavirus-response/safe-COVID-19-vaccines-europeans/eu-digital-COVID-certificate_en.

modes ultimately determined how each member state addressed the challenges of a highly contagious virus.

The future: European pandemic preparedness

The question now is whether the largest public health crisis in the last 100 years will have major consequences for how the EU will tackle public health crises in the future. On the one hand, the acute crisis caused by the coronavirus brought into public view the EU's constraints in handling the public health aspect of the pandemic. On the other hand, even this crisis may not be sufficient to break down the concerns and reservations of the member states.

COVID-19 was a major fast-burning crisis (versus a creeping, slow-burning crisis) and affected all member states since it was a symmetric crisis unlike the Euro crisis or the immigration crisis (Boin et al. 2020). In the past, EU crises built up slowly and had distinct repercussions for each member state. The global financial and economic crisis of 2008 turned into the Eurozone crisis two years later and eventually morphed into an unprecedented sovereign debt crisis for some though not all member states. In 2015, the refugee crisis overwhelmed some member states because of their geographic location as refugees crossed into Europe by sea and a handful of member states carried the brunt of the flow of migrants. Brexit was also in the making for years and had different ramifications for different member states. By contrast, the COVID-19 pandemic struck all member states essentially at once, and therefore, the shock was felt evenly and simultaneously. For this reason, we would expect that the pressures of a symmetric crisis should increase the prospects of a stronger and more coherent European disease control capacity. Nonetheless, the proposed reforms, provisionally approved by the Council and the European Parliament in June 2022, leave open the question of how or whether the European Union will be better prepared in the future.

In the fall of 2020, the Commission presented a finished draft, introducing the European Health Union, drawing from lessons learned up to that point from the COVID-19 pandemic: provide better protection for the health of citizens; equip the EU and its Member States to prevent and address future pandemics; and improve the resilience of Europe's health systems (European Commission 2020). To achieve these goals, the Commission laid out a set of steps such as improving the European Medicines Agency (EMA), upgrading the European Centre for Disease Prevention and Control (ECDC), creating a regulation that would make ad hoc emergency measures permanent, and formulating a European Pharma Strategy to avoid shortages of critical drug ingredients, medicines and medical devices (European Commission 2022). The Commission also introduced HERA (Health Emergency Preparedness and Response Authority), modelled after the U.S. BARDA (Biomedical Advanced Research and Development Authority), and responsible for responding to health emergencies through intelligence gathering and building the necessary response capacities by stockpiling medical supplies. Finally, the Commission asked for and received, a much larger budget for EU health, more than ten times the size of its previous allocation (increasing from €446 million to €5.3 billion for the 2021–27 budget cycle) (European Commission 2021). Such a sizable layout from the EU budget reassured member states that greater involvement by the EU would not be at the expense of their national budgets (Naumann 2022).

As part of the reforms, the Commission made a number of concrete proposals to strengthen the ECDC (Deruelle & Engeli 2021). First, it proposed traveling medical teams to step in during a crisis in a member state in case of an emergency. Second, it proposed giving the ECDC the authority to recommend measures for controlling outbreaks and to issue non-binding recommendations for risk management, something that had previously been prohibited. Third, it called for more financing for improving digital platforms and epidemiological surveillance, since the submission of real-time data during the pandemic had been irregular. Fourth, it proposed expanding the ECDC's activities to cover areas such as health education, health literacy, and lifestyle changes. Finally, the Commission encouraged the building of a network of EU reference laboratories to be able to collect real-time information about threats to health (European Commission 2020b).

The Committee for Environment, Health, and Food (ENVI) of the European Parliament introduced many amendments in September 2021, including mandatory guidance for member states, direct assistance for member states to improve their health systems capacities by introducing common indicators and definitions to ensure comparability, and augmenting the ECDC's mandate to include gathering information about non-communicable diseases (such as cardiovascular diseases, diabetes, and cancer) (Kopcińska 2021). Moreover, the ENVI report suggested that the ECDC should have a right to organize regular visits to the member states to assess health systems' capacity to manage health crises and to organize ad hoc inspections of the member states to verify preparedness and response plans (Scholz 2020; European Parliament 2021). In short, the EP committee proposed bolder reforms and sought to pave the way for more European integration in areas such as EU pandemic preparedness.

To be expected, the Council expressed reservations concerning a dramatic extension of the ECDC's mandate and EU responsibility for pandemic preparedness plans. Multiple rounds of inter-institutional negotiations yielded a provisional compromise in June 2022 that will lead to stronger cross-border cooperation, but not to the Europeanisation of infectious disease control and prevention (Popp 2022).

First of all, the provisional agreement strips the ECDC of its "more supervisory and prescriptive role", and reinforces its supportive or complementary mission. The Council vetoed the suggestion that the ECDC (like the U.S. CDC) covers non-communicable diseases. Instead, the compromise extends the mandate of the ECDC to improve coordination by standardising data collection and modelling. The agency is encouraged to improve its digital platforms and rely on artificial intelligence techniques to support epidemiological surveillance, though it will still be reliant on national health authorities to supply that information. The agency runs the European COVID-19 surveillance network, yet it is still dependent on the reference laboratories to share their epidemiological and virological data.[10]

One of the concessions made by the Council is that the ECDC will be able to recommend pandemic responses to the Health Security Committee, the intergovernmental committee of national health officials. This spills over into risk management, something that was explicitly proscribed in its founding statutes, since proposing countermeasures could affect national allocation for health services and care. However, the new regulation does not compel the HSC to accept ECDC's recommendations. The latter will be non-binding and the HSC is not forced to act upon the advice of the ECDC. Possibly, it will be difficult for the HSC to ignore expert advice from the European disease control agency, but it is not required to follow through with the recommendations of the ECDC. Ultimately, unless the EU changes its treaties, especially Art. 168, the ECDC cannot prescribe pandemic countermeasures, since that would be in conflict with the principle that the management of health services and medical care remains the sole responsibility of the member states. Thus, the changes in the ECDC's mandate foster stronger coordination and collaboration but do not fundamentally alter the balance of authority between European and national disease control efforts (Järviniemi et al. 2022).

The new agreement also clarifies the advance purchase agreement (APA). Individual member states will be barred from entering into parallel negotiations with the same vaccine manufacturer if those products are purchased jointly at the EU level. Under the reformulated APA Framework Agreement, member states could still negotiate with different manufacturers to purchase extra doses of vaccine, but they cannot place orders with the same company that went into contract with the Commission (Naumann 2022).

---

10 European COVID-19 surveillance network (ECOVID -Net). https://www.ecdc.europa.eu/en/about-us/who-we-work/disease-and-laboratory-networks/european-COVID-19-surveillance-network-eCOVID [Accessed 30 July 2022].

Conclusion

EU public health has historically been a marginal policy area for the EU. Frequently, the EU succeeded when it could argue that the measures both promoted Europe's health and enhanced the functioning of the single market. Since the 1990s, member states have realized that Europe's citizens are exposed to health threats that originate beyond the EU and quickly traverse the European continent. Bacteria and viruses know no borders and the EU has invested in defence mechanisms against cross-border threats to health. The EU created an infectious disease control agency (ECDC), established the Health Security Committee to improve collaboration among member states and between them and the Commission, and launched different and separate programmes to improve surveillance, rescue efforts, and cross-border coordination. In the 21st century, the EU managed to establish a health security governance regime with multiple moving parts.

Undeniably, there is a persuasive argument to be made that preventing health threats is only as effective as the resilience of the weakest member state. Yet member states prefer cooperation over integration, even though coordination may falter during the height of a health crisis because politicians are responsive to the demands of their electorate and voters expect their elected officials to protect them first.

The COVID-19 pandemic has, in the end, reinforced existing agencies and procedures, and introduced an instrument to stockpile and develop medical supplies, while allocating greater funding to pandemic preparedness. Yet many of the new initiatives are still built on the principle that collaboration is preferred and rules should not be binding. At the end of the day, member states are fearful that an expanded role for EU disease control could invite greater intervention in their health care systems, and in the worst scenario, result in subsidising other member states' health care systems for the sake of greater collaboration in public health. Unless the EU introduces treaty amendments that clear the way for greater integration in health capacity and resilience, effective and successful disease control and cross-border health threats will depend on ongoing efforts to foster closer European integration.

References

Ansell, Christopher & Vogel, David (2006): *What's the Beef?: The Contested Governance of European Food Safety.* MIT Press.
Baldwin, Peter (2005): *Contagion and the State in Europe, 1830–1930.* Cambridge University Press.

Beaussier, Anne-Laure & Cabane, Lydie (2020): 'Strengthening the EU's Response Capacity to Health Emergencies: Insights from EU Crisis Management Mechanisms', *European Journal of Risk Regulation*, 11:4, 808–820.

Bengtsson, Louise & Rhinard, Mark (2019): 'Securitization across borders: the case of 'health security' cooperation in the European Union', *West European Politics*, 42:2, 346–368.

BMJ (1998): 'Ex-ministers to face trial in French "blood scandal"', Aug 1, 1998 (317(7154)), p. 302. https://www.ncbi.nlm.nih.gov/pmc/articles/PMC1174664/ [Accessed 14 September 2022].

Boin, Arjen, Ekengren, Magnus & Rhinard, Mark (2020): 'Hiding in Plain Sight: Conceptualizing the Creeping Crisis', *Risks, Hazards & Crisis in Public Policy*, 11:2, 116–38.

Brooks, Eleanor, de Ruijter, Anniek & Greer, Scott (2021): 'The European Union Confronts COVID-19: Another European Rescue of the Nation-State?', in Scott L. Greer, Elizabeth J. King, Elize Massard da Fonseca & André Peralta-Santos (eds.), *Coronavirus Politics: The Comparative Politics and Policy of COVID -19*, University of Michigan Press, 235–48.

Bucher, Anne (2022): 'Does Europe need a Health Union?' *Bruegel Policy Contribution* (02/2022). https://www.bruegel.org/policy-brief/does-europe-need-health-union [Accessed 10 September 2022].

Buonanno, Laurie (2006): 'The Creation of the European Food Safety Authority', Christopher K. Ansell David Vogel (eds.). *What's the beef?: the contested governance of European food safety.* MIT Press, 259–278.

de Ruijter, Anniek (2019): *EU Health Law & Policy: The Expansion of EU Power in Public Health & Health Care.* Oxford University Press.

Deruelle, Thibaud & Engeli, Isabelle (2021): 'The COVID -19 Crisis: The Rise of the European Centre for Disease Prevention and Control (ECDC)', *West European Politics*, 44:5–6, 1376–1400.

Elliott, Heather, Jones, David & Greer, Scott (2012): 'Mapping Communicable Disease Control in the European Union', *Journal of Health Politics, Policy and Law*, 37:6, 935–54.

European Commission (2020): *EU4Health programmeme 2021–2027 – a vision for a healthier European Union.* https://health.ec.europa.eu/funding/eu4health-programmeme-2021-2027-vision-healthier-european-union_en [Accessed 1 August 2022]

European Commission (2020b): *Building a European Health Union: Reinforcing the EU's resilience for cross-border health threats* COM/2020/724 final. https://eur-lex.europa.eu/legal-content/EN/TXT/?uri=CELEX%3A52020DC0724&qid=1605690513438 [Accessed 10 May 2022].

European Commission (2021): EU4Health programmeme 2021–2027 – a vision for a healthier European Union. https://health.ec.europa.eu/funding/eu4health-programmeme-2021-2027-vision-healthier-european-union_en [Accessed 10 May 2022].

European Commission (2022): *Health security and infectious diseases.* https://health.ec.europa.eu/health-security-and-infectious-diseases/overview_en [Accessed 3 August 2022].

European Parliament (2021): *Amending Regulation (EC) No 851/2004 establishing a European Centre for disease prevention and control.* (A9–0253/2021 (28.7.2021)): https://www.europarl.europa.eu/doceo/document/A-9-2021-0253_EN.html [Accessed 10 April 2022].

European Parliament & Council of the EU (2013): *Proposal for a Regulation of the European Parliament and of the Council on serious crossborder threats to health and repealing Decision No 1082/2013/EU.* https://oeil.secure.europarl.europa.eu/oeil/popups/ficheprocedure.do?reference=2020/0322(COD)&l=en [Accessed 10 April 2022].

Farrell, Anne-Maree (2009): 'The Politics of Risk and EU Governance of Human Material', *Maastricht Journal of European and Comparative Law*, 16:1, 41–64.

Fortuna Gerardo (2021): 'Commission takes evasive action over Germany's vaccine side deal', EURACTIV.com. https://www.euractiv.com/section/coronavirus/news/ commission-takes-evasive-action-over-germanys-vaccine-side-deal/ [Accessed 7 September 2022].

Goldner Lang, Iris (2021): 'EU COVID-19 Certificates: A Critical Analysis', *European Journal of Risk Regulation*, 12:2, 298–307.

Greer, Scott (2012): 'The European Centre for Disease Prevention: Control: Hub or Hollow Core?', *Journal of Health Politics, Policy and Law*, 37:6, 1001–036.

Greer, Scott & Kurzer, Paulette (eds.) (2013): *European Union Public Health Policy: Regional and Global Trends.* Routledge.

Greer, Scott; Jarman, Holly (2021). 'What Is EU Public Health: Why? Explaining the Scope and Organization of Public Health in the European Union', *Journal of Health Politics, Policy and Law*, 46:1, 23–47.

Greer, Scott & Löblová, Olga (2017): 'European integration in the era of permissive dissensus: Neofunctionalism: agenda-setting in European health technology assessment & communicable disease control', *Comparative European Politics*, 15:3, 394–413.

Greer, Scott, Rozenblum, Sarah, Fahy, Nick, Brooks ,Eleanor;, Jarman, Holly, de Ruijter, Anniek, Palm, Willy & Wismar, Matthias (2022): *Everything you always wanted to know about European Union health policies but were afraid to ask.* Copenhagen: WHO Regional Office for Europe. Third, revised edition.

Guagliardo, Simona (2020): 'What role for health in the new Commission?' *European Policy Center* 04/02/2020. https://www.epc.eu/en/Publications/What-role-for-health-in-the-new-Commission~2e5554 [Accessed 7 September 2022].

Henning, Deters & Zardo, Federica (2022). 'The European Commission in COVID-19 Vaccine Cooperation: Leadership vs Coronationalism?', *Journal of European Public Policy*, DOI: 10.1080/13501763.2022.2064900.

Hervey, Tamara & McHale, Jean (2015): *European Union Health Law: Themes and Implications.* Cambridge University Press.

Järviniemi, Juuso, Scholz, Robert & Hoffmeister, Kalojan (2022): *From COVID-19 towards a European Health Union: Proposals for Treaty reform on health.* https://jef.eu/news/eu-treaty-reform-way-for-a-health-union/ [Accessed 7 September 2022].

Jordana, Jacint & Juan Carlos Triviño-Salazar (2020): 'Where are the ECDC & the EU-wide responses in the COVID-19 pandemic', *The Lancet*, 395 (10237), 1611–1612.

Kopcińska, Joanna (2021): EP Committee on the Environment, Public Health & Food Safety on the proposal for a regulation of the European Parliament and of the Council amending Regulation (EC) No 851/2004 establishing a European Centre for disease prevention and control (COM(2020)0726 – C9-0366/2020–2020/0320(COD)). https://www.europarl.europa.eu/doceo/document/A-9-2021-0253_EN.html#title1 [Accessed 5 April 2022].

Naumann, Anja (2022): 'EU Response to Fighting the Coronavirus – Coordination, Support, Action – Heeding its Citizens' Calls?', in Matthias C. Kettemann & Konrad Lachmayer (eds.): *Pandemocracy in Europe: Power, Parliaments and People in Times of COVID-19*, Hart Publishing, 243–262.

Nielson, Nikolaj (2021): 'Talks to strengthen EU virus-alert agency stall', EUObserver. https://euobserver.com/health-and-society/153401 [Accessed 30 March 2022].

Nugent, Neill & Rhinard, Mark (2019): 'The 'political' roles of the European Commission,' *Journal of European Integration*, 41:2, 203–220.

OECD, (2015). *Focus on health spending*, OECD. https://www.oecd.org/health/health-systems/Focus-Health-Spending-2015.pdf [Accessed 20 October 2021].

Popp, Dana (2022): 'European Health Union: deal on stronger crossborder cooperation', *European Parliament Press Releases* 23–06–2022. https://www.europarl.europa.eu/pdfs/news/expert/2022/6/press_release/20220620IPR33412/20220620IPR33412_en.pdf [Accessed 26 August 2022].

Rechel, Bernd (2019): 'Funding for public health in Europe in decline?,' *Health Policy*, 123:1, 21–26.

Rosenkötter, Nicole, Clemens, Timo, Sørensen, Kristine & Brand, Helmut (2013): 'Twentieth anniversary of the European Union health mandate: taking stock of perceived achievements, failures and missed opportunities – a qualitative study', *BMC Public Health*, 13:1, 1–16.

Sabbati Giulio & Dumbrava, Costica (2020): 'The impact of coronavirus on Schengen borders', *EPRS: European Parliamentary Research Service*. https://www.europarl.europa.eu/thinktank/en/document/EPRS_BRI(2020)649347 [Accessed 17 November 2021].

Scholz, Nicole (2020): 'European Centre for Disease Prevention and Control During the Pandemic', *European Parliament Briefing*, https://www.europarl.europa.eu/RegData/etudes/BRIE/2020/651973/EPRS_BRI(2020)651973_EN.pdf [Accessed 17 November 2021].

Steffen, Monika (1999): 'The Nation's Blood: Medicine, Justice, and the State in France', in Eric Feldman & Ronald Bayer (eds.): *Blood feuds: AIDS, blood, and the politics of medical disaster.* Oxford University Press.

Steffen, Monika (2012): 'The Europeanization of Public Health: How Does It Work? The Seminal Role of the AIDS Case. *Journal of Health Politics, Policy, and Law*, 37:6, 1057–1089.

Vila Maior, Paulo & Camisão, Isabel (2021): *The Pandemic Crisis and the European Union COVID-19 and Crisis*, Routledge.

Martijn Mos

13 Leader or laggard? Diversity and minority rights in a union under strain

Abstract: In the 1990s, the European Union played a leadership role on minority rights. In particular, it used the Copenhagen criteria to instruct candidate states on respecting both national and sexual minority (LGBTI) rights and recognising those minorities as a fundamental component of the EU's identity. But is the Union still a trailblazer three decades later? Although it continues to insist that third countries respect minority rights, within its own borders their commitment looks uncertain. The EU has taken few steps to advance the protection of minority rights since the 'big bang' enlargement of 2004. Moreover, the EU arguably lacks the executive powers necessary to ensure its own member states comply with the same values that it successfully imposes on candidate states. The so-called Copenhagen dilemma makes it difficult to respond effectively when member states backslide on minority rights. This chapter argues that, because of the lack of EU-level progress and national-level rights retrenchment, today's Union no longer sets the pace on minority rights. Yet, important variations exist across the main institutions. Whether the EU is a leader or a laggard on minority rights thus depends on the concrete actors that one looks at.

The chapter substantiates this argument by looking at how EU bodies responded to two issues: the Minority SafePack initiative on national minority rights and member states' adoption of anti-LGBTI policies. The European Parliament has argued that the EU must do more to protect both types of minorities. The Commission and the Council, in turn, dismissed calls for action. This remains true for national minority rights. When it comes to LGBTI rights, however, the chapter identifies lagged leadership: while the European Commission and the Council refused to intervene when Lithuania passed an anti-gay propaganda law, they have taken decisive action against similar, more recent developments in Hungary and Poland.

Keywords: National minority rights; LGBTI rights; Backsliding; European Citizens' Initiative; European Union.

Introduction

At the end of the 1990s, the European Union (EU) assumed a leadership role with respect to minority rights. National leaders assembled in the Danish capital in 1993 to formalise the requirements that candidate countries had to meet to be allowed

https://doi.org/10.1515/9783110790337-014

into an elite club of EU member states. The resultant Copenhagen criteria concerned more than economic standards and technical harmonisation; the European Council (1993) broke new ground by insisting that applicant states guaranteed "human rights and respect for and protection of minorities." The primary focus understandably lay with national minorities, given the history of ethnic strife in Central and Eastern Europe. The European Parliament, however, broadened the criteria's scope. It vowed to block the accession "of any country that, through its legislation or policies, violates the human rights of lesbians and gay men" (European Parliament 1998). What is more, in 1999 the EU drafted the Charter of Fundamental Rights prohibiting discrimination based on sexual orientation and membership of a national minority. The Charter also urged the Union to respect linguistic diversity, an issue of great concern for many national minorities. The EU thus sent out a clear message at the turn of the millennium: respect for both national and sexual minority rights is a defining feature of EU membership.

However, thirty years after that momentous meeting in Copenhagen, the EU's commitment to minority rights has come under strain. On the one hand, the EU has made little progress with the protection of minority rights. For national and sexual minorities, the current legal situation at the supranational level looks remarkably like it did before the 'big bang' enlargement of 2004. On the other hand, there is evidence of national-level backsliding on minority rights. The EU has struggled to ensure compliance with the very values that it successfully promoted during the accession process. At a General Affairs Council in 2013, Viviane Reding, then the European Commissioner tasked with fundamental rights, spoke frankly of a "Copenhagen dilemma": whereas the EU uses carrots and sticks to ensure that candidate countries meet the Copenhagen criteria, it lacks an effective mechanism to ensure that actual member states do the same (European Commission 2013a). This dilemma meant that some member states could target minorities, for example, by outlawing gay 'propaganda' or by penalising the public use of minority languages, without fear of being sanctioned by Brussels. When taken together, the lack of EU-level progress and rights retrenchment at the national level make the Union look more like a laggard than a leader on minority rights.

This chapter substantiates this assessment but nuances it at the same time. It argues that the EU can be characterised as both a leader *and* a laggard on minority rights, but that the right ascription depends on the institutional actors that one looks at.[1] The European Parliament qualifies as a leader. It has consistently called

---

1 The chapter focuses on the EU's executive and legislative bodies. To be sure, the European Court of Justice has also impacted the development of sexual minority rights. Its role can even be described as judicial activism (De Waele & Van der Vleuten 2011). However, because the Court can only interpret and clarify existing legal obligations, such activism is distinct from political or policy

for further protections at the supranational level and has reminded member states of their obligation to respect minority rights. The Council, meanwhile, has frustrated progress on the topic. It opposes collective action on minority rights because it sees the issue primarily as a national competence. Lastly, the Commission's approach to minority rights has been reactive. Wary of overstepping its bounds, the Commission has often shown deference to member states.

The chapter uses concrete examples to support this argument. With respect to national minority rights, I focus on the EU's response to the Minority SafePack. This 2013 European Citizens' Initiative put forward recommendations for legal changes that would strengthen the position of national minorities. With respect to sexual minority or lesbian, gay, bisexual, transgender, and intersex (LGBTI) rights, I analyse the EU's evolving response to anti-LGBTI legislation by contrasting Lithuania's anti-gay propaganda law with similar, more recent events in Hungary and Poland. Because they concern some of the most significant developments in the EU's internal policy on national and sexual minority rights since the 'big bang' enlargement of 2004, I use these examples to illustrate the attitudes of the different EU institutions.

The chapter proceeds as follows. The first section briefly compares the ways in which the EU administers national and sexual minority rights among its member states and in candidate countries. I suggest that two shortcomings beset the EU's approach towards its own members: double standards and limited powers of enforcement. This creates a potential for backsliding on human rights. The second section uses the example of the Minority SafePack initiative to exemplify the first shortcoming. Although the EU requires candidate countries to protect and respect the rights of national minorities, only the European Parliament is willing to adopt EU legislation to ensure that member states do the same. The second shortcoming is evident in the section on sexual minority rights. A perceived lack of competence prevented the Commission from intervening whenever a member state targeted such rights. The section also observes, however, that a surge of anti-LGBTI laws has motivated the Commission and the Council to act on the claim that LGBTI rights are EU values. This development, which I term lagged leadership, results in an increasing divergence between national and sexual minority rights; whereas the latter has received renewed attention, all EU institutions other than the European Parliament continue to give short shrift to the former. The conclusion summarises the findings.

---

leadership (Cini & Šuplata 2017). The chapter therefore does not discuss the judiciary. When it comes to national minority rights, the Court's impact has been negligible due to a lack of relevant treaty-based competences and corresponding hard law.

From the Copenhagen criteria to the Copenhagen dilemma: The potential for backsliding

The Copenhagen criteria ensured that the rights of national and sexual minorities played an important role in the accession process. It resulted in a carrot-and-stick approach, which motivated candidate countries to recognise new rights and amend or annul discriminatory policies. Indeed, scholars attributed a slew of legislative improvements to EU conditionality (e.g. Kelley 2004; Kristofferson et al. 2016). Prominent examples include the liberalisation of citizenship and language laws in Estonia and Latvia (Sasse 2008) and Romania's decriminalisation of homosexuality (Buzogány 2012).

To be sure, the EU's leverage was imperfect. Conditionality mostly failed to override domestic considerations in anti-liberal regimes, such as Vladimír Mečiar's Slovakia (Kelley 2004; Schimmelfennig 2005). The Commission's monitoring also suffered from "ad hocism" and inconsistencies, as the conditions that candidate countries had to meet lacked both clarity and foundation in EU law (Hughes & Sasse 2003: 16; Rechel 2008). More generally, minority rights were not a key priority for the EU. Latvia, for instance, was allowed to accede without having addressed all of the EU's concerns related to the Russian minority (Galbreath & Muiznieks 2009). Slovakia became a member state before it had even prohibited discrimination on grounds of sexual orientation. Notwithstanding these shortcomings , there is a scholarly consensus that the Copenhagen criteria helped to liberalise minority rights.

The EU's ability to enforce minority rights standards in candidate countries, however imperfect, far exceeds the organisation's influence in the same realm, *vis-à-vis* its own members. After accession, the Copenhagen criteria give way to the Copenhagen dilemma. The EU may expect member states to respect its fundamental values, which include LGBTI and national minority rights, but it finds itself hamstrung in the face of noncompliance. There is even a danger that newcomers will backslide. As one scholar warned, "it is possible that minority issues will again disappear from the policy agenda or, worse, that the absence of conditionality gives rise to a political backlash" (Rechel 2008: 188). A post-enlargement EU loses most of its ability to dissuade politicians from targeting minority rights.

Two interrelated factors put a strain on the EU's self-image as a community of values: ambiguity and unenforceability. Importantly, these preconditions for backlash apply to *all* of the EU's fundamental values. Indeed, some scholars have argued that the EU is experiencing "democratic backsliding" and a "rule of law crisis" (e.g. Emmons & Pavone 2021; Kelemen & Blauberger 2017; also see Bogdanowicz, this volume). This chapter shows that values other than democracy and the rule of law may experience similar strains. Indeed, resistance to minority rights contributes to what Scheppele et al. (2021: 10) call the Union's broader "values crisis."

The first stressor concerns the ambiguity in which the EU's fundamental values are shrouded (Mos 2020a). Throughout the accession process, the Commission instructs candidate countries on what compliance with these values entails. This guidance is seldom based on EU law. For example, it was not at all obvious that hosting LGBTI pride marches would become a "litmus test of Europeanness" during the accession process (Slootmaeckers 2017: 518). The demand for candidate countries to allow such marches to be organised is not rooted in the EU's own body of law and legal obligations, the so-called *acquis*. Similarly, because internal standards with respect to national minority rights were altogether absent, the EU borrowed its enlargement requirements from the Council of Europe and the OSCE High Commissioner on National Minorities (Sasse 2008). This arbitrary approach enabled the EU to tell candidate states what its values meant. It did not apply, however, to actual member states.

Indeed, scholars often speak of double standards when they contrast the formulation of external requirements with the absence of internal benchmarks (Kristofferson et al. 2016: 61; Rechel 2008). The expectation appears to be that member states are already in good standing and therefore do not need to be told explicitly what 'respect for minority rights' entails; compliance is assumed. As Müller (2013: 139) summarises it, "once inside the club, or so the rather complacent reasoning seemed to go, new democracies would count their blessings and never look back".

The presupposition that member states will behave responsibly has two important consequences. On the one hand, it takes away the need for further action. Member states already respect minority rights, so new policies would only be redundant. On the other hand, policymakers see no need to spell out precisely what the EU's fundamental values entail. They are supposedly so widely shared that their meaning is intuitive. The result is that these values, especially as they pertain to national and sexual minority rights, remain opaque. This is not just a semantic observation: because member states, unlike candidate countries, are not held to any explicit standards, they may feel encouraged to dismantle progressive policies or implement discriminatory laws (Mikalayeva et al. 2012; O'Dwyer 2012). After all, if legal standards are not written down, the letter of the law cannot be broken. As will become clear, these consequences are both evident with respect to national and sexual minority rights: there is little appetite for new supranational initiatives as well as evidence of national-level backsliding.

It is not just ambiguity that facilitates backsliding. The second relevant factor concerns the EU's limited toolkit with which it can respond to such backsliding. The Union can rely on a sophisticated system of infringement proceedings to challenge noncompliance with EU directives. For example, the Commission can invoke the

Employment Equality Directive when states discriminate against homosexuals in employment matters (Mos 2014). This directive is, however, an exception; few supranational laws speak directly to national and sexual minority rights. Such rights fall instead under the rubric of fundamental values. Member states must uphold them, but, as Hungary and Poland's persistent disrespect for a plethora of such values shows, the EU struggles to enforce this obligation. The most forceful enforcement mechanism, in theory, the famously "nuclear option" of Article 7 TEU that empowers the Council to respond to serious and persistent breaches of EU values by suspending the violating state's privileges of EU membership, has proven unworkable in practice (Priebus 2022). Scholars have suggested that there are nonetheless more circuitous ways of enforcing fundamental values, and EU institutions have taken up some of these suggestions (e. g. Blauberger & Kelemen 2017; Blauberger & Van Hüllen 2021; Müller 2013; Scheppele et al. 2020). This is not the place to describe these developments in detail. What matters here is that minority rights play at best an auxiliary role in these debates and improvised solutions. The names of instruments such as the Rule of Law Framework and the EU Justice Scorecard indicate that, among all fundamental values, the EU is primarily concerned with the rule of law. Analogous initiatives to enforce minority rights are absent.

EU institutions thus long assumed that member states do not violate fundamental values. Where candidate countries required instructions, the meaning of these values was supposedly readily apparent to member states. The latter supposedly lead by example. This makes further supranational policies to advance these core principles appear redundant. Similarly, where the EU relied on external incentives to bring applicants up to speed, the belief that backsliding would not happen made parallel enforcement mechanisms irrelevant internally. Because they are ambiguous and practically unenforceable, all EU values may come under strain. The remainder of the chapter explores how this has affected the Union's leadership on minority rights. As the next two sections show, the EU combines a lack of supranational progress on national and sexual minority rights with evidence of national-level backsliding. This blanket assessment, however, obscures important differences in orientation across the European Commission, Council, and Parliament.

The neglect of national minority rights

Double standards are conspicuous in the EU's approach to national minority rights. Candidate countries are asked to meet criteria that various member states fall short of. For example, take the Framework Convention for the Protection of National Minorities. Although this treaty is prominently featured in the accession process, four member states – Belgium, France, Greece, and Luxembourg – have neither signed nor ratified it. "Do as I say, not as I do" best summarises the EU's approach (Johns 2003). This example also illustrates how the EU relied on external standards to enforce minority rights norms: the Framework Convention is a treaty of the Council of Europe. The EU had no standards of its own to impose.

How has the status of national minority rights under EU law changed after enlargement? On the one hand, the Treaty of Lisbon codified "the rights of persons belonging to minorities" as a foundational value of European integration (European Union 2007). It also gave the Charter of Fundamental Rights, including its prohibition on discrimination against national minorities, legal force. These changes, on the other hand, have left no identifiable imprint on supranational policymaking. The fate of the Minority SafePack, a proposal for a supranational policy on national minorities, helps to explain why.

The Minority SafePack Initiative

The Lisbon Treaty's relevance lies not just in its explicit references to national minorities. It also contains articles highlighting the importance of representative democracy, which kickstarted the creation of a novel instrument: the European Citizens' Initiative (ECI) (Szeligowska & Mincheva 2012). Since 2011, this instrument has enabled ordinary citizens to submit a legislative proposal for EU action. The Commission is obliged to give serious consideration to all proposals that meet the procedural and formal requirements. Minority representatives have therefore used this instrument to underscore the importance of, and widespread support for, supranational action to protect national minorities.

The initiative 'Minority SafePack: One Million Signatures for Diversity in Europe' marks the most prominent and sophisticated attempt.[2] The Federal Union of European Nationalities (FUEN), an umbrella organisation of autochthonous national minorities spanning across Europe, first registered this initiative in 2013. The ECI calls upon the EU "to adopt a set of legal acts to improve the protection of persons belonging to national and linguistic minorities and strengthen cultural and linguistic diversity in the Union" (European Union 2017). The organisers argue

---

2 Another relevant ECI is the Initiative for the Equality of the Regions and Sustainability of the Regional Cultures (Toggenburg 2018). At the time of writing, verification of the signatures was still ongoing.

that their mission builds on treaty references to fundamental values and the respect for cultural and linguistic diversity, and that it even resonates with the Union's official motto 'United in Diversity' (European Union 2017).[3] They note that the EU often fails to live up to these lofty proclamations. Indeed, the ECI invokes the Copenhagen dilemma to underscore the proposal's urgency:

> *Because of these [Copenhagen] criteria, many new Member States in central Europe have enacted advanced models to protect their national minorities. [...] Once a state has entered the Union, however, this lever no longer works, and we have seen some worrying developments in recent years.* (European Union 2017)

The ECI thus urges the Commission to step up its support for national minorities. Thematically, its recommendations run the gamut of minority protection: language, education, culture, audio-visual media, regional policy, participation, and non-discrimination. The proposed instruments range from non-binding recommendations to binding regulations and directives (see Crepaz 2018; Toggenburg 2018). All in all, the Minority SafePack ambitiously sought to carve out space for national minority rights within the EU's treaties.

This effort came to naught. The ECI's lack of success is instructive for understanding why the Union has thus far not translated its treaty-based commitment to minority rights into concrete action. In fact, the Commission has steadfastly rejected calls for a supranational policy on national minorities. In 2013, it refused to register the Minority SafePack, which prevented the organisers from initiating the collection of signatures. The Commission all but acknowledged the unenforceability of the Union's fundamental values stating: "While the respect for rights of persons belonging to minorities is one of the values of the Union referred to in Article 2 TEU, [EU treaties do not] provide for a legal base as regards the adoption of legal acts aiming at promoting the rights of persons belonging to minorities". The Minority SafePack thus fell "manifestly outside the framework of the Commission's powers" (European Commission 2013b).

The organisers successfully appealed this decision on procedural grounds. The Commission subsequently registered the initiative and, in January 2020, received 1,123,422 valid signatures. Although the ECI cleared all procedural hurdles, it was not able to convince the Commission of the proposal's merits. Commissioner Věra Jourová avowed that "respect for the rights of persons belonging to a minority is one of the core Union values, and the Commission is committed to promoting

---

3 The ECI carefully avoids any mention of group rights. These would be incompatible with the EU's focus on individual rights, as evidenced by Article 2 TEU's reference to the rights of persons belonging to minorities.

this agenda," but did not translate this commitment into action (European Commission 2021c). The Commission repeated its earlier claim that "the EU has no general legislative competence specifically on the protection of national minorities" (European Commission 2021a). The primary responsibility for minority rights rested instead with the member states. While the Commission may provide support through programs, such as Erasmus+ and the European Regional Development Fund, it saw neither a legal basis nor a need for "further legislative action" on any of the ECI's proposals (European Commission 2021a). This rejection of the Minority SafePack demonstrates the Commission's reluctance to stretch its competences in this field. Consequently, FUEN (2021) sombrely concluded that the Commission had "turned its back on national minorities."

The Commission's reticence makes sense when one realises that it cannot rule by decree. The Commission may propose legal actions, but it is ultimately the Council, usually in conjunction with the Parliament, that decides. The preferences of these other bodies therefore drive the decision to initiate legislation; the Commission will not put forward proposals that lack political support (Kreppel & Oztas 2017). Such support for minority rights is certainly absent in the Council. Some member states, such as France and Greece, refuse to recognise some minorities altogether (Dimitras 2004). Other national governments, due to the tension between minority-majority relations in their societies , jealously guard their competences in many of the Minority SafePack's issues, such as language equality (Arzoz 2020; Mos 2020b).

In fact, some member states were so opposed to an EU policy on national minorities that they took legal action in efforts to frustrate the ECI. When the initiative's organisers challenged the refusal of registration in Court, Romania and Slovakia, both home to a sizeable Hungarian minority, intervened in support of the Commission.[4] Subsequently, the Romanian government sought to annul the registration of the ECI.[5] It not only held that most of the Minority SafePack's aims fell within the "exclusive competence of the Member States," but also insisted that some proposals were discriminatory and therefore violated, rather than embodied, the EU's fundamental values (*Romania v European Commission* 2019). These legal efforts to block the Minority SafePack proved fruitless.[6] Still, they indicate how resistant some member states are to the Europeanisation of national mi-

---

4 The Hungarian government, on the other hand, intervened in support of the Minority SafePack. See Case T-646/13 (2017), *Bürgerausschuss für die Bürgerinitiative Minority SafePack – One Million Signatures for Diversity in Europe v European Commission.*
5 Slovakia initially supported the Romanian endeavor, but later withdrew its intervention.
6 Romania also unsuccessfully appealed the 2019 ruling. See Case C-899/19 P (2022), *Romania v European Commission.*

nority rights. If a non-binding citizens' initiative already managed to ruffle feathers, the opposition is sure to be particularly intense should the Council ever scrutinise legislative proposals to advance national minority rights. This has not yet happened; the Commission, aware of the Council's misgivings, has not submitted any proposals on this topic.

This is not to say that minority activists lack allies within the EU institutions. For one, Hungary advocates for an EU policy on minority rights across multiple venues, including within the European Parliament (Waterbury 2017). Representatives of Fidesz, the party of Prime Minister Viktor Orbán, are highly active within the parliamentary Intergroup on Traditional Minorities, National Communities, and Languages. Their belief that the EU should do more to protect national minorities is widely shared. In fact, the European Parliament explicitly endorsed the Minority SafePack. In December 2020, it adopted a resolution in which it "expresses its support" for the ECI and "calls on the Commission to act on it and to propose legal acts [...] in accordance with the principles of subsidiarity and proportionality" (European Parliament 2020). MEPs, in other words, believe that there is room within the Union's competencies to enshrine national minority rights in supranational legislation.

The endorsement of the Minority SafePack is emblematic of the European Parliament's outsized willingness, relative to the other EU institutions, to protect national minorities. Already in 2005, MEPs, observing that minority rights are a core component of the Copenhagen criteria but that "there is no standard for minority rights in Community policy," adopted a resolution in which they demanded an end to the Union's double standard (European Parliament 2005). In 2018, they reiterated their belief that "the EU has a responsibility to protect and promote the rights of minorities" (European Parliament 2018).

When MEPs voice concerns on minority rights in the context of enlargement and foreign policy, the Commission typically vows to take action. Whenever they address the EU's internal dimension of minority rights, however, they are rebuffed. A sense of powerlessness pervades these replies. Thus, when MEPs provided evidence of backsliding on the language rights of minorities in Slovakia, Commissioner Leonard Orban drily noted that "the Member States remain the decision-makers with respect to their internal language policy" (European Commission 2009). He stated this despite his colleagues' intervention in similar developments in candidate states. The Copenhagen dilemma, in short, weakens the EU's hold over national minority rights after enlargement.

The example of the Minority SafePack illuminates three dimensions to the position of national minority rights within the EU. First, the Europeanisation of this issue faces strong resistance. There is no appetite for a supranational policy that would hold member states to the same standards as candidate countries. Second, the absence of hard law has a crippling effect on the Commission's willingness to counteract backsliding. Although the Copenhagen dilemma besets all fundamental values, the politically sensitive nature of minority rights makes the dilemma especially hard to solve. Third, this general assessment obscures important inter-institutional differences. Whereas resistance in some member states feeds into the Commission's reluctance to act, the European Parliament has repeatedly argued that the EU can and ought to do more to protect national minorities. The latter's exhortations, however, have fallen on deaf ears. As a result, the problems of double standards and unenforceability continue to plague the Union's core principle of respect for national minorities.

Sexual minority rights: A case of lagged leadership

The Commission, wary of overstepping its bounds, refuses to initiate supranational legislation on national minority rights. It does not have to tread as carefully on the issue of sexual minority rights, because the Treaty of Amsterdam established an EU competence to tackle discrimination on the basis of sex and sexual orientation (Mos 2014).[7] This competence already led to hard law in 2000, with the adoption of the Employment Equality Directive. Since 2008, the Commission has pushed for a follow-up directive that would prohibit discrimination beyond the employment realm, including access to goods and services, healthcare, and education. It has even published strategic documents – the 'List of Actions to Advance LGBTI Equality' in 2015 and the 'LGBTIQ Equality Strategy' in 2020[8] – that outline how the Commission integrates sexual minority rights into much of its work. In the 2020 State of the Union, Ursula Von der Leyen underscored her Commission's unwavering support for these rights:

> I will not rest when it comes to building a Union of equality. A Union where you can be who you are and love who you want – without fear of recrimination or discrimination. Because being yourself is not your ideology. It's your identity. (European Commission 2020a)

---

7 The treaties do not explicitly refer to gender, but Court rulings have clarified that sex-based discrimination encompasses gender identity (Stychin 1997).

8 The changing acronyms also reveal how the Commission's thinking about sexual diversity has evolved. Prior to 2015, EU documents spoke mostly of lesbian, gay, bisexual, and transgender people (LGBT). The Commission added intersex people in 2015 (LGBTI) and queer people in 2020 (LGBTIQ).

Evidently, the charge of double standards does not seem to apply here; candidate and member states alike must respect sexual minority rights.

At the same time, the Commission's ability to promote and protect LGBTI rights is seriously constrained. For one, its anti-discrimination competence is limited. The Commission recognises this. It admits that in some areas, such as family law, it can do little more than encourage national governments to "complement" its actions with measures "in areas of Member State competence" (European Commission 2020b). Even where it has competence, its initiatives may fall through. The proposed follow-up to the Employment Equality Directive, for instance, has lain dormant for well over a decade, in part because some member states cite "cultural incompatibilities" with respect to sexual orientation (Thiel 2015: 76). Without such a law, the Commission can only address discrimination unrelated to employment by invoking the EU's fundamental values. At this point, however, the Copenhagen dilemma rears its head. The mantra that LGBTI rights are a constitutive part of the EU's identity then proves to be merely an unenforceable illusion.

This unenforceability becomes apparent when looking at the EU institutions' efforts to curb human rights infringements. More so than with national minority rights, some countries began to contest LGBTI rights after accession. In what follows, I explore how the different EU institutions responded to such backsliding. I describe the Commission and Council's behaviour as *lagged leadership:* they initially did little to counteract anti-LGBTI developments but have more recently embraced an interventionist stance.

The EU's response to backsliding on sexual minority rights

For many candidate countries, where religious beliefs and traditional views on sexuality were dominant (Gerhards 2010; Mole 2016), the imposition of LGBTI rights was a hard price to pay to secure membership. This lay the foundation for backsliding. As O'Dwyer (2018: 900) notes, "the potential for backlash builds with the EU's endorsement of LGBT norms, but it is activated when EU leverage wanes". The backlash soon materialised. Already a year after its accession, the nationally conservative government in Poland, among other measures, abolished a government unit tasked with an anti-discrimination policy that had been created in response to the accession requirements; banned educational material that supposedly promoted homosexuality; and introduced an internet filter to prevent pupils from accessing websites about homosexuality in schools (Pankowski 2010). Anti-gay politics also played out at the subnational level, as municipal governments in Poland and also in Latvia banned pride marches.

Until recently, the response to these episodes of backlash was consistent across the main EU institutions. The European Parliament denounced the restrictions on LGBTI rights as violations of the EU's fundamental values. In various resolutions, it not only expressed its concerns over a surge in homophobia in the respective member states but also accused the Commission of standing idly by. The Commission replied that its hands were tied. In 2006, for example, Commissioner Franco Frattini stated that he was "quite sure that the Commission does not currently have the necessary powers to take action" against most of the rights violations that MEPs informed him about (European Parliament 2006). The Commission consequently took no legal measures to redress anti-LGBTI developments in Latvia, Poland, and other member states. The Council, meanwhile, stayed on the sidelines altogether.

Yet, these institutional dynamics have begun to shift in recent years. Particularly instructive is the contrast between the EU institutions' response to a Lithuanian law that prohibited the promotion of homosexuality and similar, but more recent initiatives in Hungary and Poland. The former concerned changes to a law shielding minors from harmful public information. In 2009, the Lithuanian parliament added new categories that it believed detrimentally affected the mental and moral well-being of persons under the age of 18. This included information:

> which expresses contempt for family values, encourages the concept of entry into a marriage and creation of a family other than stipulated in the Constitution of the Republic of Lithuania and the Civil Code of the Republic of Lithuania. (Republic of Lithuania 2009)

Lithuanian lawmakers, simply stated, classified same-sex families and marriages as damaging to minors (see Mos 2022). They also prohibited the distribution of information "which promotes sexual relations" (Republic of Lithuania 2009). Because the amendment originally referred to homosexual, bisexual or polygamous relationships, the lawmakers' main target was clear.

Critics decried the initiative as a "Russian-style anti-gay propaganda law" (LGL 2014). The bill attracted the ire of the European Parliament, which adopted two resolutions condemning Lithuania for running afoul of EU values (European Parliament 2009b, 2011). MEPs also urged the Commission and Council to act. As one representative put it, "We must take action to stop this. The values and laws of the EU cannot be treated like an *à la carte* menu" (European Parliament 2011).

The Council did not heed this appeal. The bill provoked some pushback from individual member states, including the Swedish Presidency of the EU, but not a collective response (European Parliament 2009b). Indeed, MEPs were told that the Council "has not discussed the matter" (European Parliament 2009a).

The Commission also did not intervene. It argued that "it is for Member States […] to ensure that fundamental rights are effectively respected and protected," and that its own competence "is limited to cases when the implementation of European Union law is at stake" (European Parliament 2013). Two human rights organisations, the Lithuanian Gay League and ILGA-Europe, complained that Lithuania had in fact violated hard law, namely the Audiovisual Media Services Directive. The Commission disagreed. Because the Lithuanian law did not affect "broadcasts from other Member States" in Lithuania – that is, there was no cross-border dimension to the LGBTI rights violations – there were "no grounds to establish an infringement" of the directive (European Commission 2016). Lithuania could keep the anti-LGBTI law on its books.

Yet, when LGBTI rights came under fire in Hungary and Poland less than a decade later, the Commission shifted gears. In June 2021, the Hungarian National Assembly approved a series of amendments that restricted communication about sexual minorities, supposedly to protect children. Under the revised Child Protection Act, for instance, it is forbidden "to make accessible" to persons under the age of 18 information that "propagates or portrays divergence from self-identity corresponding to sex at birth, sex change or homosexuality" (Venice Commission 2021). Other amendments contain similar language. Critics described these changes like they had condemned the Lithuanian bill: by labelling it as "Russian-style" legislation (ILGA-Europe 2021). Indeed, although the Hungarian amendments target gender identity in addition to homosexuality, the similarities between the two countries' bills are striking.

Similar legislation looms in Poland. Days after Hungary's restriction of LGBTI rights, the Deputy Minister of Justice announced that his ministry was preparing a bill outlawing "LGBT propaganda activities" (Rębisz 2021). In the meantime, Polish officials had found other ways of shielding children from the alleged spectre of sexual diversity by, for instance, banning adoption by same-sex couples. The most prominent initiative concerned the creation of so-called 'LGBT-free zones'. By February 2020, almost one hundred municipalities and five voivodeships had passed variously phrased resolutions extolling the virtues of the traditional family or, more explicitly, denouncing "homopropaganda" or "sexual depravity and indoctrination" (Ciobanu 2020).[9] The Lithuanian, Hungarian and Polish initiatives thus have comparable aims.

---

9 The former concerned the adoption of a Local Government Charter of the Rights of the Family. This initiative of Ordo Iuris, an ultra-conservative think tank with close ties to the ruling Law and

Whereas only the European Parliament reacted strongly to Lithuania's anti-LGBTI law, all EU institutions denounced the developments in Hungary and Poland. The European Parliament (2021a), observing a "clear breach of the EU's values", called upon the Commission and, where necessary, member states to "immediately take legal action" against Hungary. MEPs countered Poland's LGBT-free zones by declaring the EU an "LGBTIQ freedom zone" (European Parliament 2021b). These resolutions only reinforced the Parliament's supportive record on LGBTI rights.

More remarkable were the reactions of the other two institutions. The Commission's response, in particular, suggests a transformation from indecision to lagged leadership. Not only did Von der Leyen call the Hungarian law "a shame," she also saw it as discriminatory "against people on the basis of their sexual orientation" and as a clear violation of "all the values, the fundamental values, of the European Union" (Eder & Von der Burchard 2021). The Commission President similarly held that "LGBTQI-free zones are humanity free zones" which have "no place in our Union" (European Commission 2020a). The decision of the Commission's highest official to call out member states' violations of LGBTI rights marked a sea change in her organisation's management of EU values.

Moreover, the Commission did not just use words to express its indignation. In July 2021, it launched infringement proceedings against both Hungary and Poland. Concerning the latter, the Commission argued that the Polish government had, in violation of the principle of sincere cooperation, frustrated the Commission's inquiry into the compatibility of the LGBT-free zones with EU law.[10] Concerning Hungary, the Commission cited a list of legal breaches. These included the Audiovisual Media Services, the same law that the Commission had deemed irrelevant in the Lithuanian case (European Commission 2021b). The charges extended to other hard law, several provisions of the Charter of Fundamental Rights, and, groundbreakingly, "the values laid down in Article 2 TEU" (European Commission 2021b). Hungary did not address these concerns; the Orbán government even doubled down by organising a referendum in support of its anti-LGBTI policies.[11] The Commission therefore referred Hungary to the European Court of Justice (European Commission 2022). The proceedings against Hungary and Poland were still unfolding at the time of writing. Regardless of the outcome, their import is apparent:

Justice party, does not explicitly refer to LGBTI rights. Nevertheless, the project's coordinator explained that the charter, in direct response to "the threat posed by LGBT ideology," intends to "defend children from demoralisation and depravity" (Ciobanu 2020).

10 Under the EU's twinning scheme, the Commission also denied funding to municipalities declaring themselves to be LGBT-free zones (Wanat 2020).

11 Because the referendum failed to draw quorum, its outcome was non-binding.

for the first time, the Commission took legal action to protect the EU's fundamental values as they pertained to LGBTI rights.

Given Hungarian and Polish opposition, the Council has not been able to speak with one voice on the events in the two countries. Still, a majority of member states came together to denounce the anti-LGBTI laws. Following the General Affairs Council of 22 June 2021, eighteen member states (ironically including Lithuania) adopted a joint declaration on Hungary. They called the legal changes a "flagrant form of discrimination" and urged the Commission "to use all the tools at its disposal" to ensure that Hungary respects EU law (Wilmès 2021). Two days later, Viktor Orbán drew the ire of some colleagues within a European Council meeting. The Dutch Prime Minister Mark Rutte told Orbán outright to either respect the EU's fundamental values or to "get out" of the Union. That same day, sixteen heads of state expressed their "attachment to our common fundamental values" in a statement that was issued "in the light of threats against fundamental rights and in particular the principle of non-discrimination on grounds of sexual orientation" (De Croo 2021). These forceful reactions contrast sharply with the reaction to the Lithuanian anti-LGBTI law, which the Council did not even discuss.

In sum, the EU's protection of LGBTI rights constitutes lagged leadership. The European Parliament for a long period was the only institution calling for decisive action against member states that violated these rights. As the nonresponse to Lithuania's anti-LGBTI law showed, neither the Commission nor the Council wished to intervene. However, both institutions have become convinced of the importance of responding to violations of sexual minority rights. The response to anti-LGBTI initiatives in Hungary and Poland shows a newfound commitment to overcome the Copenhagen dilemma on this issue. As one Commissioner put it, "we have entered a new era in the fight for equality" (Wanat 2020).

Conclusion

The Copenhagen criteria at once enabled and constrained the EU's ability to lead by example on minority rights. On the one hand, they were the vehicle through which the Commission imposed its vision of human rights and the respect for and protection of minorities on candidate states. On the other hand, the criteria fed into a paradox: within its own borders, the EU struggles to uphold the selfsame values it so successfully diffuses abroad. As result, the EU's representation of itself as a community of values looks increasingly strained.

This chapter has addressed two dimensions of the paradox across two types of minority rights. Double standards are most evident with respect to the rights of national minorities. The EU institutions emphasise this issue during the accession process, but a post-enlargement commitment to this minority can only be discerned within the European Parliament. The varied reactions to the Minority Safe-Pack illustrated this: while MEPs endorsed this proposal for legislative action on national minority rights, the Council ignored it altogether, and the Commission, citing competence limitations, dismissed the initiative. As a result of this lack of supranational decision-making, the claim that the rights of national minorities are among the EU's fundamental values rings hollow.

The paradox's second dimension concerned the unenforceability of minority rights. This Copenhagen dilemma is well-documented within the context of democracy and the rule of law, but this chapter has shown that it also besets minority rights. The difficulty of enforcing the EU's fundamental values applies to both national and sexual minorities. In practice, however, it is predominantly the latter whose rights have come under strain. The example of Lithuania, which prohibited the distribution of public information about non-heteronormative families and marriage to minors, demonstrated the Commission and the Council's reluctance to respond to a post-enlargement backlash against LGBTI rights. Only the European Parliament saw this as a threat to the EU's fundamental values that required decisive action.

Yet, recognising that its values are under threat, the EU has begun to address the Copenhagen dilemma. The EU institutions initially focused on democracy and the rule of law in Hungary and Poland. When these two countries followed Lithuania's lead by targeting the supposed promotion of homosexuality and gender ideology, however, they galvanised the EU into defending LGBTI rights. MEPs were predictably outraged over the anti-LGBTI initiatives. The other institutions' reaction, which I have described as lagged leadership, was more surprising. A clear majority of member states castigated the two countries for violating the EU's fundamental values and called on the Commission to intervene. The Commission did just this. For the first time ever, it initiated infringement proceedings against two member states for violating LGBTI rights. This watershed moment marks an ambitious attempt to ease the strain on the Union's fundamental values as they apply to sexual minorities. Whether the attempt will succeed, and whether the EU institutions would be equally willing to take legal action in defence of national minorities, remains to be seen.

References

Arzoz, Xabier (2020): 'The Protection and Promotion of Language Equality in the EU: Gaps, Paradoxes, and Double Standards', in Thomas Giegerich (ed.): *The European Union as a Protector and Promoter of Equality*, Springer, 97–112.

Blauberger, Michael & Kelemen, R. Daniel (2017): 'Can courts rescue national democracy? Judicial safeguards against democratic backsliding in the EU', *Journal of European Public Policy*, 24(3), 321–336.

Blauberger, Michael & Van Hüllen, Vera (2021): 'Conditionality of EU funds: An instrument to enforce EU fundamental values?', *Journal of European Integration*, 43:1, 1–16.

Buzogány, Aron (2012): 'Swimming against the Tide: Contested Norms and Antidiscrimination Advocacy in Central and Eastern Europe', in Emanuela Lombardo & Maxime Forest (eds.): *The Europeanization of Gender Equality Policies: A Discursive-Sociological Approach*, Palgrave Macmillan, 145–167.

Cini, Michelle & Šuplata, Marián (2017): 'Policy Leadership in the European Commission: The Regulation of EU Mobile Roaming Charges', *Journal of European Integration*, 39:2, 143–156.

Ciobanu, Claudia (2020): 'A Third of Poland Declared "LGBT-Free Zone"', *Balkan Insight*, https://balkan insight.com/2020/02/25/a-third-of-poland-declared-lgbt-free-zone/. Accessed 21 November 2022.

Crepaz, Katharina (2018): 'The Minority SafePack Initiative: A European Participatory Process Supporting Cultural Diversity', *European Yearbook of Minority Issues*, 17, 23–47.

De Croo, Alexander [@alexanderdecroo] (2021, June 24): *Hate, intolerance and discrimination have no place in our Union. That's why, today and every day, we stand for diversity and LGBTI equality so that our future generations can grow up in a Europe of equality and respect.* [Tweet], https://twit ter.com/alexanderdecroo/status/1407977290189971457. Accessed 21 November 2022.

De Waele, Henri & Van der Vleuten, Anna (2011): 'Judicial Activism in the European Court of Justice – The Case of LGBT Rights', *Michigan State Journal of International Law*, 19:3, 639–666.

Dimitras, Panayote Elias (2004): 'Recognition of Minorities in Europe: Protecting Rights and Dignity', *Minority Rights Group International*, https://minorityrights.org/wp-content/uploads/old-site-down loads/download-47-Recognition-of-Minorities-in-Europe-Protecting-Rights-and-Dignity.pdf. Accessed 21 November 2022.

Eder, Florian & Von der Burchard, Hans (2021): "A shame': Von der Leyen vows EU will fight Hungary's anti-LGBTQ+ law', *Politico*, https://www.politico.eu/article/european-commission-legal-steps-hungarys-anti-lgbtq-law/. Accessed 21 November 2022.

Emmons, Cassandra & Pavone, Tommaso (2021): 'The Rhetoric of Inaction: Failing to Fail Forward in the EU's Rule of Law Crisis', *Journal of European Public Policy*, 28:10, 1611–1629.

European Commission (2009): *Joint answer given by Mr Orban on behalf of the Commission*, https://www.europarl.europa.eu/doceo/document/E-7-2009-3753-ASW_EN.html. Accessed 21 November 2022.

European Commission (2013a): *Safeguarding the rule of law and solving the "Copenhagen dilemma": Towards a new EU-mechanism*, https://ec.europa.eu/commission/presscorner/detail/en/SPEECH_ 13_348. Accessed 21 November 2022.

European Commission (2013b): *Your request for registration of a proposed citizens' initiative*, https://fuen.org/user_upload/downloads/20130916_ECI_Absage_MinoritySafepack_org.pdf. Accessed 21 November 2022.

European Commission (2016): *Your complaint against Lithuania*, On file with author.

European Commission (2020a): *State of the Union Address 2020*, https://ec.europa.eu/commission/presscorner/detail/en/SPEECH_20_1655. Accessed 21 November 2022.

European Commission (2020b): *#UnionOfEquality: LGBTIQ Equality Strategy 2020–2025*, https://ec.euro pa.eu/info/files/lgbtiq-equality-strategy-2020-2025_en. Accessed 21 November 2022.

European Commission (2021a): *Communication from the Commission on the European Citizens' Initiative "Minority SafePack – One Million Signatures for Diversity in Europe"*, https://ec.europa.eu/transparency/documents-register/detail?ref=C(2021)171&lang=en. Accessed 21 November 2022.

European Commission (2021b): *EU founding values: Commission starts legal action against Hungary and Poland for violations of fundamental rights of LGBTIQ people*, https://ec.europa.eu/commission/presscorner/detail/en/ip_21_3668. Accessed 21 November 2022.

European Commission (2021c): *European Citizens' Initiative: European Commission replies to 'Minority Safepack' initiative*, https://ec.europa.eu/commission/presscorner/api/files/document/print/en/ip_21_81/IP_21_81_EN.pdf. Accessed 21 November 2022.

European Commission (2022): *Commission refers HUNGARY to the Court of Justice of the EU over violation of LGBTIQ rights*, https://ec.europa.eu/commission/presscorner/detail/en/IP_22_2689. Accessed 21 November 2022.

European Council (1993): *Copenhagen European Council: Presidency Conclusions*, https://www.consilium.europa.eu/media/21225/72921.pdf. Accessed 21 November 2022.

European Parliament (1998): 'Resolution on Equal Rights for Gays and Lesbians in the EC', *Official Journal of the European Communities*, C:313, 186.

European Parliament (2005): *Protection of Minorities and Anti-Discrimination Policies in an Enlarged Europe*, https://eur-lex.europa.eu/legal-content/EN/TXT/?uri=celex%3A52005IP0228. Accessed 21 November 2022.

European Parliament (2006): *Homophobia in Europe*, https://www.europarl.europa.eu/doceo/document/TA-6-2006-0018_EN.html. Accessed 21 November 2022.

European Parliament (2009a): *Joint Reply*, Accessed 21 November 2022. https://www.europarl.europa.eu/doceo/document/E-7-2009-3865-ASW_EN.html. Accessed 21 November 2022.

European Parliament (2009b): *Situation in Lithuania Following the Adoption of the Law on Protection of Minors*, https://www.europarl.europa.eu/doceo/document/TA-7-2009-0019_EN.html. Accessed 21 November 2022.

European Parliament (2011): *Violation of freedom of expression and discrimination on the basis of sexual orientation in Lithuania*, https://www.europarl.europa.eu/doceo/document/TA-7-2011-0019_EN.html?redirect. Accessed 21 November 2022.

European Parliament (2013): *Answer given by Mrs Reding on behalf of the Commission*, https://www.europarl.europa.eu/doceo/document/E-7-2013-012158-ASW_EN.html. Accessed 21 November 2022.

European Parliament (2018): *Fighting Discrimination of EU Citizens Belonging to Minorities in the EU Member States*, https://www.europarl.europa.eu/doceo/document/TA-8-2018-0032_EN.html. Accessed 21 November 2022.

European Parliament (2020): *European Citizens' Initiative – Minority SafePack*, https://www.europarl.europa.eu/doceo/document/TA-9-2020-0370_EN.html. Accessed 21 November 2022.

European Parliament (2021a): *Breaches of EU law and of the rights of LGBTIQ citizens in Hungary as a result of the adopted legal changes in the Hungarian Parliament*, https://www.europarl.europa.eu/doceo/document/TA-9-2021-0362_EN.html. Accessed 21 November 2022.

European Parliament (2021b): *Declaration of the EU as an LGBTIQ Freedom Zone*, https://www.europarl.europa.eu/doceo/document/TA-9-2021-0089_EN.html. Accessed 21 November 2022.

European Union (2007): 'Treaty of Lisbon Amending the Treaty on European Union and the Treaty Establishing the European Community', *Official Journal of the European Union*, C:306, 1–271.

European Union (2017): *Minority SafePack Initiative: You Are Not Alone. One Million Signatures for Diversity in Europe*, http://ec.europa.eu/citizens-initiative/public/documents/1721. Accessed 21 November 2022.

FUEN (2021): *Minority SafePack: The European Commission turned its back on national minorities*, https://fuen.org/en/article/Minority-SafePack-The-European-Commission-turned-its-back-on-national-minorities. Accessed 21 November 2022.

Galbreath, David & Muiznieks, Nils (2009): 'Latvia: Managing Post-Imperial Minorities', in Bernd Rechel (ed.): *Minority Rights in Central and Eastern Europe*, Routledge, 135–150.

Gerhards, Jürgen (2010): 'Non-Discrimination towards Homosexuality: The European Union's Policy and Citizens' Attitudes towards Homosexuality in 27 European Countries', *International Sociology*, 25:1, 5–28.

Hughes, James & Sasse, Gwendolyn (2003): 'Monitoring the Monitors: EU Enlargement Conditionality and Minority Protection in the CEECs', *Journal on Ethnopolitics and Minority Issues in Europe*, 4:1, 1–36.

ILGA-Europe (2021): *Europe's Leading LGBTI Rights Organisation Calls on EU to Act as Hungarian Parliament Adopts Legislation Censoring Communication about LGBTI People*, https://ilga-europe.org/press-release/europes-leading-lgbti-rights-organisation-calls-on-eu-to-act-as-hungarian-parliament-adopts-legislation-censoring-communication-about-lgbti-people/. Accessed 21 November 2022.

Johns, Michael (2003): '"Do as I Say, Not as I Do": The European Union, Eastern Europe and Minority Rights', *East European Politics & Societies*, 17:4, 682–699.

Kelemen, R. Daniel & Blauberger, Michael (2017): 'Introducing the Debate: European Union Safeguards against Member States' Democratic Backsliding', *Journal of European Public Policy*, 24:3, 317–320.

Kelley, Judith G. (2004): *Ethnic Politics in Europe: The Power of Norms and Incentives*, Princeton University Press.

Kreppel, Amie & Oztas, Buket (2017): 'Leading the Band or Just Playing the Tune? Reassessing the Agenda-Setting Powers of the European Commission', *Comparative Political Studies*, 50:8, 1118–1150.

Kristofferson, Mattias, Van Roozendaal, Björn & Poghosyan, Lilit (2016): 'European Integration and LGBTI Activism: Partners in Realising Change?', in Koen Slootmaeckers & Heleen Touquet; Peter Vermeersch (eds.): *The EU Enlargement and Gay Politics: The Impact of Eastern Enlargement on Rights, Activism and Prejudice*, Palgrave Macmillan, 45–67.

LGL (2014): *Lithuanian Parliament to vote on Russian style anti-gay "propaganda law" in final reading*, http://www.lgl.lt/en/?p=5368. Accessed 21 November 2022.

Mikalayeva, Liudmila, Schwellnus, Guido & Balázs, Lilla (2012): 'The Revocation of Minority Protection Rules in New EU Member States: Language and Education Policy in Slovakia and Latvia', *L'Europe En Formation*, 364, 379–400.

Mole, Richard C. M. (2016): 'Nationalism and Homophobia in Central and Eastern Europe', in Koen Slootmaeckers & Heleen Touquet; Peter Vermeersch (eds.): *The EU Enlargement and Gay Politics: The Impact of Eastern Enlargement on Rights, Activism and Prejudice*, Palgrave Macmillan, 99–121.

Mos, Martijn (2014): 'Of Gay Rights and Christmas Ornaments: The Political History of Sexual Orientation Non-discrimination in the Treaty of Amsterdam', *JCMS: Journal of Common Market Studies*, 52:3, 632–649.

Mos, Martijn (2020a): 'Ambiguity and interpretive politics in the crisis of European values: Evidence from Hungary', *East European Politics*, 36:2, 267–287.

Mos, Martijn (2020b): 'Diverting Linguistic Diversity: The Politics of Multilingualism in the European Parliament', in Katerina Strani (ed.): *Multilingualism and Politics: Revisiting Multilingual Citizenship*, Palgrave Macmillan, 47–76.

Mos, Martijn (2022): 'The Anti-Gay Propaganda Law in Lithuania: Defying the European Union', in Bianka Vida (ed.): *The Gendered Politics of Crises and De-Democratization: Opposition to Gender Equality*, Rowman & Littlefield, 175–194.

Müller, Jan-Werner (2013): 'Defending Democracy within the EU', *Journal of Democracy*, 24(2), 138–149.

O'Dwyer, Conor (2012): 'Does the EU help or hinder gay-rights movements in post-communist Europe? The case of Poland', *East European Politics*, 28:4, 332–352.

O'Dwyer, Conor (2018): 'The Benefits of Backlash: EU Accession and the Organization of LGBT Activism in Postcommunist Poland and the Czech Republic', *East European Politics and Societies*, 32:4, 892–923.

Pankowski, Rafal (2010): *The Populist Radical Right in Poland: The Patriots*, Routledge.

Priebus, Sonja (2022): 'Watering down the 'nuclear option'? The Council and the Article 7 dilemma', *Journal of European Integration*, Advance online publication.

Rębisz, Karol (2021): 'Deputy Justice Minister Says Polish Government is Working on a Bill to Ban "LGBT Propaganda"', *Gazeta Wyborcza*, https://wyborcza.pl/7,173236,27266406,deputy-justice-minister-says-polish-government-is-working-on.html?disableRedirects=true. Accessed 21 November 2022.

Rechel, Bernd (2008): 'What Has Limited the EU's Impact on Minority Rights in Accession Countries?', *East European Politics & Societies*, 22(1), 171–191.

Republic of Lithuania (2009): *Law on the Protection of Minors against the Detrimental Effects of Public Information*, old.ilga-europe.org/content/download/16797/108713/file/Law.pdf. Accessed 21 November 2022.

Romania v European Commission, T-391/17 (2019): https://eur-lex.europa.eu/legal-content/en/TXT/?uri=CELEX:62013TJ0646. Accessed 21 November 2022.

Sasse, Gwendolyn (2008): 'The politics of EU conditionality: The norm of minority protection during and beyond EU accession', *Journal of European Public Policy*, 15:6, 842–860.

Scheppele, Kim Lane, Kochenov, Dimitry V. & Grabowska-Moroz, Barbara (2020): 'EU Values Are Law, after All: Enforcing EU Values through Systemic Infringement Actions by the European Commission and the Member States of the European Union', *Yearbook of European Law*, 39, 3–121.

Schimmelfennig, Frank (2005): 'Strategic Calculation and International Socialization: Membership Incentives, Party Constellations, and Sustained Compliance in Central and Eastern Europe', *International Organization*, 59:4, 827–860.

Slootmaeckers, Koen (2017): 'The litmus test of pride: Analysing the emergence of the Belgrade "Ghost" pride in the context of EU accession', *East European Politics*, 33:4, 517–535.

Stychin, Carl F. (1997): 'Troubling Genders: A comment on *P. v. S. and Cornwall County Council*', *International Journal of Discrimination and the Law*, 2:3, 217–222.

Szeligowska, Dorota & Mincheva, Elitsa (2012): 'The European Citizens' Initiative – Empowering European Citizens within the Institutional Triangle: A Political and Legal Analysis', *Perspectives on European Politics and Society*, 13:3, 270–284.

Thiel, Markus (2015): 'Transversal and Particularistic Politics in the European Union's Antidiscrimination Policy: LGBT Politics under Neoliberalism', in Manuela Lavinas Picq & Markus Thiel (eds.): *Sexualities in World Politics: How LGBTQ Claims Shape International Relations*, Routledge, 75–91.

Toggenburg, Gabriel N. (2018): 'The Protection of Minority Rights by the European Union: The European Citizens' Initiative as a Test Case', in Rainer Hofmann, Tove H. Malloy & Detlev Rein (eds.): *The Framework Convention for the Protection of National Minorities*, Brill, 49–74.

Venice Commission (2021): *Hungary: Relevant Extracts of Act XXXI of 1997, Act XLVIII of 2008, Act CLXXXV of 2010, Act CCXI of 2011, and Act CXC of 2011.* http://www.venice.coe.int/webforms/documents/default.aspx?pdffile=CDL-REF(2021)089. Accessed 21 November 2022.

Wanat, Zosia (2020): 'Respect LGBTQI rights or lose EU funds, says equality commissioner', *Politico*, https://www.politico.eu/article/lgbtqi-rights-rule-of-law-funds-equality-commission-helena-dalli/. Accessed 21 November 2022.

Waterbury, Myra A. (2017): 'National Minorities in an Era of Externalization', *Problems of Post-Communism*, 64:5, 228–241.

Wilmès, Sophie (2021): *Eighteen countries unite at Belgium's initiative to defend LGBTIQ rights in Europe*, https://web.archive.org/web/20220328070554/https://wilmes.belgium.be/en/thirteen-countries-unite-belgiums-initiative-defend-lgbtiq-rights-europe. Accessed 21 November 2022.

Jeffrey Rosamond

14 The slow-burning climate emergency and the European Green Deal: Prospects and pitfalls in the polycrisis era

Abstract: The European Green Deal (EGD) and its European Climate Law have raised EU climate ambition to new heights by making the goal of net-zero emissions by 2050 legally binding. However, the action plan was proposed in times of crisis, and competing economic, health, and geopolitical emergencies risk undermining the EU's climate objectives. In this chapter, I situate climate policy and the EGD against the backdrop of the polycrisis. I argue that crisis-era governance provides both prospects and pitfalls for EU actors to advance climate ambition. This chapter proceeds in several steps. First, I provide an overview of the EGD, the European Climate Law, and the Fit for 55 Package, discussing whether they mark a break from previous incremental steps forward. Next, I outline crisis trends that risk derailing the EU's climate ambition. Thirdly, I demonstrate the key role that each of the EU's institutions have played in facilitating the development of the EGD and the challenges they face to maintain momentum in crisis contexts. Finally, this chapter focuses on the COVID-19 crisis and Russia's invasion of Ukraine, showing that crises provide both opportunities and challenges for the EU to stay the course on advancing the goals of the EGD. I argue that actions like tying climate objectives to economic recovery and energy security plans demonstrate that the EU may have adapted to working within crisis contexts to maintain climate ambitions. However, this hopeful trend is fragile as economic and energy hardships risk exacerbating east-west member state divisions on climate policy, thereby giving the EU institutions less room to advance radical climate action.

Keywords: climate policy; European Climate Law; European Green Deal; Fit for 55; polycrisis.

Introduction

First proposed by the European Commission (hereafter: the Commission) in December 2019, the European Green Deal (EGD) is a policy package that sets the EU on a path towards climate neutrality by 2050 while also safeguarding biodiversity and eliminating pollution. The action plan marks a break from previous incre-

https://doi.org/10.1515/9783110790337-015

mental climate policy developments by raising ambition to new heights (Dupont et al. 2020). A key component of the EGD, the European Climate Law – first proposed by the Commission in March 2020 and which entered into force in June 2021 – enshrines both the goal of net-zero emissions by 2050 and the short-term objective of a 55 per cent reduction of emissions from 1990 levels by 2030 into law (Regulation 2021/1119). The Commission's Fit for 55 package compliments the Climate Law by providing an impressive array of policy proposals that guide the EU towards the 2030 goal.

The EGD is significant not only in its promise of decarbonising all sectors of the EU's economy but also in ensuring a just transition that benefits all citizens and leaves no one behind (Rosamond & Dupont 2021). The Just Transition Mechanism (proposed in January 2020) and the Social Climate Fund (proposed in July 2021) aim to cushion the economic impacts of decarbonisation, especially in member states that will feel the most pressure (Eckert 2022; von Homeyer et al. 2022). Despite climate policy developments seen since the announcement of the EGD, the action plan faces both challenges and opportunities as it moves into its implementation phase. Proposed in times of crisis, the EGD competes with economic, health, and geopolitical emergencies for political attention, thereby putting its long-term goal of a climate-neutral Europe at risk.

In this chapter, I examine the relationship between climate policy development – focusing on the EGD – and other crises impacting the EU. Previous studies argue that since the financial and economic crisis of 2008, the EU has been confronted with a series of overlapping crises or a "polycrisis" (Zeitlin & Nicoli 2020; Zeitlin et al. 2019). Others have put forward the notion that successive crises and emergency responses have created a state of "turbulence" that has become the new normal for EU governance (Dobbs et al. 2021). The financial and economic crisis, Russia's annexation of Crimea in 2014, the irregular flow of migrants into the EU in 2015, Brexit, COVID-19, and Russia's invasion of Ukraine in 2022 have all prompted immediate political responses from the institutions of the EU and its member states. However, the climate crisis has co-existed alongside each of these other emergencies as a "slow-burning" crisis (see Seabrooke & Tsingou 2019).

While climate change has gained increasing political attention over the years, it has not garnered the sense of urgency experienced by other crises threatening the European project. Previous research has shown that environment and climate policy ambition waned in the immediate aftermath of the financial crisis, as the EU institutions and member states focused on economic recovery (Burns & Tobin 2020; Burns et al. 2018; Burns et al. 2020). Others, however, demonstrate that crises can provide springboards to advance climate policy development (von Homeyer et al. 2021), including in the wake of the COVID-19 crisis (Bäckstrand 2022; Dupont et al. 2020; Eckert 2021) and the rising energy prices of late 2021/2022 (von Homeyer et al. 2022). Through this contribution, I argue that two immediate crises impacting the implementation of the EGD – COVID-19 and Russia's invasion of Ukraine – provide opportunities for the EU to advance climate policy ambition to a level that allows it to meet its 2050 goal of carbon neutrality. These opportunities, however, are fragile as simultaneous challenges risk de-railing the EU's climate goals. The institutions and member states of the EU must act in a way which mitigates the challenges arising from the pandemic and the war in Ukraine in order to stay on course in implementing the policies contained within the EGD.

Based on an analysis of recent contributions in climate policy literature, EU policy documents, and media reports, this chapter proceeds in several steps. First, I provide an overview of the EGD, giving particular focus to the European Climate Law and the Fit for 55 Package, to show how it may mark a break from previous incremental increases in climate ambition. Secondly, I discuss how previous crises, especially the financial crisis of 2007/2008, contributed to stagnation in climate policy ambition and how crises trends in general pose obstacles to momentum in climate and environmental policy development. Next, I outline the role that the core institutions of the EU – the Commission, the European Parliament (hereafter: the Parliament), the Council of the European Union (hereafter: the Council), and the European Council – have had in the realisation of the ambition enshrined in the EGD and challenges that they will face as the component policies move into implementation. Finally, I focus on the COVID-19 crisis and the war in Ukraine and argue that both crises may offer political opportunities to increase climate ambition but that political, economic, and energy challenges stand as parallel threats to Europe's green transition. The EGD offers the EU a chance to continue to lead by example in climate policy development on the world stage (Bäckstrand & Elgström 2013; Oberthür & Dupont 2021; Wurzel et al. 2017) and inspire green transitions in other countries (Bäckstrand 2022; Eckert 2021), but this chance is fragile amidst the context of the polycrisis.

The European Green Deal, the European Climate Law, and the Fit for 55 Package

In striving for net-zero emissions by 2050, the EGD elevates the EU's climate policy ambition to a level that the climate crisis calls for. According to the Commission's proposal outlining the EGD, the package is:

> *a new growth strategy that aims to transform the EU into a fair and prosperous society, with a modern, resource-efficient, and competitive economy, where there are no net emissions of*

greenhouse gases in 2050, and where economic growth is decoupled from resource use. (European Commission 2019: 2)

The action plan, therefore, calls for the decarbonisation of the EU's economy while
promising sustained economic growth. It mandates a transformational change in
all sectors of the EU's economy including agriculture, transportation, energy, industry, land use, and buildings. Though not the focus of this chapter, the EGD further
prescribes the protection of biodiversity and the elimination of pollution, recognising the mutually-reinforcing relationship between all three objectives. The action
plan also marks a break from previous climate policy development in its call for
a just transition in which all members of society can benefit from the transition
to carbon neutrality (Bäckstrand 2022; Dupont et al. 2020; Rosamond & Dupont
2021). According to the Commission proposal, "the transition must be just and in-
clusive. It must put people first, and pay attention to the regions, industries, and
workers who will face the greatest challenges" (European Commission 2019: 2).
To this end, a Just Transition Mechanism and Just Transition Fund were written
into the EGD proposal, promising the mobilisation of at least 100 billion euros to
ensure disadvantaged member states and regions can benefit from the green transition (European Commission 2020). These financial instruments fall under the
larger European Green Deal Investment Plan (EGDIP), also referred to as the Sustainable Europe Investment Plan (SEIP), which will leverage at least one trillion
Euros in public and private investments before 2030 to fund the action plan (European Commission 2020). Finally, the EGD mandates the acceleration of "'green deal
diplomacy' focused on convincing and supporting others to take on their share of
promoting more sustainable development" (European Commission 2019: 20). In
calling for an increase in green diplomatic objectives, the EU hopes to "support
a just transition globally" as part of a new green international strategic agenda (European Commission 2019: 20; Oberthür & Dupont 2021).

While all elements of the EGD support climate objectives at least partially, the
European Climate Law has been particularly significant in advancing the EU towards its goal of net-zero emissions by 2050. Despite being confronted with the
public health and economic consequences of COVID-19, the EU managed to enshrine
its 2050 goal into law while also upgrading its interim 2030 targets. The European
Climate Law was proposed by the Commission in March 2020, received endorsement from the European Council in December 2020, and entered into force in
July 2021. Under the 2030 Climate and Energy Framework, proposed by the Commission in January 2013 and endorsed by the European Council in October 2014,
the EU's climate goals were a 40 per cent reduction in greenhouse gas emissions
from 1990 levels, a 32 per cent share of renewable energy in final energy consumption, and a 32.5 per cent improvement in energy efficiency, all to be achieved by

2030 (European Council 2014). The European Climate Law strengthens the 2030 greenhouse gas emissions target to a 55 per cent reduction in emissions from 1990 levels. The Law also provides for the creation of a European Scientific Advisory Board on Climate Change, gives guidelines on setting emissions reduction targets for 2040, mandates the Commission to assess progress towards goal achievement at the EU and member state level every five years (including ensuring whether actions outlined in member state National Energy and Climate Plans [NECPs] are being implemented effectively), and tasks the Commission with liaising with sectors of the EU economy to prepare voluntary sectoral roadmaps (Regulation 2021/1119).

In July 2021, the Commission delivered a set of proposals, collectively known as the Fit for 55 Package, which are designed to ensure the EU achieves its 2030 and 2050 objectives (European Commission 2021). While the EU institutions were kept busy with a policy agenda dominated by COVID-19 and its after-effects, the Commission still managed to unveil 13 legislative proposals each contributing to emissions reductions. These include: a revision of the emissions trading system (ETS) (a cap-and-trade carbon allowance system that covers energy infrastructure, heavy industry, and domestic aviation), a revision of the Effort Sharing Regulation (outlining emissions reductions in sectors of the economy not covered by the ETS), a revision of the Land Use, Land Use Change and Forestry Regulation (LULUCF) (providing guidelines on how natural carbon capture can contribute to emissions reductions and setting the goal of no net-emissions from land use or forestry), and the creation of a new ETS covering emissions from buildings and transport (European Commission 2021). A Social Climate Fund mobilising 72.2 billion euros – funded predominantly through revenues generated by the newly developed ETS – was created to soften the economic blow that the new targets will deliver to industry and citizens in fossil fuel-dependent regions (European Commission 2021).

The Fit for 55 Package also notably proposes increases in targets for renewable energy and energy efficiency. The 32 percent renewable energy target under the 2030 Climate and Energy Policy Framework is increased to 40 per cent and the energy efficiency target for final consumption is raised from 32.5 to 36 per cent while a goal of 39 per cent is also set for primary energy consumption. A final note of significance is that the Fit for 55 Package proposes the creation of a carbon border adjustment mechanism (CBAM) that levies a carbon tax on imports that have large carbon footprints (e.g. electricity and steel). This mechanism is designed to safeguard the EU's competitiveness as it undergoes its green transition and also to eliminate the free allocation of carbon credits under the ETS (European Commission 2021).

Crisis trends: Threats to the European Green Deal and climate policy development?

Despite the leaps forward made by the EU in 2021 and 2022 in passing the European Climate Law through the EU's legislative processes and by the Commission in unveiling its Fit for 55 package of policy proposals, polycrisis trends stand as threats to the implementation of Fit for 55 and the goals of the EGD more broadly. Writing in the context of the polycrisis era, von Homeyer et al. (2021) put forward five crisis trends that may impact climate policy development: growing socio-political divisions, rising 'post-factual' forms of political communication, growing legitimacy challenges, increasing constraints on governance capacity, and wider geopolitical shifts. These trends have effectively ended the permissive consensus – or, unchallenged support from EU citizens – once enjoyed by mainstream political parties and paved the way for an increase in right-wing populist parties appealing to Eurosceptic voters (see also Bickerton et al. 2015). Such trends raise concerns about maintaining momentum towards increased climate ambition since research has shown that right-wing populist governments do not generally give support to aggressive climate policy action (Huber et al. 2021; Jahn 2021). As will be elaborated later in this chapter, central and eastern European (CEE) countries – especially those with far-right leaders in power – have been the most vocal opponents of climate action (Biedenkopf 2021; Huber et al. 2021; Skjærseth 2018).

In light of these crisis trends, it is perhaps unsurprising that in the years immediately following the Financial Crisis of 2007/2008, climate and environmental policy ambition was diluted (Burns et al. 2018; Burns et al. 2020; Burns & Tobin 2020; Skovgaard 2014). Research suggests that the Financial Crisis laid bare the east-west divide on climate policy, with CEE countries expressing their frustration over the economic burden of decarbonisation in the European Council and the Council (Skovgaard 2014). Due to such divisiveness, climate policy had largely developed in small, incremental steps prior to the publication of the EGD (Rosamond & Dupont 2021). Studies have demonstrated that the 2020 and 2030 Climate and Energy Policy Frameworks were short-sighted or "myopic" (Gheuens & Oberthür 2021) and fall short of the EU reducing its emissions significantly enough to ensure meeting its fair share of the goal of the Paris Agreement to limit global temperature increase to well below 2 degrees Celsius, and as close to 1.5 degrees Celsius as possible, compared to the pre-industrial era (Kulovesi & Oberthür 2020; Oberthür 2019). How then has the development of the EGD, which necessitates transformative change across the EU's economy, and which aims for net-zero emissions by 2050, been possible? And even more significantly, how have the EU member states and the European Parliament reached an agreement to make the 2050 goal legally binding by passing the European Climate Law?

In the remainder of this chapter, I outline the role that each of the core EU institutions have played in creating the political environment necessary for the development of the EGD, the Climate Law, and the Fit for 55 Package. I will further highlight the challenges that each face in the context of the polycrisis as the components of Fit for 55 move towards legislation. Finally, I draw on recent research and media analysis to demonstrate that the two most recent crises of the polycrisis, COVID-19 and the War in Ukraine, pose distinct challenges for climate action but, in parallel, provide windows of opportunity to maintain momentum in raising climate ambition further.

The European Commission: Seizing opportunities and balancing interests

Numerous contributions argue that climate policy ambition in the EU has advanced largely due to the leadership role occupied by the Commission (Čavoški 2020; Dupont et al. 2020; Eckert 2021; Rietig 2021; Rietig & Dupont 2021; Skjærseth 2021). According to Article 4 of the Treaty on the Functioning of the European Union (TFEU), environment and climate change policy is a shared competence between the EU and its member states. Most pieces of climate legislation must therefore pass through the EU's Ordinary Legislative Procedure (OLP) in which the Commission has the right of initiative to propose pieces of EU law and the Parliament and Council then legislate on equal footing. In seizing political windows of opportunity, the Commission has acted as a policy entrepreneur to formulate proposals that increase climate ambition while also ensuring that member states do not vote down the legislation (Bäckstrand 2022; Dupont et al. 2020; Skjærseth 2021). It also has the difficult task of taking into account the interests of citizens and industrial stakeholders in order to create balanced climate policy proposals. However, studies have further demonstrated that the Commission has facilitated the political environment necessary for the development of the EGD and passage of the European Climate Law not only via its right to propose legislation but also through its budgetary powers (Rietig 2021), policy monitoring mandate (Oberthür 2019; Schoenefeld et al. 2021; Schoenefeld & Jordan 2020), and the leadership of the Commission President (Čavoški 2020; Rietig & Dupont 2021).

In proposing landmark pieces of climate legislation – including the development and revisions of the ETS, the Effort-Sharing Regulation, the Renewable Energy Directive, and the Energy Efficiency Directive – the Commission has used policy mixes to advance its goals (Skjærseth 2021). Skjærseth (2021) defines policy mixes as processes that move policy development from narrow initiatives to coordinated policy packages; he argues that by developing climate policies combining "push" and "pull" factors, the Commission has managed to maintain support amongst member states while driving increases in ambition forward. One example of an innovative policy mix emerged during the revision of the ETS for the period of 2021 to 2030. The revised ETS came with a reduced cap on emissions and a more ambitious reduction factor, two factors increasing pressure on heavy industry and, by extension, member state governments. However, the revised ETS also included the Innovation Fund. The Innovation Fund receives its budget from revenues generated by the ETS and therefore can be used by member states to fund low-carbon research and innovation projects. As such, a policy mix was created which was designed to reduce emissions in the EU while simultaneously easing the burden of transition for member states. The second example of a policy mix can be seen in the new ETS for transport and buildings, proposed as part of the Fit for 55 Package. The new ETS similarly comes with a Social Climate Fund attached in order to supplement the Just Transition Mechanism in helping fossil fuel-dependent member states transition to carbon neutrality more smoothly. This combination of "push" and "pull" forces in climate policy legislation has contributed to the success of the Commission in, for now, keeping most member states on board with ambitious policy development (Skjærseth 2021).

The Commission has also capitalised on political "windows of opportunity" to develop ambitious climate policy proposals, thereby acting as a policy entrepreneur (Bäckstrand 2022; Čavoški 2020; Dupont et al. 2020; Eckert 2021; Rietig & Dupont 2021). The EGD was proposed at a favourable moment: the Fridays for Future protests of 2018 brought widespread attention to the climate crisis; the Fifth and Sixth Assessment Reports of the Intergovernmental Panel on Climate Change (IPCC) released in 2013/2014 and 2018, respectively, outlined the detrimental consequences for societies and economies if they do not take immediate action on climate change; a spate of forest fires devastated Europe in 2019; and the Paris Agreement negotiated in the context of the United Nations Framework Convention on Climate Change (UNFCCC) was adopted in December 2015, requiring signatories to submit nationally determined contributions (NDCs) (see Bäckstrand 2022; Rosamond & Dupont 2021; Siddi 2021; Skjærseth 2021). Each of these events increased political focus on climate change as a problem requiring a more robust response from political authorities. Research also suggests that Commission President Ursula von der Leyen herself and her leadership capacity may have helped facilitate the development of the EGD and passage of the Climate Law through the tense negotiations for endorsement in the European Council and the legislative processes in the Parliament and the Council (Čavoški 2020; Rietig & Dupont 2021). As will be discussed later in this chapter, COVID-19 and the war in Ukraine may provide further windows of opportunity to maintain momentum on climate policy development in times of crisis.

Finally, recent contributions have shown that the Commission continues to shepherd climate policy ambition through budgetary and policy monitoring processes (Oberthür 2019; Rietig 2021; Schoenefeld et al. 2021; Schoenefeld & Jordan 2020). Rietig (2021) demonstrates that the Commission managed to increase funding for climate mainstreaming (a process in which aspects of climate adaption and mitigation are integrated across all policy sectors) from 20 per cent of the EU's budget in the period of 2014–2020 to 30 per cent of the budget for 2021–2027; this increase was achieved largely through entrepreneurship and policy learning amongst actors within the Commission itself. Others have shown that the Commission's role in monitoring the NECPs of member states –and the progress of member states achieved in practice –as outlined under the Governance Regulation (established in the context of the 2030 Climate and Energy Policy Framework and reiterated in the new European Climate Law), has given the institution more power to ensure that EU countries fulfill their emissions reductions obligations (Oberthür 2019; Schoenefeld et al. 2021; Schoenefeld & Jordan 2020).

Challenges facing the Commission as the proposals of Fit for 55 move through the legislative process largely rest on balancing divisive member state and industrial interests while continuing to push forward with ambitious targets for 2040. Poland has already expressed opposition to the revision of the ETS and especially the introduction of a new ETS in transport and building sectors (Euractiv 2021a). With the Social Climate Fund funded partly by revenues from the new ETS and partly by member states, it will be up to the Commission to strike a balance that satisfies CEE member states demanding more money for a just transition and western member states who have to put money into the fund (von Homeyer et al. 2021). Members of the European Parliament (MEPs) have also expressed concern about the proposal for an ETS covering transport and building sectors; MEPs from the Greens and S&D fear that funds from the Social Climate Fund will not reach the most vulnerable members of society (Euractiv 2021b). The Chair of the Parliament's environment committee, Pascal Canfin (France, Renew Europe political group), also expressed concern that the new ETS could spark social unrest at a level similar to the 2018 yellow vests movement in France (Euractiv 2021b).

Besides reaching compromise with member state officials sitting in the Council and the elected officials of the Parliament, the Commission must also juggle the interests of industrial actors as it is regularly confronted with lobbyists asking to delay the EGD agenda (Eckert 2021). Finally, from a foreign policy perspective, the CBAM – designed to protect European industry – has not been well received by the USA and China, and also penalises neighbouring countries such as Turkey and Ukraine (Politico 2021). The carbon levy imposed on imports thus may undermine the diplomatic objective of spreading the norms of the green and just transition globally (Eckert 2021). In summary, the Commission bears the task of maintaining the ambition of the Fit for 55 Package while ensuring it is acceptable to a huge array of political actors.

The European Parliament: Climate champion in turbulent times?

The European Parliament is regularly praised as the most ambitious EU institution in climate policy terms, acting as a powerful motor for emission reduction increases (Burns 2019; Buzogány & Ćetković 2021; Petri & Biedenkopf 2021). The Parliament is one of the legislative institutions of the EU – it makes amendments to legislative proposals and must adopt the texts alongside the Council before they become EU law as per the OLP. The institution is composed of 705 directly elected MEPs from the EU's member states, divided into 8 political groups based on ideology: the European People's Party (EPP), the Progressive Alliance of Socialists and Democrats (S&D), Renew Europe, the Greens/European Free Alliance (EFA), Identity and Democracy (ID), the European Conservatives and Reformists (ECR), the Left (GUE/NGL), and non-inscrits (NI). Recent research on the Parliament's role in EU climate policymaking and the EGD has focused on whether or not the increase in far-right and Eurosceptic parties in the 2014 and 2019 elections has resulted in the Parliament watering down its climate policy ambition. According to Burns (2019), despite challenges to the dominance of mainstream political parties with the increase of populist MEPs since the late 2000s, there is limited evidence to suggest that the Parliament is watering down the ambition of Commission proposals. Rather it continues to exercise a positive influence on EU climate and environmental policymaking. Others have found that during the Eighth European Parliament (2014–2019), the institution put forward the most ambitious negotiating position on all 12 legislative acts studied (Buzogány & Ćetković 2021). Despite a rise in far-right MEPs, the mainstream political parties (EPP and S&D) remained committed to ambitious climate action and the Greens, in particular, used a more fractionalized parliament to rally support for ratcheting up climate ambition (Buzogány & Ćetković 2021). Petri & Biedenkopf (2021) further demonstrate that the EP as a whole has remained stable in advancing ambitious climate policy positions in plenary debates between 2009 and 2019, though individual MEPs express different opinions on what the EU's role should be in conducting climate diplomacy. In the context of the European Climate Law, the European Parliament put forward a target of 60 per cent emissions reductions by 2030 as opposed to the 55 per cent goal agreed upon through the legislative process. The Parliament thus once again occupied a more ambitious position than the Commission and the Council, pushing for a greater leap forward on the road towards net-zero emissions (European Parliament 2020).

The principal challenge for the Parliament as the Fit for 55 Package enters implementation and the EU moves towards climate neutrality is for the institution to retain its status as a climate and environment champion (Burns 2019). If the economic effects of the COVID-19 crisis and war in Ukraine deepen, there is a risk that far-right parties will make more gains in the 2024 European Parliament elections. Right-wing populist parties are known to weaken climate ambitions within the EU member states (Huber et al. 2021; Jahn 2021) and as such, the Parliament's status as the motor for climate action is far from guaranteed.

The European Council and the Council: Fora for political compromise and momentum

The European Council and Council are the institutions most often criticised as being reticent in terms of climate action, yet both are crucial actors in advancing the goals of the EGD and Fit for 55 Package (Rosamond & Dupont 2021; Wurzel 2021). The European Council brings together the heads of state and government of the EU member states while the Council is comprised of ministers of member states. The Council acts as co-legislator alongside the Parliament and therefore makes amendments to Commission proposals as they pass through the OLP and must approve final versions of the proposals before they become EU law. The European Council, on the other hand, does not play a role in legislative processes. Rather, it outlines the political direction and strategic priorities for the other EU institutions to follow. It is important to note that overall emissions reduction targets are seen as political decisions and therefore *must* be finalised by decision in the European Council (Rosamond & Dupont 2021; Wurzel 2021).

Research on the European Council and the Council argues that before endorsing the European Green Deal, the institutions primarily supported small, incremental advances in climate policy ambition (Dupont & Oberthur 2017; Rosamond & Dupont, 2021). However, in the context of the EGD, both institutions have succeeded in brokering compromises between ambitious western and northern member states and less ambitious CEE member states, as well as providing the political momentum necessary to drive the action plan forward (Dupont 2019; Rosamond & Dupont 2021; Wurzel 2021).

Serving as a meeting place for senior officials from every EU member state, the European Council and Council are sites of intense, deliberative negotiations and are therefore essential fora for compromises to be brokered and climate ambition to be advanced (Wurzel 2021). It is through these negotiations that details can be worked out and common solutions developed. The discourse of the member state institutions further provides political support towards the EGD and climate policy broadly speaking (Dupont 2019; Rosamond & Dupont 2021). Research on the European Council and Council Conclusions – political documents published by the institutions after negotiations – has found that the European Council and Council have advanced the "securitization" of climate change (recognising it as an existential threat) (Dupont 2019) as well as given political support to the three main elements of the EGD: an increase in climate ambition, a systemic transformation across all sectors of the EU's economy, and a just transition in which no one is left behind (Rosamond & Dupont 2021). As such, the European Council and Council have provided the political support needed by the Commission to rollout proposals like the EGD roadmap, the European Climate Law, and the Fit for 55 Package.

The east-west divide on climate policy ambition stands as an important obstacle for the European Council and Council to support further strides forward in climate policy development. With over 70 per cent of its energy supplied by coal and having a significant supply of domestic coal itself, Poland stands as a potential obstacle for the EU to implement the energy transition and emissions reductions policies contained within the Fit for 55 package (Biedenkopf 2021; Skjærseth 2018). Analysing debates within Poland's Parliament, Biedenkopf (2021) argues that Polish officials have constructed three narratives that run against EU climate policy ambition: that Poland is in a unique situation, Poland pursues an alternative pathway, and that climate policy endangers competitiveness. In fact, Poland was the only EU country that did not endorse the EGD when it was first unveiled by the Commission (Reuters 2019). However, Poland is not the only country that risks thwarting the objectives of the EGD and Fit for 55 Package. In March 2020, former Prime Minister of Czechia Andrej Babiš urged the EU to abandon the goals of the EGD to focus on COVID-19 recovery plans (Euractiv 2020). It is therefore the task of ambitious member states to work within the European Council and Council to broker compromise with reticent countries to prevent the watering down or abandonment of legislation proposed by the Commission.

The COVID-19 crisis and war in Ukraine: Prospects and pitfalls from the EGD

In this final section of analysis, I focus on the relationship between the implementation of the EGD and two crises generating immediate responses from the EU's leadership: COVID-19 and the war in Ukraine. Research has shown that despite the pandemic and the outbreak of war, EU climate policy has made significant advancements (Bäckstrand 2022; Eckert 2021; von Homeyer et al. 2022; von Homeyer et al. 2021). Despite being confronted with the challenges associated with the COVID-19 crisis, the Commission proposed the European Climate Law and the Fit for 55 package, and the Climate Law ultimately entered into force amidst the pandemic. These efforts were not undermined by rising energy and food prices caused by Russia's invasion of Ukraine; rather, the EU doubled down on its commitment to advance and even accelerate the green transition (von Homeyer et al. 2022). As such, in this section, I argue that the two crises provided both prospects and pitfalls for the future of the EGD.

COVID-19 provided the Commission and the European Council with an opportunity to push forward a 'green recovery' (Bäckstrand 2022; Dupont et al. 2020; Eckert 2021). In using the recovery package for COVID-19 as a springboard to advance the green transition, the EU capitalised on a chance that it missed during the Financial Crisis of 2007/2008 when the bloc turned its attention away from climate objectives to focus on economic health (Burns et al. 2020; Burns & Tobin 2020). The Commission links the priorities of the EGD to a green recovery through the Recovery and Resilience Facility (a recovery package falling under the auspices of Next Generation EU [NextGenEU]) as well as an expansion of the Multiannual Financial Framework (MFF). The MFF, the Recovery and Resilience Facility, the Just Transition Mechanism, and the modalities of Europe's recovery from COVID-19 were approved and laid out in the European Council Conclusions of July 2020. Taken together, the funding package mobilised 1.8 trillion Euros and member states were mandated to spend a minimum of 37 per cent of their recovery funding on green objectives (Eckert 2021; European Council 2020). By funding the EGD through a mechanism designed to provide economic relief, the Commission and European Council reaffirmed their commitment to a climate-neutral Europe by 2050 despite hardships generated by COVID-19.

While the EU has maintained momentum towards the EGD by funding it through recovery instruments, the COVID-19 crisis also poses a challenge that can undermine the green transition. The true economic outcomes of the pandemic are still not yet fully understood. Should a recession follow the end of the crisis, there is a risk that some member states may withdraw support towards aspects of the EGD or Fit for 55 package (Skjærseth 2021). As was the case with the Financial and Economic Crisis of 2007/2008, this could widen the east-west cleavage as more carbon-dependent member states would feel unable to bear the economic burden of the green transition (Skovgaard 2014). The EU has, for now, rescued the EGD through its COVID-19 recovery plans but prospects for increased ambition are fragile as the after-effects of the pandemic are still playing out.

Russia's invasion of Ukraine in 2022, exacerbating and intensifying the increase of energy and food prices across the EU, similarly provides prospects and pitfalls for advancing the EGD. As a prospect, there is hope that Russia reducing gas supplies to Europe, and the EU's commitment to wean itself off Russian fossil fuels, may spur member states to accelerate their transition to renewable sources of energy and speed up improvements to energy efficiency (Homeyer et al. 2022). The REPowerEU plan, unveiled by the Commission in May 2022 as a strategy to end EU dependency on Russian gas for energy production, proposes upgrades to both the renewable energy and energy efficiency targets of the Fit for 55 package (European Commission 2022). The proposed renewable energy target increases from 40 to 45 per cent while *binding* energy efficiency targets rise from 9 to 13 per cent. The Commission also proposes an EU solar strategy to double solar photovoltaic capacity by 2025 and install 600GW by 2030. Further commitment to an increase in solar energy is demonstrated through the proposal of a Solar Rooftop Initiative, which mandates a phased-in legal obligation to install solar panels on public and commercial buildings as well as newly built residential buildings. Besides solar power, the REPowerEU package also proposes to double the rate of deployment of heat pumps, sets domestic renewable hydrogen production targets at 10 million tons and promises the import of a further 10 million tons of renewable hydrogen, proposes a Biomethane Action Plan to increase biomethane production to 35bcm by 2030 through industrial partnerships as well as through the Common Agricultural Policy, and includes a Commission Recommendation to tackle slow and complex permitting processes for large-scale renewable energy projects (European Commission 2022). The plans are financed largely through an expansion of funding to the Recovery and Resilience Facility from other budgets, showing the Commission's continued commitment to linking economic recovery to climate and energy transitions. In framing the transition to renewable sources of energy and improvements to energy efficiency as a matter of energy security, while also funding these initiatives through economic recovery programmes, the east-west divide on climate policy may be reduced allowing greater ambition in the years to come.

Conversely, there are serious pitfalls arising from Russia's invasion of Ukraine that risk undermining Europe's green transition. Firstly, if energy and food prices plunge the EU into economic recession, CEE Member states may back down from their support towards the EGD, as was the case during the 2007/2008 Financial and

Economic Crisis (Burns et al. 2020; Burns & Tobin 2020; Skovgaard 2014). Secondly, as Russian gas supplies to the EU diminish and member states seek to end their dependency on their eastern neighbor, many are reverting back to using coal or nuclear sources to power their countries. In June 2022, Austria and Germany announced that they would re-fire coal plants that had been decommissioned in order to meet energy demands for the winter (Euronews 2022). The Netherlands has indicated that it would lift all restrictions on coal power stations as an emergency measure (Euronews 2022). Belgium, on the other hand, stated that it would have to extend its reliance on nuclear power until 2035, thereby abandoning its plan to decommission all nuclear reactors by 2025 (Reuters 2022). While nuclear energy is carbon-neutral, reactors pose safety risks to communities, and waste from nuclear power has environmental impacts. Since the REPowerEU plan also promises an increase in gas imports from partner countries – many of whom are led by non-democratic regimes – the risk of carbon lock-in for years to come remains high (von Homeyer et al. 2022; European Commission 2022).

Conclusion

In the polycrisis era, the climate emergency has run parallel alongside all other crises as the EU's "slow-burning" problem. However, calls for more ambitious policy action coming from citizens' movements like Fridays for Future and scientific authorities like the IPCC, compounded with natural disasters impacting the lives of EU citizens and the economies of member states, may have spurred a greater sense of urgency amongst policymakers in Brussels. On paper, it seems that the EGD marks a break from the incremental policy development which has previously characterised the EU's response to climate change. A commitment to achieving neutrality by 2050 and a complete transformation across all sectors of the EU's economy shows a higher level of ambition than seen in both the 2020 and 2030 packages. However, much still rests on the implementation of the Fit for 55 package and the level of ambition pursued with the next interim targets for 2040.

This chapter has outlined prospects and pitfalls confronting EU climate policy development and the future of the EGD in the polycrisis era. Despite turbulent times, the Commission managed to propose a Green Deal for Europe and the EU made the goal of net-zero emissions by 2050 legally binding through the adoption of the European Climate Law. The EU's institutions – the Commission, the Parliament, the Council, and the European Council – have each played a role in achieving these important climate policy milestones. Indeed, EU actors seem to have learned to work within the contexts of successive crises, taking advantage of windows of opportunity to stay on course for climate policy development. However, this chapter also argues that economic and energy hardships arising from contemporary crises, including COVID-19 and the War in Ukraine, may exacerbate political cleavages between member states. While prospects for climate policy targets for 2040 remain uncertain, successive crises or turbulence seem to have become the new normal for EU governance. As such, the EU must continue to find opportunities to advance climate policy through crisis tailwinds, both in the interest of achieving climate neutrality by 2050 and to demonstrate the feasibility of a green transition to countries around the world.

References

Bäckstrand, Karin (2022): 'Towards a Climate-Neutral Union by 2050? The European Green Deal, Climate Law, and Green Recovery', in Antonina Bakardjieva Engelbrekt, Per Ekman, Anna Michalski & Lars Oxelheim (eds.): *Routes to a Resilient European Union*, Springer International Publishing, 39–61.

Bäckstrand, Karin & Elgström, Ole (2013): 'The EU's Role in Climate Change Negotiations: From Leader to 'Leadiator''. *Journal of European Public Policy*, 20:10, 1369–1386.

Bickerton, Christopher, J., Hodson, Dermot & Puetter, Uwe (2015): 'The New Intergovernmentalism: European Integration in the Post-Maastricht Era', *JCMS: Journal of Common Market Studies*, 53:4, 703–722.

Biedenkopf, Katja (2021): 'Polish Climate Policy Narratives: Uniqueness, Alternative Pathways, and Nascent Polarization', *Politics and Governance*, 9:3, 391–400.

Burns, Charlotte (2019): 'In the Eye of the Storm? The European Parliament, the Environment and the EU's Crises', *Journal of European Integration*, 41:3, 311–327.

Burns, Charlotte; Eckersley, Peter & Tobin, Paul (2020): 'EU Environmental Policy in Times of Crisis', *Journal of European Public Policy*, 27:1, 1–19.

Burns, Charlotte & Tobin, Paul (2020): 'Crisis, Climate Change and Comitology: Policy Dismantling Via the Backdoor?', *JCMS: Journal of Common Market Studies*, 58:3, 527–544.

Burns, Charlotte, Tobin, Paul & Sewerin, Sebastian (2018): 'Measuring the Impact of the Crisis on European Environmental Policy', in Charlotte Burns, Paul Tobin & Sebastian Sewerin (eds.): *The Impact of the Economic Crisis on European Environmental Policy*, Oxford University Press, 1–18.

Buzogány, Aron & Ćetković, Stefan (2021): 'Fractionalized but Ambitious? Voting on Energy and Climate Policy in the European Parliament', *Journal of European Public Policy*, 28:7, 1038–1056.

Čavoški, Aleksandra (2020): 'An Ambitious and Climate-Focused Commission Agenda for Post COVID-19 EU', *Environmental Politics*, 29:6, 1112–1117.

Dobbs, Mary, Gravey, Viviane & Petetin, Ludivine (2021): 'Driving the European Green Deal in Turbulent Times', *Politics and Governance*, 9:3, 316–326.

Dupont, Claire (2019): 'The EU's Collective Securitization of Climate Change', *West European Politics*, 42:2, 369–390.

Dupont, Claire & Oberthür, Sebastian (2017): 'The Council and the European Council: Stuck on the Road to Transformational Leadership', in Rüdiger K. W. Wurzel, James Connelly & Duncan Liefferink (eds.): *The European Union in International Climate Change Politics: Still Taking a Lead*, Routledge, 66–79.

Dupont, Claire, Oberthür, Sebastian & von Homeyer, Ingmar (2020): 'The Covid-19 Crisis: A Critical Juncture for EU Climate Policy Development?', *Journal of European Integration*, 42:8, 1095–1110.

Eckert, Sandra (2021): 'The European Green Deal and the EU's Regulatory Power in Times of Crisis', *Journal of Common Market Studies*, 59:S1, 81–91.

Euractiv (2020): 'Czech PM Urges EU to Ditch Green Deal Amid Virus'. https://www.euractiv.com/section/energy-environment/news/czech-pm-urges-eu-to-ditch-green-deal-amid-virus/ [Accessed 15 June 2022].

Euractiv (2021a): 'Against the EU ETS, Poland Threatens to Veto 'Fit for 55''. https://www.euractiv.com/section/politics/short_news/against-the-eu-ets-poland-threatens-to-veto-fit-for-55/ [Accessed 15 June 2022].

Euractiv (2021b): 'EU's Timmermans Defends New ETS in Front of Sceptical Lawmakers'. https://www.euractiv.com/section/energy-environment/news/eus-timmermans-defends-new-ets-in-front-of-sceptical-lawmakers/ [Accessed 8 June 2022].

Euronews (2022): 'All the European Countries Returning to "Dirty" Coal as Russia Threatens to Turn Off the Gas Tap'. https://www.euronews.com/green/2022/06/24/all-the-european-countries-returning-to-dirty-coal-as-russia-threatens-to-turn-off-the-gas [Accessed 5 July 2022].

European Commission (2019): The European Green Deal, Com (2019) 640.

European Commission (2020): Sustainable Europe Investment Plan, European Green Deal Investment Plan, Com (2020) 21.

European Commission (2021): "Fit for 55": Delivering the EU's 2030 Climate Target on the Way to Climate Neutrality, COM (2021) 550.

European Commission (2022): REPowerEU Plan, COM (2022) 2030.

European Council (2014): Conclusions – 23/24 October 2014, EUCO 169/14.

European Council (2020): Conclusions – 17, 18, 19, 20 & 21 July 2020, EUCO 10/20.

European Parliament (2020): 'EU Climate Law: MEPs Want to Increase 2030 Emissions Reduction Target to 60%', Press Release, 11 September 2020. https://www.europarl.europa.eu/news/en/press-room/20200907IPR86512/eu-climate-law-meps-want-to-increase-emission-reductions-target-to-60-by-2030 [Accessed 20 December 2022].

Gheuens, Jana & Oberthür, Sebastian (2021): 'EU Climate and Energy Policy: How Myopic is it?', *Politics and Governance*, 9:3, 337–347.

Huber, Robert A., Maltby, Tomas, Szulecki, Kacper & Ćetković, Stefan (2021): 'Is Populism a Challenge to European Energy and Climate Policy? Empirical Evidence Across Varieties of Populism', *Journal of European Public Policy*, 28:7, 998–1017.

Jahn, Detlef (2021): 'Quick and Dirty: How Populist Parties in Government Affect Greenhouse Gas Emissions in EU Member States', *Journal of European Public Policy*, 28:7, 980–997.

Kulovesi, Kati & Oberthür, Sebastian (2020): 'Assessing the EU's 2030 Climate and Energy Policy Framework: Incremental Change Toward Radical Transformation?', *Review of European, Comparative and International Environmental Law*, 29:2, 151–166.

Oberthür, Sebastian (2019): 'Hard or Soft Governance? The EU's Climate and Energy Policy Framework for 2030', *Politics and Governance*, 7:1, 17–27.

Oberthür, Sebastian & Dupont, Claire (2021): 'The European Union's International Climate Leadership: Towards a Grand Climate Strategy?', *Journal of European Public Policy*, 28:7, 1095–1114.

Petri, Franziska & Biedenkopf, Katja (2021): 'Weathering Growing Polarization? The European Parliament and EU Foreign Climate Policy Ambitions', *Journal of European Public Policy*, 28:7, 1057–1075.

Politico (2021): '5 Things to Know About EU's Fit for 55 Climate Package'. https://www.politico.eu/article/fit-for-55-eu-5-things-to-know/ [Accessed 1 July 2022].

Reuters (2019): 'EU Leaves Poland Out of 2050 Climate Deal After Standoff'. https://www.reuters.com/article/us-climate-change-eu-idUSKBN1YG01I [Accessed 15 June 2022].

Reuters (2022): 'Engie to Work With Belgium to Study Extending Nuclear Power There Until 2035'. https://www.reuters.com/business/energy/engie-work-with-belgium-study-extending-nuclear-power-there-until-2035-2022-03-18/ [Accessed 5 July 2022].

Rietig, Katharine (2021): 'Accelerating Low Carbon Transitions Via Budgetary Processes? EU Climate Governance in Times of Crisis', *Journal of European Public Policy*, 28:7, 1018–1037.

Rietig, Katharine & Dupont, Claire (2021): 'Presidential Leadership Styles and Institutional Capacity for Climate Policy Integration in the European Commission', *Policy and Society*, 40:1, 19–36.

Rosamond, Jeffrey & Dupont, Claire (2021): 'The European Council, the Council, and the European Green Deal', *Politics and Governance*, 9:3, 348–359.

Schoenefeld, Jonas J. & Jordan, Andrew J. (2020): 'Towards Harder Soft Governance? Monitoring Climate Policy in the EU', *Journal of Environmental Policy and Planning*, 22:6, 774–786.

Schoenefeld, Jonas J., Schulze, Kai, Hildén, Mikael & Jordan, Andrew J. (2021): 'The Challenging Paths to Net-Zero Emissions: Insights from the Monitoring of National Policy Mixes', *International Spectator*, 56:3, 24–40.

Seabrooke, Leonard & Tsingou, Eleni (2019): 'Europe's Fast- And Slow-Burning Crises', *Journal of European Public Policy*, 26:3, 468–481.

Siddi, Marco (2021): 'Coping with Turbulence: EU Negotiations on the 2030 and 2050 Climate Targets', *Politics and Governance*, 9:3, 327–336.

Skjærseth, Jon Birger (2018): 'Implementing EU Climate and Energy Policies in Poland: Policy Feedback and Reform', *Environmental Politics*, 27:3, 498–518.

Skjærseth, Jon Birger (2021): 'Towards a European Green Deal: The Evolution of EU Climate and Energy Policy Mixes', *International Environmental Agreements: Politics, Law and Economics*, 21:1, 25–41.

Skovgaard, Jakob (2014): 'EU Climate Policy After the Crisis', *Environmental Politics*, 23:1, 1–17.

von Homeyer, Ingmar, Oberthür, Sebastian & Dupont, Claire (2022): 'Implementing the European Green Deal During the Evolving Energy Crisis', *JCMS: Journal of Common Market Studies*, 60:S1, 125–136.

von Homeyer, Ingmar, Oberthür, Sebastian & Jordan, Andrew J. (2021): 'EU Climate and Energy Governance in Times of Crisis: Towards a New Agenda', *Journal of European Public Policy*, 28:7, 959–979.

Wurzel, Rüdiger K. W., Connelly, James & Liefferink, Duncan (2017): 'Introduction: European Climate Leadership', in Rüdiger K. W. Wurzel, James Connelly & Duncan Liefferink (eds.), *The European Union in International Climate Change Politics: Still Taking a Lead?*, Routledge.

Wurzel, Rüdiger K. W. (2021): 'The Council, European Council, and Member States', in Andrew J. Jordan & Viviane Gravey (eds.), *Environmental Policy in the EU: Actors, Institutions, and Processes*, Routledge, 75–29.

Zeitlin, Jonathan & Nicoli, Francesco (eds.) (2020): *The European Union beyond the polycrisis?: Integration and politicization in an age of shifting cleavages*, Routledge.

Zeitlin, Jonathan, Nicoli, Francesco & Laffan, Brigid (2019): 'Introduction: the European Union Beyond the Polycrisis? Integration and Politicization in an Age of Shifting Cleavages', *Journal of European Public Policy*, 26:7, 963–976.

Andreas Eisl & Mattia Tomay

15 European economic governance in times of crisis: Solidarity, responsibility, and legitimacy in EU debt mutualisation

Abstract: Common EU debt instruments (also known as *Eurobonds* or, more recent-ly, *Coronabonds*), have often been portrayed as a panacea in EU economic gover-nance. A plethora of proposals emerged in academic and policy circles, especially in times of political and economic crisis. Limited instances of debt mutualisation have existed in Europe at least since the 1970s oil shocks. During the Eurozone cri-sis, academics and policymakers went as far as to call for the establishment of treasury-like mechanisms mutualising existing national debt and issuing new joint debt securities. Yet, leaders instead mainly implemented loans-based solu-tions, such as the European Stability Mechanism. Conversely, in 2020, amid the Covid-19 crisis, the EU managed to create an ambitious common debt programme in the context of its Recovery Plan "Next Generation EU". What changed between these crises? What factors played a role in making some proposals a reality and others unfeasible? To shed some light on these questions, this chapter presents and analyses proposals and instances of EU debt mutualisation during the Euro-zone and the Covid-19 crises. By considering their solidarity and responsibility fea-tures, it induces a conceptual framework to better understand their legitimacy, and ultimately their political and economic feasibility. It concludes by suggesting how this same conceptual framework may shed light on other domains of EU crisis response.

Keywords: European economic governance, debt mutualisation, Eurobonds, solid-arity, responsibility, legitimacy

Introduction

Economic integration has been at the heart of the European project since its incep-tion. Through a series of treaties and reforms, European Union (EU) economies have become highly integrated over the course of the last decades. While this

Note: The information and views set out in this text are those of the author and do not necessarily reflect the official opinion of the European Commission.

https://doi.org/10.1515/9783110790337-016

has allowed EU member states to reap significant economic benefits, it has also increased the likelihood of crisis transmission in the EU.

In addition, the incomplete nature of the economic and monetary union (EMU), notably the lack of a genuine fiscal union to accompany the single currency, has led to instances of economic divergence rather than convergence between member states. The Great Recession, the Eurozone crisis, the Covid-19 crisis, and the recent energy crisis caused by the Russian invasion of Ukraine have repeatedly put this set-up and its key actors under serious strain.

EU public debt has been pointed at as a potential solution to the shortcomings of EU economic governance, with debates regularly emerging in times of crisis (see Eisl & Tomay 2020 for an overview and analysis of more than 50 common debt proposals). At its most basic level, EU public debt consists of debt securities similar in design to national sovereign bonds, issued by the EU, its institutions, or (a group of) its member states acting in a joint fashion. As this chapter will show, while EU public debt is no novelty, it is a highly contested subject when its aim is to finance national budgets, public expenditures and investments, or when its guarantee and repayment structures foresee any major actual or potential transfer of resources among member states.

Prior to discussing EU public debt as an instrument of European economic governance in times of crisis, which is the core subject of this chapter, we briefly sketch out 1) why EU public debt has often been described as a panacea, and 2) why its introduction has historically been problematic.

On the one hand, three main arguments justify the creation of EU public debt. First, sovereign debt is an appropriate means to finance projects and policies of common interest. In the EU case, common debt would allow for minimising costs to finance initiatives such as trans-European transport and energy infrastructure networks, or projects contributing to the Union's transition to climate neutrality. Second, debt can serve as a means to respond to exogenous macroeconomic shocks, especially if they have asymmetric effects, i.e., affecting different economies to different extents. In such situations, EU debt would ensure that struggling member states are guaranteed access to capital markets and lower borrowing costs during times of hardship. Third, centralised issuance of debt is a crucial step of economic integration (see, for example, the significance of Alexander Hamilton's consolidation of the debt of the 13 American colonies for the creation of a federal union). As such, EU public debt underpinned by a treasury-like mechanism engaging in common borrowing and expenditure would harmonise fiscal policy and address macroeconomic and fiscal imbalances through strictly coordinated budgetary policy.

On the other hand, critics have often argued that EU public debt would lead to the emergence of moral hazard and free-riding problems. To understand why, one should note that the issuance of EU debt may entail a *mutualisation* of the costs related to its borrowing costs, its repayment, or even pre-existing national debt. In principle, this mutualisation results in a net transfer of resources among member states. Subsequently, common debt would undermine sound national fiscal policymaking as some could free-ride on the strong macroeconomic and fiscal credentials of other EU countries. Thus, in practice, prudent countries would effectively pay for the fiscal profligacy of other members, undermining the legitimacy of EU debt mutualisation among the former.

These concerns led to the introduction of a number of legal limitations on debt mutualisation in the treaty frameworks, e.g. an EU balanced budget rule (Art. 310 (1) TFEU), the interdiction to "raise loans within the framework of the budget" (Art. 17 (2) Financial Regulation) and the so-called 'no-bailout clause' which states that neither the EU nor its member states shall "be liable for or assume the commitments" of another member, with minor exceptions (Art. 125 (1) TFEU).

As Estrella-Blaya (2022) explores, these limitations have, however, not prohibited the introduction of certain joint borrowing mechanisms. In 1975, during the first oil shock, *ad-hoc* supranational debt issuance (the Community Loan Mechanism), backed by the European Community's budget and additional national guarantees, provided "back-to-back" loans to countries struggling with balance-of-payments-problems (see Horn et al. 2020). In this model, loans taken up by the Commission are "passed on" to member states at the same favourable conditions. Due to a 'several' rather than a 'joint and several' guarantee design[1], each member remained liable only for its share of the obligations, rather than for the totality (see Waibel 2016).

As the next sections explore in detail, debt instruments multiplied in the aftermath of the Eurozone debt and the Covid-19 crises. In 2010, two temporary debt instruments were established: the European Financial Stability Mechanism (EFSM) and the European Financial Stability Facility (EFSF), with a maximum lending capacity of €60bn and €440bn, respectively. In 2012, they were replaced by the European Stability Mechanism (ESM) as a permanent financial institution outside the EU legal architecture, with a maximum lending capacity of €500bn. In 2020, the Commission established the SURE ('support to mitigate unemployment risks in an emergency') mechanism, with a maximum lending capacity of €100bn, similar to previous facilities. Most notably, in July 2020, EU member states agreed on the

---

1 Under a joint and several guarantee/liability, each party is responsible for the totality of the outstanding debt, hence offering the highest level of security to investors thanks to the credibility of the strongest participants. Under a several (not joint) structure, parties are only responsible for their share of the common obligations (for a more detailed discussion, see Waibel 2016).

"Next Generation EU" recovery instrument, which went beyond, in terms of scale and ambition, any previous attempt at debt mutualisation in the EU.

This chapter analyses how debt mutualisation proposals and instruments emerged as instruments of EU economic governance during these two distinct crises. Sections two and three analyse and compare the nature and framing of the crises, the various proposals, the political controversies that accompanied the negotiations of common borrowing, and the final policy outcomes, in both economic and political terms. This will serve as a foundation to develop a conceptual framework for the study of EU debt mutualisation in the fourth section. The framework stresses (1) the key role of solidarity and responsibility mechanisms in proposals and actual instruments of common borrowing and (2) the need to achieve a legitimate balance within solidarity-responsibility arrangements to make EU debt policy work economically and politically. The conclusion suggests how this conceptual framework could be applied in the future to other EU policy fields.

Debt mutualisation during the EU sovereign debt crisis

The Eurozone crisis was characterised by two "systemic crisis waves" that brought substantial financial and macroeconomic distress to a group of Eurozone countries between 2008 and 2011 (Lo Duca et al. 2017): First, in the aftermath of the global financial burst, countries like Ireland, Spain, and Portugal came to experience large-scale bank failures necessitating substantial public and external support. Second, the deteriorating macroeconomic and fiscal profiles of countries like Greece, Cyprus, and Italy increased sovereign risk, leading to financial instability.

Widening spreads and increasing fears over sovereign defaults sparked doubts about the viability of the single currency. Despite its asymmetric nature, the crisis was perceived as an existential challenge not only to the EMU but to the EU integration project as a whole, with then Commission President José Manuel Barroso speaking of "a fight for the economic and political future of Europe [...], a fight for integration itself" (BBC 2011). In this context, policymakers and academics brought forward several proposals for common borrowing, which aimed at avoiding defaults and guaranteeing market access to struggling member states (De Grauwe & Moesen 2009; Amato & Verhofstadt 2011; Chamley 2012; EP 2012), averting contagion risks (Montaigne 2010; Beck et al. 2011; Delors et al. 2011), and completing a monetary union with insufficient fiscal coordination and capacity (Leterme 2010; Varoufakis & Holland 2011; Philippon & Hellwig 2011; EP 2012).

Proposals differed regarding technical features like institutional solutions, bond design, the scope of participation, and the share of mutualised debt. Yet, most envisioned the creation of a permanent treasury-like agency pooling a share of existing national debt and jointly issuing new debt guaranteed by participating member states. A well-known proposal in this respect was that by Delpla and von Weizsäcker (2010; 2011). Under their scheme, a share of national debt accounting for up to 60 % of GDP would be transferred to a Stability Council and transformed into an extra-safe and liquid asset, so-called 'Blue Bonds', guaranteed joint and severally (see footnote 1) by participating members. For needs surpassing the 60 % cap, countries would issue 'Red Bonds', i.e., purely national obligations whose juniority (i.e., relatively lower repayment priority) increased their risk profile and borrowing costs, intending to enhance fiscal discipline through financial markets.

Despite calls for solidarity at the political level to underpin the EU response, the crisis was largely framed as the result of the EU periphery's fiscal profligacy (Warren 2017: 8–9). The dominating narrative contrasted a dissolute south, whose fiscal recklessness was at the root of financial turmoil, against a prudent, responsible north (Laffan 2014: 276). In this context, virtually all proposals for debt mutualisation called for strong control mechanisms aimed at minimising moral hazard and free- riding issues.

Blue Bonds proponents warned for example that "solidarity with the most vulnerable [...] runs the risk of further weakening the incentives for individual countries to pursue fiscally sustainable policies" (Delpla & von Weizsäcker 2010: 1). Hence, proposals often made participation to debt schemes conditional to strict criteria, including solvency (Suarez 2011), an AAA credit rating (Erber 2012), compliance with budgetary discipline criteria (Philippon & Hellwig 2011), or agreement over budgetary planning and coordination (Montaigne 2010: 56), debt reduction schedules (Varoufakis, Holland 2011: 5, EESC 2012), or structural reform plans (Delors 2011). Other authors included even further risk aversion tools, i.e., "exit" mechanisms (Erber 2012), sanctions for non-compliance (EP 2012), the application of discriminatory interest rates reflecting the degree of solvability of each member state (Leterme 2010), and similar market-like features to enhance fiscal discipline (Monti 2010: 63).

This strong focus on moral hazard, free-riding, and the need to resume responsibility is also evident when considering the actual European responses to the sovereign debt crisis, namely the EFSM, the EFSF, and the ESM. Despite EU institutions themselves joining calls for joint debt mechanisms (European Commission 2011; EP 2012), EU governments fell short of establishing any treasury-like stabilisation mechanism. Instead, they opted for two temporary loan facilities and a permanent one to provide a mutualisation of borrowing costs and access to financial markets against strong conditionalities.

The underlying logic of these mechanisms is similar to that of the 1975 Community Loan Mechanism: mutualise borrowing costs to provide loans at favourable market rates to struggling countries, conditional to reforms. While both the EFSM and the EFSF originally only provided "back-to-back" loans, the EFSF later switched to a so-called diversified funding strategy (DFS), improving liquidity through maturity transformation. Funds were no longer attributable to any specific member but pooled and disbursed to programmes countries (EFSF 2016: 4). Except for the EFSM, guaranteed by the so-called "headroom" in the EU budget (i.e., the difference between the maximum amount of funds that the EU can request from its member states and the amount of funds actually spent), the EFSM and the ESM raised funds through several-type liability, making each member state responsible for its predetermined share. For the ESM, a paid-in security buffer enhanced creditworthiness.

As such, these mechanisms provided no genuine mutualisation of existing or new debt. Countries receiving support remained ultimately responsible for the debt incurred. Furthermore, conditionality was "the DNA of (young) European emergency assistance" (Bénassy-Quéré & Weder Di Mauro 2020: 9). Member states requesting assistance had to negotiate a detailed adjustment programme *ex ante* that was to be unanimously agreed upon by all participating parties, with the Commission and the Eurogroup monitoring compliance.

Debt mutualisation during the Covid-19 pandemic

With the outbreak of the Covid-19 pandemic, countercyclical fiscal measures addressing the socioeconomic impact of the health crisis led to burgeoning budget deficits across the continent. Eurozone countries differed in their capacity to tackle the crisis: Budget surpluses in some member states ensured adequate fiscal buffers to finance extraordinary measures, while high public debt levels in others sparked doubts about their ability to "afford" similar measures. This led to a worrying surge of borrowing costs for countries like Italy and Greece (Koranyi & Canepa 2020), before the ECB's pandemic emergency purchase programme (PEPP) intervened to stabilise borrowing costs.

This situation reignited calls for the introduction of common debt instruments. EU debt was seen as a way to lower financing costs for fragile countries (Giavazzi & Tabellini 2020; Claeys & Wolff 2020), ensure equal access to markets among member states (Nine-country proposal 2020; Gentiloni & Breton 2020), guarantee a level playing field in the Single Market (Gentiloni & Breton 2020; Spanish non-paper

2020), and even share the economic costs of a health crisis for which no member state was responsible (Hüther et al. 2020; French non-paper 2020; Grund et al. 2020).

The economic context of the Covid-19 crisis initially marginalised proposals for an overhaul of Eurozone governance. Debt mutualisation was to respond to a contingent and exogenous shock rather than to structural defects in the EMU architecture. Consequently, proposals suggested expanding the Commission's existing issuance capacity through the "headroom" (French non-paper 2020; Garicano & Verhofstadt 2020; EP resolution 2020; Franco-German proposal 2020; 'Frugal Four' non-paper 2020), or establishing temporary solutions without pooling existing debt, for example through the ESM (Claeys & Wolff 2020; Hüther et al. 2020; Bénassy-Quéré et al. 2020).

Moreover, ongoing negotiations over the multiannual financial framework (MFF), strengthened the technical links between the EU's long-term budget and common debt instruments. While early proposals (Giavazzi & Tabellini 2020; Claeys & Wolff 2020; Hüther et al. 2020; French non-paper 2020; Grund et al. 2020) called for national guarantees (either joint-and-several or several), the idea to utilise the EU budget as a guarantee, vehicle for disbursement and negotiation ground progressively consolidated as the dominant approach (French non-paper 2020; Garicano & Verhofstadt 2020; Spanish non-paper 2020; EP resolution 2020; Franco-German proposal 2020).

In terms of framing, the macroeconomic distress resulting from the Covid-19 crisis was largely portrayed as a symmetric shock (Von der Leyen 2020; Nine-country proposal 2020; ESM 2020) rather than the consequence of some member states' profligacy, in stark contrast with the Eurozone crisis. The human toll of the crisis filled political declarations and European Council and Eurogroup conclusions with references to "sympathy" and a "[spirit of] solidarity" (European Council 2020a; European Council 2020b; Eurogroup 2020a; Eurogroup 2020b).

While the framing of fiscal irresponsibility did surface, viewing the strong economic fallout in the South as the consequence of insufficient fiscal consolidation in the period up to the outbreak of the pandemic, it failed to become dominant and was soon marginalised. When a member of the fiscally 'hawkish' Dutch government, for example, suggested an inquiry over the absence of fiscal buffers to weather unforeseen shocks in the South, a backlash ensued from both abroad and at home (Khan 2020). In Germany, as Bulmer (2022:177) recounts, an adamant advocate of fiscal consolidation historically opposed to any type of debt mutualisation, "the view began to take hold that, whatever the nature of past debts accumulated in southern Europe, the pandemic was nobody's fault and if the EU could not show solidarity under these exceptional circumstances it would be disastrous for the future of both Europe and German industrial exports". Troika-like mechanisms thus gave way to crisis-contingent approaches largely driven by solidarity.

Proposals rarely mentioned conditionality or excluded it openly by pointing to the symmetric nature of the crisis. Some did introduce what can be defined as 'conditionality of purpose' (see Eisl & Tomay 2020): Countries can only utilise resources for commonly agreed actions such as recovery investment (Gentiloni & Breton 2020), or healthcare and unemployment schemes (Grund et al. 2020). An early ESM-based proposal by Bénassy-Quéré et al. (2020) foresaw a credit line whose conditionality consisted of a transparent use of funds and a commitment not to introduce non-Covid-related spending and tax cuts by the end of the crisis. Two proposals included more conservative wording: The Franco-German proposal (2020: 2) envisioned support to be *based on* (yet still not *conditioned to*) a "clear commitment [...] to follow sound economic policies and an ambitious reform agenda"; while the 'Frugal Four' non-paper (2020: 1, emphasis in original) insisted that **"strong commitment to reforms and the fiscal framework** is essential to promote potential growth", though falling short of referring to conditionality as such.

A key point of discussion surrounded the modalities of repayment of newly-issued debt. As discussed, previous mechanisms like the EFSM, EFSF, and the ESM largely rested on a loan-based logic. However, in 2020, simple on-lending could worsen the already-bleak fiscal position of some countries, at a time of necessary fiscal expansion. Hence, many recommended a grants-based approach whereby the cost of the crisis would be shared among members through a reimbursement key accounting for parameters like population, GDP per capita, unemployment rate, and the national economic impact of the crisis (Nine-country proposal 2020; French non-paper 2020; Claeys & Wolff 2020; Grund et al. 2020). To further minimise the short-term financial brunt on member states, proposals argued to spread out repayment over long periods (or even to use perpetual bonds) and to finance repayment through (new) national or EU taxes (Giavazzi & Tabellini 2020; Claeys & Wolff 2020; Garicano & Verhofstadt 2020; Spanish non-paper 2020; Soros 2020).

Notwithstanding these technical differences, the basis of such proposals shared a common understanding of a symmetric shock and a normative conclusion that its effect could and should not be endured by individual member states without EU solidarity.

The actual European responses eventually followed these considerations. Initially, however, EU institutions resorted to existing or familiar mechanisms. In April, the Eurogroup endorsed an *ad-hoc* Pandemic Crisis Support ESM facility, based on the existing Enhanced Conditions Credit Line but with weaker conditionality, as well as the Commission's SURE, an EFSM-like temporary mechanism to support national short-time work schemes. Critics, nevertheless, soon pointed to the inadequacy of these instruments alone in face of the magnitude of the shock (e. g., Giavazzi & Tabellini 2020). Moreover, following the Eurozone crisis, the ESM and the stigma of its conditionality – however minimised in the new facility – had become politically toxic in the periphery, with no member state making use of it in the first three epidemic waves (Tesche 2021).

Despite the recalcitrance of so-called 'frugal countries', leaders' discussions eventually gravitated towards a one-off new EU debt issuance, propelled by a Franco-German initiative along these lines in early May 2020. In July, the European Council reached a political agreement on a Commission proposal to temporarily (until 2026 at the latest) raise funds on behalf of the EU. Guaranteed by an increased "headroom" under the new MFF, the Commission was to raise €750bn on financial markets through an instrument called Next Generation EU (European Council 2020).

The main element of the instrument, the €672.5bn Recovery and Resilience Facility (RRF), supports measures specified in national recovery and resilience plans (NRRPs), submitted by member states to the Commission for approval, "consistent with the relevant country-specific challenges and priorities identified in the context of the European Semester" (EU Regulation 2021/241). Besides its significant financial volume, the key innovation of the instrument lies in its disbursement logic. In fact, while €360bn could finance loans with long maturities, nearly half of the proceeds (€312.5bn) are allocated to member states in the form of grants, upon the achievement of milestones and targets included in their NRRPs. While loans will be reimbursed by beneficiary countries, grants will be repaid between 2028 and 2058 through (1) newly proposed EU own resources coming from carbon border adjustment levies, emissions trading revenues, and a minimum corporate tax, and/or (2) national contributions based on a GNI-based capital key.

Conceptual framework: A legitimate balance of solidarity and responsibility mechanisms for European debt mutualisation

The previous sections analysed debates surrounding proposals and instruments of EU debt mutualisation during the Eurozone and Covid-19 crises. As explored below, these discussions circled around two key concepts: solidarity and responsibility (see Vignon 2011). These concepts inform – what this chapter defines as – *solidarity* and *responsibility mechanisms* that: (1) define the type and extent of solidarity and responsibility entailed in any specific EU mutualisation instrument, and (2) shape its concrete economic and legal design. Linking the previous discussion to these two concepts, this section builds a conceptual framework to better understand how and why EU debt emerged as a (potential) instrument of economic governance in times of crisis, and which factors determined its perceived economic and political success.

Solidarity mechanisms

Inter-state solidarity mechanisms can vary strongly in the form and extent (in terms of size and duration) of solidarity provided through risk- and/or resource-sharing (see Fernandes & Rubio 2012). As sketched in the previous sections, solidarity mechanisms in EU debt instruments may differ along several dimensions, in particular (see Table 15.1):

1. *Borrowing size:* Borrowing instruments without any limitations in size entail a higher extent of solidarity than those limited to a specific monetary amount or percentage points to GDP. The fact that all implemented debt mutualisation instruments at the European level have been limited in size highlights that 'unlimited' solidarity has been controversial so far.
2. *Mutualisation type:* the mutualisation of existing and future national public debt (e.g., as in the Blue Bond proposal analysed above) implies more solidarity than common borrowing supporting new nationally incurred public debt (e.g. through back-to-back loans, as provided by the EFSM). While comprehensive mutualisation has been politically unfeasible so far, a more circumscribed version has been adopted during the Covid-19 crisis in the form of Next Generation EU.
3. *Borrowing duration:* permanent debt mutualisation instruments provide for more solidarity vis-à-vis temporary ones as they render solidarity more stable and predictable. Depending on the concrete set-up, they would also imply more solidarity in terms of size.
4. *Guarantee design:* joint-and-several guarantees are a stronger indicator of solidarity than several guarantees, as the former provide for a more comprehensive risk-sharing.
5. *Repayment type:* a grant-based logic of debt repayment (e.g., Next Generation EU) provides for more solidarity than a loan-based logic (e.g., the ESM).
6. *Repayment duration:* perpetual common debt delivers more solidarity than common debt with short maturities.

Table 15.1: Elements of solidarity mechanisms for common borrowing

	< More limited solidarity	More extensive solidarity >
Borrowing size	Limited size	Unlimited size
Mutualisation type	Support for nationally incurred public debt	Mutualisation of all existing and future national public debt
Borrowing duration	Temporary	Permanent
Guarantee/liability design	Several guarantees	Joint and several guarantees
Repayment type	Loan-based logic	Grant-based logic
Repayment duration	Short maturities	Perpetual

Source: Own depiction

Ceteris paribus, common borrowing instruments thus provide for more extensive solidarity, when they are (1) unlimited in size, (2) mutualise existing and future national public debt, are built on a (3) permanent basis, are (4) insured through joint and several guarantees, (5) follow a grant-based logic and (6) remove the need for debt repayment through perpetual bonds.

Concrete debt mutualisation proposals do not necessarily fall clearly into the left or the right column of Table 15.1 but rather mix various elements that entail more or less extensive solidarity. Typically, they can, however, be assigned to two different but potentially complementary solidarity logics of debt mutualisation. The first more limited logic of common borrowing aims to mutualise borrowing costs (e. g., through back-to-back loans) while the second more encompassing one aims to (also) mutualise debt repayment (e. g., Coronabonds).

Responsibility mechanisms

Solidarity mechanisms are generally accompanied by responsibility mechanisms which are supposed to avert moral hazard and free-riding problems. With respect to European debt mutualisation, proposals have suggested a variety of different mechanisms to achieve 'responsible' behaviour. In particular:
1. Market discipline;
2. Fiscal rules compliance;
3. Implementation of fiscal consolidation and other reforms measures;
4. Less constraining conditionality of purpose.

First, the idea behind *market discipline* mechanisms is that unsustainable borrowing by sovereigns leads to higher risk premia, providing incentives for governments to return to lower and more sustainable borrowing. At the EU level, this mechanism is hampered due to the EU's strong creditworthiness. Some proposals have hence sought to ensure that market discipline continues to affect political decision-making, for example by capping the amount of mutualised debt and letting the disciplining effect of markets play out on the remaining national debt (see the Blue Bonds proposal discussed above), or by introducing 'artificial' market discipline mechanisms where debt service costs would reflect member states' individual fiscal standing (see e.g., Boonstra 2005).

Second, several proposals incorporate *fiscal rules compliance* as their responsibility mechanism. They suggest that access to common borrowing could be limited to countries that run fiscal policies in line with European and/or national rule requirements (European Commission 2011; Philippon & Hellwig 2011) and that adhere to long-term debt reduction plans (Varoufakis 2011).

Third, *consolidation and reform* requirements are one of the most often mentioned responsibility mechanisms in EU debt mutualisation proposals and actual instruments. Already the 1975 Community Loan Mechanism required countries receiving assistance to agree on a so-called "performance conditionality", i.e., a set of policies addressing the balance-of-payments issues they faced (see MacDougall Report 1977). Typical asks in terms of policy conditionality are strict fiscal consolidation measures and structural reforms, e.g., concerning labour market policy.

Fourth, responsibility mechanisms based on a *conditionality of purpose* are built on incentives rather than punishment, linking the transferring of funds to the compliance with commonly agreed-upon spending objectives. As seen above, this approach was largely brought forward during the Covid-19 crisis and has been employed on a large scale with the RRF.

Crisis framings and their effect on politically viable solutions

Another element highlighted in sections 2 and 3 was the difference in the dominant framings of the Eurozone crisis and the Covid-19 crisis, summarised in Table 15.2.

Table 15.2: Political crisis frames during the Eurozone and Covid-19 crises

	Dominant framing	Alternative framing
Eurozone crisis	Fiscal profligacy by peripheral Eurozone member states	Structural flaws in the design of the EMU leading to private sector bubbles requiring state intervention
Covid-19 crisis	External symmetric shock with asymmetric effects across member states	Insufficient fiscal consolidation by peripheral member states to build up fiscal buffers

Source: Own analysis

As seen, during the Eurozone crisis, many academics and policymakers framed the crisis and its potential solution in terms of the structural flaws in the EMU architecture. Eventually, however, the successful narrative was one holding Southern member states responsible for reckless fiscal behaviour laying at the root of the crisis (Fernandes & Rubio 2012: 25). While at the beginning of the pandemic, some actors maintained this same framing, the dominant narrative viewed Covid-19 as an external symmetric shock with a demand and supply component, having an asymmetric effect on member states based on their exposure and economic structure.

Together with other influence factors (the concrete economic and budgetary consequences of each crisis, the existing landscape of EU institutions and instruments dealing with public debt at the time, and the power relationships between countries providing and receiving solidarity), these dominant framings had a major effect on which debt mutualisation proposals – including their respective arrangements of solidarity and responsibility mechanisms – were finally implemented.

Table 15.3 compares the various debt mutualisation instruments adopted during the Eurozone and the Covid-19 crises, including their solidarity and responsibility mechanisms. It highlights the move from arrangements with solidarity based on the mutualisation of borrowing costs in exchange for strict conditionality regarding consolidation and reform requirements (during the debt crisis) to arrangements including solidarity based on the mutualisation of debt repayment in exchange for more lenient conditionality of purpose (during the Covid-19 crisis).

Table 15.3: Implemented instruments of public debt mutualisation during the Eurozone and the Covid-19 crises

	Eurozone crisis		
Type of crisis	Balance-of-payments crisis		
Dominant crisis frame	Fiscal profligacy of peripheral eurozone member states		
Key concepts	Moral hazard and free-riding problems		
Role of ECB	Limited from 2010 to 2012: Securities Markets Programme (SMP) Larger from 2012: Outright Monetary Transactions (OMT)		
Actual instruments of supranational public debt issuance	EFSM	EFSF	ESM
Introduction	05.2010	05.2010	09.2012
Size of common borrowing	€60bn	€440bn	€500bn
Type of common borrowing	Mutualisation of borrowing costs	Mutualisation of borrowing costs	Mutualisation of borrowing costs
Duration of common borrowing	Temporary	Temporary	Permanent
Type of guarantees/ liabilities	Several	Several	Several
Type of debt repayment	Back-to-back loans	Back-to-back loans / Loans based on DFS	Loans based on DFS
Duration of debt repayment	Long-term maturities (country-specific)	Long-term maturities (country-specific)	Long-term maturities (country-specific)
Responsibility mechanisms	Conditionality based on consolidation and re-form requirements	Conditionality based on consolidation and re-form requirements	Conditionality based on consolidation and re-form requirements

Table 15.3: Implemented instruments of public debt mutualisation during the Eurozone and the Covid-19 crises *(Continued)*

	Covid-19 crisis		
Type of crisis	Demand and supply shock		
Dominant crisis frame	Symmetric demand and supply shock with asymmetric impact		
Key concepts	Need for unity and solidarity		
Role of ECB	Large role from March 2020: Pandemic Emergency Purchase Programme (PEPP) with up to €1,850bn		
Actual instruments of supranational public debt issuance	ESM – Pandemic Crisis Support Facility	SURE	EU Recovery Instrument (Next Generation EU)
Introduction	04.2020	04.2020	12.2020
Size of common borrowing	€240bn	€100bn	€750bn (€390bn grants + €360bn loans)
Type of common borrowing	Mutualisation of borrowing costs	Mutualisation of borrowing costs	Mutualisation of borrowing costs & debt repayment
Duration of common borrowing	Temporary	Temporary	Temporary
Type of guarantees/ liabilities	Several	Several	Several
Type of debt repayment	Loans based on DFS	Back-to-back loans	Loans based on DFS / Grants with reimbursement key
Duration of debt repayment	Long-term maturities	Long-term maturities (~15 years)	Long-term maturities (~30 years)
Responsibility mechanisms	Conditionality of purpose (for direct and indirect health costs)	Conditionality of purpose (for preservation of employment)	Conditionality of purpose & reform requirements (RRF spending requirements and CSRs)

The legitimacy of solidarity-responsibility arrangements

The above discussions highlighted how any debt mutualisation proposal or instrument represents a specific arrangement of solidarity and responsibility mechanisms. In line with Schmidt (2015), we argue that for such an arrangement to be 'successful' it needs to be legitimate for decision-makers and citizens across EU member states. This includes input, throughput, and output legitimacy in both countries *providing* and *receiving* solidarity, in view of the specific responsibility mechanisms attached.

To ensure input legitimacy, solidarity-responsibility arrangements must respect fundamental requirements of national sovereignty, leaving sufficient room for democratic politics to decide on national fiscal policy priorities. This does not imply that common rules or guidelines across EU member states should be absent. Rather, it means that – inside common economic and political frameworks – democratic decision-making and priority-setting need to be protected. In terms of throughput legitimacy, procedures, and criteria for EU debt mutualisation, the spending of raised funds and their repayment need to be transparent and allow for accountability across the various levels of government. To achieve output legitimacy, solidarity-responsibility arrangements need to be economically 'successful'. This means that the extent of solidarity provided needs to address problems and achieve desired objectives, whether this means financing predefined priorities, tackling exogenous macroeconomic shocks, or harmonise fiscal policies. Solidarity-responsibility arrangements thus have output legitimacy if they can provide sufficient funds to realise policy objectives, address the crisis impact, and ensure economic growth.

The legitimacy of solidarity-responsibility arrangements during the Eurozone crisis

Many past proposals and actual instruments of EU public debt have suffered from a lack of legitimacy (see Table 15.4). In the case of the Eurozone crisis, the dominant framing and the unequal negotiating positions between countries providing and receiving solidarity (with the ECB not yet backstopping national public debt at the time), played a major part in the adoption of solidarity-responsibility mechanisms with insufficient legitimacy for countries receiving solidarity – but not exclusively. The EFSM, EFSF, and ESM provided loan-based solidarity limited in size (first on a temporary, then permanent basis) in exchange for responsibility mechanisms entailing strict conditionality based on fiscal consolidation and reforms (see Table 15.3).

The coercive nature of the responsibility mechanisms accompanying these arrangements, laid down in country-specific Memoranda of Understanding (MoU) involving member states, the EU, and the IMF, led to a significant lack of input legitimacy in crisis countries. Major social movements, for example in Greece, Italy, Spain, and Portugal, contested the austerity measures imposed by external actors (see Ramalho 2020), considered politically illegitimate due to the unpopular content of MoU conditionality, and the perceived undemocratic method of negotiation and adoption. Additionally, output legitimacy was also limited, due to considerable losses in economic output and catastrophic social consequences.

Alternative solidarity-responsibility arrangements for treasury-like mechanisms pooling (a share of) existing national public debt in exchange for stronger market discipline and fiscal rule compliance would have arguably been more legitimate for crisis countries, as they could have constituted a considerably higher extent of solidarity matched with responsibility mechanisms leaving room for national politics. Given the dominant framing of the Eurozone crisis, this approach was, however, not seen as legitimate by governments "providing" solidarity, because such an arrangement would have 'absolved' the accountability of profligate members over their excessive debt.

While member states providing solidarity largely acknowledged that this was necessary to both protect the eurozone and their own economies from negative spillover effects (Fernandes, Rubio 2012), the dominant framing rendered even solidarity provided by loans against highly constraining conditionality requirements politically difficult. This was exemplified by several government breakdowns, such as in Slovakia in 2011 linked to an extension of guarantees for the EFSF (Santa & Lopatka 2011). In the end, common debt solidarity-responsibility arrangements were nevertheless adopted, with countries providing solidarity largely dictating the extent of solidarity and the conditionalities linked to it, given the large power asymmetries during the debt crisis.

The legitimacy of solidarity-responsibility arrangements during the Covid-19 crisis

Reflections on debt mutualisation in face of the Covid-19 crisis were heavily affected by the experience of the previous crisis and the solidarity-responsibility arrangements previously implemented. Overall, the nature of the Covid-19 crisis and the early PEPP-based ECB response led to smaller power asymmetries between member states and made it difficult for some actors to reinstate the previous fiscal profligacy framing.

Table 15.4: The political legitimacy of solidarity-responsibility arrangements of debt mutualisation proposals

Solidarity-responsibility arrangements	States providing solidarity	States receiving solidarity
Eurozone crisis (dominant fiscal profligacy framing)		
Mutualising existing public debt (Eurobonds) + market discipline and/or fiscal rule compliance	Politically illegitimate because it would have approved *ex post* on a permanent basis of inefficient spending	Politically legitimate to a certain extent: Eurobonds constituting significant solidarity but mechanisms for market discipline/fiscal rule compliance questioned
Loans (permanent and temporary) + conditionality	Politically legitimate given the framing of the crisis	Politically illegitimate because of the intrusive nature of policy conditionality and lack of democratic choice

The power asymmetry between states providing and receiving solidarity allowed the former to impose their vision of solidarity-responsibility arrangements to prevail, rendering the actual instruments of public debt mutualisation (EFSM, EFSF, ESM) politically illegitimate among the latter.

Solidarity-responsibility arrangements	States providing solidarity	States receiving solidarity
Covid-19 crisis (dominant external symmetric shock framing)		
Loans (permanent and temporary) + conditionality of purpose	Politically legitimate because of the framing of the crisis' nature	Politically illegitimate because of the insufficient extent of solidarity
Grants (and loans) + conditionality of purpose	Politically legitimate because of limited and temporary nature and *ex ante* control over priorities and spending of grants (and loans)	Politically legitimate because of grant-based solidarity and the possibility to select investment and reform projects domestically (within certain limits)

The type of crisis and its dominant political framing allowed for a more balanced compromise between states providing and receiving solidarity, making it politically legitimate among both country groups.

Source: Own analysis

These more balanced negotiating premises allowed for the early adoption of loan-based solidarity with considerably softer responsibility mechanisms built on a conditionality of purpose (i. e., health and employment-related) with the ESM Pandemic Crisis Support Facility and the SURE mechanism (see Table 15.3). These instruments remained nevertheless at least partly illegitimate for countries in need of solidarity because of their insufficient size, leading to an expected lack of output legitimacy, their limited scope of application, and, as seen above, the political toxicity and lack of input legitimacy of bodies like the ESM (Tesche 2021). The new SURE mechanism, however, was perceived in a different light and has achieved broad output legitimacy due to its capacity to protect employment (European Commission 2021).

The increasing dominance of the framing of the Covid-19 crisis as an exogenous symmetric shock with asymmetric effects, matched by lower power asymmetries between member states, allowed for the development of an EU debt instrument based on a solidarity-responsibility arrangement balancing legitimacy concerns among both countries providing and receiving solidarity. Thus, Next Generation EU introduced temporary and size-limited grant-based solidarity accompanied by a conditionality of purpose, negotiated by all member states, with the possibility of suspending support when the funds are not used according to the agreed criteria and conditions.

For countries who have previously provided solidarity, this approach can be legitimated since it does not mutualise existing national public debt, is crisis-contingent, and ensures continuous control over the priorities and the spending of grants (and loans). For countries who have previously benefitted from solidarity, grant-based solidarity in exchange of conditionality of purpose and reform requirements is considerably more legitimate than the Eurozone crisis arrangements, as grants are precious additional resources for governments struggling with spending constraints, as opposed to loans adding to a country's public debt. It should be noted that the differentiation between providers and recipients of solidarity was also blurred under Next Generation EU, since all member states have requested to benefit from this grant-based solidarity, preventing both stigma and Polarization between the two camps.

Finally, while some spending priorities were defined at the European level, national governments retained significant domestic choice over the investment and reform projects financed by the common borrowing, in stark contrast to the structural-reform-based conditionality imposed during the Eurozone crisis. Input legitimacy was also strengthened by the additionality of grants provided by Next Generation EU, which reduces the pressure on member states to go through with all conditionality requirements even in the face of strong domestic contestation. While this would come with reduced pay-outs, it nevertheless gives more political room for manoeuvre for national policymakers as compared to the previous crisis.

Conclusion

This chapter has focused on proposals and actual instruments for EU public debt during the Eurozone and Covid-19 crises. It has highlighted how these are based on specific arrangements of solidarity and responsibility mechanisms setting out conditions for issuance, disbursement, and repayment. It argued that these arrangements determine the perceived legitimacy of specific instruments for EU debt mutualisation. The analysis has also highlighted how crisis framings and the broader politico-economic context affect policy options, for example by limiting policy space or affecting negotiation positions among member states.

We concluded that during the Eurozone crisis, debt arrangements lacked a legitimate balance between solidarity and responsibility mechanisms, leading to strong resistance in crisis countries. Conversely, instruments adopted during the Covid-19 crisis seemed to integrate some 'lessons-learnt', achieving a considerably more legitimate balance, improving input and output legitimacy.

At the time of writing, in the midst of the implementation phase of Next Generation EU, "yet another external economic shock with asymmetric consequences across Europe" (Redeker 2022: 1) halted the recovery: the 2022 Russian invasion of Ukraine and its effect on energy prices. As for previous major shocks, new EU debt mutualisation proposals have been emerging, calling for solidarity between member states to respond to the economic fallout of the war.

While these calls have not found broad political support yet, under the initiative "Repower EU", the Commission proposed to use the unused RRF loans to reduce energy dependence from Russia and to accelerate the green transition (see Eisl 2022). In the ongoing battle over crisis narratives, yet another ECB decision introduced new ways to address yield divergence in the Eurozone, reducing negotiation asymmetries between member states. Our conceptual framework could help analyse these dynamics, and potential future EU debt instruments to counter the energy crisis. An interesting avenue for comparative research could for example consider how the 1970s oil shock led to one of the earliest instances of EU debt instruments: the Community Loan Mechanism.

Beyond the macroeconomic domain, our conceptual framework may provide a useful angle to study other EU policy areas and EU responses to common crises. The 2015 and 2022 migration-management crises (respectively linked to the Syrian civil war and the Russian invasion of Ukraine) would be interesting instances to put the framework to test in the future. As for the Eurozone and Covid-19 crises, different dominant framings emerged regarding the arrival of asylum seekers in 2015 and 2022. There is variation regarding the nature, timing, and proximity of the conflict, as well as regarding the countries most affected by the human influx. This provides analytical leverage for the study of proposals and actual instruments of solidarity-responsibility arrangements in the area of migration, and their legitimacy on the distribution of asylum-seekers or related compensation mechanisms across member states.

In principle, the conceptual framework developed in this chapter could provide insights when applied to any type of crisis with asymmetric effects and which requires solidarity among member states. The type and extent of EU solidarity-responsibility arrangements will be circumscribed by whether a specific policy field is already to a significant extent handled at the EU level.

References

Amato, Giuliano & Verhofstadt, Guy (2011): 'A plan to save the euro and curb speculators', *Financial Times*, 03.07.2011.

Arnold, Nathaniel G., Barkbu, Bergljot B., Ture, Elif H., Wang, Hou & Yao, Jiaxiong (2018): 'A Central Fiscal Stabilization Capacity for the Euro Area', *IMF Staff Discussion Notes*, No. 18/03, https://www.imf.org/en/Publications/Staff-Discussion-Notes/Issues/2018/03/22/A-Central-Fiscal-Stabilization-Capacity-for-the-Euro-Area-45741, accessed on 02.12.2022.

BBC (2011): 'Commission president Barroso to put forward eurobonds', 14.09.2011, https://www.bbc.com/news/business-14913517, accessed on 02.12.2022.

Beck, Thorsten, Wagner, Wolf & Uhlig, Harald (2011): 'Insulating the financial sector from the European debt crisis: Eurobonds without public guarantees', *VOX. CEPR's Policy Portal*, https://cepr.org/voxeu/columns/insulating-financial-sector-european-debt-crisis-eurobonds-without-public-guarantees, accessed on 02.12.2022.

Bénassy-Quéré, Agnès, Boot, Arnoud, Fataás, Antonio, Fratzscher, Marcel, Fuest, Clemens, Giavazzi, Francesco, Marimon, Ramon, Martin, Philippe, Pisani-Ferry, Jean, Reichlin, Lucrezia, Scheonmaker, Dirk, Teles, Pedro & Weder di Mauro, Beatrice (2020): 'A proposal for a Covid Credit Line', *VOX. CEPR's Policy Portal*, https://voxeu.org/article/proposal-covid-credit-line, accessed on 02.12.2022.

Bénassy-Quéré, Agnès, Brunnermeier, Markus K., Enderlein, Henrik, Farhi, Emmanuel, Fratzscher, Marcel, Fuest, Clemens, Gourinchas, Pierre-Olivier, Martin, Philippe, Pisani-Ferry, Jean, Rey, Hélène, Schnabel, Isabel, Véron, Nicolas, Weder di Mauro, Beatrice & Zettelmeyer, Jeromin (2018): 'Reconciling risk sharing with market discipline: A constructive approach to euro area reform', *CEPR Policy Insight*, No. 91.

Bénassy-Quéré, Agnès & Weder di Mauro, Beatrice (2020): Europe in the time of Covid-19. A new crash test and a new opportunity, https://www.parisschoolofeconomics.eu/docs/benassy-quere-agnes/europe_in_the_time_of_covid-19-chap-1.pdf, accessed on 02.12.2022.

Bini Smaghi, Lorenzo & Marcussen, Michala (2018): 'Strengthening the euro area Architecture: A proposal for Purple Bonds', *SUERF Policy Note*, No. 35, https://www.suerf.org/policynotes/2733/strengthening-the-euro-area-architecture-a-proposal-for-purple-bonds, accessed on 02.12.2022.

Bofinger, Peter, Feld, Lars P., Franz, Wolfgang, Schmidt, Christoph & Weder di Mauro, Beatrice (2011): 'A European Redemption Pact', *VOX. CEPR's Policy Portal*, https://voxeu.org/article/european-redemption-pact, accessed on 02.12.2022.

Bonnevay, Frédéric (2010): 'Pour un Eurobond. Une stratégie coordonnée pour sortir de la crise', *Institut Montaigne Étude*, https://www.institutmontaigne.org/ressources/pdfs/publications/etude_pour_un_eurobond.pdf, accessed on 02.12.2022.

Brunnermeier, Markus K., Garicano, Luis, Lane, Philip R., Reis, Ricardo, Santos, Tano, Thesmar, David, Van Nieuwerburgh, Stijn & Vayanos, Dimitri (2012): 'European Safe Bonds (ESBies)', *The euro-nomics group*, https://personal.lse.ac.uk/vayanos/Euronomics/ESBies.pdf, accessed on 02.12.2022.

Brunnermeier, Markus K., Langfield, Sam, Pagano, Marco, Reis, Ricardo, Van Nieuwerburgh, Stijn & Vayanos, Dimitri (2016): 'ESBies Safety in the tranches', *ESRB Working Paper*, No. 21.

Bulmer, Simon (2022): 'Germany, the Eurozone crisis and the Covid-19 pandemic: Failing forward or moving on?', *Comparative European Politics*, 20(2): 166–83.

Chamley, Christophe (2012): 'Europe requires Eurobonds', *VOX. CEPR's Policy Portal*, https://voxeu.org/article/why-euro-needs-eurobonds-hundreds-years-reasons, accessed on 02.12.2022.

Cioffi, Marika, Rizza, Pietro, Romanelli, Marzia & Tommasino, Pietro (2019): 'Outline of a redistribution-free debt redemption fund for the euro area', *Bank of Italy occasional papers*, No. 479.

Claeys, Grégory & Wolff, Guntram B. (2020): 'COVID-19 Fiscal Response: What are the options for the EU Council?', *Bruegel Blog Post*, https://www.bruegel.org/blog-post/covid-19-fiscal-response-what-are-options-eu-council, accessed on 02.12.2022.

Codogno, Lorenzo & van den Noord, Paul (2020): 'Covid-19: A euro area safe asset and fiscal capacity are needed now', *VOX. CEPR's Policy Portal*, https://voxeu.org/article/covid-19-euro-area-safe-asset-and-fiscal-capacity-are-needed-now, accessed on 02.12.2022.

Corsetti, Giancarlo, Feld, Lars P., Lane, Philip R., Reichlin, Lucrezia, Rey, Hélène, Vayanos, Dimitri & Weder di Mauro, Beatrice (2015): 'A new CEPR Report: A New Start for the Eurozone: Dealing with Debt', *VOX. CEPR's Policy Portal*, https://voxeu.org/article/new-cepr-report-new-start-euro zone-dealing-debt, accessed on 02.12.2022.

De Grauwe, Paul & Moesen, Wim (2009): 'Gains for All: A proposal for a common Eurobond', *CEPS Commentary*, https://www.ceps.eu/download/publication/?id=6232&pdf=1823.pdf, accessed on 02.12.2022.

Delors, Jacques, Berès, Pervenche, Bertoncini, Yves & Cohen, Daniel (2011): 'Europe must use bonds to fight the debt crisis on two fronts', *The Guardian*, 18.10.2011, https://www.theguardian.com/commentisfree/2011/oct/18/europe-bonds-debt-crisis-eurobonds, accessed on 02.12.2022.

Delpla, Jacques & von Weizsäcker, Jakob (2010): 'The Blue Bond Proposal', *Bruegel Policy Brief*, No. 2010/03.

Delpla, Jacques & von Weizsäcker, Jakob (2011): 'Eurobonds: The Blue Bond Concept and its Implications', *Bruegel Policy Contribution*, No. 2011/02.

EFSF (2016): 'European Financial Stability Facility (EFSF) FAQ', https://www.esm.europa.eu/sites/de fault/files/2016_02_01_efsf_faq_archived.pdf, accessed on 02.12.2022.

Eisl, Andreas & Tomay, Mattia (2020): 'European debt mutualisation. Finding a legitimate balance between solidarity and responsibility mechanisms', *Jacques Delors Institute Policy Paper*, No. 255, https://institutdelors.eu/wp-content/uploads/2020/10/PP255_European-debt-mutualisation_Eisl_EN.pdf, accessed on 02.12.2022.

Eisl, Andreas (2022): 'An ambitious plan without adequate financing? How to address the underfunding risks for the REPowerEU proposal', *Jacques Delors Institute Blog Post*, https://in stitutdelors.eu/wp-content/uploads/2022/06/BP_220613_RepowerEU_Eisl_EN.pdf, accessed on 02.12.2022.

ESM (2020): 'Klaus Regling at Eurogroup video press conference', https://www.esm.europa.eu/press-releases/klaus-regling-eurogroup-video-press-conference-2020-03-16, accessed on 02.12.2022.

Estrella-Blaya, Laura (2022): 'The Future of Common Borrowing: A Legal Analysis', *Jacques Delors Institute Policy Paper*, No. 283, https://institutdelors.eu/wp-content/uploads/2022/10/PP283_The-future-of-common-borrowing_Estrella-Blaya_EN.pdf, accessed on 02.12.2022.

European Commission (2011): 'Green Paper on the feasibility of introducing Stability Bonds', https://eur-lex.europa.eu/legal-content/EN/TXT/PDF/?uri=CELEX:52011DC0818&from=EN, accessed on 02.12.2022.

European Commission (2017): 'Reflection paper on the deepening of the economic and monetary union', https://ec.europa.eu/commission/publications/reflection-paper-deepening-economic-and-monetary-union_en, accessed on 02.12.2022.

European Commission (2018): 'Proposal for a regulation on sovereign bond-backed securities. https://ec.europa.eu/info/publications/180524-proposal-sbbs_en, accessed on 02.12.2022.

European Commission (2020): 'The EU budget powering the recovery plan for Europe', 27.05.2020, https://eur-lex.europa.eu/legal-content/EN/TXT/HTML/?uri=CELEX:52020DC0442&rid=9, accessed on 02.12.2022.

European Commission (2021): 'Report on the European instrument for Temporary Support to mitigate Unemployment Risks in an Emergency (SURE) following the COVID-19 outbreak pursuant to Article 14 of Council Regulation (EU) 2020/672', https://ec.europa.eu/info/sites/de fault/files/economy-finance/sure_one_year_on.pdf, accessed on 02.12.2022.

European Council (2020): 'Special meeting of the European Council (17, 18, 19, 20 and 21 July 2020) – Conclusions, https://www.consilium.europa.eu/media/45109/210720-euco-final-conclusions-en.pdf, accessed on 02.12.2022.

European Council (2020a): 'Statement by the President of the European Council Following the Video Conference on Covid-19', 10.03.2020, https://www.consilium.europa.eu/en/press/press-releases/2020/03/10/statement-by-the-president-of-the-european-council-following-the-video-conference-on-covid-19/, accessed on 02.12.2022.

European Council (2020b): 'Joint statement of the Members of the European Council', https://www.consilium.europa.eu/media/43076/26-vc-euco-statement-en.pdf, accessed on 02.12.2022.

Eurogroup (2020a): 'Report on the Comprehensive Economic Policy Response to the Covid-19 Pandemic', 09.04.2020, https://www.consilium.europa.eu/en/press/press-releases/2020/04/09/re port-on-the-comprehensive-economic-policy-response-to-the-covid-19-pandemic/, accessed on 02.12.2022.

Eurogroup (2020b): 'Statement on Covid-19 Economic Policy Response', 16.03.2020, https://www.con silium.europa.eu/en/press/press-releases/2020/03/16/statement-on-covid-19-economic-policy-re sponse/, accessed on 02.12.2022.

European Economic and Social Committee [EESC] (2012): 'Opinion of the European Economic and Social Committee on 'Growth and sovereign debt in the EU: two innovative proposals' (own-initiative opinion)', https://eur-lex.europa.eu/LexUriServ/LexUriServ.do?uri=OJ: C:2012:143:0010:0016:EN:PDF, accessed on 02.12.2022.

European Parliament [EP] resolution (2020): 'European Parliament resolution of 15 May 2020 on the new multiannual financial framework, own resources and the recovery plan (2020/2631(RSP))', 15.05.2020.

European Systemic Risk Board (2018): 'Sovereign bond-backed securities: a feasibility study. Volume I: main findings', *ESRB High-Level Task Force on Safe Assets*, https://www.esrb.europa.eu/pub/ task_force_safe_assets/shared/pdf/esrb.report290118_sbbs_volume_I_mainfindings.en.pdf, accessed on 02.12.2022.

EU Regulation 2021/241 (2021): Regulation (EU) 2021/241 of the European Parliament and of the Council of 12 February 2021 establishing the Recovery and Resilience Facility, https://eur-lex.eu ropa.eu/legal-content/EN/TXT/?uri=CELEX%3A32021R0241, accessed on 02.12.2022.

Erber, G. (2012): 'Safe Conditional Eurobonds', VOX. CEPR's Policy Portal, https://www.researchgate.net/profile/Georg-Erber/publication/344264526_Safe_Conditional_Euro-bonds/links/5f61bd8d4585154dbbd572e2/Safe-Conditional-Eurobonds.pdf, accessed on 02.12.2022.

Fernandes, Sofia & Rubio, Eulalia (2012): 'Solidarity within the Eurozone: how much, what for, for how long?', *Notre Europe – Jacques Delors Institute Policy Paper*, https://institutdelors.eu/wp-con tent/uploads/2018/01/solidarityemus.fernandes-e.rubionefeb2012.pdf, accessed on 02.12.2022.

French non-paper (2020): 'The Recovery Fund: features of a EU27-common debt issuance to boost dedicated programmes of the EU budget', 06.04.2020.

French-German proposal (2020): 'A French-German Initiative for the European Recovery from the Coronavirus Crisis', 18.05.2020.

'Frugal Four' non-paper (2020): 'Non-paper EU support for efficient and sustainable COVID-19 recovery', 23.05.2020.

Garicano, Luis; Verhofstadt, Guy (2020): 'Towards a European Reconstruction Fund', *VOX. CEPR's Policy Portal*, https://cepr.org/voxeu/columns/towards-european-reconstruction-fund, accessed on 02.12.2022.

Gentiloni, Paolo & Breton, Thierry (2020): 'Coronavirus: EU must mobilise all its resources to help member states', *Irish Times*, 06.04.2020, https://www.irishtimes.com/opinion/coronavirus-eu-must-mobilise-all-its-resources-to-help-member-states-1.4221476, accessed on 02.12.2022.

Giavazzi, Francesco & Tabellini, Guido (2020): 'Covid Perpetual Eurobonds: Jointly Guaranteed and Supported by the ECB', *VOX. CEPR's Policy Portal*, https://voxeu.org/article/covid-perpetual-euro bonds, accessed on 02.12.2022.

Giovannini Group Report (2000): 'Co-ordinated Public Debt Issuance in the Euro Area', *European Commission*, https://ec.europa.eu/economy_finance/publications/pages/publication6372_en.pdf, accessed on 02.12.2022.

Gros, Daniel & Micossi, Stefano (2008): 'A call for a European Financial Stability Fund', *VOX. CEPR's Policy Portal*, https://voxeu.org/article/call-european-financial-stability-fund, accessed on 02.12.2022.

Grund, Sebastian, Guttenberg, Lucas & Odendahl, Christian (2020): 'Sharing the fiscal burden of the crisis. A Pandemic Solidarity Instrument for the EU', *Jacques Delors Centre Policy Paper*, https://hertieschool-f4e6.kxcdn.com/fileadmin/20200407_Pandemic_Solidarity_Instrument__Guttenberg_Grund_Odendahl.pdf, accessed on 02.12.2022.

Horn, Sebastian, Meyer, Josefin & Trebesch, Christoph (2020): 'Coronabonds – The forgotten history of European Community debt', *VOX CEPR Policy Portal*, https://voxeu.org/article/long-run-view-co ronabonds-debate, accessed on 02.12.2022.

Hüther, Michael, Bofinger, Peter, Dullien, Sebastian, Felbermayr, Gabriel, Schularick, Moritz, Südekum, Jens & Trebesch, Christoph (2020): 'To avoid economic disaster, Europe must demonstrate financial solidarity', *German Economic Institute*, https://www.iwkoeln.de/en/press/in-the-media/mi chael-huether-europe-must-demonstrate-financial-solidarity.html, accessed on 02.12.2022.

Juncker, Jean-Claude & Tremonti, Giulio (2010): 'E-bonds would end the crisis', *Financial Times*, 05.12.2010, https://www.astrid-online.it/static/upload/protected/Junc/Juncker-Tremonti.pdf, accessed on 02.12.2022.

Khan, Mereen (2020): Dutch PM faces dissent at home over hardline Coronabonds stance, *Financial Times*, 01.04.2020, https://www.ft.com/content/b65da5ba-7873-4d99-8fc9-589d51800f2e, accessed on 02.12.2022.

Koranyi, Balazs & Canepa, Francesco (2020): 'ECB to print 1 trillion euro this year to stem coronavirus rout', *Reuters*, 19.03.2020, https://www.reuters.com/article/health-coronavirus-ecb-idINKBN21606P, accessed on 02.12.2022.

Laffan, Brigid (2014): 'Framing the Crisis, Defining the Problems: Decoding the Euro Area Crisis', *Perspectives on European Politics and Society*, 15:3, 266–280.

Leandro, Álvaro & Zettelmeyer, Jeromin (2018a): 'Safety Without Tranches: Creating a 'real' safe asset for the euro area', *CEPR Policy Insight*, No. 93.

Leandro, Álvaro & Zettelmeyer, Jeromin (2018b): 'The Search for a Euro Area Safe Asset', *PIIE Working Paper*, No. 18–3, https://www.piie.com/sites/default/files/documents/wp18-3.pdf, accessed on 02.12.2022.

Leterme, Yves (2010): 'Pour une agence européenne de la dette', *Le Monde*, 05.03.2010, https://www.lemonde.fr/idees/article/2010/03/05/pour-une-agence-europeenne-de-la-dette-par-yves-leterme_1314894_3232.html, accessed on 02.12.2022.

Lo Duca, Marco, Koban, Anne, Basten, Marisa, Bengtsson, Elias, Klaus, Benjamin, Kusmierczyk, Piotr & Lang, Jan Hannes (2017): 'A new database for financial crises in European countries,' ECB, https://www.ecb.europa.eu/pub/pdf/scpops/ecb.op194.en.pdf, accessed on 02.12.2022.

MacDougall Report (1977): 'Report of the Study Group on the Role of Public Finance in European Integration. Volume I: General Report', *Commission of the European Communities*, https://www.cvce.eu/content/publication/2012/5/31/c475e949-ed28-490b-81ae-a33ce9860d09/publishable_en.pdf, accessed on 02.12.2022.

Macron, Emmanuel & Gabriel, Sigmar (2015): 'Europe cannot wait any longer: France and Germany must drive ahead', *The Guardian*, 03.06.2015, https://www.theguardian.com/commentisfree/2015/jun/03/europe-france-germany-eu-eurozone-future-integrate, accessed on 02.12.2022.

Monti, Mario, Dăianu, Daniel, Fuest, Clemens, Georgieva, Kristalina, Kalfin, Ivailo, Lamassoure, Alain, Moscovici, Pierre, Šimonytė, Ingrida, Timmermans, Frans & Verhofstadt; Guy (2016): 'Future financing of the EU: Final report and recommendations of the High Level Group on Own Resources', https://ec.europa.eu/info/sites/info/files/about_the_european_commission/eu_budget/future-financing-hlgor-final-report_2016_en.pdf, accessed on 02.12.2022.

Münchau, Wolfgang (2011): 'The only way to save the eurozone from collapse. The introduction of a Eurobond would be the catalyst of further political integration', *Financial Times*, https://www.ft.com/content/64eeb9c8-0c5e-11e1-8ac6-00144feabdc0, accessed on 02.12.2022.

Nine-country proposal (2020): No title, 25.03.2020.

Philippon, Thomas & Hellwig, Christian (2011): 'Eurobills, not Eurobonds', *VOX. ECPR's Policy Portal*, https://voxeu.org/article/eurobills-not-euro-bonds, accessed on 02.12.2022.

Ramalho, Tiago Moreira (2020): 'The Troika in its own words: responding to the politicization of the southern European crises', *Journal of European Integration*, 42:6, 677–693.

Redeker, Nils (2022): 'Same shock, different effects. EU member states' exposure to the economic consequences of Putin's war', *Jacques Delors Centre Policy Brief*, https://www.delorscentre.eu/en/publications/economic-consequences-ukraine, accessed on 02.12.2022.

Santa, Martin & Lopatka, Jan (2011): 'Slovak parliament ratifies EFSF expansion', *Reuters*, 13.11.2011, https://www.reuters.com/article/us-eurozone-slovakia-idUSTRE79C1IY20111013, accessed on 02.12.2022.

Schmidt, Vivien A. (2015): 'The Eurozone's Crisis of Democratic Legitimacy. Can the EU Rebuilt Public Trust and Support for European Economic Integration?', *European Commission Discussion Paper*, No. 15, https://ec.europa.eu/info/sites/info/files/dp015_en.pdf, accessed on 02.12.2022.

Soros, George (2020): 'The EU Should Issue Perpetual Bonds', *Project Syndicate*, https://www.project-syndicate.org/commentary/finance-european-union-recovery-with-perpetual-bonds-by-george-soros-2020-04, accessed on 02.12.2022.

Spanish non-paper (2020): 'Spain's non-paper on a European recovery strategy', 19.04.2020.

Suarez, Javier (2015): 'A three pillar solution to the Eurozone crisis', *VOX. ECPR's Policy Portal*, https://voxeu.org/article/three-pillar-solution-eurozone-crisis, accessed on 02.12.2022.

Tesche, Tobias (2021): Pandemic Politics: The European Union in Times of the Coronavirus Emergency, *Journal of Common Market Studies*, 60:2, 480–496.

Tommaso Padoa-Schioppa Group Report (2012): 'Completing the Euro. A road map towards fiscal union in Europe', *Notre Europe Jacques Delors Institute Report.* https://europe-solidarity.eu/documents/ES_CompletingTheEuro_Report_June2012_01.pdf, accessed on 02.12.2022.

Varoufakis, Yanis & Holland, Stuart (2011): 'A modest proposal for overcoming the euro crisis', *Levy Economic Institute of Bard College Policy Note*, https://www.levyinstitute.org/pubs/pn_11_03.pdf, accessed on 02.12.2022.

Vignon, Jérôme (2011): 'Solidarity and responsibility in the European Union', *Notre Europe – Jacques Delors Institute Policy Brief*, No. 26, https://institutdelors.eu/wp-content/uploads/2018/01/bref27_jvignon_en.pdf, accessed on 02.12.2022.

Von der Leyen, Ursula (2020): Speech by President von der Leyen at the European Parliament Plenary on the EU coordinated action to combat the coronavirus pandemic and its consequences, 16.04.2020,
https://ec.europa.eu/commission/presscorner/detail/en/speech_20_675, accessed on 02.12.2022.

Warren, Thomas (2017): 'Framing the eurozone crisis: a case of limited ambition', *Journal of European Integration*, 40:4, 1–16.

Index

https://doi.org/10.1515/9783110790337-017

www.ingramcontent.com/pod-product-compliance
Lightning Source LLC
Chambersburg PA
CBHW020524270326
41927CB00006B/441